JUAN SOLDADO

AMERICAN ENCOUNTERS /

GLOBAL INTERACTIONS

A series edited by Gilbert M. Joseph

and Emily S. Rosenberg

RAPIST,
MURDERER,
MARTYR,
SAINT

Paul J. Vanderwood

SOLDADO

DUKE

UNIVERSITY

PRESS

DURHAM

AND LONDON

2004

2nd printing, 2006

© 2004 Duke University Press. All rights reserved.

Printed in the United States of America on acid-free paper ∞

Designed by Rebecca Giménez. Typeset in Minion by Keystone

Typesetting, Inc. Library of Congress Cataloging-in-Publication

Data appear on the last printed page of this book.

For Glenn, fine friend and
dedicated fellow-voyager

American Encounters/Global Interactions

A series edited by Gilbert M. Joseph and Emily S. Rosenberg

This series aims to stimulate critical perspectives and fresh
interpretive frameworks for scholarship on the history of the imposing
global presence of the United States. Its primary concerns include the
deployment and contestation of power, the construction and decon-
struction of cultural and political borders, the fluid meanings
of intercultural encounters, and the complex interplay between the
global and the local. American Encounters seeks to strengthen dialogue
and collaboration between historians of U.S. international relations
and area studies specialists.

The series encourages scholarship based on multiarchival historical research. At the same time, it supports a recognition of the
representational character of all stories about the past and promotes
critical inquiry into issues of subjectivity and narrative. In the process, American Encounters strives to understand the context in which
meanings related to nations, cultures, and political economy are
continually produced, challenged, and reshaped.

FAITH & DOUBT

I have no living sense of commerce with God. I envy those who
have, for I know that the addition
of such a sense would help me
greatly.—*William James*

The art of faith is a constant
dialogue with doubt.—*Bishop
J. A. T. Robinson*

Thus it is not like a child that
I believe in Christ and confess
him. My hosanna has come forth
from the crucible of doubt.
—*Fyodor Dostoyevsky*

Lord, I believe. Help my
unbelief.—*Mark 9:24*

CONTENTS

W hen I first learned of Juan Soldado a decade ago, I reacted like most everyone else: "How is this possible?" How could it be that a confessed rapist-murderer who had been publicly executed for that horrible crime in 1938 had come to be venerated as a miracle-working saint at his grave site in Tijuana, Mexico, just across the border from my home in San Diego, California? It took many visits to the shrine which now covers Juan's grave, numerous conversations with those who believe in him (and some with those who do not), deep readings in religious and other literature, archival digging, interviews with priests, scholars, *curanderos*, and skeptics, and considerable personal pondering before I began to discern the contours of popular religiosity that I believe led to the devotion. This was not precisely a journey of self-discovery; I have always admired people of faith, perhaps in part because my own is less absolute. But my research did deepen my appreciation for the myriad creative ways in which humans seek to overcome obstacles in their lives and reach an accord with the Divine. Faith has the power to provide a person's passport to liberation.

JUAN LIVED AS Juan Castillo Morales. Beyond that, facts about his life are hard to establish. He was apparently born and raised in the pueblo of Ixtáltepec (then a town of twelve thousand people) deep in the Zápotec region of southern Mexico, although there is no record of his birth or baptism in the admittedly spotty parish records. Most families in Ixtáltepec farmed life-sustaining corn and beans, but capricious rains and fierce dry winds created a harsh life for them. They had rich traditions and colorful festivities, but drinkable water was scarce, and sickness endemic. Whatever his history, we know that Juan must have finished primary school because literacy was a requirement for enlistment in the Mexican army, which he joined sometime before 1938. That year found him, at the age of twenty-four, stationed in Tijuana—far from home, family, and culture—where fate overtook him.

On 14 February Juan Castillo Morales confessed to the rape and murder of an eight-year-old girl, and the army summarily court-martialed and brutally executed him on 17 February. In the aftermath, curiosity led locals to the grave of the soldier. There they reported "signs"—blood seeped up from the ground; the soldier's *ánima* (his soul) cried out for revenge—which played into that rich tapestry of religiosity that had been nurtured in these believers since childhood. They sensed God's presence in their midst. They knew of God's grace and they felt it. They erected a shrine at the site, and today it is visited by a steady stream of believers, some just to insure Juan's comfort, or to seek inner peace, but most to ask him for a favor—health, a good marriage, the repair of a broken family, a baby, safe passage into the United States, rent money, decent grades in school, a passport, driver's license, or green card, an automobile, steady employment, peace of mind, to win the lottery, to get off drugs or drink or both, to bring a son home safely from the States, to release a father from jail—all of which perfectly reflect conditions in their mushrooming metropolis of more than two million people struggling to maintain some sort of balance. Petitions at all such shrines mirror such needs and conditions, but then all religion is suffused with material wants. Meanwhile migrants and the media have spread Juan's fame across Mexico, the United States, and beyond. But when I visited Ixtáltepec in search of his family roots, residents did not know that one of their sons had been proclaimed a *santo* far to the north. When told so, an elderly gentleman quietly concluded: "They must have seen some truth in him." Indeed they have.

People have canonized their own saints since early Christianity. The official Roman Catholic Church claims sole ownership of the procedure, but popular canonizations remain quite common, even for self-confessed criminals. In the case of Juan Soldado people began to doubt the evidence against him, or at least the speed and thoroughness of the proceedings which had condemned him. They wondered at the justice of the entire hurried process, including the ceremonial, deliberately cruel public execution. Guilt to a good many witnesses mattered less than justice writ large. Some believed (as many do today) that those who die unjustly sit closest to God. Therefore, they have the ear of the Lord and are especially effective as intercessors. Devotion and petitions to Juan for personal help followed. Miracles occurred—or at least, prayers and petitions were answered—and the people proclaimed the soldier a saint. Such canonizations are the result of need, hope, aspiration, and faith. Roots of any particular devotion may be found tangled in a group of measurable realities—the politics, geography, economic conditions, social relations, and the so-called temper of the times—affecting devotees, who blend in their spiritual sensibilities to weigh, measure, and mediate these factors. Little in human experience can be explained only in material terms. There are always spiritual or religious dimensions which influence motivation and behavior.

Such is the case in the search for origins of the Juan Soldado devotion. International currents and national concerns buffeted the townspeople of Tijuana during the first part of the last century. The Depression had struck. Countrymen expelled from the neighboring United States settled in town, further straining already slim resources. The end of America's era of Prohibition had already curtailed tourism. Church and state were at war in Mexico; churches were closed, priests expelled. A new president had unleashed an unsettling radical reform program that mandated widespread land, labor, and educational reforms. Labor unions in Tijuana battled for control over workers. Moreover, the national government's moralization crusade had closed down the town's main source of gainful employment, the gambling casinos. Hundreds of heads of household had lost well-paying jobs and been thrust into catch-as-catch-can work. People adapted as best they could. Some even profited from the changes, but the stress in town was palpable. Then came the untoward rape and murder of the child. Tijuana erupted in riot and chaos.

For many, the young soldier's execution satisfied their lust for revenge. The town settled down, and people began to reflect upon what had befallen them and their community. Then came reports of wondrous happenings at the grave site and the beginnings of a devotion. Today petitions to Juan are written on scraps of paper, the backs of photos, ticket stubs, or scribbled on the walls of the shrine itself. Heartfelt and heartrending, uplifting and tragic, some funny and playful, others laden with anxiety and fear, they touch humanness. But are they answered?

Proof lies all around and inside the shrine. Its outer walls are covered with marble plaques giving thanks for miracles received. Inside lie such tokens as the crutches of the once lame who now walk, the symbolic eyeglasses of the blind who now see, the baby clothes of a child born to a couple formerly thought barren. Some have painted lovely pictures giving thanks, others donate homemade embroideries. A good many have hung necklaces around a portrait of the soldier, or the neck of his statue. A few admit that their requests have not yet been answered, but explain that Juan is busy and will answer them when he can.

THERE IS NOTHING unique about the devotion to Juan Soldado, even if many (or most) of us have never seen or experienced such practice. Instead, there is a long, fascinating history behind these sorts of enthusiasms, which permeate the fabric of Christianity and other religions. One need not participate, or even believe, in such devotions to appreciate them. Because they are so human, they nudge us in unexpected ways. Strangeness may begin to feel familiar. Whatever your predilections in these matters, it is my pleasure to introduce you to Juan Soldado.

P. J. V.

ACKNOWLEDGMENTS

M y greatest gratification in writing this book came from my visits to the Juan Soldado shrine in Tijuana, where devotees so openly introduced me to the mysteries of their faith. They helped me to appreciate that there are many ways of knowing this world. I could not have understood the beliefs of these people without the help of many others—some of them disciples of Juan Soldado, most not—on both sides of the international border. It is impossible to mention everyone who contributed to the study, but many are thanked in the endnotes which accompany the text. A paucity of written documentation made the interviews especially rewarding. History colleagues in Tijuana lent me their enthusiasm and expertise. My former student and good friend Raúl Rodríguez González, who teaches and directs the library at Centro de Enseñanzas Técnicas y Científicas, led the way. José Armando Estrada, coordinator at the Consejo de Cultura y Arte, and José Gabriel Rivera Delgado, coordinator of the city's historical archive, ironed out the wrinkles in that part of the manuscript pertaining to Tijuana's past. José Saldaña Rico, radio personality, teacher, and an aficionado of local history long interested in the Juan Soldado story, introduced me to individuals directly involved in the events of 1938. David Ungerleider Kepler, a Jesuit priest with academic training in anthropology who is assistant to the rector at Tijuana's Universidad Iberoamericana, helped me to bridge the gap between Catholic theology and the practicalities of religious life in the city. Orlando Espín, director of the University of San Diego's Transborder Institute and member of its Theology and Religious Studies Department, guided me through the labyrinth of popular religion, while archivists and researchers at the Instituto de Investigaciones Históricos of the Universidad Autónoma de Baja California (Tijuana) could not have been more cooperative in leading me to appropriate documentation. John Mraz, a highly regarded historian of Mexican photography, and Martin Nesvig, who recently earned his doctorate at Yale University, helped meet my research needs in Mexico City.

Duke University proved to be an uncommonly pleasant publisher with which to work, thanks to its acquisitions editor, Valerie Millholland, whose professionalism and encouragement are ceaseless. The mapmaking artistry of Melodie Tune, director of graphics at San Diego State University graphics department, speaks for itself. The gifted historian William A. Christian, Jr. made valuable comments on an early version of the manuscript. Ellen F. Smith proves that every writer needs a good editor. And no one can excise the glitches in page proofs more successfully than my longtime comrade Professor Carolyn Roy.

As always, my two dependable "friendly readers"—Rosalie Schwartz and Eric Van Young—weighed in with comments and criticisms, uncovered flaws, and offered me both expertise and earnestness. They know when to rein me in and when to cut me loose. No one could have had finer comrades on this long pilgrimage to Juan Soldado. My heartfelt thanks to them, as well as to other splendid San Diego friends—Glenn, Mike, Susan, and Carolyn—who joined me in various ways on the journey.

I

THE CRIME

1. Notions of Justice

D read clutched Feliza Camacho. She had sent Olga, her eight-year-old daughter, to the corner grocery to buy meat for the family's Sunday dinner, and the child had not returned home. Such errands normally took only ten to fifteen minutes, but more than half an hour had passed, and winter's daylight was fast fading. Feliza thought that her next oldest daughter, Lilia, had accompanied her sister to the store, but when she noticed the four-year-old was playing in the living room, she told her to look out the window. Could she see Olga headed up the street? "No, mama." There was no sign of the youngster.

With her third child, an infant daughter, in her arms, Feliza rushed to the La Corona grocery, whose amiable proprietor, Mariano Mendivil, was a neighborhood friend. "Señor, have you seen Olga?" "Why yes, Feliza, she was here just a few minutes ago and bought some meat. She left smiling and happy as ever. I saw her skip over a puddle as she crossed the street, and then I turned to wait on another customer."

Through the store window the mother spotted a young uniformed soldier resting on a wall at the street crossing. Separate military and police headquarters in this small border town of Tijuana stood nearby, and soldiers frequented the vicinity. Feliza approached the soldier: "Did you see a little girl near here just a few moments ago?" "No, no, señora, I've seen no one. Perhaps she went over that way," and he pointed away from the military compound. Still, no trace of Olga.[1]

What went through the mother's mind? The streets were wet from earlier rain. Perhaps Olga had been hit by a car and taken to the local hospital. But that would have caused a commotion in the neighborhood.

Or did she aimlessly wander off to call on a friend, been invited inside a home and was overstaying her visit? Not likely, as she carried meat for dinner. Feliza shielded herself from darker thoughts. Ever since the sensational Lindbergh case six years earlier, parents throughout the United States and beyond feared kidnapping. Reverberations still made front-page news.[2]

Furthermore, within the last few years there had been an alarming series of yet-to-be-solved kidnappings and murders of both children and adults in and around San Diego, California, just fifteen miles north across the international boundary. In February 1931, Virginia Brooks, age ten, had left for Euclid School carrying her lunch, four books, and a bouquet of flowers for her teacher. A month later police discovered her ravished, strangled, and deteriorating body stuffed in a gunny sack on a lonely mesa near the city. On 19 April 1931, the nude body of nineteen-year-old Louise Teuber was found dangling from the limb of a tree at the foot of San Diego's Black Mountain; she had been garroted and then hanged. In 1933 a fiend tortured to death Dalbert Aposhian, seven years old. Officers recovered the boy's mutilated and dismembered body from San Diego Bay. A year later police stumbled upon the raped and otherwise battered body of Celta Cota, age sixteen, a model student at San Diego High School, under tangled bushes in the backyard of her home. In August 1936, an assailant raped and beat to death Ruth Muir, a forty-eight-year-old secretary at the YMCA in Riverside, California, and dumped her corpse in a glade in the San Diego suburb of La Jolla.[3]

The Muir case developed a Tijuana angle in the spring of 1937 with the arrest of Charles Harvey, alias Adam Windbush. San Diego police booked Harvey, a popular twenty-six-year-old crooner of cowboy songs on a Tijuana radio station, for robbery and possible kidnapping involving three young women who had been assaulted two years earlier at a gate to the international exposition then being held at the city's Balboa Park. Police labeled him the "Kiss Thief," who sweet-talked and then kissed his victims before he stole their pocketbooks. If any of the girls had claimed bodily injury, he could have been charged under the new Lindbergh Kidnapping Act, which mandated either death or life imprisonment. Harvey was already under a $10,000 bond pending trial for attempted assault on a housewife in Chula Vista, a major suburb between San Diego and Tijuana. Police had also questioned him in connection with the rape-murders of Ruth Muir and Celta Cota. With these sorts of sordid, spectacular incidents capturing public attention throughout the region, no wonder that Feliza Camacho's thoughts turned ominous.[4] Had Olga suffered a similar fate? Was there a maniac on the loose? The newspapers that would soon cover the Camacho case drew no direct connections between the unsolved murders and Olga's disappearance but noted the similarities.

Feliza contacted her husband, Aurelio, who was at work tending bar in the Foreign Club, one of the town's most famous casinos. Aurelio rushed home, and he and Feliza spent an hour going house to house in their neighborhood, knocking on doors, talking with acquaintances, searching for news of Olga. No one offered a clue. The child had just vanished.

At 7:30 P.M. the distraught parents called local police for help. Tijuana had only a handful of paid policemen, five or six officers whose salaries came from public donations. In these sorts of emergencies, military personnel reinforced them. Word of the missing child spread through the town of hardly ten thousand inhabitants, and while some folks hastened to console the anxious parents in their home, Aurelio's labor union associates joined the authorities and other Camacho family members in the search. Roadblocks sealed off exits from the city, principally north to the border, but also east in the direction of Tecate, and south toward Ensenada. The main hospital and several clinics yielded no evidence about the girl's whereabouts, nor did a search covering several blocks around Olga's home and the grocery store (see map 1)—the last two places she had been seen. Late that evening rain fell, and as night stretched toward dawn, a February chill hovering in the low forties set in. No leads concerning Olga developed. As implications of the disappearance filtered more deeply into the community's consciousness, residents locked windows and doors and checked on their own children more regularly for fear that a sexual predator was at large in the community.

Dawn broke at 6:45 A.M. with a partially overcast sky that Monday, 14 February 1938. Increasing numbers of volunteers arrived, and the search expanded. People poked here, there, and everywhere—in thick bushes, inside buildings, and in automobiles and trucks parked on the streets. Nothing, absolutely nothing. Police and military authorities huddled to devise a strategy. Everything depended upon the discovery of some tidbit, any hint, concerning the disappearance and whereabouts of Olga. About noon their luck changed.

Señora María B. de Romero, affectionately known in the neighbor-

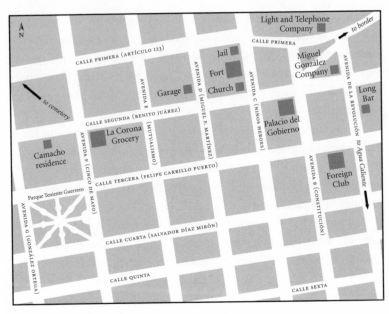

Map 1. Central Tijuana, 1938

hood as "Meimi," lived across Second Street from the Camachos. She had spent much of the previous evening with Feliza and Aurelio, comforting them. She assured them that search parties would find Olga and bring her back home. Shortly before noon on Monday, however, she experienced a powerful vision in which the Virgin Mary Herself appeared to her, revealed the child's face, and told Meimi to look for Olga in a deserted building: "I had a vision," she later said. "It told me that Olga would be found in an abandoned building. She would be found ill-treated." The vision guided Meimi to a vacant, weather-beaten, one-car wooden garage on the backside of a neighbor's property that abutted the military and police compounds and lay within two blocks of the Camacho home. Meimi did not attempt to enter the structure; instead, she gazed with apprehension between two warped boards of the exterior and saw on the wet ground inside, the bloody hand of a child, palm down, stretching from beneath a filthy sheet of cardboard that covered the rest of the body.

"I have found her. I have found her," she wailed as she stumbled toward the Camacho home. Searchers intercepted her. "Over there. In the garage," she said, and then fainted.

Soldiers and police hurried to the scene. (They never explained how they had overlooked the garage in their seventeen-hour search.) They hurled open the garage doors, saw the hand, gently removed the cardboard, and recoiled in horror. There lay Olga, her throat slashed open a full five inches by a piece of glass or a dull hunting knife, so savagely that she was nearly decapitated. A knotted rope encircled what remained of her gashed neck. Her torn, bloody dress had been pulled over her head, her undergarments removed. The child's body was badly scratched, and two deep, ragged gashes on her right arm indicated she had put up a desperate fight before her assailant subdued her. Blood had crusted around a large wound to her head.

Police agent Israel González broke up the crowd gathering at the site. And now the authorities began to find clues to the killing. Droplets of blood led from the scene to a nearby stable where the Fourteenth Cavalry Regiment had until recently kept its horses. In one of the stalls, as police moved some hay and manure to one side, they uncovered a sizable blotch of blood. At this point, General Manuel Contreras, chief of military operations in Tijuana, assumed control of the investigation. He possessed a take-charge personality, and a hint of threat edged his voice as he ordered local authorities to stand clear while the army took command.

Informed of the horrific find, Feliza crumpled in hysterical sobs on the floor of her home. Aurelio collapsed onto a chair in anguish. Police carried the girl's disfigured body to the surgical amphitheater of the Military and Civil Hospital, where Dr. Severano Osornio Camareña, the town's coroner, a military doctor educated in France, performed an autopsy. Dr. Osornio announced around 4 P.M. that strangulation and a sharp blow to the head had caused death and that Olga had been raped after being killed. Furthermore, he had found six reddish hairs, a piece of straw, and a few strands of gray cloth clutched in one hand of the child, along with human skin beneath her fingernails. Forensic experts could analyze such evidence.

Meanwhile, police and military personnel cordoned off and combed the presumed murder site for further physical evidence. They discovered a reddish material smeared on a fence abutting the garage. Some thought it blood, but General Contreras ruled it red paint. They found the clear print of a man's boot heel with a diamond-shaped design in its center pressed into the wet ground near the garage. The cardboard which covered the child was too wet and soggy to reveal a fingerprint, but then another break: a small package of meat had been tossed on the roof of a nearby shed used to store hay behind the military headquarters. A well-defined bloody thumb print lay on the discolored white wrapping paper.

As potentially incriminating evidence accumulated, Tijuana's police chief, Luis Viñals Carsi (who was also an army captain), contacted the more technically advanced San Diego Police Department. Cooperation between the two forces had ebbed and flowed over the years (and still does), but on this occasion the San Diegans sent Sgt. Edward A. Dieckman of the homicide squad, along with William Menke and Walter R. Scott of the department's identification bureau, to assist in the investigation. A former schoolteacher now dedicated to upgrading technology and training for the city's police force, Scott had pieced together a rudimentary photographic laboratory in which photos of fingerprints or footprints could be enlarged.

Before the San Diegans arrived early that evening of 14 February, police had interrogated the purportedly last person (besides the killer or killers) to see Olga alive: the owner of La Corona sundry store, Mariano Mendivil, who repeated in more detail the same story he had told the dead girl's mother. The child had bounced into the shop smiling, chatting, and in a good mood. He had sold her a slice of raw meat for a few pesos, and she had left in the direction of her home. He watched her cross the street, no one else seemed to be around, and then he had turned to serve another customer. And yes, the package now in possession of the authorities contained the meat that he had sold to Olga. He said he knew nothing else of the tragedy, and the police seemed to believe him. They probably had also questioned the customer.

About this time, the investigation might have turned to the parents of the victim for details about her life at home and events leading up to her disappearance, but the authorities declined to question them. Perhaps they believed Feliza and Aurelio too distraught to undergo interrogation. Indeed, Feliza was under a doctor's care. At any rate, no officials ever questioned the parents about the ordeal, then or later. Had they done so, they might have learned of the soldier whom Feliza insisted she saw leaning on a wall near La Corona in the early moments of her frantic search for her daughter. She could have described that army man to them.

But the police and military pursued a different tack. By two in the afternoon they had rounded up five young men said to have been at or near the scene where the murder and rape had apparently occurred. Three of the five were civilians who had spent the night shielded against the cold and rain, sleeping in hay in the old horse stalls at the backside of the military post. The *cuartel* (garrison) itself had been moved the preceding year to heights on the southern edge of town. While General Contreras and his staff still maintained their headquarters in a large rented house adjoining the old site, the distinctive stone building which had been the military post became the *comandancia* for the Tijuana police. With its turrets and parapets the structure resembled a movie set, like one of those remote desert outposts manned by the French Foreign Legion in *Beau Geste*. Commonly called "The Fort," it had been erected in 1915 on high ground along the Tijuana River to warn off foreign filibusters who had territorial designs on Baja California. An expanding town center had gradually surrounded The Fort with residences and small stores, but it still stood as a stern symbol of authority, and now became the nerve center for investigation of the murder and rape of Olga Camacho.

Besides the three young men who had sought refuge in the stalls from the night's cold, authorities arrested two soldiers said to have been in or around military headquarters about 6 P.M. or so, the Sunday evening that Olga disappeared. There had been speculation from the beginning that a soldier, or soldiers, might have been involved in the rape and slaying. At this point Baja California's federal police inspector, Jesús Medina Ríos, reviewed for eager newspaper reporters those clues that he hoped could lead to a quick solution of the crime: identification of the red hairs or woolen fibers found in Olga's hand; finding and analyzing additional fingerprints on the package of meat the girl had carried; identification of the heel print; a confession by one of the five in custody; or the discovery of blood on the clothes of a suspect.

Interrogators held the suspects incommunicado. Late that afternoon investigators announced that they had found nothing that would definitely link any of the detainees to the crime. Then around 7 P.M., after a final brusque questioning, police exonerated the three civilians as youths only in search of a place to sleep on a cold, wet night. They also absolved one of the soldiers. His mother provided an alibi for him: the boy, off duty that Sunday, had been home with her all afternoon and evening, and they could prove it.

That left only one person detained for further questioning, a twenty-four-year-old private named Juan Castillo Morales, a light-skinned *sol-dado raso* (lowest of the low in military ranks) of medium build, with dark, wavy hair and a hint of mustache along his upper lip. He had been born and raised in the small pueblo of Ixtáltepec, far to the south in the Tehuántepec region of the state of Oaxaca, a zone renowned for its Zápotec influence, although Juan's physical features were clearly mestizo. In fact, foreign invasion, colonization, and commerce had since the 1860s brought considerable racial diversity to the area.

Precisely how and why the authorities identified the private as their prime (indeed only) suspect virtually from the start is not known. The official record, such as exists, contains nary a hint. Sources of the period do not state precisely when police arrested him or whether he was in uniform. Feliza Camacho now says (but did not report at the time of the investigation) that she is sure Castillo Morales was the soldier she saw leaning on the wall near La Corona grocery, the person she had queried about her daughter's whereabouts. Others who witnessed the events of 1938 say today that Juan had been on guard duty at the comandancia earlier that fateful day and therefore needed to be questioned, but no contemporary accounts verify that point. Newspapers reported at the time, and witnesses to these happenings say now, that police knew Castillo Morales as someone who had made sexual advances toward young girls, perhaps even fondled some of them, although neither the authorities nor offended parties ever brought charges against him. It was simply rumored that he had the habit, and, therefore, the soldier's alleged sexual proclivities drew suspicions upon him. It was said that from the start of the investigation, police had identified known pedophiles, and that individuals in the crowd outside the comandancia had leaked word to interrogators that Castillo Morales had such sexual leanings. At this juncture, interrogators questioned Juan carefully on this point, and he vigorously denied any such inclinations or behavior, just as he steadfastly proclaimed his innocence of any involvement in the murder and rape of Olga Camacho.[5]

Interrogation and Confession

José Carmareña took notes at the initial interrogation of the suspect, which lasted past midnight. Carmareña had learned stenography and typing at Hoover High School in San Diego. Through his father's close personal relationship with the territorial governor, Lt. Col. Rudolfo Sánchez Taboada (the elder Carmareño was an army general), José had been appointed the personal secretary of Tijuana's *delegado*, Manuel Quiróz. Delegados—chief executive officers of major towns in the territory, Tijuana, Mexicali, and Ensenada—were appointees of the governor; no one was elected to any political office in the territory at that time. While beholden to the governors who named them, delegados held substantial local power of their own. Camareña tells his own story of the day he encountered Juan Castillo Morales:

Here I was, twenty-one years old and sent by the delegado to go to the interrogation and prepare a brief, called an *acta*, which could be used as the first step in court proceedings against a suspect. We were in a passageway of the comandancia, seated on wooden benches, and the Agente del Ministerio Público del Fuero Común [the municipal prosecutor], Moisés Oliva, was doing the main questioning in conjunction with the inspector general of police, the police commander, and several military officers. [In their function, agentes resemble district attorneys, weighing evidence and deciding whether or not it is sufficient to forward a case to judicial channels.]

The crowd outside was in an uproar. It now numbered at least a thousand, and the mob grew more and more impatient with the investigation, which it considered unnecessary, or at any rate too slow, and quite possibly headed for an official cover-up. They demanded that the police turn over the suspect to them so that they could lynch him. As their anger and frustration mounted, they began to pelt the comandancia with anything loose that they could get their hands on. We could hear projectiles hitting the walls: rocks, large chunks of wood, clumps of dirt, metal cans, and glass bottles. Windows were shattering around us. We didn't know what would happen if the crowd got inside the compound. Agente Oliva was so intimidated by the mob that he could hardly interrogate the prisoner. His mind was not on the job but on the crowd outside. He rushed his questions.

"Let's get this over with. Where were you on Sunday evening?"

"Around the military compound."

"What were you doing there?"

"Just walking around."

"Where were you headed?"

"Nowhere."

"Did you know Olga Camacho?"

"NO!"

"Did you get close to her?"

"I saw the girl, but I never got close to her."

"Did you speak to her?"

"No."

Castillo Morales had a great many lies and contradictions in his testimony. He would say one thing, and the mob outside would start yelling and screaming and threaten to break in, and he would change his mind. He was very confused under rough questioning by Oliva along with Contreras and police. He was highly nervous and could not concentrate. Almost all the questions could be answered "yes" or "no," but Castillo Morales could not afford to say "yes" to any of the questions, because if he did, it was the end of his life. The mob outside would finish him off. So he said "no." Or if he said "yes" one time, he would say "no" the next.

There were no democratic forms in the entire questioning process. Castillo Morales had no lawyer, no defender, no representation. The entire proceeding was marked by speed, the need to quell the mob. Everything was hurried. They [the authorities] just wanted to get him out of there, out of jail, out of the city. The feeling was that whether he did it or did not do it to her [Olga], it didn't matter, because he had done it to other girls. So that must be him; he is the presumed killer.

My typewritten acta was very jumbled and virtually useless for anything legal. There was no clear statement in it. It was only two pages long. Castillo Morales denied doing anything wrong. He denied raping and murdering the little girl. Castillo Morales denied everything. In my mind he was 75 percent guilty and 25 percent not.[6]

In the early hours of the interrogation, Castillo Morales understandably was under enormous pressure, not only from the point-blank questions and the nature of the crime of which he was being accused (if only by inference), but by the din of the tumult outside the walls of the headquarters, the shouts of a crowd that literally wanted his neck and was at the point of breaking into the compound. His interrogators tried all the tricks of their trade, one moment promising leniency if he confessed, the next threatening him with the harshest punishment if he did not.

Without a moment of relaxation, nothing to eat, no break for a smoke (the accused was a cigarette smoker—some said he also enjoyed marijuana and was influenced by the drug when he committed the crime), the suspect vigorously and steadfastly maintained his innocence.

With the investigation concentrated on Castillo Morales, police had gone to search his house in Colonia Morelos, near the cuartel (see map 2 in chapter 5). The majority of military personnel lived there in rented dwellings. The police purportedly found the suspect's blood-stained clothing soaking in a wash bin—some said inside the house, others outside (one of the discrepancies later noted in retellings of the events). Police also reported that they had found some of Olga's bloody clothing at the house. They later decided that the garments belonged to the soldier's common-law wife, the kind of contradiction that develops when those in search of answers jump too quickly to conclusions.

THE COMMON-LAW wife is a mysterious presence in this story. Unnamed in any newspaper, apparently never interviewed by the press, around 8 or 9 P.M. that day she suddenly assumes center stage, as would an unforeseen and unannounced ghost, delivers damning evidence, and then disappears for good, at least from historical accounts. This unidentified woman repeated for the agents what Juan had told her about his blood-stained garments. He explained that he had been cut up in a fight, hence the blood. She said her husband was mentally unhinged, but we do not know if she was speaking of the moment he returned home in blood-spattered clothing or of a more general state of mind. The woman was then taken to the comandancia, where under police guidance she confronted her husband with the evidence and denounced him.

Whether authorities might have coerced the woman into confronting her husband or offered her a bounty, or she testified voluntarily—there are many incentives for betrayal—did not seem to occur to the accused. Her presence with the clothing was the last calamitous stroke for Juan Castillo Morales, who lowered his head into his hands and sobbed that he had done the deed. When Olga had left the store, La Corona, he had hit her on the head with a rock. She began to bleed profusely. He then lifted her in his arms and carried his victim to the stable area at the rear of the military compound. There he raped, then killed her and carried her to the garage, where he cut her throat with a piece of glass. Police theorized that he had tried to stem the flow of blood from the initial head wound by raising the girl's skirt and wrapping it around her head, which explained the lack of a substantial blood trail anywhere at the site.

Following the confession, the soldier asked to be protected from the raging crowd outside, which was shouting for his head. Contreras assured him that his fate lay with the law, not the mob.

Later that night the officials invited newspaper reporters to interview the confessed rapist-murderer, who in more protected surroundings, away from the raging crowd, seemed to the journalists to be unrepentant and nonchalant about his crimes. Reporters must have been provided access to the prisoner with a proviso that they not reveal the location at which the prisoner was being held, and the newspapers kept that promise. The *Los Angeles Examiner* headed its story "Smiling Mexican Private tells *Examiner,* 'Yes, I did it.'" The report continued (omitting the full surname as English-language newspapers frequently did with Hispanics): "Morales appeared unperturbed by threats of a howling, vengeful mob, which sacked and burned the headquarters. Closely guarded in a secret hiding place, Morales shrugged and half-smiled when questioned by *The Examiner* concerning the crime: 'Oh, yes, I did it . . . I did not do anything to the little girl after she was dead, though [contradicting the findings of the medical examiner]. Everything I did was while she was alive. But I did it. I have done something like this before.'"[7] The *San Diego Evening Tribune* stated: "With calm unconcern, he [the suspect] told a reporter for the *Evening Tribune,* 'I killed the little girl to cover up my lust,' and repeated that he had 'first attacked her criminally and then killed her.'"[8]

Investigators went to extraordinary lengths to have the confession publicized by the press, as it was the heart of their case against him. Confessions extracted by police were as suspect then to the general public as they are now. It has been common police practice to announce a confession as justification for the imprisonment and then execution of a prisoner. Confessions have a way of putting an end to further investigation; they can relieve the prosecution of the need to stitch together a case based on hard evidence and sufficient motives. Suspects who confess are presumed guilty; a confession is the gemstone in officialdom's bag of evidence, sometimes all that prosecutors have to go on. Once announced, confessions carry immense weight, because they make it appear that the suspect has been self-judged and convicted.

Those who question the procedures that authorities followed in the Juan Castillo Morales case usually turn first to the confession. At this point it is doubtful that anything can be proved one way or the other about its legitimacy. All confessions carry blemishes and hairline cracks. Yet, at this point police seemed to have in hand what Inspector Medina Ríos had said earlier was what they needed for a quick solution to the crime: a confession from one of the suspects and the discovery of blood on his clothes. Pieces for the government's case seemed to be falling into place.

EARLY THAT EVENING (now it was about twenty-four hours after Olga's death) the San Diego detectives returned to their station with the wrapping paper that bore the bloody fingerprint and other bits of evidence surrounding the case. They had agreed to make blow-ups of the print, which was thought to be the one piece of physical evidence which could positively identify the killer. Tijuana police were to pick up the prints at Scott's refurbished laboratory the next day, Tuesday, 15 February. As the San Diego department still lacked a real forensic laboratory, it would have needed to send the hairs and any other sort of such evidence to the FBI in Washington, or to the state facility in Sacramento, or perhaps to a testing room in Los Angeles. As there does not seem to be any report on these matters in police files, the results of any such investigation are not known. Even more advanced laboratories could not have tested the blood samples for anything more than blood type; DNA testing was still in the distant future, and the hair samples could only be determined as animal or human, and if human, the results might indicate the person's race.[9]

Fingerprints (other than the one found on the wrapping paper) might have been lifted, if well formed on a dry surface, such as a piece of glass, but it is not known if police searched for such evidence in the Camacho murder case. Moreover, in contrast to reports of investigative procedures normally followed on these occasions, there is no indication that officials ever fingerprinted Juan Castillo Morales, typed his blood and hair (even as authorities could best deduce it at the time), or matched his fingerprints with those on his military service record, which should have been on file in Mexico City. There was nothing scientific about this investigation.

As it turned out, none of this mattered. Whatever thoughts the authorities might have had about developing proof through a photographic blow-up of a bloody thumbprint or by matching the wearing pattern of the heel print with those of the suspect's shoes or in an overall way following judicial procedures codified in civil law, they were soon challenged and hurried along by angry, unruly, threatening crowds of determined townspeople who numbered into the thousands (one newspaper estimated the crowd at four thousand, but this was most likely exaggerated). The mob demanded that the soldier in custody be released to them for their style of justice or they would storm the comandancia and take him by force. Authorities who resisted also would be hanged.

The Mob

Tijuana had swirled in rumors, suppositions, spontaneous outbursts of anger, and a general commotion since the initial disappearance of Olga Camacho and through the ensuing search for the child. But the town had never been a calm, well-run community of inhabitants living a simple life. Just the opposite: at least since the 1920s and the advent of Prohibition across the border, it had courted the reputation of a wide open, rip-roaring tourist mecca where anything went and the good times rolled. Moreover, the grinding worldwide Depression, the end of Prohibition, and the Mexican government's determination to curtail gambling had bred side effects which only further agitated the community. The Depression caused the United States to deport Mexican workers, thousands of whom then settled in Tijuana to await better times to the north. The sudden spurt of population placed substantial stress on already limited public services and employment possibilities. The resumption of the sale of alcohol in the United States hurt the local cantinas and nightclubs and forced their owners to seek other types of livelihood. Those with capital and foresight furiously competed for new opportunities in real estate and business. Others with scant financial assets relied on their ingenuity and wits to forge a new start, and in doing so frequently stepped on each others' toes. Closure of the gambling casinos, by far the town's largest source of employment, meant that several thousand unionized employees lost well-paying work. The labor unions bitterly fought the government to keep the establishments open and forcefully agitated for the job security of their membership. In this roiling atmosphere, the Camacho affair exacerbated frustrations and gave the already disgruntled a new venue (some say a pretext) for venting their wrath and parading their discontent.[10]

At first the crowds milling in the streets around the comandancia only demanded to know the names of those in custody. Photos of the throng show many in business suits and neckties, or at least dress jackets. They must have come to The Fort directly from work that Monday, 14 February, or perhaps from extending their condolences to the Camacho family. Not a faceless crowd of anonymous people: according to witnesses the participants knew each other through work, union affiliation, baseball games, civic celebrations, and social activities. Predominantly male, it exhibited most ages and walks of life, and remained cohesive and focused in the current crisis. It wanted justice, quick and certain, for Olga's killer.

When authorities remained tight-lipped about the progress of the investigation, the crowd became suspicious, and some turned surly. Was the military out to protect one of its own, a practice well known to Mexican tradition? Would the military spirit the suspect out of town and take him to a distant army base where he could be shielded from view and eventually allowed to drift into anonymity? This would not have been the first time, or the last, that the army placed its reputation ahead of justice.

When in early evening the crowd realized that the inquiry had become centered on one prime suspect, the gathering turned ugly. "Produce the murderer within half an hour or suffer," they roared.[11] Call it revenge or retribution, they wanted to assure themselves, needed to see with their own eyes, that Olga's killer met his fate *their* way, not the military's way. Police and the military urged patience, but the mob demanded its due.

Spontaneous lynchings by an angered public, of course, are not peculiar to Mexico, even at this late date. Tijuanenses storming The Fort likely remembered the infamous Brooke Hart case that brought far-flung notoriety to the San Francisco Bay area in late 1933. On 12 November of that year, Thomas H. Thurmond and Jack Holmes had kidnapped and murdered Hart, the twenty-two-year-old son of a wealthy San Jose merchant. They dumped his body into the bay, but demanded a $40,000 ransom from the young victim's father. Police soon apprehended the pair, who admitted their crime and were incarcerated in the San Jose jail pending trial. On 26 November, a mob pulled the prisoners from jail and hanged them in the name of sure justice. In fact, at the time of the troubles in Tijuana, the U.S. Senate had just deliberated an anti-lynching bill which would have allowed the federal government to prosecute state officials who willfully failed to prevent lynchings. The legislation took aim at

Southern local authorities who all too frequently looked the other way when white citizens' groups ignored the law and lynched blacks accused of violating the social codes of a community dominated by whites. Enemies of the bill launched a filibuster, and proponents could not garner sufficient votes to break it. The Senate shelved the measure until further notice.[12]

Only seven months before the Camacho murder, a mob two thousand strong had tried to lynch twenty-two-year-old Albert Dyer, suspected of ravishing and murdering three little girls in a public park in Inglewood, California. The crowd swarmed around the city jail and demanded to know if Dyer were there. A police captain responded that the suspect had been moved to a Los Angeles lockup, and when the throng demanded evidence, he opened the doors and allowed a committee of three protesters to search the jail. They found nothing, and the mob dispersed.

Meanwhile, Dyer had indeed been moved to Los Angeles police headquarters, where he underwent rigorous questioning. A Works Progress Administration worker from the East Coast of the United States and a married man, the prisoner had been a street-crossing guard at the school the girls attended. Police first suspected him while they were uncovering the bodies at the crime site. Dyer stood nearby, politely asking spectators not to smoke at such a tragic scene. Then he sobbed uncontrollably as police carried off the victims. Authorities thought his behavior off and brought him in for questioning. Under interrogation, contradictions developed in Dyer's alibi, although he maintained his innocence. Only when the officers suggested that he stand on the steps of the Inglewood City Hall and explain the contradictions to an enraged citizenry did Dyer break down: "I did it. I killed them," he shouted. In his confession he explained how over time he had become infatuated with the girls, two sisters ages seven and five, and their eight-year-old schoolmate. One afternoon he met them in a park, chatted with them, and offered them a soda. Then, one by one, he led them up a secluded canyon in the park. First he strangled and raped the eight-year-old. Then he returned to the park for one of the sisters, murdered her, and then went back for his last victim.[13] Echoes of the Dyer episode—the hounding mob, the tactics used in gaining a confession—reverberate through the case of Juan Castillo Morales.

Nor have the lynchings stopped. In an eerie echo to the rampage in Tijuana, sixty years later the same sort of fury erupted in central Mexico:

HUEJUTLA, Mexico—Hundreds of residents of this central Mexican city banded together yesterday [26 March 1998] and lynched two men accused of trying to kidnap four girls from an elementary school.

José Santos Vázquez and Salvador Valdez allegedly tried to force the girls into their pickup truck Wednesday in front of a school in Huejutla, [State of Hidalgo, less than] 100 miles from Mexico City.

Early yesterday, more than 1,000 townspeople—many drunk and some carrying guns—stormed the jail and dragged the bloodied men into the central square. They hanged one of the men from a kiosk and beat the other man to death on the ground.

Police were unable to stop the crowd because of its size.

Hidalgo state Gov. Jesús Murillo Karam, who was in town when the lynchings happened, said he begged the mob in vain to stop.

The townspeople also set the courthouse on fire and burned five patrol cars as well as the victims' pick up truck.

The local prosecutor, Omar Fayad, said 20 people were arrested.[14]

About 9:30 P.M. that troubled 14 February in Tijuana, members of the horde burst through the police cordon outside The Fort and broke down the massive wooden front doors of the comandancia itself. A few reached the entrance to the interrogation area and with crowbars and axes began to break in, but deputies, threatening to shoot, forced them back into the street. Police Inspector Medina Ríos called for military help. Fifty soldiers quickly responded to reinforce the defenders. (Tijuana's army contingent had only numbered 150 officers and men before the Minister of Defense moved district headquarters, with its 450 troops, from Mexicali to Tijuana the previous year. Still, this combined force represented a fairly limited military presence in a small town.)

The riots placed the soldiers in a difficult role, as the army men were reasonably integrated into the community. While residents of the region certainly had their complaints against the authoritarianism and arbitrariness of the military, soldiers rented their lodgings from homeowners, hobnobbed with local folks, attended their social activities, and contributed to the local economy. Now officers ordered them to level their rifles at friends (or at least acquaintances), to arrest them if necessary, and to shoot into their ranks if matters burst out of hand. It is one thing to menace a faceless enemy and another to threaten an associate or companion. Abundant evidence confirms that military personnel can be harsh with family and friends, but until taunted beyond their breaking point Tijuana's soldiers for the most part grimaced and stood back when jeered by the angry throng around the comandancia. The army wanted the crime solved and avenged as rapidly as anyone else. It indicated no thought of transferring the soldier to another post, but it did order its troops to prevent a mob lynching, and duty called. Meanwhile, inside the building nervous soldiers guarded the suspect. Officials quietly informed the distraught relatives of the slain child Olga that the case would be solved by ten o'clock that night and an official statement issued.

At that hour General Contreras stepped out front of The Fort and addressed the menacing crowd with a plea for calm and patience. Distinguished by his thick eyeglasses and with his outstretched hands urging self-control upon the throng, he promised that justice would prevail in this case, that little Olga would be avenged. Then came the announcement that Private Juan Castillo Morales had confessed to the rape and murder of Olga Camacho. Furthermore, the general said he had asked permission of President Cárdenas through the Defense Ministry to execute the guilty soldier immediately, either by releasing him to the crowd for its designs or by military execution. (It seems unlikely that Contreras ever considered surrendering the prisoner to the crowd but probably said so to placate it.) Now he awaited a reply from Mexico City.

Most of his listeners already knew how justice worked in Mexico. Contreras had contacted his superiors at the National Defense Ministry, who after consultation with the president would decide the fate of the prisoner and precisely how it was to be accomplished. Not a tribunal, but the president—then Lázaro Cárdenas—served as the highest judge in this land, which seemed to assure that his decision would be as political as anything else.

In this instance, the president could decree that the case be passed through the civil court system already established in the Federal Territory of Baja California Norte, of which Tijuana was part, but this procedure presented a potential problem in the Castillo Morales matter. The death penalty had been abolished in all federal entities, including the territory, in 1929. (Eight states and the Code of Military Justice still retained it.) Conviction for rape and murder carried a maximum penalty of twenty years in prison. Obviously, a citizenry demanding the head of the criminal would not have countenanced a prison sentence as retribution for the brutal slaying of a child. To curb the anger of the mob, the culprit must be put to death—but by whose authority and by what means? News of the affair had spread far beyond the town, and a decision could carry national and perhaps international implications. The morale of the military might be affected. Enemies of the regime could turn a misstep here against the government. Most definitely, any hint of riot in Tijuana needed to be quenched for fear that its sparks might fall on dry tinder elsewhere in the country. Local sedition can ignite and fuel a national rebellion.

Outside the comandancia, soldiers armed with 7 mm Mausers and 13-inch fixed bayonets nudged the crowds into a tense compliance, but certainly not docility. The throng continued to hurl its taunts—"Who are you protecting?"—along with occasional rocks, and the rabid rhetoric of certain impassioned voices heightened the stress. Among the most vituperative were labor union leaders such as Adrián Félix, known to his admirers as "El Güero" Félix (the blond or fair—"Blondie"), who edited the radical union weekly *La Razón,* and Octaviano Flores Contreras, who was a lawyer-without-title (that is, without a formal degree). Their Regional Congress of Mexican Workers (Congreso Regional de Obreros Mexicanos, or CROM) already stood at a breaking point with the federal government over rejected union demands concerning job security and pay.

As the standoff at The Fort seethed, official telegraph updates wired from the scene, as well as from the governor's palace in Mexicali to cabinet ministers and the president in Mexico City, vindictively implicated CROM members as instigators of the civic disturbances rattling Tijuana. Rival unions and government agencies accused CROM of cynically using the Camacho rape-murder as a pretext for fomenting the riots, which they feared might soon bubble over into outright rebellion. In response, CROM denied such intentions and urged swift resolution of the murder case, even as it decried the flagrant use of brute force against the public by the police. The exchange of accusations only stiffened backs and further polarized adversaries in an already nonnegotiable deadlock.

At 2 A.M., Tuesday, 15 February, all hell broke loose. Automobiles, their horns honking, raced up and down the streets; women and men beat broomsticks and iron rods against the metal covers of garbage containers, pails, cans, and pieces of scrap metal. The clamor was a call to action. History reminds us that in similar situations enraged rioters have frequently pounded tin cans and metal objects as a means of communication. The steady din summons comrades and solidifies ranks. Just as soldiers holler at the top of their lungs when they dive headlong into battle, the incessant clang of the cans stirs courage among rioters. It gives notice to adversaries that "we are coming" and strikes fright, if not terror, into the breasts of their foes. In this case, above the din of the crowd could be heard the shrill, clear notes of a bugle or coronet spurring the throng on, many of the protestors undoubtedly fortified with drink. It is well known that if liquor is available, soldiers swill it down before they swarm into battle. The rioters in Tijuana would do nothing less, and there was plenty of booze available in this freewheeling border town.

Toting burning kerosene-soaked rags wrapped around long poles, benches ripped from their moorings to be used as battering rams, jars filled with gasoline set for hurling, and pistols fingered in the pockets of overcoats along with a variety of inventive, hand-fashioned weapons, the throng began to assault its target. As The Fort came under siege, Police Chief Viñals Carsi urged restraint, but he was jostled aside and lost his glasses in the melee. Military and police guards threatened but then declined to fire their rifles at the crowd and backed away to relative safety; it was later said that most of the soldiers did not even carry weapons, but this seems unlikely. While some members of the mob simply rapped on glass containers just to make their angered presence known, others in a frenzied and righteous state of mind hurled fire bombs through the broken windows of the enclosure, which quickly burst into flame. Everything wooden burned—doors and window frames, beams and furniture, partitions, supports, floors, and roofing—creating suffocating smoke and intense heat.

The town's lone fire engine, probably a 1928 Seagrave pumper purchased used from the San Diego Fire Department, raced with its crew of four to the scene, but as it approached men and women lay down in the path of the vehicle and blocked its advance. Newspapers recounted that the citizenry literally "paved" the street with their bodies. When the firefighters stretched out their two-and-one-half-inch hoses as best they could to soak down adjoining buildings, members of the mob wielding axes, machetes, and knives easily hacked through the hard rubber covered with only a thin cotton fabric. Someone slashed the tires of the fire truck; another jumped aboard and cranked the siren so that it added its eerie piercing wail to the cacophony. Fires were the special bane of communities like Tijuana, constructed mainly of wooden buildings. Firemen could not get enough water on the flames fast enough to stifle the appetite of such blazes, which easily could consume an entire block before surrounding streets became a firebreak. Tijuana had no water mains and no hydrants, so water tankers supplied the pump engine. The blaze at The Fort spelled potential disaster for the entire town, but this possibility hardly deterred the crowd.

Some sixty rioters used benches as battering rams to crash into the interior of The Fort, where they smashed down partitions seeking the soldier under interrogation for the crime. In their minds, Juan Castillo Morales was guilty, and they aimed to loop a noose around his neck. Now they filled the main quadrangle, where some two dozen policemen and soldiers halted further advance. A stalemate developed. Then a blaze broke out in one corner of the building. When defenders informed the intruders that the flames approached a room where fifteen tons of dynamite had been stored, the infuriated invaders allowed firemen to kick embers and burning timbers away from the threatened area but still kept them from using their water buckets or hoses. Then police and soldiers used clubs and rifle butts to drive the rioters back toward their comrades in the streets, while The Fort continued to burn.

Caught between the flames and the howling mob, those inside the building took actions clouded from our view by the dense smoke and fumes of the moment, later rumors, and today's fragmented recollections. Certainly, no one died, and no one seems to have been seriously hurt. Some eighteen petty criminals (*juiciados*), mostly juveniles lodged there in makeshift confinement because they could not pay their fines, pitched in and helped fight the blazes. In the town jail next to the comandancia, seventy prisoners, among them three U.S. citizens—all in a frenzy like threatened, caged animals—choked on smoke, banged on the bars of their cells, and yelled for help, though the flames still remained some distance away from them. As for Juan Castillo Morales, a heavy guard spirited him out a rear door to the new military compound on the edge of town. Some say authorities dressed him as a woman to disguise his flight. One can only guess at the young soldier's state of mind at this moment. Eyewitnesses said he was more frightened at being ripped to shreds by the vengeful mob than he was at facing military justice.[15] He may have been promised leniency. There was still the possibility that he would be tried and sentenced within the territory's civil court system. Other hearsay had it that he would suffer the *Ley Fuga*—the law of flight—under which his guards, under the guise of transporting him to court or another safe haven, would shoot him en route alleging attempted escape. His destiny still lay in the ministries of government, and ultimately with the president himself.

A New Target

Dawn brought no respite in the turbulence. The government had done what it thought necessary to quell the violence: declared martial law, closed all shops and cantinas, sealed off the international border (which prevented tourists and gunrunners from crossing into town), issued periodic radio warnings that rioters would be treated harshly, and stationed police and troops around The Fort, the jail, and along important roadways and other points thought to be especially vulnerable to the crowd's fury. Protected by soldiers, firemen had managed to control the blaze within the comandancia. They cut holes in the wooden roof of the building, allowing smoke and heat to escape, and when the inside cooled down and they could finally see where they were going, they soaked the place, now largely in ruins. The extinguished fire left nasty scars, including the soot-covered outside walls which the inferno had licked black through shattered windows. Such markings reminded all onlookers of the determination of the crowd and underlined its challenge to state authority.

For a couple of hours in the early morning darkness a veil of relative calm obscured the reality that the town still seethed with rancor and a desire for revenge in search of an outlet. An hour after dawn the mob redirected its fervor against a new target: the two-story Palacio Municipal, the heart of government administration, which housed among others the offices and archives of the delegado, the tax collector, the property registrar and civil registry, the town treasury, the federal work inspector, and the departments of public works and agriculture, along with various levels of judicial personnel and the controversial Labor Arbitration Board. In other words, the essential workings of governance in Tijuana, situated only a block from police headquarters, lay vulnerable to assault.

During the previous ten days a dozen or so men and women of the CROM had waged a sit-down strike in the main inside patio of the building to protest a government decision that had gone against them concerning back wages, but with the raid on the comandancia the squatters had melted away. Now the CROM was back, proudly waving its red and black banners and leading toward the palacio a throng of perhaps twelve hundred, including school-age children. They met no opposition and stormed inside, breaking windows, hurling typewriters into the street, scattering archival records to the elements, destroying furniture, knocking down partitions, and generally creating mayhem. Then they hurled torches of rags soaked with gasoline into the structure. Flames eagerly devoured the termite-ridden framework of the building. Record books, specialized libraries, and files of documents blazed, including tax records for 1934 through 1936, the registry of street vendors, eleven files of tax receipts, and office correspondence for 1937. Papers lying loose on desks fed the fire, including letters, official forms, and memorandums on which employees had been working.[16] Present-day historians who wish to reconstruct the history of Tijuana for the 1930s can only shrug their shoulders at the loss. Throughout Mexican history revolutionaries have made a point of destroying municipal archives, which they see as both a symbol of government-gone-wrong and the repository of damaging documentation against themselves. Tijuana's turn came the morning of 15 February.

The few employees caught in the building at the time of the raid managed to escape, saving what they could with their own hands. They heard the mob coming, but in true bureaucratic fashion tried to salvage their work even when faced by disaster. José Carmareña and others heaved bound bundles of official documents out of second-story windows into the wet streets. Cleanup workers later toted a substantial cache of fire-scorched and water-soaked materials to military headquarters for safekeeping, but they apparently ended up in the town's rubbish heap. Fortunately, no one was injured or killed in the melee at the municipal palace, even if valuable testimonies to the town's history went up in flames.

A reporter for the *San Diego Evening Tribune*, Joe Pazen, ducked into an engineer's office overlooking the scene and telephoned to a rewrite man on the city desk his dramatic on-the-spot account of the turbulence:

> "The mob just arrived at the federal building [Palacio del Gobierno]. They broke windows and threw gasoline over the building. It's burning to beat the devil."
>
> "Is the fire department there, Joe?
>
> "No, they're busy keeping the flames from fifteen tons of dynamite at the jail."

"Where are you, Joe?

"Oh, I'm right across the street in an engineer's office. Hey, the flames have reached the second story. The crowd is out of hand."

[The rewrite man hears a rattling noise like the backfiring of automobiles] "What's all the racket, Joe?"

"Hell, the soldiers just arrived. They're shooting at the mob. Say, some bullets whistled past my ear. They almost hit me."[17]

A hapless fellow reporter fell victim to the chaos. At bayonet-point, soldiers ordered Earl Zahn, who worked out of the San Diego office of International News Photos, away from the riot area. The hard-of-hearing photographer did not respond rapidly enough to the command to "move on." Surmising disobedience, soldiers viciously kicked and pummeled Zahn, who limped in considerable pain from the scene, and that only with the help of a Mexican youngster who led him and two other *San Diego Sun* reporters to safety through a grocery store.[18]

Newsmen and photographers, who had to sneak into Mexico, evading the entry ban at the border, caught recriminations from both sides: rioters who wanted their cause reported but not their names, and authorities who hoped to see their official statements in print but no news of the extensive damage caused by the crowd or of the excesses inherent in police and military repression. Since officials used photographs published in newspapers to identify rioters, reporters faced the ire of the crowd as well as the demands of the peacekeepers.

At the height of the tumult rioters apprehended the lead dispatcher for the local light and telephone company, situated two blocks from The Fort, and ordered him to shut down all the town's electrical power. He agreed to comply, but said that the main switch was located in a rear room. He went back to throw the switch and when unobserved slipped outside into the confusion in the street. Cutting the power would have left Tijuana a battered island in a stormy sea, out of telegraph, telephone, and radio communication with the outside world. The dispatcher's ruse narrowly averted a calamity.

During Tuesday morning's rioting, Tijuana's fire chief phoned his counterpart in San Diego, John E. Parrish, for help in subduing the crowd. He faced an emergency, he said. Would Chief Parrish please send down his modern pumpers to douse the unruly mob with highly pressured water? "This is an international matter," sputtered Parrish, looking for an excuse to avoid intervention. The Tijuana chief assured Parrish that any international implications could be handled by Tijuana officialdom. "But if I go down there shooting water on your crowd, they're liable to shoot me," Parrish replied. The Mexican chief was ready for him, however: "If they shoot you, we'll shoot them."[19] That ended the conversation; the San Diego engines stayed put at home.

General Contreras, with six hundred soldiers and a number of police, customs agents, and quickly deputized officials at his command, ordered fifty soldiers and additional police to secure the palace at all costs, and this time the military meant business. At the sight of the troops, the crowd backed off some thirty yards, but did not retreat. Instead, they hurled a barrage of rocks, dirt clods, and insults at the soldiers, who cordoned off the building with hastily constructed barricades of benches, desks, tables, almost anything substantial they could find to restrain the throng. There stood the military with Mausers at the ready, bayonets set, challenging the mob to dare further assault.

Shouts of "Give us the killer or we will burn more buildings" proved the crowd's persistence. They yelled that they knew that the suspected killer was being held in the new army cuartel at the edge of town, and that when finished with the municipal building they would burn down the cuartel. The soldiers fired a volley over the heads of the belligerents. Still the mob menaced the soldiers and surged a little forward. The troops leveled their rifles and fired. A young boy pitched forward, blood streaming from his mouth. Someone put a hat over his face, thinking him mortally wounded. A man clutched at his stomach, staggered and fell. Others slumped to the ground. Bullets could be heard zinging off buildings, and the crowd soon discovered that ricochets can be as deadly as aimed shots. Had the military used a cross fire at this juncture, they would have counted scores of casualties. As it was, more than a thousand shots were fired—not all by the soldiers and police, although throughout the riots authorities reported no casualties in their ranks.

Confusion reigned as the crowd scrambled for safety up side streets; some hunkered behind whatever protection they could find, in doorways or behind and under cars abandoned in the streets. At least fourteen were trampled in the crowd's panicked retreat. The police began to make arrests and quickly apprehended El Güero Félix. Before they could hustle him off to jail some two hundred of his compatriots wrenched him free and hurried him into an automobile that sped the union leader toward the border less than a mile away. Police gave chase, aiming their weapons to hit the tires of the escape vehicle, but Félix reached refuge in the United States. Other union people followed the same route on foot toward the international line, then marked only by a strand or two of barbed wire or in certain places a chain-link fence. These flimsy barriers were full of gaps cut by petty smugglers seeking to avoid customs duties and others trafficking in more substantial commodities who wanted easy access from one side to the other. In effect, no international barrier existed. The one customs crossing was at best lightly manned, at times empty, and agents posted there more often than not met crossers with a greeting instead of official questioning.

At the center of the riot district, women clutched Rosary beads and other spiritual icons, fell to their knees, and implored the protection of God. Young children separated from parents and friends wailed for help. Fourteen-year-old Salvador Vásquez lay wounded in front of the Casa Blanca shop; Jesús Tirado, sixteen, crumpled next to Maxim's. Daniel Estrada, thirty-nine, collapsed in pain near the palace. A *San Diego Sun* reporter saw angry men stalk homeward and later return to hide rifles and pistols in automobiles parked near the riot sites. "Three soldiers rushed a member of the mob, slugged him with the butt of a rifle, and took from him a pistol hidden under his coat." In stark defiance of law enforcement came the cries of the bloodied-but-unbowed: "We shall return to fight as you do," meaning with guns of various makes and caliber, as well as almost anything that could be fashioned into a deadly weapon.[20]

THE CRIME AND chaos in Tijuana made front-page banner headlines in the regional press and page-one news nearly everywhere else. The three San Diego dailies had a field day loading up their editions with sidebar stories and dramatic photographs. Los Angeles newspapers, including the Spanish-language *La Opinión*, provided nearly as much coverage. Elsewhere the press largely relied on lengthy and detailed wire service reports. Those papers with reporters on the scene vied for scoops and crowed in print when they managed to secure a tidbit (it was rarely more than that) that their rivals had not captured. Such heated competition bred errors and use of poorly substantiated information, and deadlines at the printing plants caused some articles to be truncated. Reporting in such fast-moving and dangerous circumstances always has its pitfalls, and the journalists relied heavily on official sources for information about the proceedings against Juan Castillo Morales while they braved the streets for firsthand accounts of the rioting.

Assessing casualties caused by the tumult proved to be especially difficult. One newspaper had twelve dead and hundreds hurt, another counted two dead and a few injured. The *San Francisco Examiner* reported three dead and fourteen either wounded by gunfire or trampled in the riot. Government accounts tended to minimize the casualties. Governor Sánchez Taboada deliberately underestimated, reporting no deaths and only six injuries to the Ministry of Government in Mexico City.[21]

Fortunately for the town, flames at the municipal palace had not spewed embers or generated sufficient heat to ignite adjoining buildings. Firefighters, free of harassment from crowds and assisted by soldiers, had adequate water to extinguish the blaze confined to the palace itself, but not before over half of the interior had been destroyed. With flames doused and the military in charge, a more accurate casualty count could be made. One person was known to be mortally wounded by bullets: Vidal Torres, fifty-six, a married man with two children. Three others were seriously hurt but recovering at the civil military hospital: Jesús Tirado, Daniel Estrada, and Salvador Vásquez, the boy shot in the head and initially reported dead in the street. The teenager did indeed receive a ghastly wound: the bullet which felled him had passed through both cheeks and his mouth but had struck nothing vital, and he survived. Speculation circulated that many more had been injured but had been carried away by their comrades, or in other ways been transported or made their way back to their homes where families and neighbors treated their wounds.

No Mexican newspaper seems to have sent a journalist to Tijuana to report its own account of the events. Several Mexico City papers carried the Tijuana story on page one but relied upon wire services for information. (The national press headquartered in Mexico City rarely sent reporters to cover "provincial" events, although it occasionally printed such stories submitted by "special correspondents." Moreover, governors frequently paid these correspondents to keep unfavorable reports out of the newspapers.) In this case, the federal government quickly issued an official statement about the *zafarrancho* (row or ruckus) in Tijuana: It came from the Autonomous Press and Publicity Department of the Secretaría de Gobernación (Interior):

Mexico, D. F., febrero 15 de 1938: Col. Rudolfo Sánchez Taboada, governor of the Northern District of Baja California, Tijuana, telephonically informs [the ministry]:

An eight-year-old girl was murdered in Tijuana. The assassin was a soldier of the Fourteenth Battalion who was taken to jail. People began to threaten the jail, demanding that the murderer be turned over to them so that they could bring him to justice by lynching him, but the prisoner was not turned over to them. Agitation continued all night long.

These groups, which are of the CROM involved in the Agua caliente [contractual] matter, burned the towers [of the comandancia] next to the jail and the Palace of the Delegation. The federal force had to shoot at them in order to drive them away. Six wounded were recovered [by the authorities] and others were taken to their homes. Not one person was killed. In a detailed telegram, Sánchez Taboada will inform the government of the names of the wounded and others.

Furthermore, we are also assured that General Contreras, who commands the federal forces in Tijuana, has completely reestablished order, that soldiers guard the jail and the palace of the delegation, and that the [marauding] groups have been broken up.

Col. Sánchez Taboada immediately called for peace [among the populace], assuring that he will energetically proceed to bring the guilty to strict justice, and that he will inform the president in detail about the entire affair in order to avoid the publication of any scandalous reports concerning the tumult.[22]

The perfunctory official report reveals two strands of official thought toward the troubles in Tijuana: (1) a focus on the CROM, with which the government was already in serious conflict and was anxious to curtail, if not eliminate; (2) fear that the sensational events in Tijuana would cause a national scandal or even cross international boundaries, where they could be interpreted as evidence of a destabilized Mexico tending toward open rebellion. Cárdenas and his high-level advisors now deciding the fate of Juan Castillo Morales must have taken these sorts of concerns into consideration. Simply put, the situation demanded a speedy resolution that would guarantee public peace. No one should ask questions about the troubles on the border, but trust the government and forget the turbulence.

Conciliation of Sorts

A strong military presence smothered public resistance in Tijuana. At key points on street corners the army set up machine-gun squads. Soldiers also manned posts on the roofs of the buildings, including the palacio, so that they might have a clear field of enfilading fire down streets where mobs might congregate. Police, customs agents, almost anyone with an official function, and volunteers deputized into service patrolled the streets and established strongpoints at locations such as the comandancia. Hard-nosed, volatile, unpredictable *agraristas* had been trucked in from Mexicali, Ensenada, Tecate, and nearby El Rosarito to reinforce the pacification effort. Agraristas, mainly farmers and ranchers who had been granted land, secondhand guns, and other favors as part of the Cárdenas administration's attempt to build broad political support, constituted a loosely molded auxiliary armed force that could be called up in emergencies to restore public order. They had a national reputation more for creating mayhem than for calming disturbances, and the ordinary citizen kept them at arm's length. Now, at the behest of Governor Sánchez Taboada, several hundred of them had moved into Tijuana, where the garrison opened up its storehouse of late-model weapons and ammunition to them. San Diego's *Evening Tribune* summed up the scene: "An eighteen-hour reign of blood and destruction faded into quiet before the machine guns and riflery of the soldiers" and "Machine guns pointed disciplinary muzzles along streets and sidewalks."[23]

With official units in place, on Wednesday, 16 February, authorities made a show of returning the town to normality. Their implicit message was: "Everything is under control. Get back to work. Live as before." Even Aurelio Camacho urged an end to the rioting: "What is the sense," he said, "to spill more blood [in revenge] for hers?"[24] As there had been rumors about various instances of child abuse swirling around town even before Olga's death, a number of Tijuana mothers pleaded with the police and soldiers to make the town safe for their children, an indication of the mixed relationship that often develops between lawmen and the public in troubled times.

Officials unsealed the border, allowing tourists and the curious to wander into town but only after signing an affidavit at the customs crossing that absolved the Mexican government of any responsibility should they get hurt during their visit. Some cafes, grocery stores, and curio shops reopened for business, but official mandate prohibited saloons from doing so. No looting seems to have taken place during the tumult, although the *San Diego Union* reported broken windows in several stores run by Jewish merchants, a perhaps spurious comment unconfirmed by other sources. Officials strained themselves and their resources to create calm in the town, but in fact the atmosphere remained highly charged and far from routine.

How could it be otherwise? Police plucked people out of their homes and charged them with arson, inciting to riot, and in some cases sedition, all punishable by long prison terms (if not worse) on direct orders from the president. General Contreras ordered handbills circulated warning that "certain persons" who used the girl's death as an excuse to incite riots would be punished, and he broadcast radio spots that emphasized his intentions. Mob violence broke the law, and the military held a total of seventy-eight offenders at the comandancia in overcrowded conditions that lacked sanitation facilities, bedding, food, water, and lighting. The incarcerated were able to eat only because members and friends brought them meals, along with candy and cigarettes. Most of the detained were members of CROM, among them the spirited rabble-rouser Señora Guadalupe Gómez. People with reputations like hers incurred automatic suspicions in official eyes. Tension reigned because no one—neither the authorities nor the prisoners—knew where the mass detentions would take them; the whole scenario was entirely new to Tijuana.

Among those who found safe haven among friends and relatives on the U.S. side of the border was a rambunctious youth, seventeen-year-old Carlos Escandón, who had borrowed his sister's '24 Ford to join the protest on Monday, 14 February. "The rioters siphoned the gasoline from the car and used the petrol to soak rags which they lit to burn the comandancia. Torches were carried in the streets. When we confronted the military at the palacio, the soldiers shot in the air. Some shot at the ground, however, and their bullets ricocheted and killed a person or so. Some others were wounded." As the roundup of suspected participants began, Carlos headed for the border. "It was easy to cross; there were only three strands of wire at the line." He stayed in the United States for three months for fear of implication in the riots. During the self-imposed exile, Escandón made personal contacts that later helped him to establish a highly successful merchant business across the border.[25]

Olga Camacho, the rape and murder victim. (*San Diego Evening Tribune*)

A 1932 photograph of the Tijuana neighborhood where the Camachos lived, with its Catholic church and military headquarters, known as The Fort. The city jail stood to the right (by the palm tree). Residents called this the safest part of town. The car at the far right is a 1928 or 1929 model A Ford roadster, popular with local families. (Andre Williams Collection)

In their angry determination to get their hands on the presumed killer of Olga Camacho, a mob of a thousand or more attacked and burned the police comandancia, popularly known as The Fort. This photo was taken on 14 February 1938. (San Diego Historical Society)

The frustrated mob also burned and looted Tijuana's municipal building, the Palacio Municipal, still smoldering when this photo was taken on 15 February 1938. Policemen like those pictured used their weapons to repel the crowd. (San Diego Historical Society)

The slain girl's parents, Aurelio and Feliza Camacho, were inconsolable. (*San Diego Union*)

A twenty-four-year-old Mexican soldier, Juan Castillo Morales, confessed to the crime. Newspaper reporters who interviewed him at the jail where he was held said he told them, "I did it." (*San Diego Evening Tribune*)

To protect Castillo Morales from mobs which vowed to lynch him, authorities guarded the prisoner behind bars at the new military compound on the edge of town. (*San Diego Union*)

Over the grave, an unknown party erected a Christian cross labeled with the soldier's name, date of death, and the hope that he rest in peace. (*San Diego Union*)

RUMORS ABOUT THE disposition of Juan Castillo Morales continued to fan embers of anxiety and hatred in town. Contradictory reports stoked the burning concern that the army was out to protect its own—that as a soldier, the confessed killer would simply be transferred to another post and forgotten. There is not a scrap of evidence that the army ever intended to follow that tack, but custom and tradition raised warning flags in public sensibilities. The *San Diego Union* reported that

> While authorities speeded arrangements of trial for [Castillo] Morales, the soldier maintained an air of indifference. It was indicated that he would be brought before a [civil] court of Primera Instancia [the initial court to hear these types of proceedings] within two weeks, and if evidence proves sufficient, the case will be referred to the Supreme Court in Mexico City. Maximum penalty under Mexican law is 25 years [most other reports reduced it to 20], unless the president issues a decree of execution.[26]

According to press accounts, few people expected this case to follow Mexican law.

Other scuttlebutt had it that Juan would be tried by the military and then subjected to the Ley Fuga, certainly not a public execution, but in the accustomed way, outside of public scrutiny. Juan would simply be "disappeared." Yet other rumors had him being turned over to the public to satisfy its blood lust. It was all up to Cárdenas and his confidants. The president had shown some leniency in other capital cases, commuting death sentences to life, but political realities juggle the priorities of all rulers, and at the moment the Cárdenas administration appeared to be foundering. The national economy was weakening, and Cárdenas's reform programs, faced by increasing resistance, had lost much of their inspiration and forward momentum. Moreover, conflicts with foreign companies over exploitation of the country's oil reserves were at a crucial stage, and former political associates now threatened rebellion against the regime. Finally, the dark clouds of World War II, with all their uncertainties, were gathering on the horizon. How much deliberation might one reasonably expect a president to give to riots, now contained, and a rape-murder case in the small border town of Tijuana? Whatever Cárdenas considered and then decided, no "smoking gun" has been discovered, no evidence that indicates, or even intimates, his decision. We only know what happened, but it was so out-of-the-ordinary, so deliberately crafted, the use of the Ley Fuga at a public execution so unique to the Mexican experience, that it must have been masterminded, or at least approved, by people in highest places.

Actually, the authorities had proceeded toward civil justice, a gesture best characterized as a slight nod. José Carmareña had typed up his skimpy, jumbled acta quoting the exchange between the interrogators and Castillo Morales in the early stages of the investigation. Though hounded by questioners, the soldier had maintained his innocence. Carmareña judged the acta to be useless but did his duty and passed it on to his boss, the town's delegado. The delegado apparently made no comments on the matter; it was not particularly his role to do so, and he forwarded the case to Moisés Oliva, whom we first met interrogating the suspect in the comandancia. As acting prosecutor, Oliva was responsible for deciding whether or not there was sufficient evidence to warrant a hearing in the Court of First Instance. Oliva equivocated, hinting that whatever his duty in the matter, the case would be concluded by the Ley Fuga anyway. Without recommendation concerning prosecution, therefore, he simply passed the case on to the judge of first instance.

Carmareña picks up the thin legal thread being followed here:

> When the judge of primera estancia received the acta, which was weak and in no way conclusive, he washed his hands of the entire affair. Because the defendant was a soldier, he turned the entire case over to the military. Actually, he had authority to do so, because the town was under martial law, which meant that the governor had decided that civil authorities had lost control of the town, and therefore it should be placed under military supervision. Normal civil guarantees had been suspended. Of course, the judge could have clung to the case, but he did not. Instead, he said: "He's a soldier. It's not my duty to hear this case."[27]

Official accounts of these procedures rather cursorily stated that the judge had relinquished his authority to the military, as if this were an everyday occurrence, which it certainly was not. Juan Castillo Morales was to have a special military court martial, which meant a fast, secret, and decisive trial. Now we can see what the Cárdenas regime had decided for the soldier.

Meanwhile, Olga Camacho had been laid to her final rest. In keeping with customary funereal practices, burial occurred the day after death:

TIJUANA, Feb. 16 (Special). . . . Funeral services were conducted for Olga yesterday [Tuesday, 15 Feb.] afternoon. Danger that the rites might fan the wrath of the mob into a new riot failed to materialize.

While 400 soldiers, police, agrarista civil deputies and customs guards patrolled the streets, hundreds of men, women and children marched in long queues to the cemetery behind the motor hearse which bore the child's ravished and mutilated little body to the grave.

At the grave site the lid of Olga's little coffin was pushed back for a moment. The hundreds, heads bowed reverently, filed slowly past for a last glimpse of the tragic figure before the coffin was closed and lowered beneath the earth. Many, including little children carrying small bouquets clutched in tightly clenched fists, laid flowers on the grave.

As night came, those who had milled in angry, destroying throngs all day, slowly began returning to their homes. Lights began blinking from windows.

Much of Tijuana had turned out for the funeral.[28]

The Trial

With the case of Juan Castillo Morales firmly within military jurisdiction, the court martial began at 5 P.M., Wednesday, 16 February, at the rented home and office of General Contreras near The Fort. Nothing is known of the proceeding itself, since it was held in secret; if there is a trial record, its whereabouts are unknown. However, the court did publicly announce its verdict and punishment. The charges presumably remained the same as those presented in the civil court: homicide and statutory rape. The army might have couched these allegations as "disgracing a soldier's uniform," a military catchall open to broad interpretation and, along with treason or desertion in time of war, subject to capital punishment. Regardless, presidential discretion superseded military sentencing authority.

Normally, the military court selected an army officer with legal experience to defend a soldier accused of a capital crime. In this case, the court designated Luis G. Martínez, a prominent local resident, to be the defendant's attorney. Perhaps no military personnel with knowledge of the law were available in the district. The court, in a hurry to dispose of a case which was roiling the community, was probably loath to await the arrival of an army lawyer from another post. As for Martínez, he was one of the town's fourteen lawyers and at the time occasionally served as public defender in the court system, especially in high-profile cases with international implications. For instance, he had successfully defended Samuel Dubin, a naturalized Mexican citizen who lived a somewhat mysterious life on a rancho outside of Ensenada, against U.S. extradition attempts; the Americans allegedly wanted Dubin for swindling a U.S. citizen, but the real reason was probably because he was thought to be a German spy. But attorney Martínez was best known as secretary to the Chamber of Commerce, where he labored to boost tourism and other profit-making ventures in the city. As did all of the town's entrepreneurs in the present crisis, he urged a quick return to public order, which coincided with what seemed to be the directive to the military court from Mexico City: "Do whatever needs to be done to restore tranquility in Tijuana." It was just a matter of how this might best be accomplished.

The court martial reportedly lasted twelve hours, well into the next morning of 17 February. Did the tribunal actually weigh evidence? Did Martínez forcefully defend his client or at least plead for leniency in sentencing? He could have emphasized the defendant's state of mind prior to the killing, the result of a traumatic series of family deaths. His father, Jorge, had died of natural causes only a month before the murder of which his son now stood accused. Then, only two weeks later, his mother died. And just a week before Olga's death, his younger brother, twenty-year-old Manuel, was killed in an automobile accident. In sum, the entire family of the accused had been wiped out in the month preceding his trial, and he now stood before his accusers very much alone.[29]

A Tijuana weekly newspaper, *La Epoca,* made just this point. It noted the sudden demise of the soldier's family and asked: "Would not this number of sad occurrences foist a terrifying cloud on the mind of the youth and terrible criminal and induce him to commit the barbaric murder?"[30] When it came to the sentencing, none of these events seem to have been introduced by the defense as mitigating circumstances and probably would not have mattered if they had been.

Assuming that the court was following the country's constitution, Martínez could have stopped the trial, at least temporarily, by petitioning the nation's Supreme Court for a hearing on a constitutional issue. He could have claimed, for instance, that the defendant's constitutional rights were being violated by the court's procedures. This plea for an *amparo* has been and still is most often employed by defendants to shift their hearing from state to federal jurisdiction, or as it would have pertained to Castillo Morales, from a military to a civil court. Given the temper of the moment, it seems unlikely that the amparo would have been granted, but the high court had been known on occasion to confound the wishes of government. It would have slowed down the military steamroller in Tijuana, at least, but Martínez did not apply for such relief on behalf of his client. Public peace must have been uppermost in his mind, along with a return to business-as-normal.

Did the court maintain contact with Mexico City for instructions throughout the hearing? Was this a fair trial or a farce? These sorts of questions cannot be answered because the trial was held behind closed doors. Practically nothing about the trial itself appears in press accounts of the entire affair. Reporters either asked no questions about the procedure or received no response, official or otherwise, to their queries. It took twelve hours of hearings to do what? The daughter of Luis Martínez says she never heard him discuss the case after its conclusion.

There are gaps in all historical reconstructions, and these are yawning. The military court walked a tightrope. It aimed to underscore governmental and military authority and power, and without question it did that. It wanted to insure the nervous and incredulous citizenry of Tijuana that it could trust the tribunal to bring Olga Camacho's rapist and killer to justice, and it certainly achieved that. Above all, the tribunal wanted to restore public order to the town, and it accomplished that. The tribunal also wished to leave the impression that legal forms had been honored in the proceedings against the defendant. Some individuals believed this; others did not; and for the majority of the populace it did not seem to matter. They would have preferred the certainty of their own lynch party, but a military execution would do. Still, the secrecy, inconsistencies, and equivocations surrounding the case, added to the swiftness with which it was consummated, could not help but breed conspiracy theories, and ever since the trial such conjecture has abounded.

Relying on official statements, the press reported that the court martial ran into the early morning hours of Thursday, 17 February, and if so, it left Juan Castillo Morales only a few hours to live. The sentence was death by execution, specifically by the Ley Fuga, set for shortly after sunrise. It was decreed a public execution, to take place in the town's public cemetery. Once again, Martínez could have slowed the onrushing tide by requesting a presidential pardon, but he did not do so. The press was invited, assured that the ritual would not take place until the sun was high enough in the sky to permit good picture taking. If ever an execution in Mexico was specially crafted for public fulfillment, it was that of Castillo Morales. When one thinks of it, it was nothing less than extraordinary.

Punishment

By the end of the nineteenth century, most countries in Europe and the Americas had outlawed public executions as cruel, inhumane, revolting, and uncivilized spectacles. Being "modern" meant, among many other things, the elimination of those earlier vulgar, circuslike gatherings of thousands which had spawned debauchery and petty crime among the spectators and far too often for official taste had led the crowds to jeer the hangman and cheer the condemned. Public executions excited crowds, made spectators nervous, and in the long run brutalized those who witnessed the rituals. Performing such rites behind prison walls or at least out of public sight seemed more humane and politically preferable. By removing executions from public gaze, authorities limited attendance and obviated the problem of crowd control. Nevertheless, debate over the value of publicizing these episodes as a deterrent to others still rages on.

Mexico, along with other nations, had virtually eliminated public executions. People still remembered, if only from school texts, the ceremonial, public execution of Archduke Maximilian and two of his ranking Mexican allies outside of Querétaro in 1867 (immortalized by Manet's painting). And throughout much of the nineteenth century it was not unusual for people traveling country roads to encounter the decaying corpse of a bandit hanged from a tree as exemplary punishment. In line with the dictates of being modern, however, at the approach of the twentieth century Mexico moved its penal executions inside prison walls but still invited journalists to view and write about the ritual. Newsmen zestfully reported the details, such as those involving the demise of J. Jesús Negrete, "El Tigre de Santa Julia." Negrete and several cohorts engaged in a shoot-out with Mexico City police in October 1906; four died, and three were wounded. The court sentenced Negrete to death in 1908 and rejected his appeals for a new trial; after the president denied him a pardon, a firing squad executed El Tigre on 8 December 1910. Some complained the judicial process had been too slow, since Negrete died nearly five years after the crime, and two years after sentencing. But unlike Juan Castillo

Morales, Negrete knew, or had a lawyer who understood, how to string out the judicial process.

The night before Negrete died, he wrote poetry and a letter to his sister in which he said though near death, he did not fear it. He regretted his crimes and asked God to pardon him. Negrete then thanked his priest and ended the note with a "Viva México!" Then the capital's daily newspapers described the execution itself: Negrete smoked a Havana cigar given to him by the governor of the federal district at the condemned man's request. He wore a black *charro* (cowboy) outfit that he also had requested, and was escorted to the garden of the Belem Penitentiary. He took a long puff on his Havana, uttered "Adios a todos [goodbye to all]," and heard the firing squad ordered to fire. But the soldiers were not accurate and Negrete had to be administered a mercy shot. He was buried in the sixth-class section of a local cemetery, but not before he was decapitated so that scientists could study his brain (albeit badly mutilated by the mercy shot), a criminological practice of the day. Printed details of the execution were meant to dissuade other criminally inclined individuals, but it was said that the death frightened "honorable" people more than it deterred delinquents. Still, circumstances surrounding the execution of Negrete were far distant from the raucous atmosphere that had attended public executions in the past, and not a few Mexicans prided themselves on the nation's march toward modernity.[31]

Mexico experienced a spate of public executions during the Revolution, which raged from 1910 to 1917, but none of them incorporated the Ley Fuga, as occurred with Castillo Morales some twenty years later. Photographs of staged executions during the rebellion were rapidly converted into picture postcards that were reproduced by the thousands and enjoyed wide circulation on both sides of the border. The prisoners were often shot standing in front of an adobe wall displaying pock marks from previous executions. When new prisoners were shot, people simply said that the victims had been "dobied."

The new constitution that emerged from the Revolution limited capital punishment, and in succeeding years state after state, along with the federal district (Mexico City) and territories, eliminated it altogether. By the time of the Castillo Morales affair those states that retained the extreme penalty did so only for specific crimes such as parricide or premeditated murder, and even then they used it sparingly. The military, of course, wrote its own code of justice, but even it hesitated to escort its own soldiers to a firing squad. It usually did so only to enforce discipline in times of national crisis, and increasingly has preferred to release to civil jurisdiction soldiers who commit crimes covered by civil law. In every way, the handling of Castillo Morales ran counter to countrywide trends, which could only raise serious questions of justice about the case.

Regimes have undoubtedly used variations of the extralegal Ley Fuga (sometimes referred to as Ley de Fuga) to rid themselves of political challengers and social outcasts since time immemorial. It has allowed governments to dispose of unwanted individuals without the rigamarole and uncertainties of a judicial process subject to public review. Although generally condemned by society at large, its use has been widespread. Perpetrators of the Ley Fuga have been labeled criminals, but proof is hard to come by. Understandably, those involved rarely, if ever, admit a deed which is normally committed as clandestinely as possible in an out-of-the-way place.

The practice gained high notoriety in the early 1870s when Julián de Zugasti was named governor of Spain's Córdoba Province with the special assignment of ridding the territory of banditry. Zugasti pursued his mission with fanatical zeal, using the Ley Fuga as one of his tools. The governor kept a diary of his successes, which yields a good deal of information about his methods. He claimed, for instance, that bandits tried to free prisoners being escorted to jail under armed guard, and that in the ensuing skirmish prisoners were killed. None of the potential liberators or members of security forces seemed to die in these rescue attempts, only the prisoners.[32]

But Zugasti did not invent the Ley Fuga as many supposed; it had been in use long before his tenure as governor. Mexico's President Anastasio Bustamente employed it against two men who rebelled against his government in the 1830s. The insurgents had surrendered on the promise that their lives would be spared. Bound hand and foot, and escorted by twenty dragoons, they were taken on mule back to the outskirts of Mexico City, where, according to the official report, they were shot while attempting to flee. The steady drum beat goes on to this day, and certainly not only in Mexico. When in April 1968 police arrested the Black Panther Bobby Hutton in Oakland, California, eyewitnesses swore that officers ordered him to run from the spot of his capture to a nearby police car, and when he ran they shot him down. Hutton died with ten bullets in his body, five of them in his head.[33]

NOW IT WAS Juan Castillo Morales's turn to run. In what seems to have been an unprecedented twist, his execution by Ley Fuga was planned as a public event. The soldier's end was to be witnessed by hundreds of spectators, many of them specially invited for the occasion. These unusual preparations harked back to those carefully orchestrated, gory spectacles of torture and execution of the late Middle Ages. Now in Tijuana the army, under orders from the Cárdenas administration, was doggedly determined to parade its brute force before those who dared to riot against its authority and at the same time to assure the townspeople in the most open way that Olga Camacho had been avenged.[34]

The special court martial had completed its deliberations at 5 A.M. General Contreras immediately informed Justo Verduzco, warden of the jail to which the defendant had been moved, of the verdict: death by execution. What was told to Juan Castillo Morales at this point is not clear. When escorted by two soldiers to the black police wagon, known as a *julia* in Mexico, he may have thought himself headed for civil court, where he would have the opportunity, if he so chose, to defend himself against the charges. Regardless of his plea before the judge, he would know that the worst he faced was a prison sentence. Castillo Morales may even have been told as much to keep him calm. Having just been through a military court martial, the prisoner should have known differently, but absent an official record there is no way to discover anything the tribunal might have told him. He had a breakfast (again, its contents are unknown) and about 8 A.M. thirty soldiers escorted him to the waiting van. The military wore overcoats against the morning chill, which ranged into the mid-fifties and was accompanied by a light, variable wind.

Once under way, Castillo Morales, dressed in a khaki army uniform stripped of its insignia, seems to have understood that he was headed for an execution spot and told his guards that he was not afraid to die. When the julia arrived at the cemetery and the back doors opened, the accused hesitated. It was said that more than anything else he feared being turned over to the mob, of literally being torn apart, limb by limb, kicked and trampled, by enraged townspeople.

The time and place of the execution must have been publicly announced, since hundreds arrived for the drama, a once unruly but now largely silent crowd that displayed little movement or emotion—pensive, one would think, but it is impossible to discern their thoughts at this suspenseful moment. Soldiers had to nudge Castillo Morales from the vehicle, and as he stepped down, he may have felt faint but was quickly propped up by his guards. Then he requested and was given a cigarette, perhaps one laced with the marijuana for which he was said to have a taste.

The walled municipal cemetery lay about a mile from the center of town and within several hundred yards of the international border. It covered about half a square block with an open field in which youngsters played baseball at the western extremity. Only partially filled with irregularly arranged grave sites, the cemetery sloped rather steeply from its vacant southern edge, then not considered sacred ground, downward toward a more level area which contained the graves amidst a few trees. A complete reorganization of the cemetery, now called Number One, has occurred since these events. Cemetery Number One is now almost filled, and Number Two lies just down the street.

The two execution squads, each with seven riflemen and an officer-in-charge, were stationed near the bottom of the slope toward the back of the cemetery. Normal military executions with a stationary target required only one firing squad. In this case the soldier would be running for his life, so the commanders took no chances and readied two teams of executioners. Soldiers shoved, even partially carried, the prisoner by his armpits toward the slope, away from the spectators, and ordered him to run—to try to escape. Castillo Morales hesitated; he knew what awaited him. Then with tears streaming down his cheeks he bolted for freedom like a frightened deer. About that time, directly in the prisoner's path of flight, an eleven-year-old child appeared, pulling a cart with two cans of garbage meant for hog feed. He was cutting through the cemetery in apparent fulfillment of a regular duty. The condemned soldier waved the boy off, shouting for him to advance no further. The startled boy understood, abandoned his wagon, and hastily retraced his steps. The soldier leaped across a low barbed wire fence, one of several meant to keep grubbing animals out of the cemetery, away from the graves themselves and their decomposing contents.

The first volley hit him in the back and knocked him down. He dropped to his knees, stumbled up, and staggered on for some fifteen yards, crossed the second barrier of wire crying for mercy, and a few seconds passed before the next barrage felled him, face down. He lay there for a moment, and then, his mouth open, made one final, agonized attempt to regain his feet when the third volley of bullets sapped what life was left in him. An officer administered the coup de grâce. A few in the crowd cheered as the mercy shot burrowed into the earth beneath the victim's head. People later said a large caliber bullet must have been used because it left such a large nick in the soil where the soldier's head had lain. Spectators at public executions have always been extraordinarily interested in the details of the event, which frequently carried religious significance for them. In Tijuana, the cool morning of 17 February 1938 proved to be no different.

A doctor stepped up to declare Juan Castillo Morales dead. Soldiers picked him up and carried him to his prepared grave site not more than twenty yards from that of Olga Camacho. They dumped him into a plain wooden box, which rested on the bottom of a shallow grave, and covered it to ground level with dirt excavated from the site. Some people who saw the execution still maintain that the corpse carried few bullet wounds. The executioners, they say, all enlisted men and military comrades of Juan, had declined to shoot one of their own. Though they fired their modern Mausers, all but one or two deliberately missed him. None of this can be verified, since no one performed an autopsy on the corpse. More probably the claim is only one of the various stories which arise from these sorts of happenings, where spectators watch the same shocking event but see different things as emotions swirl their senses.

A Christian cross was immediately placed at the head of the grave and carried a plaque reading: "Juan Castillo Morales, died the 17th day of February 1938 at the age of 24. *D. E. P.*"—"Descanse en paz" or "Rest in peace." So onlookers saw a final note of formal recognition for the fallen soldier, a remembrance of his humanity, the continuance of deeply felt religious tradition. The military would not have placed that cross there as the curtain fell on its ceremonial performance, although some say it was erected by a military buddy who doubted the justice received by his friend. Whoever the donor, the eternal symbol must have been prepared prior to the execution by someone who cared for the soul of Juan Castillo Morales and did not want the young man to be forgotten. One thing is for certain: no one took the cross down.

2. Aftermath

Within days of the execution several U.S. newspapers proclaimed their appreciation for the judicial procedures followed in the case of Juan Castillo Morales. They wished their own country's courts could be as expeditious, and application of the Ley Fuga seemed to them a fitting conclusion to the case. The *San Diego Evening Tribune* headed its editorial "Quick Justice":

> We may all have our own ideas of Mexican court procedure and various phases of law enforcement below the border, but there is no getting around the fact that justice was dealt without delay in the Tijuana case which came to a climax yesterday. Doubtless, the fact that the prisoner was a soldier simplified matters. Convinced beyond a doubt of his guilt, his comrades, unwilling to await the slow grinding of the courts, permitted him to "escape," but exercised their military privilege of firing at a deserting soldier. Thus they saved the community the expense of a trial and further imprisonment and appeased the wrath of the citizens who had sought to take the law into their own hands.
>
> There are many who will call the Tijuana method primitive and protest that real justice was short circuited. But none can fail to realize that punishment, when certain, doubtless will have an arresting affect upon any others who might have similar criminal tendencies.[1]

The *San Ysidro Border Press* also lauded the expeditious handling of the entire case, asking, "How does this compare with the justice for such murders in the United States?"[2]

Other papers concentrated on the meaning of the riots. The pugnacious and sensationalist *San Diego Herald,* which in previous months had relentlessly pilloried Tijuana as "sin city," wrote that the rioting pointed "to a deep distrust which may result in a definite effort to change not only the government of Lower California but of the republic of Mexico as a whole."[3] Such comment, however, only amounted to the *Herald's* wishful thinking. Unrest existed in Mexico, but events in Tijuana neither spawned nor aggravated it.

The *San Diego Union,* ever mindful of labor troubles, which fifteen years earlier had ripped its city apart and left still visible scars, took an opposite tack and headlined its editorial "The Law Wins" and continued:

> One feature of the outbreak of violence in Tijuana is worth noting. Although buildings were destroyed and several persons were wounded, one seriously, it appears, the individual accused of the crime which precipitated the riots still is held by the authorities.
>
> Law and order were challenged below the border by a mob moved, evidently, by a smouldering resentment born long before the murder of a child set off the explosion. Plenty of damage was done, but, in spite of threats and open rebellion, the authorities of this isolated Mexican frontier post stood firm, dispersed the mob and restored order without making terms with excited citizens who demanded that all law be suspended at least temporarily.
>
> As a result Tijuana's local government is stronger than before the outburst. The officers who refused to take orders from a mob have set an example to all officers on both sides of the border who might face a lynching party.[4]

For the *Union,* the demands of public order superseded all else, and the newspaper chose not to comment on the trial and execution itself.

Tijuana's weekly, *La Epoca,* headlined its piece on the execution: "The Ley Fuga has been applied to Juan Castillo Morales" and then added: "Justice has been done." In its description of the affair, however, it reported that when the terror-stricken soldier descended from the julia and took a few steps with his escort, he suddenly bolted for freedom. He ran only twenty yards before the firing squad cut him down. This attempted escape was not reported in any other accounts of the execution and seems to represent the publisher's shameful manner of exculpating the military of its blatant use of the generally detested Ley Fuga. Indeed, authorities brooked no criticism from the press reporting on the troubles. When this same publisher accused the military of making indiscriminate arrests during the riots, authorities briefly detained him with other prisoners in the holding yard.[5]

The only newspaper to question judicial procedures in the Castillo Morales case seems to have been Mexico City's *Excelsior*. A few days after the execution, a reporter asked an unnamed high-ranking military officer (today he would be called a "reliable source") about the trial and the use of the Ley Fuga in Tijuana. The officer bristled; the military, he assured the journalist, had not applied the Ley Fuga in this case. Due to the gravity of the offenses and the riots which followed, a special military court at which the accused was prosecuted, defended, and allowed to speak in his own behalf, had sentenced the soldier to death, and he was executed in accordance with military law then in effect. The officer admitted that the entire procedure might have lacked "some" legal processes, but the case demanded rapid closure in order to satisfy the public desire for vengeance, and therefore the court had to work with speed and diligence. The officer assured the reporter that all Mexican society would appreciate the rigor with which the investigation and trial had proceeded. Not only had troops prevented a public lynching, but evidence had established the guilt of the prisoner, and justice was promptly fulfilled.[6]

The officer's denial that the Ley Fuga had been administered in Tijuana was to be expected. The use of the Law of Flight was never admitted publicly. I was warned by one person I interviewed about the happenings in Tijuana not to accuse the military of deliberately using the Ley Fuga in the case of Castillo Morales. "To do so," my source insisted, "would be impugning the honor of the military, and you could be in serious trouble for doing it." Nevertheless, despite the denial by the officer in Mexico City, abundant evidence confirms that the military purposefully employed the Ley Fuga in Tijuana and did so at a public execution, undoubtedly at the orders of superiors all the way up to the president.

The officer being interviewed for *El Excelsior*, however, admitted that some shortcuts had been taken in the proceedings against the convicted soldier. In the determination to bring the Castillo Morales case to a quick conclusion, just what were "some" of these overlooked legal processes? Whether or not investigators continued their search for material evidence after receiving the suspect's confession is not known. The press reported no new findings. Whether authorities ever questioned friends, acquaintances, and neighbors of the accused cannot be ascertained without the trial record. Journalists did not mention any such encounters. One example of how judicial treatment in this case veered from codified law can be gleaned from differences between the way military regulations of the time stipulated a soldier convicted of a crime and sentenced to death should be executed and the public execution by the Ley Fuga accorded Castillo Morales. The Code of Military Justice, promulgated 1 July 1933, contains nine articles pertaining to the "Procedure for the Execution of the Death Sentence," and it is worth quoting them in full.

Article 158—When a death sentence has been pronounced and the order given for its execution by the Garrison Commander, or Commander of the unit or column above that to which the delinquent belongs, the Judge of Instruction will notify the prisoner, accompanied on his visit by the Secretary of the Court and a small escort, which will remain at attention and with arms at order. The sentence will then be read to the prisoner, or he will be instructed to read it himself if able, after which the prisoner will be turned over to the Security Guard, which will have been duly detailed.

Article 159—After the prisoner has been notified of the sentence he will be permitted to communicate with the minister of the faith which he professes, whenever this is possible.

Article 160—The sentence will be executed on the day following the notification; but in campaign or on the march, the execution may be hastened if circumstances require it.

Article 161—The day and place where the execution is to take place will be made known to the troops by General Order with instructions that a constituent group from each unit be present to witness the act and form a square. Mounted troops will attend the execution dismounted.

Article 162—At the hour set for the execution the troops will be at the appointed place, the group from the Battalion or Regiment to which the soldier belongs being stationed at the right, and the others taking up their places in the order of their arrival. Three sides of a hollow square will be formed facing the center, so that the escort conducting the prisoner will occupy the open side.

Article 163—At the same hour, the Judge of Instruction, with the secretary and a competent escort under the orders of a garrison assistant ("Adjutant"), will go for the prisoner and escort him to the place of execution.

Article 164—As soon as the prisoner reaches the place where he is to be executed, he will be blindfolded and the escort will form in two files facing front. The firing squad will also take up position in two files three meters distance from the prisoner. At a signal from the Assistant, the first row will fire, after which, if the prisoner still shows signs of life, the second row will also fire, aiming at the head.

Article 165—When the sentence has been carried out, a small escort will remain to take custody of the body in front of which the troop will march in single file at quick time with eyes toward the body, repairing immediately to their quarters.

Article 166—There will be present at the execution besides the Judge of Instruction and his secretary, a physician who will certify that the prisoner is actually dead; also four ambulance soldiers with a stretcher for carrying the body to the military hospital and place of burial.[7]

It takes but a glance to see where the military both fell short of and went far beyond the rules that it had set for itself for the execution of a soldier convicted of a crime and sentenced to death: no formal reading of the death sentence in the Castillo Morales' case, no minister, none of the carefully prescribed rituals of execution, but instead a public performance of the extra-legal and despised Ley Fuga.

A Consul Reports

United States consuls, especially those stationed in small out-of-the-way posts, were (and still are) placed there to promote and protect American business interests, and as a distant second task to assist their countrymen and women in need. William Smale was a low-level career diplomat who had given long service in Mexico and the Caribbean. First posted to Mexicali in 1919, duty then took him to Nogales and Guaymas in Mexico, Havana and Matanzas in Cuba, Nassau in the Bahamas, and Montreal. In 1931, then a widower with two-year-old twin daughters, he returned to Baja California, and was stationed in Ensenada with jurisdiction north to the border. Judging by his reports to his superiors, Smale was a scrupulous bureaucrat who not only completed his monthly political reports dutifully on the appropriate printed forms, but from time to time drew on his experience in the region to render insightful comments on local conditions.

Since the previous century, Americans had eyed Baja California for both political and economic exploitation. As one annexation scheme after another failed, entrepreneurs had launched substantial business ventures along the border, such as the Colorado River and Land cotton-growing enterprise outside Mexicali, and gambling casinos with all of their accompanying attractions (horse and dog racing, boxing matches, bullfights, spas, and glittering, cabaret-style entertainment) in Tijuana. But with the advent of the Cárdenas regime's land and moral reform programs in the mid-1930s, the Colorado company and casino operations collapsed. Land-hungry agraristas squatted on the cotton fields, leading to expropriation of the entire operation, and the government's ban on types of gambling closed the casinos. These highly visible setbacks to U.S. business left American consuls in northern Baja with both diplomatic and practical problems on their hands.

Tijuana had never been particularly anti-American. Mexican workers demanded wages comparable to those paid their American counterparts, and official agencies protected their turf against what they considered to be American incursions, but because of its dependency on tourism and goods and services only available on the U.S. side of the boundary, overt anti-Americanism was minimal, or at least controlled. "Somos amigos"— we are friends—was and still is the impression that most Tijuanenses cared to convey.

Rioters, however, often vent deeply felt and long-repressed emotions. When in 1938 the riots in Tijuana surged out of control, Consul Smale understood their destructive force and potential for unleashing anti-American sentiments. Should the strong military presence in San Diego be placed on alert? What were the implications of Mexican fugitives seeking refuge in the United States? Were American business interests threatened? Were any U.S. citizens caught in the mayhem, or complicit in the riots themselves? What about those Americans jailed in buildings being fire-bombed?

Smale was at his home office in Ensenada when the disturbances erupted. As the upheaval subsided under military pressure the afternoon of Tuesday, 15 February, he ventured into still-smoldering Tijuana to inquire about the three jailed Americans there. General Contreras assured him that the prisoners were unscathed and protected. Just to make sure, Smale spent the night in Tijuana (or perhaps across the line in the safety of San Ysidro), where he prepared his report on local conditions, to be airmailed to the embassy in Mexico City. Next morning he returned to Ensenada and telegraphed a copy of his findings to the Secretary of State in Washington:

Tijuana, 7 P.M. [16 February]—Tijuana under martial law tonight following voluntary closing practically all establishments today resulting from clash between mob and police and military early hours this morning after mob demanded delivery to them or execution of rapist and murderer of young Mexican girl. Commander of Second Military Zone [Contreras] addressed the crowd and promised request of President's permission to execute soldier confessed to rape and murder and solicited peaceful conduct of crowd. Mob shortly thereafter disregarded pleas of Commander of Second Military Zone and set fire to Municipal Palace and Police Headquarters in an effort to seize confessed offender. In ensuing skirmish a number of persons were wounded by gun fire of the soldiers and police but at late hour today none have died. . . . Agrarians have been called in to reinforce military and military reinforcements from Ensenada and Mexicali have also been brought to Tijuana. Fracas appears to have originated as much through conflict between CROM and Federal authorities following expropriation of Agua Caliente [gambling casino] property as through desire of vengeance for assault and murder. Later tonight it is reported that President has stipulated that alleged offender not be executed but be subjected to appropriate civil trial and that rioters captured be subject to vigorous prosecution. Am remaining in Tijuana tonight to observe activities. Not impossible that further disorders will occur tonight although CROM leaders appear to have departed for the United States.[8]

This matter-of-fact statement, in the main culled from newspaper accounts, amounts to nothing more than a short summary of political happenings, perhaps because Smale had left his code book at home and therefore was forced to send his message *en claire*. Furthermore, Smale knew that his transfer to the consulate in Toronto was imminent, so why indulge in an on-the-scene, independent investigation of a controversial tumult? In his follow-up telegraph to the State Department, sent two days after the execution, the consul noted that the rioting had stopped and that only one person had since died. He seemed surprised that despite official announcements that the case against the soldier would be sent to civil courts ("in accordance with the law," he noted) the suspect had been tried by military court martial, found guilty, and executed. Smale then estimated that twenty-five to seventy-five rioters (representing a rather large spread in his estimate) were now in jail, most of them members of CROM. He said two of the highest-ranking CROM members, who had been ringleaders in the riots, were fugitives, probably hiding in the United States. Then the consul's appraisal of the entire affair hoisted several warning flags:

> I reiterate that the disturbance was more a demonstration against the government by the dissatisfied elements in Tijuana than by persons fundamentally affected by the crime committed, and that the crime simply offered the opportunity for inciting the riot.
>
> The effect of the entire incident is likely to result in killing of the open opposition of the CROM to the Government, but may increase its secret activities. Because the Military was required to call upon the agrarians in support, it is not unlikely that the agrarians in the near future will be even more bold and insistent than at present with respect to their demands upon the government. For these reasons the writer is of the opinion that while the immediate incident has passed, it leads up to what may be even more serious trouble within the next few months.[9]

"Secret activities," "bold and insistent . . . demands upon the government," "serious trouble"—from the consul's point of view, the Cárdenas administration was losing its grip on the opposition as well as on some of its major support groups.

In his overall monthly review for February 1938, Smale remarked that authorities were seeking the CROM leaders thought to have been instigators of disorder. A number of lesser union people remained in jail, and "A high ranking army officer is reliably reported to have declared that if found guilty some of them will be executed." Meanwhile, "Labor conditions are fully as bad now as at this time last month when unemployment was greater than at any time during recent years." He then continued,

> The result of rioting in Tijuana on February 15th is still being felt by those catering to the tourist trade—ordinarily the chief source of reve-

nue there. Decision of the United States Government to withdraw the right for residents to bring four quarts of liquor into the United States once every thirty days, when returning to California, undoubtedly will decrease not only the number of tourists visiting Tijuana and Ensenada but to an even greater extent, the sales made to tourists. Owing to this great amount of unemployment there is little circulation of money in stores and credit generally is strained to the limit.

In the nearby countryside Smale described conditions equally as threatening: "Although there have been no definitive expropriations which the Consulate has been able to learn of, hundreds of agrarians are occupying land provisionally given to them by the Governor or simply squatting on land affected by agrarian proceedings."[10]

The consul's reports reflected his concerns with CROM, the powerful union that had challenged American business practices in Tijuana, among them the failure to hire a sufficient number of Mexicans or to pay them salaries comparable to those of American workers. Who knows what CROM hoped to gain by further fueling the firestorm? It was getting publicity, which it always craved, but most of it was unfavorable and had to be refuted by the labor confederation. Still, a wounded union in pain can be a dangerous beast. As for the agraristas, they had support in high places and no one knew on whose property they would next choose to squat. Absent from the reports is any mention of anti-Americanism connected to the riots. While participants undoubtedly had different motives for joining the fracas, they seemed to be fired by two issues: justice for the killer of Olga Camacho and the union's grievances with local government. One supposes some of the rioters would have ransacked grocery stores had they been hungry or pillaged the finer shops if they wished to pilfer property they were unable or unwilling to buy, or simply to make a social statement, but none of this occurred.

Only one newspaper had commented on the causes of the riots at the time they occurred. In a front-page article at the height of the unrest, the pro-labor *San Diego Sun* headlined its piece "Hungry Tijuanans' Revolt Ignited by Murder Spark. Anger Smouldered for Months in Hearts of Workers over Government's Labor Policy." Then the paper explained: "The story behind today's mob violence is seated in the stomachs of the hungry Tijuana workers, whose real interest is not in an eight-year-old child, but in getting some food in their stomachs to keep their belt buckles from rattling against their spines." The article then recounted the history of the struggle over pay and job security between CROM and the government, which centered on the official forced closing of the major Tijuana gambling casino. " 'This [the murder] is just what they have been waiting for,' was the consensus of observers. 'This just touched it off.' " But not all those questioned had any such sympathy for the union workers: " 'The government has been giving the workers too much leeway,' someone said. 'They have lost their respect for authority.' " Such comments reflected political reality throughout Mexico. The government's policies favoring labor had splintered public opinion. Opponents of the regime were becoming more vocal, which made the prompt return to tranquillity in Tijuana just that much more important.[11]

WHILE STILL SEARCHING for the leaders of the riots, police released without charges some forty of those held in jail. Seventy-eight people, who were labeled radical communists, still remained incarcerated for questioning, and several were warned that if they did not talk, they might "get the same as the soldier," meaning they would be eliminated by way of the Ley Fuga. Rumors had it that as prisoners they would be marched toward Mexicali in a *cuerda*—a kind of chain gang—with ropes looped around their necks instead of chains around their ankles. In the Rumorosa, those ruggedly inhospitable mountains above that town, they would be shot in the back "while trying to escape." Three women accused of beating up policemen were among those jailed. After several days of harassment and the grim physical facilities of the jail, a Mexican federal court ordered released all but the ringleaders implicated in the riots, and by 25 February only four, including Juan Pérez Torres, E. Ruiz, and Francisco Rincón, were still being held for arson. Soon afterward the federal government sent funds to finance the repair of buildings damaged in the riots, as well as to improve roads, dig sewers, and initiate other public works projects to soak up a portion of the town's unemployed, including rank and file members of CROM. The estimated fifty residents who fled Tijuana for the United States when authorities first began to arrest riot suspects remained hidden in San Ysidro; that is, they were safe from authorities but available to the press. Labor leaders lodged in the border community denied any complicity in the disturbances but dared not return home. The Mexican government asked California authorities to apprehend those fugitives wanted for crimes in connection with the

Tijuana riots, but no such arrests seem to have been made. If the newsmen knew the whereabouts of the hunted, certainly American police must have known the same, but for their own reasons they declined to become involved.

THE SORROWFUL FUNERAL of Vidal Torres, who was, astoundingly, the only fatality in the riots, was held in the town cemetery the afternoon following the early morning execution of Castillo Morales. Torres had died the previous day of bullet wounds received in the confrontation outside the government palace, but had not been buried earlier because authorities feared that a generalized grief for him and his family, along with residual anger toward his killers, would ignite another outburst of anger against the police and military.

An official of the civil registry, Felipe Mora, recorded the deaths of Olga Camacho and Juan Castillo Morales on the books. He wrote down the soldier's occupation as "labrador" (farmer). The military had ordered him expunged from its rolls; it wanted no part of him, not the slightest remembrance of him as a military man.[12] Public opinion, however, reacted differently. By themselves and in small knots, people mulled over the unsettling happenings of the past few days. So many questions remained to be answered.

Inklings of Grace

There were now three freshly filled graves in Tijuana's public cemetery, all in close proximity to one another. The one drawing the most attention was that of the executed soldier—not only his grave, but the spot on the upper reaches of the cemetery where he had finally fallen and where his blood had stained the muddy earth. People pointed out the site for journalists, who were preparing their final comments on the sensational saga of the past few days. Captured in contemporaneous photographs, those pictured at the scene of the execution display no overt emotions, but there is no way to gauge what they thought. Some unknown person placed a few flowers at the site, a common expression of sadness and remembrance. Did any cross themselves as the religious are wont to do in such circumstances? Did some person ask God to pardon and have mercy on the fallen soldier?

While most of those still living who witnessed these events say today that they are quite certain of the soldier's guilt, others must not have been so sure. The editor of a Tijuana newspaper at that time, Antonio Morales Tamborrel, headlined an article published soon after the execution with "HABIA MUERTO UN INOCENTE CLAMANDO JUSTICIA"—"An Innocent Demanding Justice Has Died." Furthermore, he provocatively labeled the victim a *chivo expiatorio* (scapegoat). Tamborrel was a frequent critic of government, so his remarks may have been calculated to embarrass the authorities as much as anything else. On the other hand, they could have reflected an undercurrent in public thinking that was gaining strength.[13]

All occurrences like those in Tijuana in mid-February 1938 are bound to spawn rumors that nourish speculation about conspiracy. Such untoward occurrences beg for explanation and open new expanses into which the creative imagination can wander, prejudices can be aired, and grievances weighed. In this case, thoughts like "inocente"(innocent), "injusto" (not fair), and "chivo expiatorio" began to circulate and inspire perceptions that challenged official explanations and procedures. For certain, there are still a multitude of intriguing, unanswered (perhaps unanswerable) questions about the case of Juan Castillo Morales.

Whatever their motivations, individuals and small clusters of people began to visit the sites of the soldier's death and burial. Many paid their respects at the grave of Olga Camacho, certainly, but most attention was riveted on the places where Juan Castillo Morales died and was buried. More flowers and votive candles covered the site. And then stones appeared—neither pebbles nor large rocks, but smooth stones that could be held comfortably in the palm of one's hand. A mound of stones began to rise at the place where the soldier had finally fallen.

Origins of the practice of placing stones on graves seems lost to time. Many cultures and religious groups did and still do practice the rite. Touring Mexico toward the end of the nineteenth century, the anthropologist Frederick Starr found stones piled at hundreds of shrines in out-of-the-way places. While the Church labeled the practice "non-Christian," Starr thought it the remnant of an ancient rite whose origins and meaning had been forgotten, even by practitioners. Many now say the living meant the ritual for those who departed earth violently, unexpectedly, or otherwise in an anxious state, their souls so agitated that they could never rest in peace. Some of these unfortunates do not even recognize that they are dead. Therefore, out of concern visitors contributed the stones to anchor a skittish soul in place, encouraging it to calm itself toward a restful tranquillity in order to begin its long journey to eternity. Others remark that stones were piled on grave sites to protect remains from foraging animals, like dogs and pigs.

Similar observations occur at the chapel dedicated to Jesús Malverde in Culiacán, the capital city of the west-coast state of Sinaloa. A bandit with Robin Hood qualities, Malverde was captured and hanged there early in the twentieth century. The state governor ordered that the brigand not be buried in sacred ground (the local municipal cemetery), and therefore Malverde's executioners left the body to decay at the spot where he was hanged. Observers who thought this unfair, unsanitary, or disrespectful covered his body with stones, and the pile grew vast as veneration of the dead brigand also grew. Today Malverde is said to be the patron saint of drug dealers, both petty and lordly, but the faithful with an assortment of concerns kneel at his shrine.[14]

More common today is the belief that stones are placed on graves as a sign of respect for a life well lived or for a sacrifice well received. The finale of the motion picture *Schindler's List* shows those who survived the Holocaust through the efforts of Oskar Schindler placing stones on the man's grave in Israel. Afghan soldiers honor fallen comrades with a sacred memorial of stones and tattered clothing outside of Khvajeh Ghar. Travelers passing the grave site of a former voyager along the tranquil Appalachian Trail in the United States or on a barren hillside in Lesotho, the small independent kingdom nestled within the country of South Africa, are encouraged to leave a stone there to honor the departed. These latter two examples, and many others like them, carry an implied threat that failure to set a stone at the site could cause the traveler danger further down the road.

Those people who laid down stones at the Castillo Morales site did so, for the most part, with their hearts as well as their hands. Many seemed to feel some sense of obligation. Others, like Ramón Camacho, a young boy at the time, remember the stone-placing ritual more as a local fad. Ramón went with his buddies because "It was the thing to do." Because Ramón was Olga's cousin, his father ordered him not to go near the cemetery and certainly not to place stones on the grave of her murderer, but Ramón and his friends could not resist. Such was the lure of the place, for a mélange of reasons.[15]

Then extraordinary phenomena, commonly called signs, began to appear at the grave and the death site of the young soldier. Within a day or so of the execution visitors to the cemetery reported signs that witnesses understood and appreciated. Quantities of blood began to seep up through the earth where Juan had fallen and then through the rocks laid at the grave site. Furthermore, the soldier's angry, anxious *ánima* (soul) hovering at the place of execution was heard crying out for vengeance.[16]

Flowing blood surrounding violent death carries immense religious significance for many Christians, portending the presence of the Crucified Christ, a sign that the Almighty not only exists in the abstract, but is nearby and has shed His grace on the fallen one. They believe that martyrs sit close to God. In 1981 unidentified parties murdered an American Jesuit missionary, Stanley Rother, in the parish house of the Guatemalan town of Santiago Atitlán. A dedicated and outspoken liberation theologian, Rother was revered by thousands of Tzutuhil-speaking Maya Indians in his congregation and was equally reviled by the country's military for his leftist sympathies. In death, the townspeople declared him a martyr. They put his heart in a glass jar filled with a liquid preservative and placed it on the church altar, where it was venerated. Eyewitnesses declared a few days later that the stilled heart began to bleed, and steadily so, a sign of Christ's living presence. The blood confirmed what they already knew: that the Lord had taken this martyr to His side.[17]

Visitors to the grave of Juan Castillo Morales who saw the streaming blood felt much the same way. The Son of God, who had suffered injustice and shed His blood for mankind, now was showering His grace on the fallen soldier who had died a martyr's death, not necessarily for the faith, as the Church would have it, but through grave injustice.

Morticians explain the emergence of blood from graves in less extraordinary ways. If a human body placed in the earth is not embalmed, gases quickly accumulate in the body's cavities as decay occurs. The gas expands, seeking an outlet until the body bursts. Then blood, along with body tissues, may well seep to the surface, especially if the grave is shallow. The corpse of Juan Castillo Morales was not embalmed; his body was placed in a coffin which was then buried in a shallow grave, just a foot or so below the surface. Individuals may choose to believe what they wish about the flow of blood that followed. In the end, the source of these signs does not matter as much as the behavior they provoke. However, the appearance of blood was not the only sign of otherworldly presence at the grave.

There are many beliefs about what happens after death, but much of mankind believes in the existence of the soul, even if personal perceptions are framed by disparate cultural traditions. Souls inhabit the domain of the unseen, outside the realm of science but rooted within that of the spiritual. Hispanics refer to their own souls as "my *alma*"; the souls of others they call *ánimas*. Each year on 2 November, Mexicans welcome the ánimas of family members back from their ethereal place for a heartfelt and poignant Day of the Dead celebration at the grave sites of their departed ones. They light many candles to insure the ánima safe passage to the celebration. It is the moment when only the thinnest of veils separates mortal and spiritual communicants. Heaven meets earth. In respectful remembrance, wandering musicians might be paid to play a favorite song of the deceased, while the family picnics on food and drink (tequila is a favorite) enjoyed by the honored one. There is nothing at all strange about the return of the soul for a family visit, especially on the Day of the Dead.

But not all souls are deemed to be at peace. For a variety of reasons— violent or unexpected death, unfinished earthly business, the need to exact reprisals—some souls are restless, meandering, unfulfilled, pesky, revengeful, or demanding. These disturbed ánimas are not always welcomed or beloved by the living. They might return to insure that an inheritance is properly distributed or to say farewell to a loved one missed at the ánima's hour of death. They could reveal where the deceased had secreted money and forgotten to tell a trusted one about it. But ánimas have been known to scold an ungrateful relative, to settle a debt or grievance, or to seek vengeance or justice. You do not find ánimas; they find you. They can move things in your home, make noises, shove your bed, or come to you in your dreams. We all die with tasks undone, and Mexican ánimas seem especially determined to tie up the loose ends.

Animas may also be perceived as *purgando* (being purged of sin) or *sola* (alone). Images of ánimas purgando are common in churches. Normally they depict a maiden waist-deep in flames, her arms and eyes raised in supplication. Despite the inferno, she does not appear to be in pain. Her countenance is serene, for cleansing by fire precedes ascendance toward heaven. She deserves (and needs) the prayers of the faithful and in return may pass on the requests of the earthbound to the Lord.

An ánima sola—a pitiful soul who has died far from home and family and has no one to pray for his or her deliverance toward final glory—may do the same. Animas solas are not to be forgotten, and on the Day of the

Dead some households erect a special shrine to such an ánima outside their homes or at the grave site of the deceased. In this way the ánima sola becomes family. Today devotees of Juan Castillo Morales frequently refer to him as an ánima sola. They also recall his ánima's cries for justice.

Poignant stories about returning ánimas pass from generation to generation. A grandmother from rural Querétaro filled the ear of a *nieta* (granddaughter) who now lives in California:

> Mama Lolita would say that if an ánima needed help and decided that you might be the one to give it, the ánima would not leave you alone until she [or he] got it. Grandmama said you should not be afraid of them, just ask them what they want. Then the ánima would tell you what she was after, and God forbid if you did not comply. Mama Lolita had a cousin who got her mouth twisted because she did not order a three-priest Mass for an ánima.
>
> Mama Lolita was well aware of the fickleness of ánimas. There was a man in her town who saw a fire burning in a cornfield, and when he went over there to see what was going on, he found an ánima that needed a message delivered to his [the ánima's] widow. The man carried the information to the widow and then stayed on to help the woman with her chores. Later on he again saw the cornfield burning, and when he went to investigate, the same ánima told him that if he dug at that spot, he would find a pot filled with gold coins. He was told to split the money with the widow. The man did so; dug down, found the pot of coins, and shared them with the widow. He became rich and at the same time saved the widow from poverty. Mama Lolita always said that an ánima was someone who had pending business on earth and therefore could not leave [for the hereafter].[18]

Why the ánima did not himself bring the hidden money to his widow is not known. Instead, he chose to test the good will of a stranger (and teach a moral lesson). No doubt, ánimas can be pesky and disconcerting. With their unfathomable aspects, their idiosyncrasies, desires and demands, their humor and yearnings for fulfillment, as well as their good and bad intentions, they resemble the living in many ways. It is risky to ignore them and not do their bidding.

People raised in this fertile tradition swear that the soul of Juan Castillo Morales returned to the cemetery crying out for justice and vengeance. Today visitors to the soldier's grave relate stories passed down which insist that the soldier shouted, "Soy inocente"(I am innocent) as he stepped from the julia to face the firing squad. Others have him pleading for "justicia" (justice) as he ran from the inevitability of the Ley Fuga. Another account says that before he was made to run, he told a military comrade, "Promise me, promise me that you will demand that the truth comes out," and that the friend agreed to do so, thus sowing the seeds for the creation of a new myth and a new religious devotion.[19]

The curious began to weigh the signs—the blood, the soul crying for justice—at the grave of Juan Castillo Morales. They placed flowers at the site, and stones. They said the Rosary, novenas, and other more personal prayers; performed customary Catholic rituals along with rites of unknown origin. Profound veneration began; devotees asked favors of the fallen soldier, made promises, and gave thanks for miracles received. How quickly these new religious devotions can develop; they are virtually spontaneous, even if their features can be traced across time. In our narrative we are still well within 1938, less than six months from Olga's death and the execution of her presumed murderer.

Juan Soldado

In the later 1930s a reporter who nicknamed himself "Abajo Frontera" regularly wrote a front-page column featuring Tijuana news and culture for the weekly *San Ysidro Border Press*. November 1938 found him at the town's municipal cemetery. Perhaps he had received a tip about inexplicable happenings at the town's graveyard, or maybe he just decided to cover the traditional Day of the Dead rituals at the site. Regardless of the reason for his presence, he was astonished by what he found:

ACROSS the BORDER [Tijuana]—On All Souls Day [Day of the Dead] the most popular place in any Latin American town is the graveyard. Last week Tijuana was no exception. In fact, it seemed as if at least half the population of the city climbed the steep hillside just west of the Escuela Obregón [the town's secondary school] to decorate the graves of their dead and say a few prayers for the souls of the departed. That is the way it always has been and the way it was this year. But this time one thing took place that is, to say the least, extraordinary.

It seemed as if fully half of the people visiting the cemetery stopped to pray at the grave of Juan [Castillo] Morales. [Castillo] Morales, in case you don't remember, was the soldier executed last February for the murder of little Olga Camacho. He was shot while attempting to escape and was buried where he fell. The crime for which he died was the most brutal, the most horrible, that had ever occurred in the history of Tijuana. Indeed, it was exactly on a par with the more sordid deeds that have taken place in the United States since the turn of the century. Though his trial was not marked with much formality, there is little doubt that [Castillo] Morales was guilty of the deed. All the evidence was against him, and to cinch the case he made a full confession of the crime.

In view of all that it seems scarcely credible that such numbers of people would pray at his grave on All Souls Day. But the cause, as nearly as we have been able to discover, is that many believe [Castillo] Morales to have become an angel. Though some offer as their reason for the prayers that the soldier's soul had greater need of them [the orations] to escape from purgatory than those of others who were buried there, many are of the firm opinion that [Castillo] Morales died innocent of any crime. Some even say that when they knelt at his grave they could hear the voice of the dead soldier talking. These hold that the crime was committed by another, and that [Castillo] Morales, as a Christian act, decided to take the blame upon himself.[20]

There you have the published account of an incredulous eyewitness reporting from the scene of these remarkable events. Some devotees assumed that Juan had repented at the hour of death and that his ánima had gone to purgatory to be delivered from its sinfulness, and since the soldier had committed a particularly serious transgression, he required more prayers than most to expiate his wrongdoing. Others thought Juan innocent of the crime. They surmised that as a good Christian he had deliberately taken blame for a crime committed by another. As a martyr to an implacable injustice, he therefore sat with other martyrs especially close to God. In any case, proof of Almighty favor with Juan lay in the miracles granted.

It is not known when his followers first began to call their santo Juan Soldado—John the Soldier—"Juan" because that was his name, "Soldado" because he was a soldier. Quite conceivably the label had already been adopted by the time the reporter visited the cemetery in late 1938, but the journalist either did not catch it or thought it unimportant. Today, few of those who venerate Juan Soldado know the soldier's real name as Juan Castillo Morales. When asked, they say that his name is not important. What is meaningful to them is the devotion itself and its rewards, and so today the veneration of Juan endures as fervently as ever, even if renovated over the years to meet the ever evolving concerns of the faithful.

THE STEPPING-STONES of this narration are set in the title, "Juan Soldado: Rapist, Murderer, Martyr, Saint." But how did these markers come to be shaped and placed as they were, and who has trod or shunned them over time? New religious devotions, such as that which began to bud in Tijuana in the wake of the public execution of Juan Castillo Morales, are born of both immediate and long-term circumstances as well as traditional and contemporary belief. Examples of each have briefly been encountered in the story as told so far. Circumstances affecting the configuration and flow of events, as well as the ways in which people interpreted them, were in motion at all levels, national, local, and international: the sweeping changes that the Cárdenas administration brought to land tenure and labor rights; its closure of gambling casinos as part of a determined moralization program, one meant to teach Mexicans to behave responsibly; the struggle between unions like the CROM and authorities in the town itself; the impact of the worldwide Depression, which flooded Tijuana with needy workers expelled from the United States. As for belief, the exceptional strength of the spiritual was experienced in the flow of blood from the soldier's grave as well as in the pleas of his ánima for revenge. Notions of the military, family, honor, and the afterlife pervade the scene. Vigorously conflicting feelings of injustice and justice well served to penetrate this unfolding drama. Circumstances and belief have been separated up to this point, but only for convenience in recording the narrative. In reality, the two are always inextricably mixed in human experience: they are like scrambled eggs. Nevertheless, in order to comprehend and ponder the origins, existence, and power of the Juan Soldado devotion, it is necessary to expose the building blocks of this new religious observance—first the circumstances and then the beliefs—before they can be assembled into the edifice of faith and pragmatic necessity which continues to serve the needs of so many believers in Tijuana and well beyond, on both sides of the international boundary.

A Mother's Lament

Following the death of Olga, the Camacho family did not immediately return to their saddened home. They went, instead, to an unannounced location to share their grief in solitude. A Roman Catholic priest, Father Torres, visited to offer condolences. Three years earlier, radical labor unionists had forced him to flee his parish in Mexicali, and rather than return to the anticlericalism of 1930s Mexico he had chosen self-exile, saying mass and offering sacraments across the border in San Ysidro. He urged Feliza to show compassion for her daughter's assailant, to grant him forgiveness, but she could not. The tragedy turned her from God and the Church for many years. Today at age ninety, she has regained her strong faith and reembraced her earlier spiritual practices. Her patron saints are Santo Niño de Praga, the cherubic child Jesus, resplendently crowned, reigning over all in radiant glory, and San Judas, sometimes called Judas Thaddeus, who in the twentieth century became the saint of hopeless causes. Aurelio, her husband, never could shed the heavy cloak of sadness and died prematurely in 1955 at age fifty-six. Olga was his firstborn. When she died, his light went out.

Life has treated the Camachos harshly. First, Olga was dreadfully murdered. Then Lilia, three years her junior, who was playing in her home's living room when Olga was first missed, died of heart problems at age fifteen. Gloria, born in 1935, contracted measles and died at age seven in her doctor's office when he prescribed the wrong medicine for her illness. The couple's only son, Aurelio III, born in 1945, died of cancer thirty-nine years later. Feliza has suffered so much ill fortune with her family that for a long time she feared that God was punishing her for not accompanying Olga to the grocery store on that fateful late afternoon. But three daughters survive: Irma with three daughters of her own in Guadalajara, Alma and her son in Cancún, and Conchita in Tijuana.

Feliza is today a gracious, soft-spoken lady, alert of mind and with a good memory to accompany her charming smile. Only now, for the first time since the death of Olga, and at the urging of her daughter Conchita, who believes it is time for her mother to unburden herself, has she chosen to speak of the melancholy times. Feliza recalls quite buoyantly her early life, the whirlwind courtship and marriage to Aurelio Jr., the move to Tijuana, her motherly duties at home, and journeys to San Diego for chicken potpie and movies. Feliza remembers that her first child, while cheerful, outgoing, and active most of the time, could also become deeply absorbed. On one occasion shortly before the tragedy, she found Olga in the living room in deep meditation—really a trance—before the family's home altar. Sitting on a chair with her legs crossed, her head cradled in her hands, she stared at statues of saints and the Virgin Mary. Frightened at her daughter's silence, Feliza grabbed one of the little girl's arms saying, "What is happening, Olga?" The child became upset when she realized that her mother was standing close by and talking to her. Then Feliza took her daughter in her arms, and the child looked at her mother with her beautiful green eyes and said with a sweet smile, "Nothing is happening." Feliza was startled but also moved; it was the first time that her daughter seems to have had a special religious experience. Later, Feliza wondered if the occurrence was in any way connected to what soon would follow, but she appreciates the mystery in the world; not everything need be explained.

Señora Camacho has had any number of dreams over the years about her victimized daughter. In one, Feliza's sister-in-law, Lila, saw a soldier pursuing Olga and sought refuge with the child in an abandoned house. The soldier followed them inside, and when he went to seize Olga, her older companion pushed the child to safety out of an open window—and at that moment Feliza awakened. Another dream has been recurrent, with little change of detail:

> I was walking through a forest, not a dense, dark forest, but a lovely one full of space and light, in search of my daughter, Olga. Then I came upon a beautiful river, quite wide but gently flowing, hardly moving. Toward the other side of the river I saw little Olga standing up to her knees in water. She was beautiful. I stepped into the shallow river and began to move toward my child, but God appeared above the girl's head, and moving His own head from side to side said: "Olguita is with me." I was frightened, so I left the river, ran a short distance down the bank, and reentered the water from another direction, but the same thing happened. God appeared saying that Olga was with Him, and that she was doing very well in heaven.

That vision transformed Feliza. Although still in much distress because of her loss, she returned to God. As she says, "I was able to approach God and then to take better care of my three other daughters, whom I had been neglecting because of my loss."[21] Conchita says it was a moment of liberation for her mother: "She finally was able to let go of Olga, of her grief and guilt, and come to know in a very loving way her other children. As you can see, it remains that way."[22]

Much of the story concerning Olga Camacho and Juan Castillo Morales unfolding in this book owes its detail to the good will and warm kindness of Señora Camacho, who still sheds a tear when Olga comes to mind, and can be quite fierce in condemning her presumed killer.

II

CIRCUMSTANCES

3. Tijuana

Devotion such as that accorded to Juan Soldado often develops in small, out-of-the-way places, frequently locales with soiled reputations (typically for backwardness or bawdiness), and in areas dominated by the political brawn and economic weight of better-known, much-larger and more-important neighboring cities. Such tendencies are evident at several humble nineteenth-century apparition sites that since have grown into renowned shrines, including the once-innocuous grotto outside the remote French hamlet of Lourdes, situated high in the Pyrenees near the Spanish frontier. La Salette, also French, lies in the wilderness of the French Alps near Grenoble. Similarly, Marpingen, a large but unremarkable village in Germany's Saarland, was long overshadowed, if not smothered, by the more vibrant and commanding towns in the district. The twentieth century too had its apparitions in places well off the beaten path: Fátima, formerly little more than a cluster of pastoral homesteads in central Portugal, and more recently Medjugorje, which at the time of the sightings of the Virgin Mary in 1981 could only be reached by cart-track through rugged mountain territory south of Mostar in what was then Yugoslavia, now Bosnia and Herzegovina.[1]

Closer to Juan Soldado, the U.S.-Mexico border is dotted with miracle-working sites, all of them in what were, at the time their devotions originated, tiny outpost communities (see map 3 in chapter 7). Three are in southern Texas: the True Cross shrine to the crucified Christ, El Señor de los Milagros, established in San Antonio when the town had fewer than two thousand inhabitants and still belonged to Mexico; the chapel to the Virgin in San Juan, merely a hamlet dwarfed in size and

importance by neighboring McAllen; and the devotion to Pedro Jaramillo, who worked miracles on a commonplace ranch outside of Falfurrias, then just a whistle-stop on a regional rail line. Don Pedrito's followers have canonized him a saint, a devotion which still thrives, as do all
of these centers of spirituality and belief.

Popular canonizations have created shrines in numerous other out-of-
the-way places. In the 1970s local Cajuns and busloads of inquisitive and
hopeful outsiders began to venerate a deceased teenaged girl named
Charlene in the tiny community of Richard, outside of Lafayette in rural
southwest Louisiana. Her devotees also consider her to be a saint despite
the hesitations of the official Church. Arizona was still a territory when
devotion to El Tiradito (the little discarded fellow) began in the frontier
settlement of Tucson. Although now muted, it continues to this day.
Tucson's Chamber of Commerce has proclaimed Tiradito as the only
criminal to reach sainthood, but even many official saints have their
warts.

Across the Rio Grande, not far from the industrialized giant of Monterrey, El Niño Fidencio, worshiped alike by Mexican presidents and the
destitute in the 1930s, founded his mission on arid wastelands at a lone-
some site called Espinal, and today his shrine draws a steady stream of
pilgrims who call him a saint.[2] The attraction to Juan Soldado is equally
steady, not only for the faithful, but also for the curious and disdainful, as
well as media people in search of a good story.

A Small Border Town

Urban dwellers tend to see provincial villages as more remote than they
really are. In the 1930s, observers in Mexico City viewed Tijuana as a
woebegone dot on the border to be tolerated, if distastefully so, only as a
revenue-yielding customs port abutting the United States. Even today, it is
still seen as a needed national moneymaker, but "not really Mexico." When
devotion to Juan Soldado began, Tijuana fit the pattern that corresponds
to a surprising number of shrine sites. It was small then, with hardly ten
thousand inhabitants, many of them fairly new arrivals. While perhaps
not remote, it sits distant from the center of national affairs and inextricably tied to its burgeoning foreign neighbor, San Diego. The town was
widely renowned for vice and corruption, and many considered it to be
little more than a piquant playground for tourists. It had acquired that

image in a boomtown-like frenzy which had begun only two decades before the tragic death of Olga Camacho. The seeds of this reputation had been planted earlier, and looking back one can detect the emerging bent, but the sharp, sudden acceleration of pace after 1915 was unforeseen and largely uncontrollable. When money beckoned, the opportunists jumped.

Tijuana lies at the extreme northwestern corner of the Baja California peninsula, that slender and deformed finger of land that dangles southward from the western extreme of the U.S.-Mexico border for nearly eight hundred miles. Seen from space orbit, the peninsula is the most distinctive piece of terrain in the Western Hemisphere, and it is indeed unusual. Mountainous for most all its length and virtually bone dry, Baja California is inhabited to any significant degree only along its northern border and southern tip, with a string of largely isolated small towns, formerly mission posts, in between. Its ruggedness has limited settlement and tourism. It did not have a paved transpeninsular roadway until 1972. Bounded by the Pacific Ocean on the west and separated from the Mexican mainland by the Sea of Cortez to the east, most of Baja California remains unspoiled, much of it pristine. It is a naturalist's paradise. Barren, dry, mountainous, and hostile to travelers, it still offers a pastel blend of exotic plant life and wondrous panoramic views not found anywhere else in the world. Unexpected sights abound for the determined visitor: the forbidding sand dunes of the Vizcaíno Desert, a rattlesnake without rattles, a grizzled prospector panning for gold, or better yet, inquisitively poking around for church treasures rumored left behind by Jesuits expelled in the eighteenth century. Tourists might spot a bat that fishes, or lo and behold, outside the small fishing village of Abreojos more than halfway down the Pacific side of the peninsula, a freshly painted chapel honoring Juan Soldado and a local devotion to his miracle-working powers going strong.

Of course, long before Spanish explorers began to probe Baja California for its potential gold deposits, the peninsula was home to native groups—physically small, mobile, elusive hunter-gatherers about whom too little is known. They might be called primitive until their colossal and astonishing artwork leaps into sight, etched and painted in caves and on the overhangs of cliffs stretching down into deep canyons. New discoveries are still being made. Stick figures, some thirty feet tall, their arms upraised; deer, bighorn sheep, mountain lions, birds, rabbits, and fish sought by the natives for food; a huge, rounded blotch resembling a whale; and other designs which both excite and challenge today's imagination. In yellow and red ochre colors produced from local plants and minerals, along with charcoal black scraped from fire pits, the paintings cover sandstone surfaces and are at times superimposed one atop another. These stupendous murals run hundreds of feet in length; they are nothing less than museums in the mountains. Local people used to say that the Gods painted them, but today's observers think the natives must have used scaffolding. The baffling matter remains unresolved.[3]

Indefatigable Roman Catholic evangelists—Jesuits, Dominicans, and Franciscans, in that order—built a remarkable chain of missions south to north on the peninsula, starting at the end of the seventeenth century. Whether they used the cave paintings to better understand the natives is not known. Franciscans, who established their first mission at San Diego in 1769, held jurisdiction over the Tijuana River Valley and the few Indians who roamed there. The valley proper, a mile or so wide, contained quite fertile agricultural and grazing land fed by two rivers, the Alamar and the Valle de las Palmas. These joined to form the Tijuana, which then broadened out on its seven-mile run to the sea. Beyond the sloping banks the terrain rose abruptly into sinuous hills winding and twisting in convoluted folds, and surging upward into small mountains deeply cut by arroyos leading to the river. It is the sort of topography that one would expect in a region where grinding tectonic plates beneath the sea are relentlessly pushing up a crazy quilt of irregular mountains. Walkers still find sea shells in the broken hills of Tijuana.

The topography of Tijuana assures that the core of the town, situated on a flat plain on the west side of the river, offers only limited living space before it butts up against abrupt, sharply rising ascents, sheer cliffs in some areas. Nowadays the slopes around Tijuana are covered with residences, but colonization into the broken hills was just beginning in the 1930s, spawned by thousands of repatriates driven from California by the U.S. government's forceful reaction to pressures of the Great Depression. The exodus gave rise to an entirely new colony in Tijuana, named Libertad, creatively jerry-built on the topsy-turvy, unwelcoming terrain tilted toward the international line on the east side of the river. Disillusioned, hungry, and sometimes angry unemployed exiles peopled the new colony, and they proved to be a demanding lot who wanted schools, streets, water, jobs—items already in critically short supply in the town. Local authorities urged patience, but those who suffer deprivation are willing to tighten their belts only so far, especially when the downturn among their lot has been so sharp and sudden. In February 1938 the relative newcomers joined others venting their frustration in those destructive riots—spontaneously occurring yet deliberately fanned—which left Tijuana's police comandancia and municipal palace in fire-gutted ruins.[4]

Tijuana's early history, as much as its geography, helped to determine the town's own sense of connection to the nation to the north rather than to mainland Mexico. When Mexico won its independence from Spain in 1821, territorial governors like California's José María Echeandía rewarded their soldiers and friends with land grants, which is how eight years later Santiago Argüello acquired twenty-six thousand acres of ranchland in the Tijuana River Valley. Argüello, the son of a prominent California politician, married and the father of fifteen children, was a military officer who became commander of the garrison at San Diego, and over the years held a series of high political posts in the district. Like other ranchers with large holdings, Argüello raised cattle and horses. Treaty negotiations at the end of the U.S.-Mexico War in 1848 fiercely debated the western terminus of the new, arbitrary international line which was to stretch from Yuma to the Pacific. Each side coveted San Diego with its valuable harbor, but the Americans won the point, and the final boundary ran right through Argüello property before it met the ocean just below San Diego Bay. Santiago, who was not unhappy with the turn of international political events, retained holdings on both sides of the new line, but over decades, sales, expropriations, litigation, and theft steadily diminished them. A retired military officer with loyalties and sentiments that bridged the border, Santiago died in Tijuana in 1862 and was buried in San Diego.[5] Diplomatic formalities may have split the estate but not the family or the communities. The Argüellos saw Tijuana and San Diego as one, as do many in the region today.

Eyes on Baja California

One route that fed the mid-nineteenth-century California gold rush led through Baja California, and when the mines up north played out, the gold-seekers began to peck around in the territory. They did not get rich, but they found some tracings here and there in the northern part of the region. As a revenue raiser, Mexico's federal government established a customs house at the border in 1874. Prospectors complained that the agents charged more duty on their belongings than they were worth. Merchants traveling the laborious wagon route from San Diego to Yuma, which traversed the Tijuana River Valley before swinging due east along the international boundary had the same complaint. To Mexico City, however, the innocuous crossing meant much more than collecting taxes. It raised the nation's flag on the border and warned scheming interlopers to stay out.

There have always been Americans who have seen Lower California as part of Upper. Ever since the Treaty of Guadalupe Hidalgo separated the two territories in 1848, there have been numerous schemes, propositions, and scams aimed at making Baja California American. A few have gone even further. Twice—with William Walker and his filibusters in the 1850s and then a motley group of adventurers, opportunists, and Radical Leftists in 1911—bands of Americans invaded Baja California intending to establish an entirely new, independent country. Most expansionists, however, called for its annexation to the United States. Some Americans, convinced of Japanese or German military interest in the peninsula, saw Baja California as a defense outpost, which periodically led Congress to consider proposing the purchase of Baja California from the Mexican government. Just such legislation was pending in February 1938, when the troubles broke out in Tijuana, but the project made no headway in the U.S. Congress.

Capitalists thought Baja California a good investment in mining, salt, fishing, and agriculture, or at least hoped to interest investors in such possibilities. Toward the end of the nineteenth century, when Mexico was inviting foreign investment to help modernize the country, J. P. Morgan interests based in New York purchased 3.5 million acres of public lands in Baja California in hopes of a bonanza. The corporation thought the United States might buy the immense holding from them for military defense, or that American business would be interested in its mineral or other economic potential, but prospective buyers took one look at the inhospitable terrain and backed off.[6]

In response to threats to its sovereignty, the Mexican government repeatedly and vigorously proclaimed Baja California not for sale. Fearful that colonization might lead immigrants down the same path taken by Texans, who had declared and won their independence before annexation by the United States, a succession of administrations promoted colonization packages calculated to populate the peninsula with Mexican nationals, along with a few limited and carefully controlled foreign enterprises. None of these colonization schemes—British, French, American, or national—worked out. The land was simply too tough to farm, the mountains too forbidding to mine, communications too difficult and expensive to establish, and the entire peninsula too arid to sustain a large population. These failures eventually pushed Tijuana further under San Diego's sway. While Mexico City feared the consequences, it could do nothing to reverse the trend. Still, the customs post provided a federal presence and assured the nation an official stake in protecting its rights. It also marked the birthplace of Tijuana as a settlement.

A land boom struck southern California in 1885. The great ranches of a colorful past were broken up into parcels and put up for sale. Major railroads, which had been given land in exchange for establishing rail networks, divvied up leftover real estate and offered it for purchase. Overblown (and sometimes less than erudite) newspaper advertisements aimed at potential investors heralded the year-round good weather and exaggerated economic opportunities in places like San Diego and its environs:

> [It] has oranges of finer flavor than those of Cypress, rustling corn equal to that of Illinois, lemons superior to those of Italy, figs more delicious than those of Smyrna, grapes more lucious than those of Portugal, olives equal to those of Italy, vines like those that creep and trail along the castled Rhine, peaches like those of Delaware, finer pears than can be found in Maryland, apples not inferior to those of New England, prunes unequaled in any land, vegetables to which for size and quality, Southern California only can lay claim. Soft and pure mountain water is within a few feet of the surface of the soil, hence there can be no necessity for irrigation nor lawsuits over riparian rights. The land of peace and plenty.[7]

Soon a pilgrimage, mainly made up of Midwesterners, headed west by the thousands to buy into the benefits of the promised land. When they got there, their dream quickly soured. San Diego had little industry, and they found no work. The land parcels they purchased were too small to farm profitably. Finally, though there was the ocean and its beaches, there were not a great many other things for diversion and recreation. Put plainly, there was not anything to *do* in town. San Diego was Dullsville . . .

but just down the road there lay a strangely quaint border crossing that afforded the chance to plant a foot on foreign territory. The lure was irresistible.

BECAUSE THEY INTERRUPT a traveler's journey, often in annoying ways and for considerable periods of time, customs crossings tend to cultivate stop-off communities of their own. Soon after opening, the post at Tijuana developed a sprinkling of modest hospitality outlets; a place to buy a beer, some bacon and eggs, a carne asada torta, some tobacco, a serape, or a sombrero, and to rent a bed for the night. The U.S. side, also called Tijuana but spelled "Tia Juana" (and renamed San Ysidro in 1916), featured a general merchandise store and a post office.

For the first few years, the flow of traffic through the border was steady but limited. With the land boom, however short-lived, all that changed. An inquisitive, energized population with spending money branded Tijuana for good with tourism. Entrepreneurs quickly captured the mood and enhanced the draw. The International House with fifty-three rooms (one of them used as a school) appeared on the U.S. side, while across the line Alejandro Savín built a curio shop offering piles of goods, among them seashells strung together into homemade jewelry, rudely woven but colorful woolen blankets, little horses crafted from the long arms of the tule cactus, and wooden canes with nonsensical, mystical etchings of strange faces and animals, which only made them more attractive to buyers. The store turned Savín a substantial profit, approaching a small fortune.

Vendors sold *comida* (savory Mexican food) and hard drink in wooden and adobe huts, and there was novel spectator sport to boot: bullfights in a small rickety arena, horse races on a makeshift track laid out in an open field, bloody cockfights that drew spirited betting. A converted barn on the U.S. side featured a boxing ring, where on 3 May 1886, promoters scheduled a bare-fisted slugging match between a longshoreman named O'Neal and Tom Nugent of Liverpool, England. As the law banned such matches in San Diego County, on the big day sheriff's deputies forced the event just across the line into Mexico. Once there, a contingent of Mexican soldiers halted the proceeding for lack of legal permits. The promoters, however, knew how to handle that sort of shakedown. They gave the soldiers sixty dollars, ostensibly for permissions but actually for *mordidas* (bribes), and the fight went on. After four rounds, the referee, none other than Wyatt Earp (who was in the San Diego area looking for a land deal), declared O'Neal the winner.[8]

The much ballyhooed match helped to generate a reputation for Tijuana and captured the spirit of the border existing to this day: the thrill of witnessing an exciting, even naughty, event proscribed by one's own country, if not by an individual's professed morals. Sightseers got what they wanted and had a titillating time getting it. The presence of celebrities spiced the atmosphere. Permission could be obtained to stage a spectacle banned across the border, but at a price often paid off spontaneously, more or less under the table. A tense working agreement persisted between law-enforcement authorities on each side of the international line. The border has never necessarily been a hindrance; as much as anything else it has provided opportunity.

THE ARGÜELLO HEIRS to Rancho Tijuana were not about to let this occasion for substantial income pass them by. Whether the Mexican government paid them for the land on which the customs house sat is not known. Those who lived in and ran the gaggle of shops that appeared out of nowhere at the crossing were in the main squatters, but the Argüellos had bigger money on their minds. They leased mineral hot springs bubbling at a delightful 104 degrees on their property to a San Diego conglomerate headed by Dr. David B. Hoffman. The group built a hotel and ministered mainly to "one lungers," Americans suffering from tuberculosis. Others wallowed in mud baths said to alleviate rheumatism. The Argüellos then made the major decision to subdivide and sell their most valuable property, which covered the relatively level expanse of mesa land on the west bank of the Tijuana River. They hired an engineer to plot out a town for the site, and sales began in 1889. The first buyers were merchants from Ensenada who recognized the tourist potential of the sprouting town.[9] From across the border, American entrepreneurs sensed similar possibilities.

In 1887 the financier John D. Spreckels arrived in San Diego, aiming to prosper on land prices, and when boom turned to bust the following year, he amassed a fortune in discounted property. His itchy financial fingers forecast countless projects for the city. Among other things, Spreckels saw San Diego as a winter tourist haven. He hoped to attract wealthy "snowbirds" from the East to spend not just the holiday season at his resorts, but at least two or three months a year there. Toward this goal, in 1890 he acquired the fabulous Del Coronado Hotel, which had opened two years earlier and is still a San Diego landmark and historical gem.

As magnificent as The Del was (and is), tourists staying there wanted to see sights around town, and among the most popular diversions was the day tour to Tijuana (which then still enjoyed a fairly wholesome reputation) in "Old Mexico." A writer for *The Nation* magazine provides a rollicking personal account of one such trip he took to fledgling Tijuana in 1889:

> Twice a week or oftener, opportunity is given the guests at the Coronado to put a foot on Mexican soil. A steam dummy [a locomotive with a boxed-in engine, reducing noises which frightened passengers and passing horses] with open cars, starts from the hotel, goes down the peninsula [today called The Strand, a thin strip of land that separates the Pacific from the lower half of the bay] and up the other [east] side of the bay, as far as National City, and then branches off, first to the great Sweetwater Reservoir with its remarkable dam, nine stories high, and then to Tijuana. The tourists on this excursion were richly mined [hounded] by alert local operators, who at each stop, pelted the newcomers with real estate circulars [meant to get tourists thinking of a second residence in the San Diego area]. It would be difficult to imagine a more delightful excursion than this 70-mile round-trip in open cars.
>
> Once at the border, the change was distinctly perceptible. . . . Near the boundary line are some yellow pools, in one of which a water snake darted out its angry tongue. . . . The first thing I saw after leaving the train was a young burro with silky hair and no longer than a Newfoundland Dog. . . . The dividing line is occupied by a restaurant which bears the modest name of Delmonico's [after one of New York's finest]. Opposite is a cigar store which has the suggestive title of Last Chance. There are more saloons in Tijuana than buildings. . . . Some are in tents, open in front, with a counter in the center and empty beer barrels for seats. There were only so many Mexicans with their ponchos and serapes seated on their haunches. I told myself: "My God, this is a desolate place."[10]

Desolate, perhaps, but how peculiar was that little burro with the silky hair, not to mention those stereotypical Mexicans in their ponchos and serapes (the writer must have missed their sombreros), all with just a hint of danger in those yellow pools with their angry water snake, a laughable touch of the absurd in a restaurant that dared to call itself "Delmonico's," and the amazing sight of more saloons than buildings. Seedy, strange, slightly degenerate, mind-boggling, but quite intriguing, definitely different, and great fun—these sorts of observations and emotions paved the tourist trail to Tijuana and set the tone for what tourists wanted and expected to see, sense, and do in 1889 (and even now) at the border crossing. The town of Tijuana itself on the other side of the river was still in the planning stage, although a few structures had started to appear along what was to become its main street. Today it is a bustling hodge-podge of well more than two million inhabitants, but any number of tourists still call the place "desolate."

A Matter of Morals

Toward the beginning of the twentieth century, Tijuana had become a "must-see" for tourists visiting Southern California, and a "must-see-often" for residents of the region. One visitor wrote:

> No one leaves San Diego without having been in Tia Juana. There is nothing much to see in Tia Juana, nor is there much to do, but it is foreign soil, and as it is only fifteen miles and one dollar from San Diego, the trip is looked upon as an adventure. The foreign soil idea is immensely attractive to the tourist who has never been out of his own country. It is something to say that he has been—well, anywhere, even in Mexico.[11]

Eavesdrop today on sightseers riding the trolley from San Diego to the border or the Great Red Bus from a car park on the U.S. side to the bustling main tourist district of Tijuana, and you will hear these same sorts of comments.

On 26 February 1891 a series of cloudbursts in the back country raised the Tijuana River fifteen feet, swept away what little town there was, and forced builders and entrepreneurs to reconstruct on higher ground to the west. There a main street, connected to the border by a new bridge over the river, developed with a complement of bars, hotels, curio stores, restaurants, street vendors, hawkers, and hookers. Public lighting with oil lamps arrived in 1903, and by then a telephone line ran from one of the sundry stores to a counterpart on the U.S. side at the border crossing.[12]

Barely seven hundred people claimed the place as their residence, and they lived off the main street in simple, wooden dwellings where they raised families and tended gardens. Ranches farther out provided vegetables and meat, which was supplemented by purchases from stores at the customs post. Clothing and sandal-type shoes were quite often homemade, and there was normally someone available who knew how to shoe a horse, fix a wagon wheel, or wrap a broken arm. But the business of the pueblo was tourism, and that meant postcards, colorful serapes, straw sombreros, cheap wooden and onyx carvings, bad paintings, real corn tortillas, steamy menudo, carne asada tortas, strong (or weak) coffee, beer, tequila, fake folk dancing, boxing, cockfights, gambling, dog and horse racing, prostitution, bullfights, and even opium. No doubt about it, tourists could choose from one full plate of offerings.[13]

Across the line, moralists who called themselves "Progressives" or at least "Reformists" had already experienced at least some success in curbing open vice in California. State law there prohibited horse racing, cockfights, bare-knuckled boxing, and bullfights; some counties and towns (such as Calexico on the U.S. side of the border from Mexicali) outlawed public liquor sales; and police raided well-known and highly patronized red light districts, leading politicians to declare the end of prostitution, which everyone knew was a foolish claim. Still, as Progressives gained political strength in the second decade of the century, reform winds intensified, and the list of prohibitions grew. Those who made a living (and often a substantial one) in such business ventures began to search for alternative venues. Tijuana immediately came to mind. By reputation no prohibitions existed there, politicians were on the take, deals could be made. American tourism, meanwhile, was on the rise, and Tijuana eagerly welcomed visitors out for a step on foreign soil in search of different sorts of souvenirs, food, drinks, and entertainment; yearning to bet on horses or dogs or to plunk a coin in the slots, and out to have a terrific time wondering (some salivating) about all those "stories" concerning what went on behind the scenes in places on premises outside the main attractions.

In 1912 an American syndicate, working in accordance with Mexican gambling laws, made a bold move to establish a huge, multifaceted tourist attraction in Tijuana. The proposition was audacious because it came at a time when a highly destructive civil war was convulsing Mexico and only a year after Tijuana itself had been invaded by a band of adventurers, opportunists, and radical leftists from the United States who intended to take Baja California out of Mexico and refashion it as a republic of their own. The interlopers had been repulsed and dispersed, but the stench of gunpowder and the threat of further upheaval still filled the air. These were hardly times for a major capitalistic venture in Mexico, but both sides gave each other their assurances of intentions and success. According to the contract drawn up, American financiers would get their highly profitable gambling concessions in Tijuana, but they would have to pay a substantial price for permits, plus fees for various events, and agree to finance public works and other projects in the district. These public works included a first-class automobile highway and an electric or steam railroad between Tijuana and Ensenada, a steamship line between San Diego and Ensenada, an army barracks, and three schools, including money for instructional costs. Giving the package a personal touch, an unspecified government official was to receive four purebred stallions each year of the twenty-year lease. The resort was to be a Mecca for sports lovers of many preferences: horse, bicycle, and auto races, aviation meets, bullfights and cockfights, and boxing matches. Although it never came to fruition, this agreement exemplified the manner in which the tourist industry developed in Tijuana: Mexican and American investment collaboration and profit-sharing at the highest levels, touches of personal gain covered by a veneer of civic improvements, all of which left interstices for small businesses to reap a return as well. The federal government also foresaw political gains: Baja California would produce significant tax revenues and federal ties to the capital would be tightened.[14]

The next year, 1913, four Texans incorporated the Baja California Investment Company, which expeditiously received official permits to open a saloon with gambling and began to develop plans for a racetrack. They faced stiff competition from Marvin Allen, Frank Beyer, and Carl Withington, who under pressure by reformists had abandoned their brothels and saloons in Bakersfield, California, modestly labeled their new corporation ABW, and begun to reestablish in Tijuana the sort of business they knew best. They were not the only bidders, however, and soon a free-for-all followed, much of it outside the law.[15]

Sunny Jim and the Governor

Among the most aggressive rivals in the mix was a gregarious and ruthless boxing promoter from San Francisco, James Wood Coffroth, better known as "Sunny Jim." An elegant-looking, fast-talking man of forty-three, distinguished by his red hair and blue eyes, he was a legend in U.S. boxing and entertainment worlds. Seeking respectability for his sport, Sunny Jim put boxers in silk robes and referees in tuxedos. At the same time, he profited handily by making and selling movies of the bouts he staged. Coffroth also earned notoriety when he paid San Francisco's city boss $50,000 to expedite permits for his matches.

In 1915 Coffroth visited San Diego, which was reveling in the impressive hemispheric exposition that celebrated the opening of the Panama Canal. The promoter took a side trip to Tijuana, where the enterprising Antonio Elozúa had opened a *feria típica mexicana,* a folkloric Mexican fair. Elozúa had already prospered from tourists' taste for curios and correctly gauged that the San Diego exposition would attract thousands of sightseers from throughout the United States and elsewhere, many of whom would delight in a step on foreign soil and a chance to acquire things Mexican. At the feria, with its mariachi bands, jumbled market stalls, and stylized "indigenous" dancers, Elozúa also offered gambling, bull- and cockfights, Latin rhythms at a classy nightclub, and for children a circus imported from San Francisco. Furthermore, he also sponsored boxing, and it was probably the long-awaited match between Jack Clark and Mexican Kid Carter that lured Coffroth to ringside and whetted his appetite for moneymaking possibilities in the town.

The entertainment world is about networking, and Sunny Jim had cultivated powerful and wealthy friends. Among these were Baron Long, who owned San Diego's Grant Hotel as well as several high-profile restaurants that catered to movie stars and politicians in Los Angeles. Commonly known as The Baron (which says something about the man), Long had arrived in California from the Midwest as a pitchman for a patent-medicine company. In other words, he sold snake-oil remedies. The Baron soon worked his way into horse racing, the hotel business, and then with the help of the ex-heavyweight champion James J. Jeffries, moved into boxing.

Aware of expanding liquor prohibition and other Progressive reforms, Long yearned to invest in Tijuana, not only in food and drink but also in gambling casinos and his special passion, horse racing. After establishing himself south of the line, he purchased a large ranch called Viejas east of San Diego, where he became one of America's most famous breeders of thoroughbreds. (Native Americans subsequently reclaimed the property and in 1991 opened a thriving gambling casino there. Undoubtedly, The Baron would have approved.)

Long and Coffroth eased the four Texans out of their plans for a race track (the details are unknown), joined with ABW to form the Lower California Jockey Club, and with the financial backing of Mr. San Diego himself, John Spreckels, planned to open a racing season on 1 January 1916, at a hastily constructed track on the Tijuana River flats, just on the Mexican side of the international line, only one-quarter of a mile from the customs crossing.[16]

New Year's Day that year broke crisp and sunny. An astounding ten thousand spectators attended, most brought there by Spreckels's transportation services. Long insured that Hollywood stars attended: comedians Charlie Chaplin and Eddie Foy, along with the popular pugilist William Farnum. Coffroth attracted other sports figures: the famous race car driver Barney Oldfield; his friend James Jeffries; and Frank Chance of baseball's Tinker-to-Evers-to-Chance trio, who three years later would be tarred with the infamous Black Sox gambling scandal. Los Angeles Sheriff J. C. Cline represented U.S. law enforcement, while Venustiano Carranza, whose faction had emerged victorious in Mexico's revolution and who would soon be invested as president, sent a special envoy to the meet. The political dignitaries and film stars stirred excitement, but most honored of all proved to be the territorial governor, Lt. Col. Esteban Cantú, who had signed the concession for the track with gambling in the adjoining clubhouse. Swollen by heavy rains in mid-January that year, the Tijuana River washed out the racetrack just two weeks after it had opened, prompting San Diego preachers to praise The Lord for purging the region of horserace gambling, but the promoters, encouraged both by their profits and by Governor Cantú, quickly reconstructed the complex, which reopened in mid-April and just three months later had to be remodeled and expanded to accommodate a rush of betting spectators.

WHILE REBELLION RAGED elsewhere in Mexico, Cantú was credited with maintaining peace in Baja California. Now he was touted as addressing the needs of development and prosperity for the territory, known to most as Cantú's Kingdom.[17] Indeed, Cantú ruled Baja California like a private fiefdom. He distanced himself and the territory from Mexico City and allied it to Southern California. Some had inklings that he intended Baja California Norte to secede and become independent or even annexed to the United States. Today some Mexicans consider him to have been an opportunistic traitor, while others credit him with public improvements that never would have been financed from Mexico City. Actually, the federal government did not mind his making money on gambling and tourism from Americans, but it demanded its share of the spoils and abhorred the man's arrogance and autonomy.

A native of the northern state of Nuevo León, Cantú had been trained at the nation's prestigious military college and in 1911 was ordered to Baja California to help repel the mixed bag of filibusters from the United States. Three years later an interim government in the capital named him governor and military commander of Baja California, just at a time when ardent reformers in the States were forcing purveyors of certain kinds of sports, entertainment, and tourism to seek an outlet south of the border, beyond the reformers' reach. The confident thirty-four-year-old Cantú offered them a new home for a steep price, and he regulated their activities in an attempt to appease moralists like May Bliss, the sister of Michigan's former governor, who had written to the mayor of San Diego: "I have been all over Europe and America, in the slums of Paris and London and every large city in this country, but I have never seen anything so openly insolent, corrupt and defiant of order, law or decency as Tijuana."[18]

Undoubtedly, a good many people who read that letter in the press said to themselves, "That's my kind of place," but Governor Cantú received his own copy and responded as politicians often do: he announced a cleanup. Freelance con artists, bunko men, and street hustlers were jailed and then expelled to the U.S. side of the border. Racial segregation in nightclubs was enforced, prostitutes licensed. The governor established his own elite military force, fifteen hundred strong, and paid members a substantial $1.50 per day to provide public security as well as to maintain his tenure in office. Tijuana was declared safe for tourists, whatever they wanted from the place.

From humble cantina to opulent casino, all operations were taxed. So were both exports, such as cotton grown around the territorial capital at Mexicali, and imports, including opium moving through town from Macao on its way to San Francisco. Millions of dollars poured into the territorial budget, the pockets of promoters, and undoubtedly those of public officials. In 1916, Tijuana's racetrack and casino complex alone paid the territory $105,000 in taxes, in addition to other earnings from its operation. As their token of appreciation, the owners gave Cantú one thousand shares in the Jockey Club. Meanwhile, in the same year Mexicali's Owl Club paid $8,000 a month for its gambling and prostitution concession and the next year $13,000. While roulette wheels spun, dice were tossed, and horses ran, the territorial government built schools, roads, parks and playgrounds, municipal structures, and The Fort, which would become the focus of so much public anger in the 1938 riots. The regime issued concessions to finance light rail and trolley systems and steamship services along with radio, gasoline, water, electricity, and telegraph installations. It approved fishing and guano-collecting contracts. Both Mexicans and Americans profited, and there was work for everyone. The Catholic Ladies Society of Mexicali staged a bullfight to raise funds for the town's first Catholic Church. A vibrant way of life developed on the border, and local people joined in, declaring Tijuana (and other locales) their home. They did not seem much concerned about matters of remoteness, reputation, or disparities with San Diego. In fact, the thriving little town attracted migrants from other parts of Mexico, people and families who intended to stay and make a living there.[19]

In the midst of World War I, rumors began circulating about German and Japanese intrigues in Northern Baja, and when the United States entered the war in 1917, it sealed its border with Mexico. Immigration officials boasted: "Tijuana, as a tourist town for Americans, will cease to exist during the war."[20] Indeed, tourism temporarily collapsed, but smuggling continued, along with illegal migrant entries, while gambling promoters simply bided their time. By war's end, San Diego had become a major West Coast naval base, and sailors knew where liberty could be entertaining. When naval authorities sought to ban the men from the libations and pleasures of Tijuana, the sailors threatened to take their leave dollars north to San Francisco. Sensing the potential loss of revenue, San Diego's Chamber of Commerce worked out an understanding with the Navy, and Tijuana remained open for the diversion of servicemen. Cantú was equally practical when pressed by moralists to clean up the border town. He offered to create a two-year, twenty-mile vice-free zone across northern Baja California in exchange for $400,000 to compensate for lost taxes. The governor made his point, but it soon became moot. Prohibition was around the corner.

U.S. Progressives confirmed the pleasures of Tijuana with the passage of a national prohibition on public liquor sales by constitutional amendment in January 1920. Tijuana became a pilgrimage site for liquor drinkers, sellers, producers, and smugglers. Stuck with huge inventories, California dealers paid off customs officers and smuggled their wares into Tijuana by the train carload. Along the main tourist street, the number of cantinas doubled from thirty to sixty in four years. Saloons like El Caballito, the Klondike Saloon, and the Black Cat sprang up. The most elegant was said to be the San Francisco, with its oversized crystal windows, copper doors, mahogany floors, and sumptuous restaurant where Lon Chaney and John Barrymore came to dine on dove. On the other hand, it was said that one day the Devil himself put in an appearance with customers at The Aloha. The boxer Jack Johnson ran two night clubs. One, the Newport Bar, catered to blacks only. He called the other The Main Event. A small winery, Bodegas de San Valentín, which had produced 10,000 liters of red and white wines when founded in 1912, upped its output to 650,000 liters a year in 1920. Hollywood stars frequented the racetrack, the singing cowboy Tom Mix and the outrageous Fatty Arbuckle among them. To celebrate U.S. Independence on July 4 that year, an estimated 65,000 Americans visited Tijuana. As showing off one's automobile was part of the celebration, 12,654 cars crossed into Mexico on that one day. Trying to fuel them all, San Diego literally ran out of gasoline. By evening only emergency vehicles could obtain fuel, and out-of-towners had to make an unplanned overnight stay, to the joy of the city's hotel proprietors.[21]

No wonder people went to Tijuana for diversion, "to cast off restraint and kick up their heels." By the early 1920s social reformers in the States had dug deep. In Los Angeles, for example, they had even convinced city police to govern the behavior of dancing couples: "Dancing with the cheek or head touching one's partner was forbidden. The male could place his hand only on his partner's back, between the shoulder and waist. The female could place her hand only in partner's left hand. No music 'suggestive of bodily contortions' could be played. Moreover, women were forbidden to smoke in any room or place adjacent to a ballroom or dance academy."[22] How morals and manners have changed. Today's blaring discos along Tijuana's main tourist street are called the "best" in the West. Bodily contortions rule, and slightly embarrassed sightseers still venture a peek.

A New Yorker Visits Tijuana

A *New York Times* reporter, Stephen Chalmers, captured the panorama of the town in his 1920 article in the paper's "Arts and Entertainment" section. Clearly, here was a man who deplored hypocrisy and liked a drink:

> South from San Diego, Cal., there runs a road. It is not a straight road, nor is it narrow. Broad and crooked, it winds a more or less serpentine way to Tia Juana, across the international line in Old Mexico. . . . Against the paving of that road, against smoothing out the ruts in the way of the transgressor, the clergy of Sunshine City [San Diego's nickname] have thundered protest, and to that road to Tia Juana the pulpit has given a name which, to the joy of the irreverent, has stuck— "The Road to Hell."
>
> And because wickedness has a charm of its own and human nature was not changed by the Volstead Act [Prohibition], the auto-stage companies and livery stables of San Diego and Los Angeles are sowing a whirlwind and reaping a harvest. They do not have to advertise that particular route—all who visit San Diego must "do" Tia Juana.
>
> For at Tia Juana, just sixteen miles from the arid lands [dry San Diego], "there ain't no ten commandments." There the weary and law-oppressed may find an oasis in the desert, a place where he may rest his tired foot on a brass rail and drink to the health of Pancho Villa, or whoever it was that invented Mexico.

The correspondent then took the reader through customs, across the rickety wooden bridge that crossed the Tijuana River and ended at the main street in town, which he depicted as a cross between a Bret Harte mining camp and Coney Island:

> Imagine a wide main street after the old Western style, or the Spanish plaza of colonial pueblos. On either side is a succession of saloons, dance halls, movie picture barns, and gambling dens. In other places, not so largely advertised, one may cook a pill [opium] or otherwise dally through the lotus hours. The air reeks of dust, warm humanity, toilet perfume, stale tobacco and that curious congenial aroma which makes the camel twitch his nostrils afar. And also the welkin rings and vibrates with the laughter and chatter of abnormal good spirits, the noise of an occasional fracas, the whirl of the roulette

wheel, the clatter of the little white ball seeking its owner's salvation, the musically liquid swickety-swish-swish of the American cocktail, the tap-tap-tap of hammers where joy palaces are being shot up over-night to accommodate the business of this prohibition boom town. . . .

And the people—ah, the people!—they that dwell in Tia Juana. All nations! But the American, the Mexican, the Chinese and the "colored gem'man from the Souf" predominate. . . . But there are others not in keeping with the general kaleidoscopic picture—wide-eyed damsels, who, clinging to escorts, have come across the line to "do" Tia Juana. [Chalmers spotted a lady at the roulette table, where she collected a quick win but then settled into a string of losses; two hours later, her escort tried to get her to leave] and Dearie pleads, "Oh, just once more. I just KNOW I'm going to win next time . . ."

The gambling? Every form of it ever invented in [humankind's] vain but still persisting efforts to beat Chance at her own game. Even the humble shell game, playing openly on sidewalks—that is, any old place where there's parking room—finds "comers" still. For excepting always the professional gamblers, touts, &c, who make permanent camp at Tia Juana, most people visit the place in the spirit Mr. Barnum [P. T. Barnum of circus fame] discovered and patented. They know they are being humbugged, and like it. They are wise enough some-times to come with a limit in mind, and prolong the agony of being "trimmed" of that fixed sum for as long as possible.

To the seriously minded newcomer it is staggering, however, and intoxicating, this passing recrudescence of wild and wooly [18]69. It is no place for a St. Anthony, for the wheel and the stacks of bright, new-minted dollars make one dizzy, and the brass rail [in cantinas] fasci-nates by its very shininess.

But it was time to go home:

If you have a liking for the sort of life that once made the Bowery [in New York City] famous you may linger in Tia Juana until 10 P.M. until repassing the gates of respectability on the north side of the river. You may, if your taste runs that way, explore other and more devious channels of Tia Juana life. But along about 5 in the evening there is usually a rush for the line before dark, as that crazy bridge must be negotiated, and one by one the cars are halted at United States Customs for search. As frequently from 500 to 1,000—oh, sometimes more—automobiles from the United States side are parked like a mass of black beetles at Tia Juana, your chances of getting back to San Diego are slim.

[When you do pass through customs,] you are halted in that narrow alley, which is the only official entry and exit point. You are requested to step out of the car—ladies too—sometimes ladies in particular. An urbane official, while perhaps smiling at the possible faint exhalation of ambrosia, deftly runs his hands over your clothing, perhaps lighting [lifting] your hat for you, if it happens to have a high crown, while another officer opens up the hood of the car, sounds the radiator, studies the tires, peeps into the horn, removes cushions, investigates the tool box and even examines the spark plugs, sometimes, or peers under the rubber matting in search of opium. [Regulations permitted each traveler only one package of liquor and that in the form of personal apparel.] Hence, the "package" is frequently as much as a single-bodied man can carry unassisted.

Then, if your bill is clean, you can go ahead, free to enter a respectable republic, where the demon, buried alive still turns in his coffin and makes strange noises.

How Chambers decried "the worse effects of prohibition," one being those large road signs along the "Road to Hell . . . , which point at the sinner with a kind of goading insolence and cry: 'Do Not Attempt to Bring Liquor into the United States.' "[23]

Other Perspectives

Not only the moralists but Mexico's federal government observed Tijuana, its independence, and revenues. Carranza had been deposed in the capital, and in 1920 the new interim president, Adolfo de la Huerta, acted to bring Cantú in line. It was not only that the governor's administration was siphoning off revenues meant for federal coffers, but also that he had a habit of conducting his own foreign diplomacy, in this instance with American oil magnates and congressmen over Mexican petroleum rights. When told by Mexico City to step down, Cantú balked, so the president ordered the army to depose him. Before any armed conflict occurred, however, the governor fled in exile to the United States. His replacement was Abelardo Rodríguez, who had joined the Revolution on the winning side and who belonged to the dynasty from the northwestern State of Sonora which came to rule the nation in the aftermath of the fighting. It was under Rodríguez that Tijuana truly flourished, not only as "American doughsville [moneytown]," as it was called, but as a burgeoning town in its own right, with its civic improvements, fierce business competition, labor conflicts, and vivid, vital daily life.

Tourism and entertainment continued to set the pace, although justices of the peace also had a steady clientele of those wishing a quick marriage or divorce. The ABW "border barons" had already bought the Monte Carlo casino from Antonio Elozúa when they added the sumptuous Sunset Inn to their border racetrack complex. The Inn, where the rich and famous mingled with the hoi polloi, featured fourteen card games, eleven roulette wheels, ten craps and two poker tables, four chuck-a-luck outfits, and two wheels of fortune. The likes of Gloria Swanson and Norma Talmadge, the acerbic, humorous social critic Will Rogers, and the comedian Harold Lloyd graced the faces in the crowd, often a thousand strong in the main hall alone. In 1923 the millionaire cosmetician Helena Rubinstein hosted an exclusive party for twenty-four at the gambling complex; among her guests were David P. Barrows, the president of the University of California, along with Cornelius Vanderbilt Jr. and Hollywood kingpins Carl Laemmle and Joseph Schenck. One's gaming luck could also be tested at the Foreign Club, its private rooms reserved for high bettors where Schenk was a regular. Restaurants in these big clubs featured fillets of game animals such as deer, while the Foreign Club went a step further with rattlesnake stew.[24]

Bars, cantinas, saloons, all laden with slot machines, angled for distinctiveness; among them was The Ballena, better known as The Long Bar because it boasted what the owners claimed to be the longest bar in the world, 215 feet in length. It took ten bartenders and thirty waitresses there to tend to customers, who drank their beer out of glass jars at thirty cents a drink. (By the 1970s, The Long Bar was only a shadow of its former self, but the curved mirrors up front, which distorted the images of patrons as they entered, still provided a humorous welcome.) Soo Yasuhara, a Japanese migrant, owned and operated the most famous brothel in town, the Moulin Rouge, clearly identified by the windmill on the roof. Its employees—Mexicans as well as whites, Asians, and blacks of various nationalities—worked the clientele for a negotiable price.[25]

The Flor de Italia, which opened in 1927 in the Hotel Comercial (later renamed Caesar's Palace), was touted as the best among many good restaurants in town and was patronized by movie stars such as Rudolph Valentino, Clark Gable, W. C. Fields, Rita Hayworth, and everyman's tough guy, James Cagney, as well as the well-known aviator, Billy Mitchell. Besides these notables, regular customers also included U.S. navy pilots stationed in San Diego. Alex Cardini, his brother Caesar, and Paul Maggiora ran the Flor. Alex had been a pilot in the Italian air force during World War I, and following the conflict he migrated to Tijuana to open the restaurant. Possessed of a fine singing voice, Alex, while waiting on patrons, might break out with a famous operatic aria, "Vesti La Guibba" from *Pagliacci* or "La Donna E Mobile" from *Rigoletto*. The Flor had class. Alex was also known for his experimentation with salads. One day he mixed grated Parmesan cheese, boiled egg, garlic, olive oil, lemon juice, anchovy paste, and seasonings and poured the concoction over lettuce with fried bread croutons. He called it his "Aviator's Salad," but as its fame grew, Alex renamed the salad in honor of his brother, Caesar.[26]

Tijuana was not only inventive in cuisine, but modernized horse racing with its first electric starting gates, the photo-finish camera, Sunday racing, large purses up to $100,000, the calling of races on a public-address system, and wetting the track by sprinkler car. In other words, the high-spirited atmosphere of Tijuana stimulated innovation and experimentation. Unfortunately, not enough is known or appreciated of the painting and literature, the poetry, photography, and theater that emerged from this epoch. The town was often the set for silent and then sound movies. As a remembrance, tourists bought picture postcards, many of them hand-drawn and hilarious, and sufficient examples of creative photography remain to prove some photographers were as much artist as entrepreneur. Family-owned newspapers came and went, but the four that were being published in the 1930s recorded and commented, often with literary flourish and commendable flair, on local politics and social life. Regrettably, only tantalizing, scattered fragments of these journals remain for our perusal, examination, and delight.

A handful of outsider journalists recognized Tijuana to be more than a tourist haven. In its 1922 inaugural edition, *The Wanderer,* a tourist magazine published in Los Angeles, offered a more a balanced overview of the town. Certainly it recapped the goings-on along the main tourist street, but then it roamed down side streets and off the beaten path, and found that

The city already possesses a good school and Catholic Church as well as a residence district in which no concessions are permitted, and where many highly cultured Mexican families live and prosper. There is a first-class hotel in operation, and stores where all the necessities of life may be purchased. At the meat market, for example, good meats are on sale at prices much below those in San Diego.

This illustrates the prevailing viewpoint of Tijuana's best citizens. Those saloons [they say] are provided for those who ask to patronize them, [but] there are also places like the "The Big Curio" store which are full of interest for the traveler and which form the base of the town's attractions.[27]

Permit fees and other taxes, even higher than those imposed by Cantú, paid for the town's public improvements during the 1920s. ABW alone paid $65,000 annually for licenses to run its enterprises, among them the racetrack with its adjoining casino, the Foreign Club, and the Tivoli Bar, all notable gambling places. Each saloon paid a minimum tax of $1,000 a month, plus $2 on every bottle of liquor sold. The racetrack paid $2,000 daily during its hundred-day racing season.[28] These were the major sources of municipal income, but every business paid its price, enabling Tijuana to pave some of its major streets, to build new, impressive schools, and to lay out a handsome downtown park, the Parque Teniente Guerrero, with its traditional Mexican design and landscaping, which became the center of the community's social activities and civic celebrations. Local authorities bought a fire truck, dug water wells, constructed and furnished a municipal palace to house a variety of administrative offices, walled the town cemetery (where Juan Castillo Morales later died), began installation of gutters and water mains, and most important, started work on a high dam a few miles up the Tijuana River. This dam would control the periodic flooding along its route through town as well as provide a reservoir that would guarantee the growing town a substantial water supply.

Taxes and payoffs also financed a new bridge crossing the river between the border customs post and the main part of town. It was called "La Marimba," because autos traveling along the wooden cross-ties "played" the bridge like a musical instrument, making a distinctive sound that may have been just a "clunk" to some but carried a humorous tune for others. In dealing personally with American gambling interests, Governor Rodríguez and others in high places no doubt grew rich, but his administration also provided the town with an infrastructure that induced civic pride. Regardless of what moralists and some outsiders said, the people of Tijuana liked their city, earned a good livelihood there, and despite the town's gaudy and salacious attractions, enjoyed a family life steeped in traditional Mexican customs. Although it was characterized as such, Tijuana was not really a "boomtown." It did not boom and bust as did so many legendary gold and oil towns. Without doubt, in these early years it was heavily dependent on tourism, but population growth was steady, and those who came declared the town their home; in other words, they had come to stay.

The showpiece of civic advancement was the new secondary school named for Mexico's President Alvaro Obregón, who in 1928 was about to begin a second four-year term when an assassin's bullet cut him down. Obregón was not the town's first or only school. There were several primary schools: Miguel F. Martínez, located in a residential area toward the center of Tijuana, and two or three one-room school houses in outlying settlements. Martínez, named for a progressive educator in late-nineteenth-century Mexico, employed respected instructors, most of them Americans, who were given land and homes to encourage them to teach there. It attained a reputation for excellence, although enrollment was limited. Olga Camacho was among the many youngsters in the community who even by age eight were not attending school, even if some today claim to have been her classmate.

Before the establishment of the Obregón School, those who wanted a secondary education had to go to San Diego or Mexico City, and few did so. Pupils went four years to primary school and there they stalled. Parents could not afford or did not care to send them away to school, and the young people themselves did not sense a need to further their education because decent paying work was quite available in town, and given the tourist trade, ingenuity provided ways to further opportunity.

Some, of course, desired a profession. A number pursued normal school studies in southern Baja California and later directed their own schools, but most young people settled into work near home. Governor Rodríguez meant to expand their horizons, however, so when he was invited to the inauguration of a new high school in Yuma, Arizona, he asked to borrow the architectural plans for that school in order to construct a replica in Tijuana. The result was the $250,000 Alvaro Obregón mammoth, a two-story structure, mainly financed by casino proceeds. Soaring columns graced the entranceway, making it by far the most imposing building in town. The school housed twenty-one classrooms, an auditorium, a library, a kitchen, a dining room, a gymnasium, administrative offices, a museum which displayed dissected animals, and the requisite bathrooms, including a heated one for teachers. Students received both general and practical education at Obregón, and when it opened in 1930, it signaled Tijuana as much more than a bawdy tourist town. There it stood on the west side, high on a steep bluff overlooking the entire community, as a symbol of culture and modernity for the *new* Tijuana. Today the building, no longer a school but still a landmark, is an active cultural center for the greatly enlarged city.[29]

THE PACE AND turbulence of Tijuana's tourism industry naturally bred grievances and protest. A shrill outcry could be expected from the moralists, both in Mexico City and on the other side of the international line. Mexican presidents periodically launched "moralization campaigns," occasionally out of some personal conviction, but always laden with political purpose, either to "save the reputation and soul of the nation" or to "rescue our working people from vice," but more realistically to bring fringe areas and their resources more firmly under central control.

Church and reform groups on both sides of the border lambasted Tijuana for its wickedness, but observers like Duncan Aikman caught the saccharin odor of hypocrisy in their pronouncements: "I find in all these towns [like Tijuana] no sins more gorgeous than those enjoyed by every Massachusetts Lodge of Elks at its annual fish-fries prior to 1920 [Prohibition]." Noting that most of the American tourists to Tijuana were "middle-income people—babbits—from the mid-west," Aikman wrote,

> They have either sorrows to drown or pleasures to accelerate in a way that is relatively difficult and expensive and sometimes socially inexpedient at home. . . . The more one frequents the Mexican border resorts, the more one is brought to realize that the great American gift for depravity is for playing devilish rather than being it. . . . The real thing, obviously and always sought in a border debauch, is to carry the memory of from two to nine drinks back to some town like Coon Rapids or Memphis, and to be able to say at the next gathering of cronies or lodge brothers: "Lemme tell you, li'l ole Juarez [or Tijuana]

is some town to raise hell (feminine equivalent: raise the roof) in, and boy, we sure raised it."[30]

Of course, such doses of satire never curb moralists, even if their harangues only make a place more inviting to many tourists.

The residents of Tijuana may have been bruised by some of the more slanderous outbursts against their town, especially those which carried racial connotations, but they were not about to let moral accusations affect their livelihood. When an American got in trouble in Tijuana, or when the U.S. government cared to do some moral policing, or when national politics dictated, U.S. authorities might limit the hours that Americans could cross into Mexico or entirely shut down the border, as during World War I. In 1920, Navy Secretary Josephus Daniels complained to the Secretary of State that "Tia Juana has become one of the most infamous vice resorts on the Western Continent," and requested the use of "every resource at your disposal for protection of the Naval forces."[31] The threat of closure was a club periodically wielded by American authorities to bend Mexican border cities to their will, although the Mexicans frequently countered with special charges and closures of their own. There are many examples of these customs wars over the years, but the infamous Peteet case in 1926 proved to be pivotal.

On Saturday, 30 January 1926, Thomas Peteet, age fifty-five, who operated a moneymaking popcorn and peanut stand in San Diego's delightful Balboa Park, took his wife, Carrie, and their two daughters, the twenty-six-year-old Clyde and the nineteen-year-old Audrey, to Tijuana by car. They checked into the San Diego Hotel for a weeklong vacation and spent their days eating, drinking, and gambling. Each afternoon Tom returned home to feed the family cat and then went back to his family in Tijuana. On Wednesday, February 3, Carrie was not feeling well, so Tom and the girls left her at the hotel and went out carousing. At 8 P.M. they found themselves at the Oakland Bar. So did Tijuana's police chief, Zenaido Llanos, who joined them at their table and offered them some drinks. These, it later was said, turned out to be Mickey Finns that drugged the three tourists into a stupor. There are various versions of what happened next—Tom somehow made it back to his hotel, or his wife found him slumped in the street outside the Oakland. At any rate, their daughters were missing, and the parents searched for them without success.

Shortly after midnight Audrey returned to the San Diego Hotel; police brought Clyde there early the next morning. Both women claimed to have been raped, implicating seven men, including Chief Llanos and the Oakland bar owner. The Peteet family returned to their home in San Diego, and on Saturday, 6 February, committed suicide by gassing themselves to death. All but Clyde died immediately; she slipped into a coma and died three and half days later in a hospital. Investigators found a hastily written will and two farewell letters in the home.

As might be expected, an international furor ensued. California's governor and a congressman from the state demanded justice. San Diego's city council urged closing the border from dusk to dawn to protect American citizens. The U.S. Treasury Department agreed, closing the border from 6 P.M. to 8 A.M. In response, Governor Rodríguez petitioned Mexico's president Plutarco Elías Calles to close the border completely, but Calles declined to go that far. The impact of the early closing imposed by the Americans could be felt on business in Tijuana, but the racial slurs hurt Tijuanenses more. The town's Chamber of Commerce wrote to President Herbert Hoover: "We do not consider ourselves an inferior race whose contact means danger at night, nor as a body afflicted with an infectious plague, and consequently request equal consideration and the same treatment accorded other people." But the U.S. government did not budge, and the shortened hours remained in effect until 1933, when President Franklin D. Roosevelt removed all such restrictions as part of his welcomed "Good Neighbor Policy."

On 10 February 1926, Mexican authorities arrested seven men in connection with the rape of the Peteet girls. A week later, they charged two of them, Chief Llanos and the bar owner, with rape, violent assault, and concealing a crime. Officials accused two other men of cover-up and dismissed complaints against the remaining three. At a subsequent trial, a jury acquitted all the accused, but President Calles moved quickly to deflect criticism. With a flick of the wand of morality, so beloved by heads of state, he ordered fifty-two of the town's seventy-five bars closed, five hundred foreigners (most of them bar girls) deported, and twenty-five Mexicans sent for various offenses to the dreaded island prison of Tres Marías off the Pacific coast, but without trial or sentence. Nothing is known of these twenty-five unfortunates, who probably ranged from petty criminals to political adversaries. They now lie among the disappeared.

Subsequently, historians have reviewed the case and uncovered discrepancies and contradictions in the evidence given police and reported in the press at the time. They have discovered the Peteets themselves to be less than your average American family, but any inferences that a loose lifestyle caused the tragedy seem unwarranted, especially in the absence of Mexican police and trial records.[32] As is evident from the Olga Camacho murder case, cooperation existed between San Diego and Tijuana law enforcers, but it only went so far, as it does today.

TRENCHANT HUMORISTS LIKE Will Rogers ridiculed his own government's efforts to clean up—or make the Mexican government clean up—Tijuana:

> Americans don't want to drink and gamble. They just go over there to see the mountains, and these scheming Mexicans grab 'em and make 'em drink, and make 'em make bets, and make 'em watch those horses run for money. It seems that Americans don't know these places are over there at all, and when they get there these Mexicans spring on 'em and they have to drink or the Mexicans will kill 'em. . . . We come nearer to running Mexico than we do New York State. . . . For the love of Mike, why don't we let Mexico alone and let them run their country the way they want to!
>
> If we have to admit to the world, that we are raising people that don't know enough to take proper care of themselves, we will have to do it by another Amendment [to the Constitution], as follows: "Americans are not allowed anywhere they will be subject to evil influences."[33]

Americans (or enough of them) agreed with Will Rogers, and Tijuana's business hardly stuttered in the wake of the sordid Peteet case. Just the opposite: tourism picked up, and people wanted to see and fantasize about where "it" happened.

4. Mexico for Mexicans

While Americans owned (with Mexican associates) the major moneymakers in Tijuana—the casinos and the racetrack—any number of Mexican entrepreneurs also profited handsomely from the business of Tijuana. Miguel González, for example, started in a curio shop in 1922 and seven years later built one of Tijuana's best hotels, La Comercial, famed for catering to internationally revered bullfighters. In between, he founded the town's Banco del Pacífico in partnership with Governor Rodríguez, and along with the two American entrepreneurs Carl Withington and Ed Henderson, he owned the Mexicali Brewery. González, reputed to be the wealthiest man in town, was also the proprietor of La Ballena, the Long Bar. The Savín clan also started in curio shops and expanded into liquor stores, backroom casinos, and a brothel. Enrique Aldrete owned the expansive Comercio Mixto, a general goods store called "mixed" because it sold everything from medicines to bread to ornamental iron, lumber, and haberdashery. Aldrete was also mentioned in some liquor smuggling scandals. In 1927, the Laniados founded the town's first perfume shop, featuring European imports, along with crystal, porcelain, and other sophisticated objets d'art. Brothers Ruben and Manuel Barbechano owned the local light and telephone company and operated it from an imposing three-story building, while the Ruiz brothers, Wulfano and Humberto, ran two cantinas with restaurants and the Ben Hur and El Nogales cafes, noted for their Latin orchestras specializing in Caribbean rhythms. The year 1934 found the Ruizes dickering for property on which to build a casino in the heart of Mexico City. Mariano Escobedo owned the two-story cantina and casino next to El Bazar Mexicano. Six Tijuanenses—Miguel Bujazán, Cornelio Díaz, Angel Fernández, Luis Rojas, Francisco Martínez, and Carlos Gómez—incorporated a motion picture company in 1937 and the next year produced their first film, shot in Tijuana. These are only a few of the more prominent Mexican ownerships. Many others owned small places up and down the main street, and just off it along the little *callejones*, or alleys, that darted off into the jumbled interiors of city blocks. In sum, although there were complaints that the Americans had acquired the town, a substantial number of Mexicans, along with Armenians, Syrians, Japanese, Spaniards, Italians, and Chinese, found ways to profit.[1]

Tijuana's Chamber of Commerce, which was founded in 1926 and had one of the American border barons as a vice president, insisted that Mexican merchants receive their due. When it complained that the opulent American-owned Monte Carlo casino and racetrack at the border was siphoning off tourist revenue before it could reach the center of town, the casino was closed. The entrepreneurs, however, quickly constructed a replacement, The Tivoli, on the main street, which became Avenida Revolución in 1932 and remains so today. Such accusations were common—that one place or one group of people, usually Americans, were being favored and getting more than their share of the proceeds. Labor unions were especially strident in this regard, charging that "Gringos" had frozen them out of their operation or that Americans declined to hire Mexican workers, or if they did, paid them less. Nationalism naturally became entwined with protest—Mexico for Mexicans—but the issues concerned opportunity for work and fair wages more than national pride. Workers did not necessarily want the Americans out, but they demanded their share of earnings.

In the wake of the Revolution unionization in Mexico gained significant strength because politicians from presidents on down in their search for constituencies encouraged union formation and militancy. The overarching federation of syndicates was the CROM (Congreso Regional de Obreros Mexicanos), the group so instrumental in the rioting which rocked Tijuana in 1938. Labor unions in northern Baja were not industrial but mainly service syndicates representing waiters, bartenders, taxi drivers, agricultural laborers, port workers, bakers, musicians, and others. Since each of these unions had individual needs and goals, at times in conflict with one another, there was normally a good deal of elbowing and bullying going on beneath the umbrella called CROM. So the confederation mediated as much with its membership as it bargained with management. The Tijuana taxi and horse-and-buggy drivers who attended tourists organized first. The Mexicans complained, with reason, that while American taxi drivers could carry their fares into Tijuana and back, Mexican drivers were not allowed to cross the international line. So American tourists usually stuck with the cab that brought them or picked up an American taxi which could carry them back through the border crossing and closer to home. In protest, the Mexicans formed a Chauffeurs' League in 1922 and within a year had negotiated an acceptable sharing agreement with the owners of the American cab companies.

A broader local grievance concerned equal employment opportunities and pay for Mexican workers throughout the whole spectrum of businesses. It was true that in the early 1920s American patrons preferred English-speaking American service, which they understood and trusted, and at the time Americans occupied at least 80 percent of the jobs in casinos, bars, and restaurants—at least those jobs that brought them into contact with American customers. Governor Rodríguez adjusted but did not exactly rectify the disparity on 1 May 1924, when he decreed that at least 50 percent of the workers in all establishments must be Mexican. Four years later, he ordered that the workforce erecting the gigantic dam on the Tijuana River be no less than 80 percent Mexican.

As Mexicans became more familiar with American customs, idiosyncrasies, manners, and language, the majority of service positions came to be occupied by Mexicans, although Americans retained many of the most lucrative jobs. Still, the pay scale for comparable work by Mexicans was among the highest in the country, and all salaries were in U.S. dollars. An advertisement for the Tijuana Brewery Company in 1933 claimed that it had thirty-three employees, all protected by workingman's insurance, who worked eight-hour days and earned $3 to $8 a day. A year later, still in the midst of the Great Depression, waiters in Tijuana earned $100 a month and gardeners $150 at about the same time that a waitress in California received $64 a month, and New York set the minimum wage at eighteen cents an hour for a fifty-hour week.

One Mexican worker remembers that in the 1930s the unemployed would go to Tijuana's cantinas just to scoop up coins and bills dropped on the floors, and that waiters at the best restaurants made so much money that when they needed rest, they would sell their position to a friend for $200 a day until they recuperated and came back, normally within a day or two. As in all such work, it was not the salary but the tips that counted, and there are legendary stories about the tips left by Americans, both the famous and infamous. The gangster Al Capone, for instance, once gave a $50 tip to a hatcheck girl. Per capita income for Tijuana has normally been among the highest in Mexico, which is one reason why the place attracts so many migrants. Certainly many newcomers arrive en route to work on the U.S. side of the line, but increasingly migrants have come to Tijuana itself to work and stay.

Wages could be uneven, of course, and complaints of other sorts of inequities occurred frequently enough. At the huge dam-building project started up the Tijuana River in 1928, for instance, Mexican carpenters earned $2.50 daily, while American carpenters received $6.00 for similar work. On 11 September 1923, some 100 to 150 unionized Mexican men stormed the Tivoli casino to protest their own government's general favoritism toward U.S. business. They turned over gaming tables, tossed about the tools of gambling, and hurled packets of money in the air, but kept none (it is said) for themselves. They made their statement and dispersed when police arrived. In the following decade, workers on the Tijuana-to-Ensenada roadway complained that their American manager insulted and mistreated them.

The CROM persistently found ways to make its presence known and felt. In 1933 it charged that airplanes and hydroplanes from the United States flew over and dropped bombs on Mexican territory, a reference to U.S. Navy Air Corps training exercises, which remained offshore but still in the general area. Two years later it organized a boisterous protest over increased telephone and telegraph prices. Then the full force of the union's fury exploded in February 1938, using the Olga Camacho murder as the occasion to discharge other resentments.[2]

Tijuana's working people also had their concerns and complaints as community residents. They wanted a fair share of benefits, so when they felt they had been abused or cheated, they brought their charges to higher authorities. Most concerned claims that customers had failed to pay for items or merchants had failed to deliver purchased goods or overcharged for them; against public employees the common charges were bureaucratic incompetence or corruption. Any number of these accusations were rooted in longtime rivalries and personal conflicts. Moreover, although local people well knew what was going on along main street and did not seem to disapprove—after all, most of it provided their family income—they nonetheless expected that the shameful aspects would be kept in their place. They did not want gambling and drinking joints in their residential neighborhoods, and they insisted that the large movie houses be located off the main tourist district so that their children could attend a film in neighborly surroundings. When improprieties occurred, especially sexual ones, the people demanded official action. They denounced a townsman who had received permission to turn an old church building into a social service center but instead used it, or at least some of its rooms, as a whorehouse. One woman deplored that an exotic dancer at one of the cantinas in the tourist area was using emblems of the national flag as pasties to cover her breasts and pubis.[3] The outsiders were permitted their entertainment, but the residents meant to retain their respectability and traditions. Of course, local people, especially males, periodically (or regularly) slipped off to join the activities on tourist row. Looking back today, older men admit their indiscretions with a wink.

Regular People, Daily Life

In the early 1930s everyday life for residents of Tijuana was a churning mixture of traditional small-town habits and routines and the excitement, insecurities, surprises, and disappointments of a burgeoning border community. In the core of town, but away from the main tourist street, people like the Camachos lived in moderately sized, one-story wooden houses. The lumber to build them came from the U.S. side of the line. Most wooden houses were built from sections assembled in San Diego and brought by truck or wagon to Tijuana through a yawning gate called the Puerta Blanca, located a mile or so west of the customary port of entry. (As the main border crossing at San Ysidro had permanent customs structures to control both foot and vehicle traffic, an overhead arch to mark the boundary, and clusters of stores in the immediate vicinity, large, bulky items such as houses entered through the Puerta Blanca, which had a duty station to one side but no obstruction to free passage.) Once in place in accordance with the crude town development plan, the houses were put together. A few homes were of rolled tin, others English-style with gables and flat tiles. All lacked drainage. The toilets were typically sump holes, and people took baths in portable tubs. Sanitation was a problem, which led to frequent stomach and intestinal disorders, too many of them deadly.

In the newer colonias on the steep hillsides, residences and their facilities were even more rudimentary. People built with what they could find: cardboard, straw, packing crates, metal signs, bricks, wooden poles, and cloth hangings. An entire conglomeration of flimsy cardboard shanties (nicknamed *cartolandia* in the 1960s) arose in the flat plain of the river on the edge of the main town. Floods periodically washed it away with devastating consequences for the dwellers and their belongings. Because tourists crossing the bridge from the border to entertainment row recoiled at this human misery, soldiers from time to time drove the squatters out at gunpoint, but as they had few alternatives, the homeless and destitute came right back.[4]

If possible, residents grew at least some of their own chiles and beans in gardens around their homes. With sufficient space, especially on the outskirts of the town, they might also have a few chickens, a pig or two, goats and a calf, plus the inevitable cats and dogs, most of them running wild. There were grocery stores in town, run mainly by Chinese, at which one could buy pastas, bananas, grapes, and peaches when in season, and a great many street vendors peddled their wares (though there were no taco stands), but fruits and vegetables were fresher, more plentiful, and of greater variety just a mile or so across the Marimba Bridge at San Ysidro. Tijuana did not have papaya, pineapple, or serrano chiles in those days, but communities around San Diego grew watermelons, cantaloupes, California green chiles, apples, bananas, and oranges, and sold them at the border.

Bread: there was only one bakery in Tijuana, but in the afternoons, after the streets had been wet down by one of those whimsical examples of Mexican inventiveness—in this case a jerry-rigged watering truck—the baker-boys would walk house to house with their delivery of fresh *bolillos* (bread rolls) and *pan dulce* (sweet buns). Tortillas could be purchased at any of fourteen small outlets or made at home with masa purchased at the local nixtamal plant. Tamales were homemade in the traditional way.

Water supplies were always short. Lack of water is nature's cruelest curse on Tijuana, indeed on all of Baja California. Wells were dug in the river plain at places where subterranean flows had forced their way toward the surface. Water was free of charge, but had to be hauled in heavy jugs from an outlet to one's residence. Normal use for a family of four or five required two barrels of water daily.[5] Water towers arose here and there, and for a fee water trucks served a number of the residences, but in times of shortage one could not irrigate a vegetable patch or tend to other necessities outside the essentials. People eyed the new dam eagerly as a secure source of water, but engineering problems, financial shortages, and political whims created frustrating delays. It took more than a decade to build the dam, which finally opened in October 1938. In the meantime, sewage, drainage, pumping, and potable water predicaments festered. There simply was no water to wash them away.

Ill health, therefore, remained a persistent and fearsome problem. As late as 1940, average life expectancy in Tijuana was only forty-two years. More men than women died each year, because so many males worked in hazardous conditions; they were also more prone to suffer shootings, knifings, and cirrhosis of the liver. The mantle of death, however, weighed most heavily on the newborn and very young. Infant mortality in 1936 was a devastating 148 per 1,000 live births. And in 1931, of the ninety native Tijuanenses who died there, seventy-six perished of infectious diseases like bronchopneumonia, dysentery, and tuberculosis in their first two years. Another eighteen were born dead, five from syphilis, and others because the mother was overworked or the midwife had erred in delivery. Only six of the ninety died in adolescence or adulthood. Parents never recover from the grief of losing a cherished baby, and nearly everyone in Tijuana bore these scars of misfortune.

Poring over deaths recorded in the civil registry for the 1930s one finds few individuals living into their sixties and seventies. Most adults died in their thirties and forties, a significant number of rheumatic heart disease, caused by a strep infection passed from person to person. Now the disease is controlled; the infection can be fought with antibiotics, and new heart valves may be installed, but not in those days before penicillin, when less than two percent of the town's population lived long enough to die of a heart attack.

Many died of gastrointestinal disorders which came from bad water and improperly prepared food. Diseases such as cholera, salmonella, and shigellosis are caused by bacteria in food or water that when consumed initially cause high temperatures, diarrhea, and vomiting. Victims lose fluids, are unable to keep in new ones, and cannot maintain their blood pressure, eventually going into shock, then heart failure. Death comes quickly, usually within two days, at times overnight. Children are highly susceptible, which is why the town's infant mortality rate was so alarming. Today people afflicted with gastroenteritis are given blood transfusions and fed intravenously, but none of that was available seventy years ago in Tijuana.

The town in 1940 had only one hospital, the Civil and Military, with ninety-six beds, and three private clinics with a total of thirty-nine beds, hardly enough to handle a steady stream of patients suffering from gastroenteritis and heart diseases, along with others dying of tuberculosis and pneumonia.[6] When it came to death and dying, Tijuana was probably no worse off than many other communities in the world, but the grim reality places a human face and a sobering shadow on the glitter and tinsel of the town.

Adequate work with decent reward, however, can ameliorate the negatives of a place and shepherd people through personal troubles. The jumbled, cluttered, unregulated, energized conditions in Tijuana whetted the appetite and stimulated the creative proclivities of a populace that engaged in all sorts of work for pay, some of it unsavory to be sure, but also in other refreshing pursuits. A charming example comes to mind: the ownership of those burros painted with zebra stripes with which tourists still crave to be photographed. Origins of the burro-zebra are not certain, but they are said to have been inspired by zebras seen by a Tijuana photographer in the San Diego Zoo during the 1920s or perhaps the 1930s. Whatever the precise date, white and coffee-colored burros accustomed to pulling carts as taxis acquired black stripes, first through vegetable dyes and later hair tint. The double hybrids were hitched to colorful carts and stationed at intervals along the main street, where they became an immediate hit with tourists. Visitors who climbed on the cart, donned a broad-brimmed sombrero, and draped a brightly hued serape over one shoulder had themselves photographed against a backdrop of some outrageous, supposedly indigenous mythic scene. The picture became not so much that of a funny, striped zebra but a souvenir of Tijuana, that somewhat zany, slightly off-color border town where Americans might escape their routines and inhibitions.[7]

Many women took advantage of paying jobs in the service sector. Imagine how a young girl (some recently arrived from a rural district of interior Mexico) felt as a hatcheck girl in a glamorous casino, or as a waitress in a fancy restaurant, or selling French perfume along with cashmere scarves. Making beds and washing laundry day after day might be back-breaking routines, but for many it must have beat hoeing weeds in a parched field or sweeping animal mess from a dirt floor. Besides, urban life itself had its excitements, then as today.

Most of the married women stayed home with their chores and children, like Feliza Camacho. There was plenty to attend to around the house. Buying groceries might entail a trip to San Ysidro; water had to be drawn from the river-bottom wells. Women tended to make and mend parts of the family's wardrobe. They cooked meals, cleaned house, tended gardens, and cared for animals, often with the help of their younger children. In emergencies they helped their neighbors delivering babies, comforted them in times of grief, and watched children when parents were called away. Outside the tourist area, but still at the core of the community, the ambiance of Tijuana was still strikingly small-town in the 1930s. People knew one another and their business, kinship ran deep, compadres confirmed their loyalties, and the citizenry felt secure. On the fringes of town, with their rising and ebbing flow of migrants, there was less stability, less commitment, fewer material assets, but at the center there was a sense of well-being and good fortune.

School Lessons and Community

Tijuanenses valued education. Schools not only taught reading and writing but also good manners, how to behave both at home and in public. Pupils learned to think their ways through difficulties and how to better their lives. And education also conferred status. Regardless of wealth or talent, people respected those with titles that came with diplomas.

Schools were too few to serve the town's entire population, so many children learned only from their parents and through experience. Those fortunate enough to be enrolled in the progressive Miguel F. Martínez primary school studied beyond reading, writing, and arithmetic, and in class mulled over themes such as laziness, hygiene, and drunkenness. The First Primer used in Mexican schools stressed the need for punctuality and work: "Birds, bees and spiders must work to live. If you observe other animals, you will find that each one works in his own way. You too must work." The Second Primer told a story: "Despite being tired on coming home from the field, Pascual feels happy. By means of incessant work, he betters his position. Scarcely three years ago he received a plot of land when the territory in his district was being divided. By means of steady work, he has gotten good crops." Loyalty and appreciation for government was an essential part of this lesson. Love of family was underlined by a poem:

I adore my dear mother
I love my father too,
No one loves me in this life,
As I know they do.
If I sleep, they protect me,
If I cry, they too are sad,
If I laugh, their faces are smiling.
My smile is the sun to them.[8]

The Third Year primer emphasized the need for fresh air and sufficient food eaten at regular hours, and the depravity of alcoholic beverages.

Though separated by sexes, the Martínez school was a mix of cultures; the roster included surnames like Yasuhara (Japanese), Basso, Anfuso, and Ferrari (all Italian). Education-minded foreigners who lived in Tijuana made sure their children received a formal education. School lasted eight hours a day, from eight in the morning to noon, then a lunch break, followed by four hours in the afternoon. Pupils learned practical things, the girls to sew, the boys to do carpentry and plant crops. They were expected to memorize their lines for songs and plays (among them the socialistically inspired "Himno a la Agricultura," "La Historia de un Agrarista," and "El Corrido de los Campesinos") presented for parents and friends in the school theater. Fiestas marked Christmas, New Year's, and Mother's Day. There were no organized sports.[9]

RESIDENTS CERTAINLY ENJOYED sightseeing on the main tourist street in town, but the hub of their social life was blocks away, well off the beaten tourist path, at Parque Teniente Guerrero, where more traditional Mexican festivities reigned. Built by the army and named for Second Lt. Miguel Guerrero, a military hero in the 1911 clashes with invading separatists from the United States, the attractive park featured an ornate, two-story gazebo as its centerpiece. Men played boliche with compadres in the park, while women sitting close to one another on concrete benches gossiped, not infrequently on matters of a sexual nature. On weekends and holidays people set up little stands to sell homemade candy, pan dulce, sandwiches, pozole, tostadas, tacos, sodas, and beer. Festive civic celebrations, usually preceded by parades through town, packed the park. The parades featured floats with comical, commercial, and patriotic themes, dancing troupes of schoolchildren in traditional dress, mariachis with their distinctively Mexican yelps, choral groups, and of course the highlight, the Queen of the Fiesta, exhausted but dutifully smiling and waving a hand at the appreciative crowd. Kids darted everywhere, teenagers met up, parents watched but lost track as some of the boys wandered off to pool halls.

In the gazebo, the talented Tijuana municipal band, or a military or school band, performed those splendid, frequently rousing tunes that may seem slightly discordant to the uninitiated but which responsive onlookers had heard dozens of times. Trumpets, saxophones, tubas, clarinets, coronets, trombones, cymbals, and drums; marches, hymns, vigorous political anthems such as "La Internacional" (au courant for the times), songs from the regions, arrangements of operatic overtures and arias, music by contemporary Mexican composers all combined to etch out the *paisaje sonoroso,* the extraordinary musical landscape of Mexico. Nowhere else in the world is there anything like a *banda típica mexicana.* It exudes passion and a local sense of belonging.

Politicians gave their expected, interminable, and tedious speeches in Parque Teniente, but few listened. Beer flowed, gestures became more animated and exaggerated; "cabrón" (son of a bitch), "guey" (smart aleck), and "chinga" (screw you) were heard more boisterously as the day wore on into evening and noisy fireworks arched overhead. Here was genuine Mexico. People who claimed that there was really nothing Mexican about Tijuana did not know what they were talking about. More kindly, they were ignorant of Mexican customs and behavior. Most tourists never experienced any of these periodic popular celebrations, and did not care to do so. They never knew what they missed.[10]

The locals engaged in all sorts of leisure, recreation, and entertainment activity, some of it organized, like the Boy Scout troop, but much of it on a whim. There were three large movie theaters in town. Entrance to the Cine Concordia, across from Teniente Park, cost each patron ten cents U.S., while tickets at La Zaragoza and the Cine Ideal were a little more. A fourteen-year-old boy played piano at silent films, and as most of the sound films shown in the 1930s featured Hollywood stars, Tijuanenses especially appreciated seeing *Allá en el Rancho Grande* made in Mexico City by and for Mexicans. Legitimate theater attracted some of Mexico's

An ad to visit Tijuana. Most such advertisements featured "booze and babes." (Andre Williams Collection)

Tourists showed off their cars as part of their entertainment in Tijuana. This 1913 Overland, model 69T, had gas headlights and kerosene side lights. Note the right-hand drive. In this epoch, deep ditches alongside bad roads were more of a challenge to drivers than were passing vehicles. (Andre Williams Collection).

As a symbol of authority and security, in 1915 the governor of the district erected The Fort, an extraordinary structure burned in 1938 by rioters determined to avenge the horrible death of Olga Camacho. (Andre Williams Collection)

Prohibition in the United States spawned glitzy entertainment along Tijuana's main tourist street: casinos, bars with slot machines, girls for hire, fine (and common) restaurants, curio shops, import houses, and fancy hotels and flop houses, as well as supporting barbershops, grocery stores, gas stations, shoe and auto repair places, and chapels for quick marriages and divorces. The first automobile, lower left, is a Hudson (1925–28). Those further along the line are Model T Fords (1920–25), indicating a presence of less affluent tourists or Mexican owners. (Andre Williams Collection)

La Ballena (The Whale), better known as the Long Bar. Its owners claimed it was the longest bar in the world, 215 (some say 241) feet in all. Ten bartenders manned the stretch. (Andre Williams Collection)

Those who "overdid" spent a night or so in the town jail, experiences now remembered in song, amateur poetry, and lore. (Andre Williams Collection)

As a symbol of civic pride, Obregón Secondary School, modeled after the high school in Yuma, Arizona, stood on a high bluff overlooking the town. Today it has been remodeled as a cultural center. (Andre Williams Collection)

With its eclectic but still sumptuous architecture, the Agua Caliente resort rivaled Europe's best. The well-to-do, including celebrities, flocked there for horse and dog racing, high-stakes gambling, spicy entertainment, horseback riding, exotic meals at reasonable prices, personal dalliances, and to see and be seen. (Andre Williams Collection)

Who could resist the goddess of chance? (Andre Williams Collection)

HOTEL AGUA CALIENTE
Tijuana, Mexico

PATIO SPECIALS
Clicquot Champagne Cocktail 25c
Clicquot Champagne Cup $1.50 (Serves Four)

LUNCHEON
$1.00
or bottle of "O. K." Beer

California Season Salad Fine Herb Marinade

Lamb Gumbo Glasgow
Cream of Fresh Mushrooms Saint Denis

Selection of:
Boned Speckled Seatrout fried in Butter white wine sauce
Veracruz

Venison Potpourry en Casolette with Braised Celery Florian

Mexican Specialty
Pipian Sabroso de Pato Salsa con Ajonjoli
Papas Doradas - Frijoles Refritos
Potted Long Island Duckling in Mex. Sesame seed sauce & Fried Beans

Spiced Prime Beef Kernel with Cornfritter
Sauce with Grapes Lithuanienne
Porkloin Medaillon grilled & glazed with Fresh Pineapple
& Sweet Potatoes
Fresh Vegetable Selection, Minced Capon Croquette
Cold Boiled Fresh Lobster Mayonaise
Cold Roast Milklamb Italian String Bean Salad

Potatoes Fondant Persilles - Buttered New String Beans

Southern Ginger Cake
Tutti Frutti Ice Cream or Raspberry Sherbet
with French Macaroons
Coffee

Saturday, November 24, 1934.

A menu from the Agua Caliente restaurant. Thousands visited the resort weekly just to sample its inexpensive gourmet meals. (Andre Williams Collection)

The *haute cuisine* at the casino resort was decidedly international; something for all bourgeois tastes: French, Italian, British, American, along with a daily Mexican special. (Andre Williams Collection)

leading performers to Tijuana, as did operettas (spectators favored *La Traviata* sung in Spanish), and the Cine Bujazán frequently offered stage shows—audiences especially delighted in vaudeville—in conjunction with its movies, most of them made by thriving film industries either in the capital or in Los Angeles and San Diego. Tijuana itself provided the setting for any number of moving pictures. Sergei Eisenstein inspected the pueblo as the potential site for his heralded but never completed *Que Viva México!* in 1932 but then rejected the idea. *The Champ* with Wallace Beery and Jackie Cooper was made there in 1931, and four years later *In Caliente* starring Pat O'Brien, Dolores del Rio, and Leo Carrillo. Residents earned a few dollars a day as extras in these films. A circus periodically came to town, as did boxing and wrestling matches which packed the Arena Aloha. Dances, meanwhile, filled the Salón Alfa. Between songs, mothers and daughters sat on benches holding hands at the edge of the dance floor. Boys impatiently strayed outside the perimeter, but once the music began the young men rushed to find a partner and rarely were refused. Bailes, as they are called, are an indispensable part of the Mexican way of life. Again, they help define community.

Baseball was a favorite sport, and the town had two well-tended ball fields along with a host of sandlots. Soo Yasuhara, a native of Japan who came to Tijuana at age eighteen, organized the town's first team and named it after the famous Molino Rojo or Moulin Rouge, the elegant brothel (nowadays a school) that he owned and operated. Mexico frequently nicknames its sports teams for the companies that sponsor them. At the time, Mexicali Beer had its Cerveceros, and the Royals represented the Bar Palacio Royal. Yasuhara, who played second base for his team, was a tough competitor and stocked his lineup with Mexicans and North Americans who played in the Liga Latina de los Estados Unidos in California. He supplied all the uniforms, bats, and balls and paid his players five to eight dollars a game for their competitions against semi-pro teams from San Diego and Los Angeles. Admission to the ball park, located next to the whorehouse, was free. San Diegans who played in these games as teenagers remember how much fun it was playing in Tijuana. After the game, there would be a beer bust in a cantina, and some players were said to have wandered off to the Molino Rojo. Tourists paid the sport no attention, but Mexicans reveled in it. Some years back, I met a young Mexican from a border state who thought that "home run" and "baseball" were Spanish words. The locals also played pick-up basketball and occasionally volleyball, but soccer (*fútbol*) did not arrive in any big way until the 1940s.[11]

Families went on excursions to broad open mesas below the Rodríguez Dam site to fly kites, or to San Diego for window-shopping, to see a movie in one of the city's five splendid art-deco houses, or to eat some southern fried chicken. At night boys hunted frogs in the Tijuana River bottom, especially near the Marimba Bridge, and sold them for $1.50 each to one of the town's most exclusive restaurants, La Mariana. Later people swam and fished in the lake formed by the impressive dam, an engineering marvel of its own.

Much of the town's social life, often mixed with business or other concerns, revolved around fraternal and social organizations. The Masons, Rotarians, and Lions had branches there, all in close contact with their San Diego counterparts. (Tom Mix financed the town's Masonic Temple.) There was a woman's group, a Club Hebe for young women, and small Catholic and Protestant associations. The Woman's Catholic Union raised money and other donations for the sick in clinics and the hospital, while the Japanese Association also had its charities. The powerful Chamber of Commerce and the labor syndicates, often at odds with one another, also had their more genial social get-togethers.

Town governance was more open than one might think. As a federal territory, the top officials—governor, delegado, judges—were appointees, but beneath their level there was a good deal of give-and-take debate in meeting rooms at the Palacio Municipal about needs and conditions in the community, along with its future. Interest groups did not hesitate to speak their minds vigorously in these sessions, which were not exactly town hall forums with forthright full public participation, but down-to-earth, round-the-table discussions among local leaders. Casino owners and their partners held the big money card in town, but they certainly did not play a free hand.

In the 1920s and 1930s most of the adult population of Tijuana had come there from elsewhere, mainly from other parts of Baja California (principally Mexicali and Ensenada) and the State of Sonora. Smaller groups came from the neighboring United States, Mexico's west coast states of Sinaloa, Nayarit, and Jalisco, and those just to the east, Durango and Zacatecas. Finally, there were scatterings from the Federal District, Chihuahua, and San Luis Potosí. Foreigners, besides Americans, included Chinese and Japanese, Middle Easterners from Turkey (Armenians) and Lebanon, and, of course, Europeans, representing Germany, Romania, Russia, Italy, Spain, Greece, and other countries. Most came to Tijuana at the behest of relatives who already lived there.[12] Word-of-mouth traveled along family lines and drew relatives to the border town, among them the Camachos.

The Camachos: Typical Baja California Migrants

Olga Camacho's grandfather, Aurelio Sr., enjoyed strong political connections in his hometown of Hermosillo, Sonora, and when in the early 1930s an opening occurred as administrator of the government hospital in Mexicali, he accepted the position and moved with his wife and children to the busy border town, where he soon invested in farmland on the outskirts. His son, Aurelio Jr., Olga's father, first went to work in a general store across the line in Calexico, but a cousin who owned a butcher shop in Mexicali convinced Aurelio Jr. to open his own grocery store nearby, which sold fresh vegetables along with staples such as salt, pepper, and canned goods. Mexicali was a young bachelor's delight, and according to Feliza, Aurelio lived it to the fullest.

Feliza grew up in the rural Nayarit pueblo of Acaponeta, where her mother died and her father remarried. When her father divorced his second wife, he and his daughter moved to Mazatlán to care for his aged mother. At age fifteen, in 1926, Feliza was invited by a cousin to reside with her in Mexicali. Feliza wanted to learn English and saw this as her chance. With her father's permission, she moved to the border town. There she practiced her English by listening to American radio. The shy seventeen-year-old had a limited social life, no dancing, not much singing. One April afternoon, she went to Aurelio's grocery to buy vegetables and met the proprietor. They did not speak much at the time, but she admits to admiring his green eyes. That night he hired a Norteño trio to serenade her, and flowers followed every day. On three different occasions over the next three months he asked her to marry him, and she finally agreed. Because a militant labor union had occupied the only Catholic church in town, Aurelio and Feliza drove nearly three hours to Yuma, Arizona, to be married by a priest. More than seventy years later, she still smiles when she thinks of the event.

Aurelio changed jobs; he gave up his grocery and went to work as a bartender and waiter in the picturesquely boisterous beer garden run by the Mexicali brewery. Olga came along in 1930. Three months later they moved to Tijuana to escape Mexicali's summer heat, which regularly rises to 115 degrees and stays there day after day. Aurelio's sister worked as a telegrapher in Tijuana and helped the newcomers to find a house; Aurelio managed a liquor store and tended bar. Soon after that his father, Aurelio Sr., whose agricultural holdings had been seized by uncompromising agraristas, moved his finances and the rest of his family to Tijuana. He invested in nightclubs and bars, one of them the famous Foreign Club, where Aurelio Jr. was working as bartender the evening that Olga disappeared.[13] So the Camachos had been in Tijuana six or seven years before Olga's death. They had incorporated themselves into the economic, religious, and social life of the town and built a network of friends, neighbors, and colleagues in the community that tourists never saw. The outpouring of grief and anger over the rape and murder of the little girl was so heartfelt and profound throughout the town that such emotions could not help but clash with the veneration and canonization of her convicted murderer which soon followed.

Border Religion

Even if they could not (or did not) regularly participate in church services and activities, Aurelio and Feliza Camacho got married in a Catholic church in Yuma to affirm their ties to religious tradition. As a group, the citizens of 1930s Tijuana were not extraordinarily devout, at least not in any organized way. In keeping with the tendency of all migrant groups, relocation altered their religious behavior. There were extremes: some broke with old traditions altogether; others clung to the past with ferocity. Protestantism had chipped away at Roman Catholic foundations in Tijuana; there were nearly fifty evangelical Baptists in town. Masons, long known throughout Mexico for their anticlericalism and political ambitions, continually griped about the partisan political activities of the Catholic Knights of Columbus. At one point, the Masons officially petitioned for the removal of all Knights from public employment throughout the district, charging that their loyalties lay more with the Pope than with the Mexican state.[14] Law forbade Church intervention in politics, but the measure was enforced unevenly, and the Church always found ways to play politics in its own favor.

The great majority of Tijuanenses professed to be Roman Catholics but occupied a spiritual middle ground. While they abandoned many of the rituals associated with religious practice as taught them by priests and parents, their faith remained strong, even as they reshaped their devotions to suit their new needs. They did not go to Mass as much, but religious icons adorned their homes. Quite possibly the meaning of "sin" changed in their new setting. Church doctrine carried less weight, but they certainly continued to call themselves Catholics, claimed to have been baptized Catholic, and hoped to die as such. Even those who found solace in another denomination remained Christian, reserving to themselves the right to return to former religious customs.

Following national independence, the Mexican Church largely ignored scantily populated Baja California, and it took one of those larger-than-life priests, Padre L. Osuna, to establish a Church presence on the peninsula. Osuna had been exiled from Mexico around 1860 for refusing to adhere to the country's new constitution, which separated church and state and proscribed many of the Church's habitual activities. He then spent some twenty years working among Native Americans in northern California; during that period a Father Ubach, working out of San Diego, intermittently delivered the sacraments to the faithful at the Baja California missions.

By the 1880s the Mexican government had relaxed its enforcement of constitutional prohibitions against the Church and allowed Padre Osuna to serve Baja California. In doing so, he roamed the entire length of the peninsula, much of the time by himself. Distinguished by his long gray hair and beard, curled like that of a Nazarene, he traveled in a horse-drawn light spring wagon, in which he carried a portable altar and a lockbox that contained the vessels, candles, vestments, and other accouterments needed to say Mass. At night he staked out his horse, rolled up in blankets beneath the wagon, "sleeping securely within the circle of a horse-hair lariat over which no reptile will venture." He used clerical dress only for his sacred duties, preferring ordinary traveling clothes otherwise. When meeting a dignitary he donned a business suit and wore a white, high-peaked sombrero on his head. He spoke English, Spanish, and several Indian dialects. While in northern Baja California he also visited friends and acquaintances in San Diego. As there was not yet any Tijuana to speak of, around 1886 he built an adobe chapel near the customs crossing, where he stored his books.[15] The little chapel became the subject of picture post cards, even as it succumbed to the weather. Tourists mentioned the building but not the priest, who certainly would have been a highlight of any trip to the border. What a pity. We crave to know so much more of this remarkable pioneer, but he has faded from historical view.

In the early years of the twentieth century, Italian missionaries tended to the spiritual life of Baja California, assisted by U.S. priests along the northern border. When in 1917 a new national constitution placed radically new prohibitions on the Church and its priests, the revolutionary government expelled the Italians, but some, like Severo Alloero, could not abandon their duties. Alloero escaped at night by boat from Santa Rosalía, halfway down the peninsula on the gulf side, and made his way to Tijuana, where two other priests were already at work at a new adobe church constructed toward the center of town. Not one to enforce federal edicts he didn't care about, Governor Cantú permitted Father Alloreo to organize a women's guild and expand the size of the church building. A few years later, heightened pressure from Mexico City (with Cantú himself now in exile) forced Alloero across the border to San Ysidro, where in 1925 he organized a new parish, serving Americans in the tiny border community, as well as Mexican Catholics from Tijuana.[16]

With Alloero gone, Tijuana's only Catholic church was shut tight, but in 1929, when church and state negotiated an uneasy truce, a refugee priest, José Resendo Núñez, tried to resuscitate religious life in Tijuana. Born in Zacatecas, he was attending seminary there in 1914 when Pancho Villa and his henchmen rode into town, killed several priests, and moved on. José Núñez returned to his pueblo, studied with underground priests and in 1922 was ordained. When armed conflict between church and state (the savage Cristero rebellion) erupted four years later, he fled from Zacatecas to San Diego and soon became the first pastor of a new parish in nearby National City. Mexican church-state relations eased in 1929, and Father Núñez recrossed the border to rebuild a parish and church in Tijuana. It was not to be, however, doomed by lack of funds. Tijuana's Catholics had become accustomed to paying American priests for services, and the Americans declined to relinquish the income. Núñez complained to the bishop in Los Angeles that the Americans were breaking canon law, but his protests proved futile. Frustrating as this must have been for the priest, there was worse to come.

In a new burst of antichurch enthusiasm, the Mexican government in June 1932 limited the Church to only one priest per fifty thousand population. This amounted to one for all of northern Baja California and that one to be stationed in Mexicali. The secular administration encouraged Núñez to finish building his new church in Tijuana, but then he would have to leave the country. Everyone knew what the federal government was up to: it would sanction the structure, then confiscate and turn it into a public building; some observers mentioned its potential as a library. Núñez, however, declined to play along. He suspended work on the structure and, in a dramatic display of defiance, openly carried the Holy Eucharist across the line to San Ysidro, where he joined the parish of his old Italian friend, Father Alloreo.[17]

IT IS ONE THING to observe how the faithful practice their religion and another to reflect upon how they think and feel about it. Religiosity is so rich and personal, idiosyncratic and diverse, that generalities about spiritual belief can become banal and misleading, but life histories provide insights. Here is an eloquent sample from a migrant Mexican woman who crossed the border into the United States in the late 1920s; a person like many of those who inhabited Tijuana at the time, she gave the kind of personal testimony heard at the Juan Soldado shrine today:

> As I was educated in Catholicism, I am Catholic, but I am tolerant not fanatic. What is more, as a result of my reading and general studies, I believe only in an all powerful Being, God. I wouldn't attempt to define it, but I know that there is something superior to us which rules the destiny of mankind and of the universe.
>
> I pray every night. It doesn't matter that I have gone to some festival or that I had danced, I pray the evening Rosary, a litany, and other prayers before going to bed. I pray for my husband, not because I believe that his soul is suffering, but for a certain personal feeling which draws me near to him and our happy past; that is the only reason why I pray.
>
> I don't believe in the sanctity or in the purity of priests, or that they are invested with superhuman powers. To me they are men [human beings] like all the rest of us. That is why I don't pay any attention to their preachings.
>
> I make a confession once in a while, but not because I have committed sins—I don't believe that I have any—but to talk with an intelligent man [such] as the priest, to whom I make confession. When I go to him in the confessional, the priest doesn't know me. If he asks me of

what sins I wish to accuse myself I say, "Father, I haven't killed, or robbed, or spoken ill of my neighbor, and I accuse myself of all the other sins for I am a woman, or rather a human being." Then I talk for a long time with the priest, if he lets me, always trying to keep him from knowing me. I unbosom all my troubles to him and tell all that I can't tell my parents or my friends, so that I talk in a shrine where everything that I say stays. After one of those confessions I am happy, as if I had been freed from a load.[18]

Here is a woman of free conscience who believes in God, calls herself Catholic, and relies on rituals of the Church, such as saying the Rosary, reading her prayer book, and praying before going to bed; who treats sin on her own terms; and who does not consider priests to be particularly holy, but who still needs one with whom to discuss her concerns and troubles, even if in the secrecy and sanctity of the confessional. During the first decades of the twentieth century most Mexican migrants remained Catholic, but with personal variations based on background, experience, and perhaps gender and class. This is apparent in statements drawn from their individual life histories:

I am a Catholic because my parents taught me the faith. But to tell you the truth, since I left Mexico, I have not gone to a single church, nor do I pray except when I think of it.

I am a Catholic and although I almost never go to Mass or pray, I do keep Holy Thursday and Friday every year for I am accustomed to do that. At home I was very Catholic but that was because of my parents.

I am Catholic but I do not even pray. I believe mainly in God.

I believe in God, but I have my doubts, for I was convinced [by what I learned] in Catholic school that all those beliefs are useless. [This person wanted a practical education; he aspired to become a doctor, but complained that all he learned in Catholic school was to pray.]

My religion is Catholic, but I do not go to church except in Lent. Then I even take the sacraments, confess myself and tell the priest all my sins, but that does not do me any good, because I commit them again.

I am a Catholic and pray in my house, but I hardly ever go to church for many reasons [among them, his work schedule].

I am a Catholic but I almost never go to church. Sometimes before coming to the dance hall, I go to church, even if it only be to pray a little. I think that I have only confessed myself four times in my life.[19]

The testimonials are overwhelming, the evidence convincing. Living in a new place, away from priest and parents, these migrants practiced their faith in original ways, clinging to those past habits and traditions that still served some purpose, but shucking those that no longer did so and developing other ones that made more sense in their own situations. No doubt, as Mexico modernized, these same tendencies took root throughout much of the country, but they were accelerated along the border, especially among those who crossed into the United States.

Weighing the Origins of Devotion

Even had they wanted to, Tijuana's Catholics would have had difficulty maintaining sustained contact with the official Church. There was a small church building in town, next to The Fort and just down the street from the Camacho family home, but due to a lack of priests in Baja and because of the strife between church and state in much of the country, it was open only sporadically, and parishioners never knew when a priest might be in town to celebrate the sacraments. Once Father Alloreo left for San Ysidro, the church remained in limbo, visited at the most once a year by the priest from Ensenada to say the Mass. It was not until the 1940s that a full Catholic life was reinstituted in Tijuana. Today the city's main cathedral (Tijuana now has a bishop) stands on the site of the original church.

It was up to Catholics to pursue their religiosity as best they could. Some held neighborly prayer meetings in their homes; such sessions were not secretive, simply people getting together to say the Rosary. A priest might come to town surreptitiously from the U.S. side to perform last rites (at a substantial fee), or authorities might just look the other way when a known priest arrived in street clothes to perform a religious rite or to visit friends. The threat of arrest or interference remained, and while most priests seem to have kept their distance, the local historical record reveals no official sanctions taken during this period against church personnel. Those Tijuanenses who wished to do so could cross the line for regular Catholic services—as Feliza and Aurelio went to Yuma to be married—and many people regularly did so. Holy images adorned the dwellings of residents, and some, like the Camachos, had home altars. None of this, however, approached remembrances of Catholic life back home, where the church building itself—often a large, remarkably distinctive structure which housed revered paintings and sacred images—was the center of life, much of it attuned to and regulated by the clanging of church bells. Tijuana did not even have a patron saint, no holy figure to celebrate, to pray to for favors and protection, no one special to intercede for citizens before The Lord. Perhaps they felt no need for one; in any case, the town's Catholics were for all practical purposes on their own.[20]

But did it matter? It is tempting to draw a direct line from formal religious deprivation in Tijuana to the origins of the devotion to Juan Soldado. One could say that the people needed a saint and so created their own, but this explanation is much too simplistic. Other towns experienced the same sorts of general conditions which stirred Tijuana, yet no special devotion developed in them. Tijuana's Juan Soldado seems to have been unique in this regard. Furthermore, it is one thing for latter-day onlookers to judge the town and declare it wanting, and something quite different to understand and appreciate what the populace felt about itself at the time. Just how badly did migrants miss the strong Catholic presence of previous times? Judging by their comments, not very much. Many said they were Catholics because their parents raised them in the Church, and they were perfectly willing to respect those wishes. Migration, however, had loosened the ties and allowed them to practice their faith as conditions permitted and in their own ways. There is no reason to suspect that Tijuanenses (themselves largely migrants) did not do the same. Catholicism-as-missed-or-forgotten did not create the Juan Soldado shrine, but was among a series of lenses, some quite murky, through which people viewed the horrendous events of mid-February 1938. It was only one of the circumstances that defined the town, its populace, and its thinking at the time.

FACTORS SUCH AS remoteness, neighborly dominance, and reputation, which seem to have spawned shrines elsewhere, also have only limited application here. Tijuana may well have seemed remote as viewed from Mexico City or Washington, D.C., but it had transport connections to other locations on the peninsula, as well as to the main part of the country to the east and south, and also telegraph, telephone, and radio stations to spread communications even further out. A steady if limited flow of merchandise arrived from the interior. Residents read books and newspapers. One weekly paper, *El Hispano Americano,* carried a page of highlights from Mexico City in each edition. The 1940 census reported the town's literacy rate at an astounding 67 percent, among the highest in the republic.[21] Tijuanenses regularly listened to their local radio station XEBG, on the air from 9 A.M. to 11 P.M., and just as fervently folks relished movies and traveling shows. Thousands of tourists, moreover, reminded them every day of their connection to a wider world. They understood that they were a long way from Mexico City, but that was not all detrimental. They wanted to improve communication with other places mainly for economic reasons, and the border could complicate but certainly not isolate them from their neighbor to the north. Yet there is no indication that the residents of Tijuana considered themselves remote, especially in the sense of being out of touch.

People also found good and bad in their proximity to San Diego. When juxtaposed against fast-growing San Diego's much larger population (in 1940 approaching 200,000), its more diversified economy, its entertainment and culinary possibilities, and the fabulous harbor that guaranteed its future, Tijuana certainly seemed to be overshadowed. But while the two urban neighbors enjoyed important working relationships, each maintained its own identity, and Tijuanenses could be quite feisty in protecting their interests, whether at the customs post, in police investigations, the marketplace, employee relations, or in regional politics. Tijuana was largely dependent on San Diego for essential supplies, money, livelihood, and emergency services, but its residents struggled against that dependency by clinging to values, morals, habits, and customs they thought the best of Mexican society. While they knew that they were economically dependent, they did not feel socially, politically, or psychologically dependent. They proudly flew their nation's Tricolor and despite complaints against the central government, especially its judicial system and overall arrogance, at civic celebrations and other occasions they proudly insisted "We are Mexicans," and demanded respect for their country. Thus, in the case of Tijuana, "overshadowed" did not mean "dominated by."

As for reputation, moralists and others considered Tijuana to be the devil's playground, a town of vice and sin. Its reputation as seen through these eyes was pitch black. But for the great majority of outsiders Tijuana's hue was more subtle, perhaps a bit off-color, fuzzy, but not unappreciated. Many of the American migrants who came to Southern California in the 1920s saw their new home as a golden land of opportunity. They did not migrate out of desperation; they were not driven west by dust bowl conditions as their comrades were in the next decade. These earlier immigrants followed the same imaginary path that had been trod in gold rush days, and they were reasonably well-off middle-class people, often self-starters open to change and difference. They may not have had thousands to invest, but they had money to spend, and coming out of largely rural Oklahoma, Texas, Kansas, and Missouri, their California dream included a chance to kick up their heels some.[22] Tijuana was certainly a place to do that.

Tijuanenses have long decried labels such as "vice" and "sin" wantonly applied to their city, mainly because there is so much more to their town than the main tourist street, and also because those sorts of negatives can be found in any town or city. Many practices considered sinful or unlawful in the United States, furthermore, have solid cultural foundations in Mexico. For example, most Mexican towns and cities had (and have) their *zonas de tolerancia* (red-light districts). Challenging lady luck at the lottery or elsewhere is a national pastime; when the government tightened gambling laws in 1935, Tijuanenses wondered whether or not the new restrictions applied to neighborhood poker games. Cantinas, of course, are no stranger to Mexicans of whatever social distinction. Mexicans love their fiestas—the drinking, jokes, spontaneous singing, and bantering in words *de doble sentido* (double meaning), often with sexual innuendos. There is no comparison between a Mexican fiesta and an American party.

Tijuana's Chamber of Commerce and other agencies have over time been trying to ameliorate the community's negative image among outsiders by stressing the cultural and entertainment diversity in town, but at they same time they fear that too much "cleanup" will hurt tourism, that is, sterilize a place that thrives on a little bit of dirt. The city recently hired a Los Angeles public relations firm to help refashion its image, but only so far.[23]

Residents do not appreciate being called *provincianos* by Mexico City. The truth is that they are hardly country rubes. They cannot hope to acquire the political power and cultural strength of Mexico City, but they can elect opposition candidates, strive to run their own affairs, and gather economic strength which raises eyebrows in the capital. They certainly did not feel in the 1920s and 1930s that they were living in Sin City. Although memory has its way of scraping the barnacles off former times, older Tijuanenses recall a secure, neighborly, small-town past in which people used inventiveness and fortitude to forge a respectable community in turbulent years.

5. Riding the Roller Coaster

By the late 1920s, Tijuana's tourism was booming. Both the seedy joints and the more elegant restaurants and casinos enjoyed unprecedented prosperity. The town itself had barely eight thousand residents, but streams of inquisitive, fun-seeking tourists tripled the population almost every day. Easterners touting their supposed sophistication became accustomed to visits west, and for Southern Californians a day out on the town frequently meant a trip to Tijuana.

These trends did not escape the border barons and their well-placed Mexican friends. The genius of the ABW gaming syndicate, Carl Withington, had died in 1925 but was replaced by Wirt G. Bowman, an aggressive man of equal promotional skills who knew Tijuana and had even better contacts within the country's power structure. Bowman had earlier worked for a railroad in the northern State of Sonora, married there, and by the time of the Mexican Revolution had moved to Nogales, Arizona, the little town literally split in two by the international border. There he made a fortune brokering cattle deals with rebel leaders like the future president of Mexico, Plutarco Elías Calles. The Sonoran dynasty that ruled the country from 1921 to 1935 included individuals Bowman had helped with his U.S. banking connections both during and after the fighting. (It is said that Bowman facilitated gun-smuggling to these Sonorans in their struggle against Pancho Villa.) Then in partnership with the territorial governor Abelardo Rodríguez, also considered to be a member of the ruling clique, Bowman and associates conceived a dazzling, luxurious gambling, entertainment, and recreation complex that would be constructed in Tijuana and rival the best in Europe. By 1928,

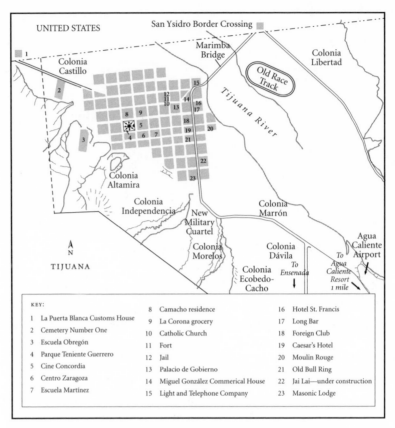

Map 2. The Town of Tijuana and Vicinity, 1938

they had formed the Compañía Mexicana de Agua Caliente and enrolled five hundred investors, among them Calles, who although no longer president, was still the nation's most influential political leader. They hired the governor's brother Fernando to build a $10 million complex to include hotel, spa, and casino. Two thousand unionized Mexican workers were paid $2.50 daily to do the work. Over the next two years—and for an additional $7 million—the group added an Olympic-sized swimming pool, golf courses, greyhound and horse tracks, gardens with singing tropical birds, massage clinics, an airfield to fly in guests, and an outlandish bell tower that resembled an Islamic minaret as the resort's symbol of greatness. Mexicans did most of the construction, and the government provided the requisite permits and concessions for the activities. A California-style resort emerged—a touch of this, a taste of that: mission revival exteriors, French Louis XV or Italian Renaissance interiors, elaborate tiles, precious woods, charmingly crafted wrought iron fixtures, beautiful imported stained glass, and the Moorish-style bell tower which stood at the entrance to the resort. When guests complained that the tower's ringing bells disturbed their sleep, it was moved to the back part of the property, but the bells continued to bong because Baron Long liked the sound.

Agua Caliente was truly a scene to rival that of Monaco's Monte Carlo or San Sebastián's Trépot. Advertisements blurted out their excitement over the Shangri La "at the end of the rainbow in Old Mexico." Daily horse racing became the "greatest of all sporting events in the southland." "All the nation awaits the outcome" of the golf tournament. The spa outdid "in charm and luxury the watering places of America and Europe." Luncheon on the "World Famed Patio" featured "an unexcelled cuisine offering the delights of a European table and tempered with Spanish music" that provided "an hour of never-to-be-forgotten enjoyment." Most important, time spent at the resort was deemed important for one's psychic health:

> People who vary their existence get a great deal of enjoyment out of life. Many are finding this change of pace in a few hours or days spent occasionally at Agua Caliente. Whether you come to rest or play; for the relaxation of flower-filled patios or the excitement of the Casino, the "change of pace" will refresh you in mind and body. The complete sports ensemble here will satisfy your every whim. Bring your visiting guests to Agua Caliente, for to come to California without seeing Agua Caliente is like dinner at the Ritz minus the hors d'oeuvres—they miss the thrill.

And the price was right. Admission to the racetrack was only $2, half that on Wednesdays and Thursdays, ladies free on Tuesdays and Fridays. Horseback rides along beautified bridle paths also cost $2, use of the pool and gymnasium 50 cents, and you could rent a bathing suit for another half dollar. Patio luncheons were priced at $1 daily, $1.50 on weekends and holidays, and admission to dinner dances in the main dining hall of the casino was a reasonable $2.50 per plate. And what remarkable fare lay on that platter: a choice of fresh lobster cocktail or olives and celery hearts, and then Maryland-style soft-shelled crab fried in butter or broiled sirloin steak covered with fresh mushrooms, followed by a vegetable salad, dessert, and coffee. For a beverage, a magnum of champagne was offered at $10 to $15.

Rooms in the hotel, bungalows, and apartments ran from $5 to $12 a day. As in most such establishments, management aimed to draw crowds with low food and accommodation prices to be more than recouped in gambling returns. People of all means thronged Agua Caliente by train, airplane, ship, Greyhound bus, and thousands of cars—Fords, Dodges, and Willys Overlanders and Oaklands for average people; Cadillacs, Packards, and Pierce Arrows for the well off. Large numbers of visitors gambled, although many came just for the sights and a chance to mingle for a moment with the likes of the debonair Clark Gable; Douglas Fairbanks (father and son); the Marx brothers and lovable Jimmy Durante; the movies' Tarzan, the muscular Johnny Weismuller; Dolores del Río (herself of Mexican heritage); and suave Dick Powell. The extravagant Gold Room was reserved for movie titans like Carl Laemmle, who might bet $10,000 on the turn of a card, or Joe Schenck, who risked $100,000 a day. Outside of these closed circles, a visitor might catch a glimpse of the actress Jean Harlow, who once tossed a record thirty-four straight passes at the dice table.[1]

Posted rules at any hotel are instructive (and often titillating) because they indicate what kind of mischief guests are up to under the management's nose. In this regard, Agua Caliente prohibited men from receiving women in their rooms and vice versa. In fact, "No guest is allowed to share his room with anyone without first notifying the management and making proper arrangements." "Servants" were an exception, but guests were responsible for the conduct of these servants. On the other hand, children "must not be allowed to leave their rooms without an adult person to watch over them to avoid damage and trouble." There was to be no wandering to and from the swimming pool in "Bathing Costumes." "No dogs, birds or other animals [were] permitted." Prior to cashing a check, guests needed to fill out a credit form, "giving us time to investigate," and "All guests upon registering at the Hotel agree to leave their baggage as guarantee of payment." In summation, "those whose conduct conflicts with the standard of morality of the Hotel" would be immediately expelled. One would like to know how rigidly management enforced these rules. By all indications, Agua Caliente's "standard of morality" was exceedingly elastic. At least such was its reputation, and the place thrived on it.[2]

THE PEOPLE OF Tijuana also joined in the engaging atmosphere of Agua Caliente. They did not seem much attracted to the resort's mud-bath cures, nor did they frequent patio dining or bet on the horses—those sorts of things were for the tourists. But they threw dice and spun the roulette wheel. Employees, however, never gambled at the club where they worked. Owners prohibited such activity because they feared accusations that they were stealing back their employees' pay at the gaming table. Wages were high, especially in comparison with other work in Mexico. At Agua Caliente alone more than fifteen hundred Tijuanenses worked in over a hundred different jobs—as musicians, dishwashers, waiters, launderers, electricians and carpenters, gardeners, bartenders, in the kitchen, on the golf course, and at the gas station on the premises. The main chef and his chief assistants, hotel registrars, carpenters, and electricians earned at least $5 daily; bartenders and the pastry chef, $6 or more; musicians and some department heads, $8–9, all with one day a week off at somewhat more than full pay. Dishwashers, kitchen helpers, ironing employees, maintenance crews, and those who watered the golf course received about $3 a day, plus one day off a week with regular pay.[3]

Unions representing the various groups set the salary schedules, which were then negotiated with management by representatives of the umbrella labor confederation. The CROM drove hard bargains and did not hesitate to call strikes. Workers at the new racetrack struck for better wages and working conditions on opening day, December 28, 1929, but twenty-five thousand fans, mostly Americans, passed through the picket lines and the races ran as scheduled. There were other sorts of complaints against Agua Caliente, as well. Business competitors, for example, claimed that the resort sold food and liquor, and rented rooms, at such ridiculously low prices that they were driving restaurants, hotels, and liquor stores in the main tourist district out of business. They likened Agua Caliente to a huge sponge sucking up business and profits from other parts of town. The new conglomerate challenged other entrepreneurs no doubt, but it never held a monopoly over tourist spending, and despite some grumbling and occasional protest, most residents seemed to appreciate the resort's worldwide reputation, which attracted money-spending visitors from everywhere.[4]

As Tijuana flourished on the tourist dollar, individuals improved their lives and those of their families. Per capita purchasing power was said to be greater than in New York City, or even Monaco with its famed Monte

Carlo. Elías Mardirosian, a pastry chef at the complex, earned enough to invest in a shoe store and build a house. The Avakians, also of Armenian background, who initially operated a shoe shop, bought Caesar's Hotel. Boloyan's grocery store gained a monopoly on a brand of U.S. mayonnaise and with the returns went into the wholesale goods and tobacco business. A pretty teen-aged girl named Rita Cansino danced in a revue at Agua Caliente, attracted the attention of a movie studio which brought her to Hollywood, renamed her Rita Hayworth, and helped make her a movie star.[5]

Not only did individuals profit from the affluence, but fees and taxes assessed upon the owners of such establishments financed public works projects like schools, roads, and waterworks in town and throughout the territory. Governor Cantú had set the pace ten or fifteen years earlier, but as Tijuana plunged into the 1930s, the little town prospered in expanded ways, although a horrendous gap still existed between the ostentatiously rich and the pitifully destitute. A cost of living higher than in most other parts of Mexico affected everyone, as did the slowly devaluating peso. Some Americans were plainly resented for their profiteering and profligate spending power. Also, it did not sit well with the town's populace when in 1931 soldiers forcibly removed squatter families from the dilapidated horse stables that had become their refuge at the abandoned border racetrack. These hapless folks were simply part of the spillover from thousands of Mexicans deported from the United States as a consequence of the Great Depression, and Tijuanenses felt for their countrymen even as their presence strained local resources.[6]

The Great Depression

During Mexico's great revolution and in its immediate aftermath, thousands fleeing the rapaciousness and vengeance of that time took refuge in the United States. Others migrated from violence-wracked Mexico for work or a better life. By 1923 more than 150,000 Mexicans lived in the Los Angeles area alone. Three years later, conflict between church and state in Mexico (another sort of no-holds-barred civil war) pushed another 80,000 into Southern California. Over the next few years thousands more crossed the border, often at the urgings of family and friends already established in the region. Then the Depression hit, and Californians began to worry about the future of their livelihoods. Migrants caught the brunt of their concern and prejudices. It had happened before (and has since) in the Golden State, throughout the country, and beyond. In more flush periods migrants had been welcomed, even invited, but when times went sour, the newcomers, especially non-whites, were the first to go. There was nothing selective about the massive roundups and deportations that followed. Families were split up, homes wrecked, personal lives crushed, and any number of legal American citizens caught in the net. In 1934 Los Angeles's Catholic bishop estimated that fully 70,000 Hispanics in his diocese, which extended through San Diego to the border, had been deported or otherwise had returned to Mexico. The forced repatriations amounted to one of those national tragedies that following generations decry but rarely learn from.

Relatively few of the deported Mexicans crossed the line at Tijuana, for most thought it best to return to their former residences deep in Mexico. To do that they needed railroad connections out of larger places like Ciudad Juárez, across from El Paso, Texas. From Tijuana, the only decent travel links ran north, back into the United States. A considerable number of expelled Mexicans, however, preferred to stay close to the border where they could keep in touch with former employers, or friends and relatives left behind, in hopes that the economic downturn would soon ease and they could return to their former lives. Tijuana was attractive because, small as it was, it offered job opportunities into which the new arrivals could fit and wait out the storm. These were the families who filtered into the new Colonia Libertad, founded on the steep, ragged hills and tilted mesas on the east side of the river.

Tijuana, of course, felt the reverberations of the Depression. Employees lost jobs and had to relocate, but the town was not devastated as were places with a larger, more concentrated population employed in factories and mills, substantial agricultural ventures, shipyards, railheads, financial centers, and the like. Tijuana was a small tourist town, an entertainment and service center, and found itself among those places least affected by the crisis. No doubt tourism declined as travelers more carefully guarded their disposable income. They were wise to do so, but while long-distance tourism shuddered to a near halt, regional visitors continued to patronize (and periodically throng) their favorite haunts on the other side of the line. If they could afford a break from their troubles, Tijuana provided fantasy, diversion, and even a chance to win some cash.

Even in good times, world-famous tourist attractions—museums, zoos, theme parks, eating and entertainment centers—depend upon local patronage for their existence, and as had been the case all along, Southern California furnished the regular, steady tourism that Tijuana needed to keep going. Certainly Hollywood's upper crust, along with other well-to-do people, did their share of spending in town, and just as importantly, they polished its aura. But it was the flow of more ordinary people of lesser means that provided the energy and expenditures which enabled the numerous less-heralded shops, bars, and restaurants up and down La Revolución to ride out the aftershocks of the financial crash heard round the world. In 1932 alone nearly five million tourists visited Tijuana, an average of 13,408 daily. Mainly they came in automobiles, nearly four thousand cars each day, or one and one-half million for the year. If each tourist spent only $5 (a modest estimate) they generated nearly $25 million in income for the town. On Labor Day in 1934, more than forty-two thousand tourists came to town and spent an estimated $80,000 there, and all this in the midst of a worldwide, if unevenly experienced, economic depression.[7]

San Diego's Depression

San Diego itself suffered less than many other cities during the global downturn. It had no industrial base to speak of—certainly nothing in the sense of Detroit's automobile production, for example—and therefore did not experience the massive layoffs which caused so much misery, frustration, and angry unrest in other places. The Depression convulsed its fledgling aircraft and shipping industries, but even they were about back to normal by the mid-1930s. What really saved San Diego, however, was its commitment to the military and vice versa. By this time, the U.S. Navy owned one-third of the city's coastline and had spent millions dredging the harbor and building massive installations along its perimeter. Ever since the spring of 1915, when he visited San Diego as Assistant Secretary of the Navy, Franklin Delano Roosevelt had felt a special fondness for the place. Now, as president of the country, he honored his commitments to the city, which during the Depression years received more than its share of government assistance through the Works Progress Administration, nearly $1 million. While other cities paved streets, dug sewers, and constructed public buildings with government funding, San Diego laid out golf courses.

San Diego was squarely a Navy town. In 1930 nearly thirty thousand permanent personnel lived there, and by the end of the decade the figure approached forty thousand. In 1929 the city's military payroll reached $17 million, and ten years later, $30 million. When ships arrived from a tour of duty, they unloaded leave-starved sailors on the town, many of whom sought and found entertainment in Tijuana. At the time, U.S. destroyers carried crews of nearly three hundred fifty men; battleships from eight hundred to more than two thousand sailors. As the ships sailed in squadrons, it meant that when they docked in San Diego, sailors and marines on leave in Tijuana could easily more than double the population of the town. In 1935 a group of 114 warships landed in port, returning sixty-three thousand officers and men back home after two months at sea. Miffed by the high-minded reforms of San Diego's moral guardians, the sailors forthrightly told the city's Chamber of Commerce that they would rather spend liberty anywhere but San Diego, and Tijuana awaited them. Navy regulations prohibited them from wearing their uniforms while enjoying themselves south of the border. Military police tried to enforce prudent behavior on the sailors, and the Department of the Navy railed against the evils of diseased women, hopheads, and dope fiends, but the sailors did what sailors do after months at sea and boosted Tijuana's economy in the process.[8]

Tijuana's leadership, however, realizing that free-spending sailors contributed only so much to the local economy, persistently sought more steady, substantial, and far-reaching support. When the Depression struck, officials went to Mexico City with the backing of the state governor to request the establishment of a formal free-trade zone to stretch across the entire northern tier of the federal territory. A free zone meant the relaxation of customs duties charged on certain merchandise, mainly primary goods like food and clothing, but also building materials and equipment, coming from the U.S. side of the border. The delegation noted that duties raised prices for Mexican merchants, who passed on the costs to customers, who in response did their shopping in San Ysidro and San Diego. It was clear, they insisted, that Tijuana business suffered because of the tariffs.

The president of the republic and his ministers professed sympathy with the petitioners, but replied that given the hard times the national budget could not afford the loss of any customs revenue. Prepared for that argument, the delegation noted that smugglers carried many goods requiring duty payment across the line and paid no customs anyhow. For instance, people who went to San Diego to buy their hats, dresses, shoes, suits, shirts, and sweaters simply dressed in the new clothing, declared them personal items at the customs crossing, and strolled home duty-free. Indeed, smuggling in both directions was a given at the time. Customs officials made a habit of looking the other way when local people (some of them acquaintances, others quite poor) crossed the line with goods intended for personal and family use.[9]

The idea of a free zone to encompass Tijuana was still being pondered in 1932, when Abelardo Rodríguez, the former governor of Northern Baja California who had so successfully tied gambling to territorial development (and grown rich doing it), became the president of the republic. That event seemed fortunate for Tijuana, but then a new calamity smote the community: the repeal of Prohibition in the United States. The Great Depression had rocked the town, albeit relatively lightly, but the repeal of Prohibition to the north stunned the community.

The End of Prohibition

Beset by the Depression, Americans still needed a drink. The folly of trying to dictate and police public drinking habits and morals had become ever more obvious, as did the ways in which Prohibition had bred rabid gangsterism along with more genteel illegalities. States began to repeal their prohibition statutes, and by December 1933 the process of ratifying a new constitutional amendment to repeal the earlier one that had mandated Prohibition was completed. Americans could once again drink liquor in public places, and they did so with renewed fervor and a sassy "I told you so" attitude. So much of Tijuana's reputation rested upon the glitter and glamor of high-stakes gambling in the casinos (along with prostitution) that few had recognized how much the town's economic health and stability depended upon the everyday consumption and sale of alcohol. To the casinos, drinking was peripheral: cheap drinks were served to lure gamblers, but to almost every place else on La Revolución, drinking produced the real revenue and the slots only supplemental amusement for customers.

Once Southern Californians could legally drink closer to home, many abandoned Tijuana. California repealed its own antiliquor law on April 8, 1933. By June, one hundred fifty businesses in Tijuana had closed, including sixty of the one hundred saloons. Owners of the ABC beer brewery closed their operations in town and moved to San Diego. Thousands lost their jobs and were thrown into penury overnight. Old-timers remembered many dark moments in Tijuana's history, but these were the darkest. The town had reached its nadir.[10] Local leaders did what they could to right the ship; after all, the town still had its tourist attractions. Entertainment was lavish and prices cheap, and the Chamber of Commerce launched a vigorous campaign billing Tijuana as a tourist Mecca. Meanwhile, official authorities continued to press for the free-trade zone they hoped would stimulate the economy.

Agua Caliente, labeled "America's Deauville [referring to the elite French resort] where the door to romance opens," remained the centerpiece of the Chamber's propaganda: "Here modern gaiety finds expression in a setting of Old World luxury and splendor. The freedom and life of continental Europe [is] but a few hours from Los Angeles" by auto—three or four to be exact. Summer room rates ranged from $3 for singles to $4 and up for doubles. As we have seen, lunch, including a bottle of beer, could be had for $1, while a Danzant Delux dinner, including a cocktail before and a cordial after, was $2.50 per plate.

Once in town, the visitor should plan to stay for a few days. Auto camping cost only $3 and up daily; meals at any number of restaurants ran from 25 cents to $1.50, gas was 20 cents a gallon, and oil 15 cents a quart. A large glass of beer at The Border bar cost a nickel, a pint 15 cents, and a shot of whisky a quarter. The Aloha club featured Hawaiian hula dancers, while Vick's Place promoted a bolero dancer. The menu at Flor d'Italia offered French-style "Duck a la Press," complemented by wines from Europe. Mexican fine art was displayed for sale, along with French perfumes and Omega and Mido watches. Prominent signs reminded tourists that they could take home $100 worth of purchases duty free, including up to three hundred cigarettes or fifty cigars—but only one bottle of each brand of perfume, and no liquor (until Prohibition ended), flowers, or fruit.

Taxis were accommodating: 25 cents from town center to the border and back, and 75 cents round-trip to Agua Caliente; or they could be rented by the hour for $2.50. Those who wished to drive their own cars into Mexico now could stay for up to three months; permits were issued at customs and a bond was no longer necessary. "For any difficulty in regard to traffic violations or police regulations, all tourists and visitors should get in touch with the Pro-Tourist Committee of the Chamber of Commerce."[11] The town had twenty or twenty-five policemen and four traffic officers, enough to provide safety and security, but not enough to spoil a visitor's day. While these sorts of reminders helped, tourists already knew Tijuana by reputation, and in 1934 more than four million Americans spent about $20 million in Tijuana, providing five thousand Mexicans with jobs. At the same time, resorts and other types of businesses in town bought $300,000 worth of supplies each month from San Diego. So significant reciprocity between these neighbors benefited both towns even as the tentacles of the Depression still gripped many other places.[12]

As much as anything else, the Great Depression and Prohibition's demise forced Tijuana owners out of one type of business into another. It put liquor stores, bars, and some of their tourist trade ancillaries—barber shops, money exchanges, laundries, meat shops, hotels, rooms for rent, car garages, and outlets for soft drinks—out of operation. At the same time, it created more gift shops and perfume and tobacco outlets largely aimed at tourists, and clothing stores, gasoline stations, beauty salons, two furniture stores, an auto repair shop, and two small stationery stores that served the community as well. It also spawned small haberdashery and saddle-making factories. While such changes can be painful for the individuals involved, many thought them good for the town at large, for they shifted Tijuana from such notable dependence on liquor sales to a variety of other business ventures. Some viewed this in a moral light: the town was better for youngsters with less liquor around. Others saw it as the beginnings of a new Tijuana, one in which locals produced for them-selves rather than solely for outsiders. Tourism, of course, remained the town's number-one business; everyone knew that Tijuana could not exist without its visitors, and most did not want it any other way. Still, a heady sense of self-reliance crept into town, as people looked for ways to wean themselves from too much dependence on foreigners. In this spirit, they vigorously pressed their case for the creation of a free-trade zone sur-rounding the town.[13]

Free-Trade Zones

Mexico's federal government, especially with Abelardo Rodríguez as president, did not oppose a free-trade zone for Tijuana or other cities along the border. Variations had been tried since the nineteenth century, but they had come and gone in keeping with economic realities and political mood shifts. Nonetheless, authorities had always thought them a good way to strengthen border towns against political and economic dominance from the north, to make such towns more Mexican and less gringo, and to bring them more firmly under control of the capital. Establishing free-trade zones, however, involves difficult questions: how large should the zone be, what sorts of merchandise should be exempted from customs duties, who gains and loses by the establishment of such a zone, how long should exemptions last? Implications are serious and solutions need to be negotiated. Merchant houses deeper in the republic —in Puebla, Mexico City, and Monterrey—feared the loss of sales to cheaper, duty-free goods from elsewhere. As industrialists always do, they argued that such zones only create an artificial life for those involved, that no district in the country should receive special benefits, that improved transportation and communications routes would render them unnecessary. Baja California's fishing industry demanded protections against duty-free imports; farmers just outside the projected zone wanted gasoline and equipment free of customs; investors within the zone wondered about the long-term commitment of the government to a free-trade zone. If entrepreneurs were to start a business based on free-trade imports, might not a government hungry for customs duties suddenly extinguish the zone and place such enterprises in jeopardy?

Not all such questions can be thought out and answered on paper before the inauguration of a free-trade zone, but proponents weighed the possibilities of broad and sound economic development in border cities against their dependence upon gambling, gasoline, and alcohol consumption. Specifics have to be worked out in reality, in field experience, which is why such zones get off to such a nervous start; Tijuana was no exception. But the initiative plunged ahead by presidential decree on 30 August 1933. To assure investors, the decree established a ten-year term. To mollify manufacturers in industrialized Mexico, it exempted from import duties no goods that cost more than $30. It protected from taxes products of Tijuana's fledgling food-processing industries, such as beer, malt, and canned shrimp, but not primary necessities like milk and flour. After consideration, authorities decided not to grant a liquor exemption. The free zone was limited to the core of the town itself.

Early results proved quite dramatic. Small businesses dealing in such merchandise as groceries and clothing that Mexicans had established in San Ysidro moved to Tijuana, and the border community on the U.S. side dried up. At the time, farmers grew onions and oats on 75 percent of the farm land on the outskirts of town. Their main customer was the horse track, but with the elimination of duties on such food items, the owners preferred to buy from U.S. sources, so the farmers lost their outlet and many moved to town. With the exception of beans, the cultivation of most crops disappeared. Federal inspectors assessing the impact of the zone recommended that farmers be given exemptions from taxes on seeds and gasoline.

These same inspectors noted that within a year or so commerce in town had greatly improved, along with the earnings afforded owners. In the grocery business, for example, in 1933 few possessed assets of $500, but two years later sixty-three groceries did so. Moreover, Mexicans had replaced Chinese (some of whom were being deported at the time for lack of proper credentials) as the majority of shopkeepers. The number of small sundry shops grew from one to eleven, all run by Mexicans. Clothing stores increased from two to seven, and while they formerly handled cheap nationally produced goods sold to residents who could not afford purchases in San Ysidro, they now handled luxury items from Europe and the Far East. The one large merchandise outlet in town, the Casa Rodríguez, with capital of $100,000, sold, among other things, English cashmeres and riding outfits; imported gloves, ties, stockings, and shoes; French perfumes, clothes, and silks; and linens and gift items of Chinese porcelain—all wares sought by the wealthy from Los Angeles at prices well below those in the States, plus the $100 customs exemption at the border. Such stores were also well stocked with American goods bought through reduced price arrangements with American producers.

Other businesses did not seem to be much affected by the advent of the free zone. Ice stores, carpenter shops, boutiques, public baths, watch and shoe repair shops, milk stores, kerosene vendors, tailors, funeral parlors, and bottled-water sellers all maintained themselves, and a few did better than before. Still, there were problems. Although prices for basic items declined, they did not do so as sharply or as far as residents had hoped. Much of this was due to the cartel practices of local merchants, who held prices high and declined to undercut one another. Furthermore, the inflationary practices of the Roosevelt administration in Washington made dealings with the American economy more expensive. For consumers, decent wages made up much of the difference; business employees and other urban workers earned $3.50 daily, and farm workers

$2.50. Yet buyers suffered because most cash transactions were made in U.S. dollars, and owners juggled the exchange rate to their advantage in rapid transactions that could baffle a customer.

If the possibility for profit was so strong, one wonders why businesses did not proliferate. The main reason was a lack of confidence in the Mexican federal government. Investors suspected the government would eliminate the zone when political or economic necessity demanded. Meanwhile, federal agencies constantly tinkered with the workings of the system, especially with revenue producers like liquor. As Tijuana's health depended on tourism, bar and cabaret prices needed to be kept low and steady. The inspectors thought gambling and drinking prejudicial to youth, "but that is the best that Tijuana can do for now." The answer lay in the development of industry, commerce, and farming at a distance from the entertainment hub. Toward that end, fledgling light industry and workshops within the free zone needed tariff protection, including the town's eight bakeries, pillow factory, tin workshop, three small soft-drink factories, the pasteurizing plant, and establishments that produced lard, sweets, whiskey and beer, as well as the *nixtamal* (*masa* or dough) mill. Federal regulators considered each case separately, and as each inevitably had its pros and cons, official decisions came slowly, were tentative, politically sensitive, and subject to change, creating an insecure environment for local business investors. The truth was that it proved extremely difficult to establish industry in Tijuana because the large commercial houses in San Diego and Los Angeles sold radios, stoves, furniture, electrical appliances, and similar merchandise directly to customers below the border. Through agents they offered discount sales and deferred payments for buyers who preferred to deal directly with them rather than one of the town's two banks.[14]

THE EFFECT OF the free zone on the regional economy may best be gauged by the loudness of the howls it attracted from the U.S. side of the line. All one need do is read the pleas printed in capital letters in the *San Diego Herald*: "GIVE SAN DIEGO A CHANCE! GIVE SAN DIEGANS A CHANCE! KILL THAT MEXICAN FREE ZONE! KEEP SAN DIEGO MONEY AT HOME! HELP THE *SAN DIEGO HERALD* HELP SAN DIEGO." The newspaper had long railed against Tijuana as a haven for depravity and a drain on San Diego's economy, but with so many visitors in the city for the Exposition of 1935–36, it wanted those tourist dollars kept at home.

The *Herald* predicts—for the event is already foreshadowed—that San Diego is about to feel the heavy hand of Tijuana competition along all lines. TIJUANA HAS GOT TO DO THIS OR GO BACK TO THE DUST OF THE DESERT WHENCE IT AROSE. There is no need for any San Diegan traveling 17 miles for a highball, and San Diegans won't do it. [A clear miscalculation of local drinking tastes.] But the lure of the free zone, of the high quality of the goods and of the increasing range of offerings will bring them to Tijuana anyhow.

THE BLOW WHICH WILL KILL THE FREE ZONE MUST BE DELIVERED BY THE FEDERAL GOVERNMENT OF THIS COUNTRY, AND TO BRING ABOUT FEDERAL AID IN THIS LIFE-AND-DEATH MATTER, SAN DIEGO MUST SHOW A UNITED STAND.[15]

Tijuanenses ignored *The Herald's* bombast; they were accustomed to the newspaper's tirades against their town. Free trade was helping them through troubled times, and they welcomed it.

IN OVERVIEW, Tijuana experienced the Great Depression and the end of Prohibition in its own way. Undoubtedly there were hardships. Some people lost jobs, left town, and returned to former homesteads in search of security and relief. Others stayed but had to shift employment. Overall, however, steady tourism, which peaked when most needed, and the creation of a duty-free zone cushioned for Tijuanenses the fast, sharp slide downward and the slow crawl out into recovery suffered by so many in the industrialized world. Business and social readjustments took place, but rather than sink into despair, people relied on new opportunities and their own ingenuity to carry them through, and if possible to better themselves. A lifelong resident still working today in a curio outlet on La Revolución put it this way: "In the 1930s, when someone moved from one town to another to start over again, it normally took eight years to get reestablished. In Tijuana, it could be done in three. In three years you could have a piece of property, a house, and a car."[16]

This agitated atmosphere naturally launched some creative schemes. A Los Angeles lawyer, José L. Navarro, concerned that the repeal of Prohibition would diminish tourism in Tijuana, suggested that the town could become even more popular if Mexico loosened its family laws and appointed well-paid judges to speed up the divorce process. Others worked the new trade zone for a side-profit. One such opportunist was

Mariano Mendivil, owner of the La Corona grocery, who waited on Olga Camacho shortly before she disappeared. He bought duty-free goods for his store, smuggled them south of the zone's boundary line, and peddled them at a discount, still earning a good profit for himself. Such smuggling was rampant at the edges of the zone.[17]

All in all, most residents of Tijuana did not seem overly concerned about their material circumstances by the mid-1930s. If events had forced a diversification of businesses, toned down drinking, and weeded out some ne'er-do-wells and low-income people, so much the better. Residents had not come to Tijuana just to fill their pocketbooks. By this time, three thousand families had made the town their home. (Tijuanenses have said for some time that newcomers who arrive to stay have "tomado agua de la presa," meaning they have drunk the water from Rodríguez Dam.) There was, however, uncertainty in the community in the mid-1930s. Their main protector and benefactor, Abelardo Rodríguez, who knew the territory like no one else, departed the presidency in late 1934, and his successor, Lázaro Cárdenas, had announced widespread reforms bound to challenge and rankle the nation.

Cárdenas's Rule

For the most part, there was little new or innovative in the new president's program; most of his policies had been tried in fits and starts since the end of the Revolution, but this administration aimed to actually bring reformist ambitions to fruition and to enhance its political power in the process. First of all there was agrarian reorganization—the state would break up larger properties and redistribute land to the landless. At the same time, the government encouraged labor to heighten and broaden its demands on management. In keeping with strong international currents, it mandated for schoolchildren a practical, down-to-earth education with a socialistic bent. As with all such so-called progressive agendas, this one was larded with moralistic justification: Mexicans must rid themselves of religious superstitions, engage in honest work, recognize and fulfill their family obligations, be loyal citizens, and support the state. For many folks, this meant changing their beliefs and way of life.

In important ways, the program aimed to make Cárdenas independent of the previous regime, and an exceedingly powerful president at that. The Church was to be further distanced from political power and education. Popular support for the regime would be fashioned from new labor and agrarian organizations. The political strongman of Mexico—Plutarco Elías Calles—and his cohorts must be driven from the scene. Much of this campaign did not sit well in Tijuana. Calles had been a good friend of Abelardo Rodríguez, with whom he shared investments, and the ex-president's labor mainstay, the CROM, weak and fragmented in other parts of the country, still held sway in Tijuana, despite a degree of infighting. Certainly the new president's program had unleashed demons: agraristas squatted on private properties and considered them their own; a militant labor congress, the Confederación de Trabajadores Mexicanos, known as the CTM, arose to challenge the CROM, and when management refused its demands, unionized workers took over plants. Schoolteachers scattered into the countryside to implant socialist education, and in reply Catholics erupted in armed rebellion against state incursions into their religious practices, classrooms, and political power. Mexico was awash in agitation, and the government had its eye on Tijuana for both its union recalcitrance and political sensitivity.

The practical and secular goals of socialist schooling meshed with those of Tijuana's leadership and educators. Such a program had already been installed at the new Obregón secondary school, which resembled a trade school. We may presume the instruction there to be like other such schools in the country, at which teachers outlined evolutionist theory concerning the origins of mankind, and with the help of a doctor taught about venereal disease and the control of sexual conduct. Pupils also learned about worker solidarity, a society without classes, and collectivism, where the individual subordinated his or her desires to the common good. Capitalism was questioned but not attacked. Pupils read Mexican and world literature, especially works that ennobled rural people (farmers) and discussed the origins of private property and the division of work. Even a fourth-grade primer carried the story of a strike called in a silk mill after fifty workers had been discharged. It told how the laborers organized their protest and with the help of the government won the day against management.[18] A review of school texts indicates what the education ministry and school boards wanted students to learn, but says nothing about what and how they were actually taught, nor what lessons pupils took from the classroom. Yet in Tijuana there does not seem to have been any protest against the model, while in other parts of Mexico anger at such teachings often became deadly.

When it came to agrarian takeovers and labor union competition, Tijuana and the region were as inflamed as many other places in the 1930s. The most spectacular expropriation in the area occurred in the cotton fields of the Colorado River Land Company outside of Mexicali. It was the only truly immense private landholding in the territory; it was also American-owned and therefore a lightning rod for agrarista action. In the attack on the land company hundreds of surrounding much smaller properties owned by Mexican rancheros (such as Aurelio Camacho Sr.) suffered a similar fate. As we have seen, the grandfather of Olga Camacho lost his holdings south of Mexicali to squatters, which caused him to move his family to Tijuana. Properties in the immediate vicinity of Tijuana were so small and barren that even the agraristas shunned them; however, farther south toward Ensenada, there were takeovers that brought complaints to authorities and roiled the general ambiance.[19]

Rivalries among labor syndicates in Tijuana were as cutthroat as anywhere else in the country. CROM still dominated at mid-decade, but other syndicates nipped at its heels. The bloody riots that accompanied the Olga Camacho affair in February 1938 laid bare the vicious competition. CROM got blamed for everything. The CTM and other syndicates stalked their powerful but deeply wounded adversary like hungry hyenas challenging a fallen but still dangerous prey. They bombarded the Cárdenas administration with telegrams accusing the CROM of instigating the riots and challenging civil authority, a line of attack quickly parroted in official explanations of the mayhem released to the country's press.[20]

Reveling in encouragement proffered by the regime, many unions supported the Cárdenas program beyond their immediate concerns. Just before the president's inauguration in 1934, union leadership in Mexicali took umbrage at the local priest's criticism of socialist education, drove him across the international boundary into exile, seized the church building, and turned it into union headquarters. For the next few days, men entering the building removed their hats as they customarily did in church but quickly put them back on when ridiculed by spectators. The priest, Juan Torres, salvaged icons and records from the church and took them to the Catholic parish in San Ysidro, where he administered the sacraments along with Father Núñez, who earlier had been driven by federal edict from Tijuana.[21] Following the murder of Olga Camacho, civil authorities allowed Padre Torres into Tijuana to console the dead girl's mother, but his advice to her to forgive and trust in the Lord met with steely rejection by the mother, as did, at that time, the notion of God Himself.

The expulsion of Torres left the northern territory without a priest. Núñez wrote the president in March 1935, asking that he be allowed to pursue his religious commitments in Baja, but was turned down. For the next three years no Mass was said openly in the territory, and the faithful who crossed the border for services discovered that Latin Catholics were not always appreciated in San Diego's parishes. The basic complaint against Hispanics attending church on the U.S. side was that they did not fulfill their financial share of parish burdens. When in the 1920s the Mexican government decreed that its civil service bureaucrats must reside on the Mexican side of the line, the priest at Calexico noted he had lost seventy (decently salaried) Hispanic families from his church, "practically the only ones of [all] the Mexican people [parishioners] who were of any financial benefit to the parish." A refrain repeatedly echoed in the next decade at Our Lady of Guadalupe Church in San Diego was: "So many Mexican families in the colony are without work and are no longer able to assist in maintenance of the church, and hundreds of the parishioners have been sent back to Mexico [under the policies of repatriation], thus leaving the burden of the parish on a few."[22] A more general complaint concerning Hispanic presence emanated in 1930 from the Anglo Catholics in Calexico:

> Cannot something be done for the American Catholics of Calexico. For three years now we have been crowded out of the church pews by people who do not even live in the United States. For the last two or three weeks, we have not even heard our language spoken, or it is spoken in such a way that we cannot understand what is being said. Some American Catholics are leaving the church with bitterness in their hearts, while the younger ones refuse to come at all because of these conditions. As law-abiding American citizens helping to support our state and federal government, we feel we should have something different from what exists now.[23]

So much for goodwill and brotherly love.

Severe trouble between Hispanic Catholics and their Anglo bishop erupted in 1937 in the newly created Diocese of San Diego. Formerly, all of Southern California lay in the Diocese of Los Angeles, but four large counties, including San Diego, were separated that year to form the new diocese—63 percent of its membership Latino—with Bishop Charles Francis Buddy as its first episcopal leader. Our Lady of Guadalupe Church was the center of San Diego's large Hispanic parish on the southern edge of the city, and since the start of the decade, Spanish Augustinian Recollect brothers had run the parish, but much too loosely for Bishop Buddy's liking. A power struggle—a genuine donnybrook—developed between the Augustinians and the bishop, full of innuendos, slander, machinations, and from the bishop's side a not-too-subtle racism. He charged the Augustinians with financial laxness and noted in disgust that an ex-Augustinian lived with his woman friend in a residential section close to the church building. Equally serious, the brothers had allowed Latinos to engage in "vulgar and immoral" dancing at religious celebrations, a degradation of the Catholic faith. Dancing, of course, had long been a staple in the overlap between religious festivities and social life in Mexico, and still is. Though the Church has declared such dancing a deviation from piety and stamped it with unsavory sexual connotations, folks who consider themselves good Catholics still keep dancing regardless of criticism.

Bishop Buddy demanded of their superiors that the Augustinians be withdrawn from their San Diego duties. Parishioners countered that they needed Spanish-speaking priests who understood their culture. Buddy produced testimony that Spaniards did not understand Mexicans, and the parishioners carried their case to Rome, embarrassing the new prelate and forcing him to explain further. Buddy did so by minimizing his opposition and labeling his major accuser as unrepresentative of the congregation and mentally unstable. The result of the fracas was that an Irish priest who knew no Spanish and little of Mexican culture, but was unswervingly loyal to Bishop Buddy became pastor at Our Lady of Guadalupe, to the disappointment of many parishioners.

By 1940 Tijuana's church had reopened with Father Torres in charge, and parishioners from Our Lady began to celebrate their marriages, baptisms, and confirmations with one of their own. Torres complained to the Church hierarchy that Buddy was neglecting the welfare of the Mexican laity in his diocese, and the outraged bishop told Torres to limit his activities to Baja California, not to return to San Diego, in short, to mind his own business. Good neighbors these two clerics were not. Buddy's mentor in Los Angeles, Bishop John J. Cantwell, advised him: "You need not be anxious about Mexican conditions, even though Mexicans complain," which seemed to sum up the attitudes of Anglo prelates in Southern California.[24]

Political Vendettas

The Tijuana–San Diego sector also became the focal point of Cárdenas's determination to escape the shadow of previous administrations, particularly that of the long-time political oligarch Plutarco Elías Calles and his minions. At first a nervous detente existed between the two leaders of state, both members of the ruling political party. However, when Calles began to spar with the president and bitingly criticized the fast pace of his reforms, Cárdenas, backed by militant laborites and the loyal army, exiled his rival, who settled with his daughter and son-in-law in San Diego. Calles claimed no interest in returning to Mexican politics, but rumors persisted that he was secretly mounting a rebellion—at least releasing trial balloons toward such ends—from the U.S. side. His friend Abelardo Rodríguez was said to support the scheme, but the former Baja California governor managed to walk a tightrope between the political enemies. Still, Tijuana stirred with plots, and one can understand the administration's resolve to snuff out quickly any riots or raucous disorder that might burst out in the border town and prod protest toward revolution.

There is no doubt that the radical reform program of Lázaro Cárdenas splintered old configurations and then polarized adversaries in Mexican society. Some groups enthusiastically endorsed his measures; others detested them and their promoter. Tijuana felt the prevailing winds blowing across much of the country—agrarian unrest, labor disputes, political challenges—but the government had done some good things in town, such as carving out the free zone, even if details continued to rankle certain people and needed to be worked out. Also, $30,000 in federal funding had been received for public works during the first half of 1937, though much more was needed. Despite the Depression and the end of Prohibition, residents had readjusted and entered new lines of work, which diversified and strengthened the local economy. Economists advised that in one way or another too much business still relied on tourism, but proprietors welcomed visitors, who continued to come in significant numbers to see the sights, to enjoy the entertainment, or simply to step on foreign soil. Each of the radical reforms unleashed by the administration affected Mexican communities in various ways and in different intensities. Some subscribed to and soaked up the changes better than others. Tijuana felt the hot wind of substantial change, some gusts more unsettling than others, but it was the moralization campaign that struck the town with the force of a hurricane.

Moralization Politics

Since the Revolution, the country's political leaders had endeavored to create a so-called "new Mexican," one who was thrifty, patriotic, industrious, sober, literate, and responsible. Education was the answer, but legislation would help to push people in the right direction, and casino gambling that was said to distract workers from fruitful labor and waste their income became an obvious target. While on the presidential campaign trail, Cárdenas, as guest of the Border Barons, had visited the sumptuous Agua Caliente casino in Tijuana, taken a yacht ride with Baron Long, and consulted with Plutarco Elías Calles at the ex-president's estate outside of Ensenada.[25] The experience must have confirmed what Cárdenas himself already felt—that casinos were an unsavory enticement and repugnant example for working-class Mexicans. He also knew that Calles drew financial support from the foreign casino owners, which made the ex-president even more of a political threat. Now thirty-nine, Cárdenas, who was married and had a son, was a tireless, frugal worker who took an occasional drink but did not smoke. He had spent the year traveling the country, chatting informally with dirt-poor peasants about their needs and aspirations, and pondering ways to help them. The contrast between the lives of these ordinary rural Mexicans and the extravagance and opulence of Agua Caliente could not have been more obvious to him. In his inaugural radio address on 1 December 1934, he condemned vice and corruption, and hardly six months later closed the country's casinos by presidential edict.

The Border Barons did not believe his conviction, or thought that he would change his mind or that he could be inveigled with convincing incentives to grant them an exception. The president stood firm, however, and the following year, on 20 July 1935, his administration closed the doors of the casino at the Agua Caliente complex, as well as the other two casinos in Tijuana. The barons refused to accept their fate and decided to test the president's resolve. They declared their operation at Agua Caliente financially unfeasible without gambling and shut down the entire premises. In effect they proclaimed a lockout, and at a moment's notice fifteen hundred employees lost their jobs.[26] Well more than half the town's population was directly affected. The barons got the strident anti-Cárdenas protest they invited, hoping to move the administration to a reasonable compromise, but none was forthcoming. Even the current territorial governor, Gen. Agustín Olachea, pleaded for relief; budgetary resources (not to speak of his own rake-offs) were drying up, but the president stood firm.[27] So did the barons. Tourism declined, and the populace suffered. Casino dealers accustomed to earning $25 to $30 a night went to work as common laborers at $1.50 daily. People accustomed to buying Stetson hats; Hart, Shaffner and Marx suits, and Florsheim shoes—who thought the money would never stop—lost their jobs. Some families left town, but most decided to wait it out and looked to their labor confederation, the CROM, for relief.

Cárdenas sympathized with the suffering. In mid-1935 he deposed Governor Olachea, whose loyalty he already suspected, and sent one of his most trusted allies, the renowned Zapatista General Gildardo Magaña, north to assess the damages and recommend a resolution. To remove any doubts about the government's intentions, on arrival Magaña announced: "Never again will there be legal gambling in Mexico. The personal convictions of the president are against it. So are mine." But where to go from here?

Over the next three months Magaña and his staff drew up a recovery plan for Tijuana. Casinos no longer contributed to the local budget. Moreover, the closings had diminished tourism so that other businesses could not pay their taxes. Together, this meant that the town carried nearly a $100,000 budgetary deficit that required immediate replenishment by the federal government. Furthermore, Magaña found the town in serious disrepair that only massive spending on public projects could remedy: Obregón School needed painting and repairs, and so did the municipal palace, police headquarters, jail, and slaughterhouse. One rural school had already closed for lack of funds. Two more primary schools needed to be built, along with a sports park and a kindergarten building. The firehouse required expansion. Newer colonias lacked potable water and electricity; roads and drainage required repairs and improvements; and workmen needed tools to do the job. The total cost of repairs was estimated at $300,000, which Magaña noted represented less than half of what the government had spent over the past three months subsidizing the daily salaries of 1,329 unemployed workers in Tijuana. The acting governor also recommended that the annual federal subsidy to the territory be increased, the free zone be extended, and that in the interest of tourism, the liquor tax be dropped. Finally, Magaña asked that an infantry battalion be garrisoned in the town, a sure sign that he feared unrest in the community.[28]

Deliberately or not, Magaña held out some hope to residents of the town that Agua Caliente would be reopened and employment resumed there. He toured the resort grounds with members of CROM, walked in a parade held in his honor, promised fair consideration of the district's problems, and advocated a conference between union officials and the Border Barons. The U.S. consul at Mexicali wired Washington on 21 October 1935:

> It is reported on good authority that Gov. Gildardo Magaña, who left for Mexico City to consult with Cárdenas on economic situation in Baja [California] will offer his resignation unless he can secure re-opening of gambling in Tijuana and Mexicali. The governor has concluded that due to lack of natural resources and industrial possibilities, the city [Tijuana] cannot survive without tourist dollars. Only alternative is a mass government subsidy.
>
> It is rumored that due to unemployment, Cárdenas will agree to reopening but no concessions will be granted [to the Border Barons]. It [the president's decree] would permit installation of gambling tables in any establishment able to procure a license and pay the necessary fees and taxes. Local government formerly received an important part of its revenue from taxes levied on gambling concessions.[29]

The exchange between Magaña and the president has escaped the historical record. President and trusted advisor quite probably had different priorities. Magaña had been out of politics for fifteen years and was writing a book about agricultural economics, which undoubtedly influenced his thinking. He saw that Tijuana had neither industry nor agriculture and depended almost exclusively on tourism. As fair as that assessment may have been, Cárdenas had to blend political realities into the mixture. Gambling taxes may have been the town's principal source of revenue, but they also supported his main political rival, Calles. Federal subsidies were much preferable; they would alleviate misery while drawing the border town more closely toward central control. But the national treasury was depleted, other reform programs expensive, and the Mexican economy displaying sure signs of stress. It was a dilemma, and a year of waffling ensued.

The president replaced Magaña as territorial governor with Gen. Gabriel Gavira in February 1936, but Gavira's wide-scale reorganization of officialdom (meaning the appointment of friends to government positions) angered unions and other well-established groups. He suspended work on public projects started by Magaña and offered the discharged workers $10 to leave Baja California and find their fortunes elsewhere. His proposal to depopulate the territory came at a time when the U.S. Congress was about to consider an initiative to buy the entire peninsula. Workers railed against the governor: Did not Gavira understand that if Mexicans abandoned Baja California, it would be more vulnerable to America's territorial appetite? Under pressure, Gavira offered to resign, and President Cárdenas, no doubt to the governor's surprise, accepted. He had lasted only four months.[30]

Gavira's replacement was Gen. Rafael Navarro Cortina, a native of the president's home state of Michoacán, whose long military career had most recently included command of the essential garrison in Mexico City. Once in Baja California, he curried favor with locals by allowing gambling to take place despite the federal ban and undoubtedly got rich doing it. U.S. Consul William Smale caught the stench and reported to his superiors: "It has been a matter of general knowledge for some weeks that gambling houses equipped with all kinds of the prohibited games of chance have been in operation publicly in Tijuana, while games of chance have been in clandestine operation in the 'red light' district of Mexicali. Rumors have been prevalent for some days that complaints have been forwarded to President Cárdenas against Navarro concerning his complaisant attitude toward gambling in the territory."[31]

But the complaints did not stem from moral or legal issues; rather, they arose because of a dispute between the new governor and Rosendo Herrera, chief of immigration in Mexicali. It seems that Herrera had been accustomed to receiving payoffs from the town's gambling houses, but when Navarro Cortina became governor, according to Smale, he had diverted that income from Herrera to "officials closely associated with the [new territorial] government. This is what brought the gambling situation to the attention of Cárdenas [yet again]." The president's own officials were undermining his moralization campaign. The governorship of

Northern Baja California had become a revolving door. The district was in turmoil, and any spark of protest could ignite a conflagration. Smale's political report for January 1937 captured the spectacle:

> Continued gambling at the Hotel Playa Ensenada, later opening of games at Rosarito Beach, and during the month of January the opening of a few tables of so-called permitted games at the Foreign Club in Tijuana indicate a relaxation of the moral attitude maintained by the administration of Baja California since President Cárdenas took oath. Strong rumors abound to the effect that the present governor [Navarro Cortina] is not vigorously opposing illegal schemes and practices. It is even reported that close relatives are involved in narcotic traffic. Thus the administration appears to be reverting to that of former times when governors have used their office largely to advance their own economic position.[32]

In the midst of scandal in Baja California, Cárdenas announced a "New Deal" for the territory, promising funds for industrial development and public works. He was no friend of CROM, nor it of him, but he needed to quell union protest in town before it escalated and invited disturbances elsewhere in the republic. With this in mind, he considered the resumption of gambling on a limited, highly regulated basis, but the improprieties of Navarro Cortina scuttled any such possibilities, and CROM continued to fume. Tijuana had to be regimented and brought into line. In March 1937 the president replaced his errant governor with another general, Rodolfo Sánchez Taboada, forty-three years old and a close political and military ally, whose only stain lay in his probable complicity in the assassination of Emiliano Zapata. Concurrently, for the first time in the district's history, a president separated civil and military responsibilities. Former governors had performed both functions, but now Sánchez Taboada's sphere was limited to civil affairs, while General Manuel J. Contreras commanded the military. They would work together but at the same time keep an eye on one another, and when it came to dealing with the rioting that beset Tijuana in early 1938, they did just that. Contreras himself handled the repression, while Sánchez Taboada maintained administrative contact with his superiors in the capital.[33]

Despite the high-level political upheaval and the unsettling demands of the CROM, Tijuana continued its readjustment to the challenges presented by the Depression, Prohibition's demise in the United States, and the closing of the casinos. The California-Pacific International Exposition in San Diego's Balboa Park drew large and enthusiastic crowds during its run from the summer of 1935 to September 1936, and thousands of visitors took a side trip to Tijuana. As members of the fair's planning committee, Tijuanenses had deliberately planned it that way, insuring that their hometown staged activities certain to attract visitors. The tactic must have worked, for *The Herald* hurled a salvo at Tijuana's success: "Tijuana is flourishing like the green bay tree" in the absence of a vibrant San Diego night life, but also due to the existence of the international Free-Trade Zone.

> BUT NEVERTHELESS, TIJUANA IS REAPING MILLIONS FROM THE EXPOSI-
> TION WHILE SAN DIEGO BUSINESS MEN AND TAXPAYERS ARE STARVING
> [an exaggeration, to be sure]! Now we are finding out that it
> [the exposition] has been opened for the benefit of Mexico and Baron
> Long. His holdings at Agua Caliente, and the holdings of all Ameri-
> cans in Tijuana gambling [sharply curtailed by the Cárdenas reforms],
> are insignificant in comparison with the holdings of Mexicans—some
> of whom are bitter haters of everything American. When, therefore,
> American money goes to Baron Long he only gets part of it. He
> is only a front for rich and arrogant Mexicans who are taking the
> cream.[34]

In this way, the newspaper proclaimed the border baron Long and conniving Mexicans the culprits. Anxious to invigorate business at their entertainment centers in Tijuana, they had somehow willed the San Diego exposition into existence. No doubt Long and the others had their Mexican interests in mind while promoting the world's fair, but even as the newspaper lambasted them, they were about to lose their most lucrative enterprise, Agua Caliente.

When the gambling casino closed, along with others in town, tourism dipped in Tijuana, but by 1937 the town had largely returned to accustomed commercial activity. In the spring that year hope for a further economic stimulus surged: Agua Caliente would reopen on a three-month trial basis. There would be no casino gambling, at least no games outside the law, but horse and dog races would be resumed, so-called legal games of chance allowed—billiards, chess, bowling, and dominoes, on which people could place bets—and the resort with its spas, dance halls, dining rooms, and guest accommodations restored to its earlier splendor. There was a lot of repair work to be done. When it had closed nineteen months earlier, CROM claimed that the Border Barons owed workers severance pay, and, rebuffed by the owners, the unionists had taken over the resort, much as the Cárdenas administration had encouraged aggrieved industrial workers to do with factories in other parts of the country. CROM had considered running Agua Caliente on its own, but members knew nothing of operating such a complex and so negotiated with the Border Barons and their business partners for a reopening. In the spring of 1937, one of those partners, E. S. Neidhart, an avid and rich San Diego sportsman, made a deal with CROM. The union leased the racetrack to Neidhart for two years for $132,000 with an option to buy. More than five thousand fans attended the reopening in May. That happy day crooner Bing Crosby had two winners from his own stable, and four hundred Mexicans went back to work. One week in June the track drew seventy thousand spectators who spent an estimated $100,000 in town, a reminder of past glories.

Meanwhile, Baron Long was maneuvering to reopen the hotel and gaming casino with legal games of chance: roulette, black jack, dice, and the rest.[35] While his agents lobbied in Mexico City for expanded gambling rights, he contracted with CROM to employ some six hundred additional Mexicans at substantial pay, even if at a level 15 percent less than what they had received in the resort's heyday. Union workers felt resurrected, but their joy was short-lived. After the three-month trial, horse racing alone had not produced expected revenues, and the track once again closed. Dismissed workers demanded severance pay in accordance with Mexican law, but the company argued that as the track had reopened only on a trial basis, no such wages were due. About this time Baron Long pulled familiar political strings in Mexico City and announced that the casino would renew operations with gambling at the year's end. Where he received such assurances is not known, and perhaps he was just floating one of his famous trial balloons, but President Cárdenas would have none of it. His patience exhausted and with other much more troubling affairs of state on his mind, he declared that enough was enough, and on 18 December 1937 expropriated the Agua Caliente complex, all but the racetrack, and announced he would pay the owners in bonds over the next ten years. He then turned the resort over to the Secretary of Education with orders to redesign it as an industrial trade school.

In response to Cárdenas's edict, on 2 January 1938 four hundred irate workers and their families occupied Agua Caliente. *The San Diego Sun* described the poignant scene:

> The workmen, their wives and children trailing after them, marched into the spacious grounds and said they would hold the resort until they were provided new jobs in protest to the government seizure.
>
> Eight men were posted at the padlocked gates to the grounds, and they told reporters that they intended to stay until removed forcefully by soldiers. Carrying their possessions in bandana handkerchiefs, the workers and their families trudged along the three-mile route from Tijuana [town center] to Caliente last night [January 2, 1938] and turned into the grounds.
>
> Waving from staffs a few carried were the flaming red flags of CROM, a labor union. They forced entrance to the numerous small bungalows, laid down their bundles, and made themselves at home.
>
> The small, expensively furnished cottages became the temporary homes of people of whom some have lived all their lives in window-less, dirt-floored huts along the Tijuana River bank. Bare feet of scores of children pattered over the thick rugs. Soft, heavily cushioned chairs held in comfort men who formerly entered the cottages with trays on their hands.[36]

For a livelihood, the union proposed to operate the bar, dining room, spa, and souvenir stores as a workers' cooperative. The government could use the golf courses for military aviation. Should their demands not be met, the workers threatened to enter every building on the grounds, looting anything of worth and selling the booty in order to maintain themselves. They professed no fear of the army, and told reporters: "Let the army come. They have only 28 [soldiers]. We have 400 people here and 5,000 more in [downtown] Tijuana."[37] Then they began to dismantle the premises. The company had hoped to remove more than a million dollars worth of liquor and furnishings from the resort, but the workers beat them to it. We are now less than two weeks from the rape and murder of Olga Camacho, and the town is tense, with hundreds of rebellious workers at a standoff with authority.

During the first week of their occupation, the workers consumed and sold an estimated $4,000 worth of meat and food supplies from the resort's commissary. They drank the best liquor on the premises, but seem to have left the gilded ornaments and other expensive artifacts in place. One still wonders whatever happened to them. Soldiers posted around the grounds and buildings prevented further theft from the storerooms, and the workers formed their own vigilance committee to curb looting among the membership. For its part, the government offered to employ one hundred workers to convert the hotel into the planned school, promising that they would be permitted to remain on the grounds until the school was complete and then would be removed to farms or other public works projects.[38] These sorts of tentative, carrot-and-stick negotiations did what governments intend them to do—they split the membership of the union. Some members shrugged their shoulders, swallowed hard, and thought of their families and the need for work, while others determined to stand their ground. No doubt about it, Tijuana was a tinderbox.

The government spotted the fissures in the opposition, and the next week upped the pressure. Cárdenas refused the proposal to run any part of the resort as a workers' cooperative, standing by the expropriation and his determination to turn the site into a school. He met with a delegation of the CROM in Mexico City, warmly welcomed them in his presidential office, and then sternly ordered them to forget the casino and to get to work as farmers on land provided by the government outside the town. The workers chafed at the rebuke. Campesino life was not all that inviting; a good many of the workers had come to Tijuana precisely to escape its drudgery and limited compensations.

Then the second shoe fell. On 24 January, the local labor arbitration board ruled for the foreign-owned corporation and against severance pay for the discharged workers. Because the resort had been reopened on only a three-month trial basis, the board agreed that severance pay laws did not apply. These two acts—the quashing of the cooperative and the board ruling—lit the wick. The government thought that the adverse decisions would bring the confederation to heel, but instead they solidified the ranks of unionized workers throughout town.[39]

Four days later, on January 28, several thousand workers—former employees of Agua Caliente and their sympathizers representing every trade union in the confederation—paraded down Tijuana's main street to the old boxing arena alongside the Foreign Club. At the head of the procession "mourners" carried a coffin draped in black which bore the inscription, "Labor laws in Mexico are dead." Once at the assembly ground they ceremonially burned the coffin and its banners, and from the speaker's platform union leaders, one after another, flayed the government for its failure to provide jobs for unemployed hotel workers and daily provisions for the families now lodged at the resort. They decried that some of the destitute had been temporarily forced to board their children with better-off relatives and acquaintances. Speakers demanded that conciliation board members resign or be removed, and called for a general strike. Workers should not send their children to school. Members of CROM would not pay taxes on their homes and water services. All those out of work would demonstrate, night and day, banging on pots and pans outside the municipal palace. They developed a plan to occupy the structure itself, at least to stage an as-long-as-it-takes sit-down strike in the main patio of the town's most important government building. The challenge to authority could not have been more clarion; Tijuana had never seen the likes of a general strike. Soldiers and police patrolled the perimeter of the surly throng but dared not interfere. Cárdenas himself was urging patience upon the country's disgruntled workers. He explained that he could not devote all his attention to their problems, "because there are many problems in the nation; not only labor but some of international scope," including the petroleum dispute with foreign oil magnates. Then he scolded the proletarians: "You laborers do not realize that yours is not the only problem in the country, and that the peasant class lives in the same situation which prevailed years ago—a situation of misery."[40] Tijuana's strikers must have scoffed at such a put-off.

On 9 February—now only five days before the horrible crime and the ensuing riots—CROM occupied the municipal palace. Families of workers, women and children, set up camp in one corner of the patio, their presence marked by the union's red and black flags, their symbol of defiance. Supporters sent in supplies, and armed men manned the post at night. These aggressive actions further splintered the union's membership, even more severely than before, but the leadership remained firm and threatened reprisals against those who did not participate.[41]

The general strike never materialized as envisioned by the militants, but squatters were still planted inside the palacio when Meimi Romero discovered the mutilated corpse of eight-year-old Olga Camacho in the dilapidated garage near the child's home and when the young infantry soldier Juan Castillo Morales confessed to the crime.

THESE, THEN, were among the more obvious (and verifiable) long-term and short-term circumstances that affected ways in which Tijuanenses pondered the shocking events enveloping them in February 1938. When combined with belief, they led (for some) to the worship of Juan Soldado. Surely additional circumstances such as background and personal experience influenced individuals. We can never see what they saw, know what they knew, feel as they felt. Social science techniques can carry us only so far into their realm, but then must be abandoned to possibilities (and probabilities) and faith, along with the unknown and unknowable. Nonetheless, we still have our curiosity, instincts, humanness, and (hopefully) good sense, informed by the wisdom and intelligence of ageless sages, with which to examine and ponder the transcendental.

beyond

III

BELIEF

6. Witness to Execution

Nothing more strained and strengthened the web of circumstances and belief for Tijuanenses than the execution of Juan Castillo Morales that chilly February morning in the town's public cemetery. Extraordinary events such as these invite introspection and can heighten (as well as challenge) belief. Naturally, the event itself and the violence that preceded it were on people's minds, if not their consciences. Widely discussed in planned get-togethers and chance meetings of the citizenry, the occurrences provoked reactions ranging from vociferous debate to a hushed indecisiveness approaching bewilderment. Differences of opinion surfaced, along with conclusions of varied intensity. A good many thought the soldier guilty and deserving of death. Retribution reigned in their minds. Others found Castillo Morales culpable but harbored reservations about the procedures that had brought him to justice—the rapidity of the investigation, the suddenness of the announced confession, the secretive court martial, the staged execution. Some doubted his guilt; conspiracy theories abounded. Could Juan have been the scapegoat for a higher-up? Then, in 1938, most found him guilty. Today virtually all his devotees declare him innocent. However, Olga Camacho's relatives certainly do not, and townspeople at large simply utter, "It is said that . . . ." They pass no judgment on the case and avoid further consideration with that famous Mexican phrase of avoidance, "¿Quién sabe?"—who knows or who cares?

In this atmosphere of uncertainly and conjecture, devotion to Juan Soldado began, so quickly in fact that people must have wanted and been ready for it, or perhaps been shocked into it. The seeds had long been sown in belief and circumstance, but an unseemly event had caused the scatterings to germinate. Remember the execution itself. The army, certainly on orders from superiors in Mexico City, designed the setting. First and foremost it was to be a public execution; all were invited. Authorities timed the pageant to insure sufficient daylight for photographers. They could have shot the soldier behind the walls of the cuartel or elsewhere out of sight, in keeping with habitual military practices. If concerned that Tijuanenses would demand proof of execution, they then could have displayed the victim's body, even if that exceeded army regulation. No, the military wanted to fulfill the demands of the lynch mob and to forcefully demonstrate the unmitigated power of the state while doing it. To do so, it reverted to a ritual of execution that had long been reviled and outlawed in much of the Western world as barbarous and of uncertain deterrent effect. Now the Mexican army was about to reprise a sordid episode from the distant past.

Why perform the ritual in the town's lone cemetery? Why on sacred ground, where spectators gathered among their own beloved departed ones to witness the extraordinary execution of Castillo Morales? That in itself is enough to give one pause. Perhaps the army felt its options limited. If this was to be a stationary execution, it could have performed the ceremony against almost any wall in the town. Authorities had determined to apply the Ley Fuga, however: the accused would run for his life and then be shot down in flight as if "trying to escape." Such staging required ample space; the safety of spectators had to be assured. Moreover, burial would be rapid and convenient among the scattered graves of other townspeople, including that of the ravished child victim herself. Actually, the accused's flight may not have occurred on what was considered to be sacred ground: the exact bounds of the burial area are now unknown and were indistinct even then. Castillo Morales was ordered to run at the south end of the cemetery, below a low hill line and beyond grave sites that existed at the time. The place where he fell for the last time, where the mercy shot was fired, and where his blood stained the ground soon became the first site of major veneration, and now there is a second shrine in his honor near that spot. But following the execution, his corpse was dragged, or carried, perhaps thirty or forty yards down to sacred ground and dropped into the shallow hole prepared for it. Someone almost immediately placed a large, handmade wooden Christian cross at the site, naming upon it the soldier who lay below. That act alone may be seen as the precise moment of the origin of devotion. Some person or persons felt that Juan, innocent or not, at least should have a proper Christian burial.

While on the one hand military and civil authorities certainly never envisioned the blossoming of a strong devotion at the grave site of a confessed and convicted rapist-murderer, on the other hand, they never attempted to restrain its development (beyond laughing it off as silly superstition). One wonders whether or not religiosity in any way entered their hastily planned script for the execution, specifically the decision to bury Juan in sacred ground. Had they not learned a lesson about the dawns of devotion to Mexican criminals denied interment in sacred ground? Best known to them would have been the story we have already encountered of Jesús Malverde, the bandit who ranged through the mountains above Sinaloa's state capital of Culiacán early in the twentieth century, robbing the rich and aiding the poor, according to his wor-shipers. When Malverde was finally captured and hanged in 1909, the governor, in keeping with historical precedent, refused to permit any burial of the corpse at all. There it dangled from the limb of a tree as an example to others who might defy authority until it decomposed, tore apart, and dropped piece by part to the ground. The governor still denied the putrefied remains a decent burial, and so within days passersby began to place rocks and stones on the decayed body. A few rocks quickly grew into a pile, then a mound; devotion began, and the people canonized Jesús Malverde as *their* saint. Homage to him continues in a most ardent way to this day, not only in Sinaloa but throughout Mexico and beyond. Some, on both sides of the law, consider him to be the patron saint of drug dealers.[1]

Closer to San Diego and Tijuana we recall the story of El Tiradito, billed by Tucson's Chamber of Commerce as "the only sinner to become a saint." Like all such tales, that of Tiradito is shrouded in murky memory, creative retelling, and reflections of changing times. In the latter part of the nineteenth century, so the most frequently told story goes, a young ranch hand named Juan Oliveras, cowpoking outside Tucson or in north-ern Mexico, became infatuated with his stepmother, his father's wife, and she with him. A sexual liaison developed, and one day the father caught them making love. As the youngster sought to escape the entanglement, his father cleaved him with an ax and had the corpse tossed away to rot. Another version has the young man escaping to Tucson, where his avenging brother eventually caught and killed him. In all tellings, however, the body of the fallen lover was buried haphazardly where it fell. The callousness of the boy's fate in all of these versions relates to the sympathetic connotation of "Tiradito"—a young fellow tossed away like garbage.

Mexican and Mexican-American Catholics thought the burial of Tiradito unholy. His remains lay in unblessed earth, and therefore his soul would suffer in Purgatory forever and be denied its final glory. Pious neighbors placed candles on the grave (which tradition locates in the historic quarter of Tucson) and in their prayers commended the soul of the slain sinner to God. Devotion soon brought personal requests and miraculous rewards. A shrine now exists, "Dedicated to the soul of a sinner buried in unconsecrated ground." The manner of death and place of burial carry profound religious meaning for any number of believers for whom more secular notions of justice and fairness are also inextricably intertwined.[2]

Justice, but . . .

Let us witness again the arrival of the *julia,* the windowless paddy wagon, soldiers clinging to sidebars above its running boards, and inside the terrified convicted rapist-murderer being hurried to his execution site. A murmuring crowd of townspeople, nearing a thousand men, women, and youths, in addition to several squads of soldiers lined up for duty, await him in the cemetery on the outskirts of town. As the julia pulls up and stops at the main gate, a hush settles over the scene. Soldiers fling open the back doors of the julia, and a couple of enlisted men drop to the ground from inside. Then the accused appears, forcefully prodded by soldiers from behind. Juan Castillo Morales knows what awaits him; he hesitates to leave the julia, but soldiers push him to the ground. His knees weaken. Is he about to fall? Soldiers prop him up, and photographers take their pictures. Tears stain his cheeks. The crowd watches, but nary a shout, only a nervous shuffling.

Juan Castillo Morales is led, virtually dragged by his armpits, to an outer edge of the area marked by grave stones. Two firing squads of eight men each await him there. He asks a member of his escort for a cigarette and is handed a lighted one. He takes a few nervous puffs. Then comes the command: *Run.* No more wasting time. But Juan does not want to run; he does not want to die. Bayonets nudge him to run. *Run, Juan*

Castillo Morales. Run for your life. The twenty-four-year-old tosses down his cigarette and takes off like a frightened deer. He spots an unsuspecting lad entering the cemetery from another direction and warns him off. The quarry then leaps over a low barbed-wire fence meant to keep prowling dogs and pigs from the graves, and dashes toward open space ahead. He must know what awaits him, but does he dare think about it at this moment? The Mausers are already aimed.

Does Juan Castillo Morales hear the order to fire? *Fuego!* The crowd does, but does the target? What does it matter? The first volley, or at least a part of it, catches him square in the back and knocks him down. But with great effort he pulls himself up and staggers across another strand of barbed wire before the volley from a second squad of executioners— *Fuego!*—fells him for good. But life has not yet fully drained from his riddled body. He raises his head and then an arm, a final clutch at freedom. His pain is palpable. The firing squads are ordered to finish their duty: *Fuego!* for the third time. Juan Castillo Morales lies on his back, his arms stretched out to his sides, slightly raised, seemingly in some sort of supplication. An army officer steps forward, presses his high-caliber pistol to the head of the fallen one and fires the coup de grâce, the so-called mercy shot that supposedly finishes any semblance of agony for the wretch.

As the body of the soldier is dragged or carried to the waiting grave, a few in the crowd shout "Bien!"—well done, he got what he deserved. But for the most part the crowd is silent—some of them, at least, immersed in that stunned silence which inevitably invades public executions. We know in some detail what these people saw that cool morning in Tijuana's main cemetery. They saw a public execution in a country that had, with most of the Western world, long abandoned such practices in the name of humanity as well as uncertainty about their effect on the viewing public. "Modern" countries no longer abided public executions. Moreover, the crowd not only observed a public execution widely condemned as un-civilized, but it also witnessed a performance of the Ley Fuga—the detestable Law of Flight—that was flagrantly outside the law and highly despised by a populace which had suffered its consequences for too long.

In the Mexican mind (and ample literature), the Ley Fuga stood for brute authoritarianism, for officialdom that had no respect for the law, for the crass manner in which authorities rid themselves of troublesome subjects without reference to judicial procedures. It had a historic reputation for wanton usage in the country. Its image was especially attached to the era of the dictatorship of Porfirio Díaz (1885–1910), but the revolution that ousted him as a tyrant was supposed to have changed all that: no more Ley Fuga. It certainly did not altogether disappear, however, and was firmly lodged in the memory of those who witnessed the execution of Juan Castillo Morales in 1938. Such forms of violent punishment carry past meanings for people and can inaugurate new ones.

Odious as it was, the Law of Flight was meant to be carried out clandestinely. A prisoner in transit would simply be "disappeared." The official explanation was that the prisoner was shot while trying to escape (always in some secluded spot or at least some distance from possible witnesses), but everyone knew what had happened. If the government had ordered Juan Castillo Morales transferred under guard to Mexico City for trial and then reported him shot dead while attempting escape, it would have been understood as a classic case of the Ley Fuga, but in Tijuana the ritual of the Ley Fuga was performed onstage, in public. It is quite possibly the only such case in Mexican history. Those who saw the execution of Juan Castillo Morales participated (surely everyone at these sorts of staged demonstrations is a participant) in a unique event, the playing out of a scenario that historically they detested. Those present almost certainly had never before seen the Ley Fuga administered, and suddenly they were there, watching, feeling, thinking as participants in the drama.

What was the government trying to prove with this ritual? Undoubtedly it meant to affirm its stand for justice, so that Olga's horrible murder would be avenged in kind. Also, that the public need not fear that the accused would be transferred to another military jurisdiction, that the armed forces would simply cover up when one of its members had gone bad. Furthermore, army and civic officials needed to emphasize that beyond any doubt they would not countenance any challenge to their authority. Moreover, the military aimed its rifles at the CROM as much as the soldier. "When you kill the dog, the rabies disappears." The idea was to restore official control and then salve wounds after the fact. The public seemed to understand those messages.

At the same time, witnesses at the execution also saw a poor young man, at least one not well-off, whose entire immediate family had been wiped out in a series of tragic events in the two months preceding the brutal murder of Olga Camacho, whose details they had read about in the local press. Spectators saw a frightened young man, far from home, relatives, and friends, bereft of any support, all alone; a soldado raso, lowest of the low in military parlance, tears flowing freely down his face, pleading for mercy but forced at bayonet point to run for his life while his executioners (his military comrades) cocked their rifles—streaking across the outer edge of the cemetery, hurtling across a barbed-wire fence, racing for the freedom he knew he would never reach, and then the sharp report of rifle fire interrupted his flight. He is knocked down but struggles on only to receive another volley of bullets. Fallen, grievously wounded but not yet expired, and then a third round of shots strikes its mark. Life leaves; death arrives. An officer strides up, pistol in hand, and delivers one final blast. Unceremoniously Juan the soldier is tossed by his fellow army men into a shallow waiting pit, his final resting place.[3]

This is what spectators at that execution *saw*; the question is how did they *feel*? How might *you* feel? Feelings can inaugurate devotion. What meanings did these witness-participants take from the execution of Juan Castillo Morales?

Public Executions

Damiens had lifted his hand against the king of France, Louis XV. He meant to stab His Majesty to death, but guards intervened, and so on 2 March 1757 he was publicly executed. An officer of the watch remembered the scene:

> Then the executioner, his sleeves rolled up, took the steel pincers, which had been especially made for the occasion and were about a foot and a half long, and pulled first at the calf of the right leg, then at the thigh, and from there at the two fleshy parts of the right arm; then at the breasts. Though a strong, sturdy fellow, this executioner found it so difficult to tear away the pieces of flesh that he set about the same spot two or three times, twisting the pincers as he did so, and what he took away formed at each part a wound about the size of a six-pound crown piece.
>
> . . . Then the ropes that were to be harnessed to the horses were attached with cords to the patient's [sic] body; the horses were then harnessed and placed alongside the arms and legs, one at each limb. . . .
>
> The horses tugged hard, each pulling straight on a limb, each horse

held by an executioner. After a quarter of an hour, the same ceremony was repeated and finally, after several attempts, the direction of the horses had to be changed, thus: those at the arms were made to pull towards the head, those at the thighs towards the arms, which broke the arms at the joints. This was repeated several times without success. ... Two more horses had to be added to those harnessed to the thighs, which made six horses in all. Without success. . . . . The horses gave up and one of those harnessed to the thighs fell to the ground. . . .

After two or three attempts, the executioner Samson and he who had used the pincers each drew out a knife from his pocket and cut the body at the thighs instead of severing the legs at the joints; the four horses then gave a tug and carried off the two thighs after them, namely the right side first, the other following; then the same was done to the arms, the shoulders, the arm-pits and the four limbs; the flesh had to be cut almost to the bone, the horses pulling hard carried off the right arm first and the other afterwards.

When the four limbs had been pulled away, the confessors came to speak to him [to learn if Damiens had made his peace with God]; but the executioner told them that he was dead, though the truth was I saw the man move, his lower jaw moving from side to side as if he were talking. One of the executioners even said shortly afterwards that when they had lifted the trunk to throw it on [*sic*] the stake [to be burned], he was still alive. The four limbs were untied from the ropes and thrown on the stake set up in the enclosure in line with the scaffold, then the trunk and rest were covered with logs and faggots, and fire was put to the straw and mixed with this wood.

. . . In accordance with the decree [of the court], the whole was reduced to ashes.[4]

One might expect that an attack on the sovereign (hence his sovereignty) would demand the harshest retribution, and the public execution of Damiens is but one of many accounts that have filtered down to us from those earlier examples of human disgrace. Red hot pincers tore at flesh; axes, swords, and sawtooth blades dismembered the bodies of victims.

On August 21, 1741, a certain Pietro Costiola was condemned to "be led on a cart to Piazza Maggiore [Bologna], his back being twice flayed with red hot tongs. There he would be hanged until dead, and his head and left hand cut off and set up in an iron cage atop a wooden pole" at the site of his most heinous crime. Giovani Battista Torriggia, on the other hand, was sentenced on June 4, 1767, "to be dragged at a horse's tail to Piazza Maggiore . . . and there broken on the wheel, which will be raised so that his body will [be] left on public display for the whole day."[5]

Similar spectacles with different details but the same results occurred on many of western Europe's main squares. Women too were executed. In Venice on 19 May 1410 authorities found Bona Tartara guilty of poisoning her master. For that deed they ordered her tied to a stake and paraded down the Grand Canal on a raft, a crier all the while announcing her crime. Then she was tied to a horse's tail and dragged along the ground to Saint Mark's Cathedral, where she was burned to death. A century later, Bernadina, found guilty of murdering her husband, was taken down the Grand Canal on a raft to the Venetian barrio in which she lived, where her right hand was cut off and hanged around her neck. Then officials escorted her to Saint Mark's, where she was to be quartered—but the axe of the executioner did not quickly accomplish its task, so her tormenter had to cut her throat and then plunge his knife into her heart.[6] The horrific litany goes on, and on, and on. One can still sense the misery and hear the cries.

PUBLIC EXECUTIONS BEGAN to wane toward the end of the eighteenth century, and within a hundred years they had largely disappeared. "Killing criminals, especially in public, came to be seen as a revolting spectacle, as people began to appreciate the humanity of those being killed, and hence to empathize with the humiliation and degradation wrought by their punishment."[7] Nineteenth-century people thought of themselves as being more civilized and spoke of the barbarity of former times. They felt more acutely the pain of those being mutilated and openly put to death and came to see them as fellow human beings, more like "us." If wrongdoers were to be tortured and executed, it should at least be done beyond public sight. Executions themselves became quicker, the procedures more bureaucratic and less ceremonial. Public executions did not entirely die out of course. One of the last ones in the United States occurred on 14 August 1936, in Owensboro, Kentucky, when some ten to twenty thousand spectators from as far away as three surrounding states attended the hanging of a twenty-two-year-old African American, Rainey Bethea, who had confessed to murdering a well-to-do seventy-year-old white woman. While imprisoned before the execution, Bethea joined a Christian church and at the scaffold knelt toward the rising sun. A priest held a cross in front of him. When the trap was sprung, down he went, the snap breaking his neck—and his heart continued to beat for another sixteen and one-half minutes. At the time in Kentucky, authorities decided whether or not such hangings should be conducted privately or in public. In Bethea's case they announced with no explanation that the execution would be public. It was the first public hanging in the county's history.[8]

On 21 May of the following year, officials hanged Roscoe (Red) Jackson, a black man of thirty-six, in a public ceremony before fifteen hundred witnesses in Galena, Missouri. Jackson had confessed to shooting a traveling salesman to death. With a Catholic priest at his side, he begged forgiveness: "I guess it's asking too much for everyone concerned to forgive me, but I want all to know that I meet death with a heart free of all hatred. I blame no one for this but myself, and the law is merely doing its duty." As the sheriff sprung the trap, Jackson shouted, "Goodbye, folks!" It took him ten minutes to die.[9]

One year later Juan Castillo Morales suffered the Ley Fuga in Tijuana, but his public execution harked back to much earlier times; it carried all the hallmarks of torture, protracted pain, humiliation, degradation, and dehumanization evident in those earlier festivals of blood. No priest, no final words, although some later said that Juan had shouted out, "I am innocent! I am innocent!" And then as he lay mortally wounded, he had wept for mercy. In response, an army officer dutifully delivered the coup de grâce. Who among the spectators could not help but feel some pity for the fallen lad?

The brutality of state-sponsored executions and the spectacle of pain such as that perpetrated upon Juan, along with many others over the centuries, frequently kindled a compassion that touched compelling devotional longings—not for all witnesses, of course, but for those so inclined. "The signs of the body in pain were not just a shameful side effect to be tolerated for a sake of justice; they were instead the focal point of comprehension [in a Christian context] which gave the spectacle its religious meaning."[10]

Crowd Expressions

One of the reasons, perhaps the major one, that authorities moved executions from city plazas to enclosed prison interiors was because the reactions of spectators to public executions proved to be so unpredictable. Those in political command of public executions understood the threat and frequently stationed guards around the scaffolds and guillotines, while soldiers pushed mobs away from the machines of execution. The nineteenth-century change, therefore, may well have had less to do with reformed sensibilities toward torture and pain or the enhancement of compassion for fellow humans in anguish (I look at you and see myself suffering) than it did with maintaining domestic order. Even when raucous mobs surrounded the scaffolds and pyres and celebrated the grisly death of the condemned, there were those among them who jeered the executioner and cheered the victim, especially a condemned wretch's shouts of defiance. Spectators fainted at the unanticipated or underestimated gruesomeness of executions, and swooned at the terror-stricken sobs of the condemned. Even while justice demanded retribution, they sympathized with the doomed convict. Some expressed repugnance at the sight of the gory executions. In 1773 an anonymous pamphlet appeared in Amsterdam after "Justice Day," 6 November, when six criminals were hanged and one other broken on the wheel. The author had attended the spectacle for unknown reasons, was not related to the condemned, and knew them to be malefactors, but the cruelty of the scene he witnessed weighed keenly upon his sensibilities:

> Be quiet, I see the multitude pressing; they all fix their eyes simultaneously on the spot where the sufferers have to enter the scaffold. No wonder, one of the guilty is already presented there. But good heavens, what a frightening spectacle! I am indeed overwhelmed by pity for the state you are in. . . . This one having finished his breath [been hanged], is followed by others numbering six, who have all been condemned to the rope because of their wicked acts. How full of fright was my soul! How affected I was, when I saw them climb the ladder one after the other! I was cold, I trembled at every step they took. I often turned away my face and distracted my eyes from the mortal spectacle to the endless number of spectators. I thought that I noticed in some of them the same horror at such a terrible spectacle. The same repugnance

which I felt. This raised an inner joy in me: it gave me a positive view of my fellow-creatures again.[11]

The father of Albert Camus witnessed a public execution outside of Algiers shortly before World War I. A man in Algiers had wantonly slaughtered a farmer and his family, including children. So heinous was the crime, it was generally agreed that decapitation was too mild a punishment for the murderer, but authorities prepared the guillotine for the execution. Camus's father had never before attended a public execution, but was so enraged by the murders, especially of the children, that he resolved to attend the beheading. Afterwards, he returned home, "rushed wildly into the house, refused to speak, threw himself on his bed, and suddenly began to vomit," distraught at the repugnant ritual that had been played out before his eyes, regardless of the guilt of the condemned party.[12]

Some twenty years later in Tijuana a well-known, tough-minded militant labor leader, Octaviano Flores Contreras, firm in his dedication to the CROM and a participant in the riots which shook the town in early 1938, suffered a similar reaction at the ghastly death of Juan Castillo Morales. He returned home sick to his stomach and then suffered *susto*, an overpowering fright said to drive a person's spirit or soul from the body. Weakness occurs, and then the victim becomes wobbly or drowsy, can get a raging headache or develop nausea, indigestion, or anxiety. In such cases, curanderos are frequently called upon for relief. Flores eventually recovered, but his system had been severely jolted, and he never forgot this macabre episode in his life.[13]

Another witness to the execution recalls that among those soldiers assigned to shoot down Juan as he ran for his life, many wept and did not fire their rifles. He was their buddy, and they believed someone else must be guilty, so they did not pull their triggers. Finally one fired, and brought him down. But as a result of their reluctance, the victim had few bullet holes in his corpse.[14] Details of this account may be contested; they are not confirmed elsewhere, but the sentiments, even if they developed after the spectacle, are clear.

Following the execution of Rainey Bethea in Owensboro, Kentucky, townspeople said they felt "let down by what we have done here."[15] They were sorry they had gone to the hanging. And finally, regarding one of the world's seminal public executions, Biblical scholars say that some in the mob who had spat upon and otherwise reviled Jesus Christ must have believed his punishment unjust; that the spectacle saddened others who sympathized with its victim. Some in the multitude did not mock Him, and returned home striking their breasts in sorrow, if not contrition. One's role at public executions may vary; nonetheless, all such participations assuredly leave scars.

OFFICIALDOM COULD ALSO never be certain of the deterrent effect of such executions (an issue still under strident debate) or how spectators might receive and interpret the intended official message embedded in such elaborate rituals. Authorities understood that public executions could have unintended or even subversive results, but they went ahead with them anyway. The Spaniard don Juan de Benavides had distinguished himself as a military officer until 1634, when, unfortunately for him and Spain, he lost his entire fleet to the Dutch off Cuba. In an attempt to raise the courage of Spanish mariners, the king had his disgraced admiral publicly executed, but witnesses did not respond enthusiastically to the event. Elites especially complained about the unseemly death of one of their own.[16]

In another Spanish case, one of many public executions with unanticipated conclusions, Rodrigo Calderón was riding high (and loose) in the court of King Phillip III early in the seventeenth century. His protector against intrigues and machinations within the administration was the Duke of Lerma, a close personal friend of the king, but when Lerma fell from favor, Calderón's crimes and corruption were exposed. Phillip might have pardoned him, but died in 1621 without having done so. His son, Phillip IV, who had no love for his father's courtiers, needed a victim to highlight his own intention to reform the royal house. He chose Calderón to be publicly executed with due pomp and ceremony. When he learned of his fate, Calderón went into nothing less than a devotional frenzy. Riding a mule to his execution, he displayed great humility. His bravery and devotion moved spectators to tears. They likened his travail to the passion of Christ, and his execution brought not regeneration but condemnation to the new regime.[17]

PUBLIC EXECUTIONS CARRIED religious significance for many witnesses. As with Calderón, the spectacle of a suffering sinner on the verge of a painful death could move entire audiences to tears, even if the anesthetic of secularization has dimmed such images for us. Those who worship Juan Soldado today relate the death of the young soldier to the travail of Jesus Christ. They do not know of the passion of Christ from the gospels. Generally, they do not read the Bible; scripture reading is left to the "hallelujahs," the evangelicals, some of whom visit the shrine of Juan Soldado but say they are not devoted to him. Instead, Juan's followers have learned of and in some sense experienced the passion of Christ through their parents, or perhaps a priest, or through icons and statues at home or in church, many of which display a realistic, life-sized crucifix designed to display Christ's sufferings. The Mass itself is a remembrance and celebration of Christ's passion. Most of all, they have come to appreciate Christ's suffering in those magnificent Holy Week processions, massively attended by believers (and undoubtedly a good many nonbelievers) who have come to witness a spectacle such as the one during Semana Santa 2001 in the lovely colonial city of Antigua, Guatemala.

Beautifully embroidered banners carried by *cofradías* (religious brotherhoods and sisterhoods) announce the religious society sponsoring the procession to follow. Members of the brotherhood line each side of the street to hold back the pressing spectators, five or six deep, many of them with family in a festive mood. *Carpetas* (carpets) of local vegetation and flowers molded into intricate designs and images familiar to the populace cover the cobblestone streets over which the procession passes. The floats, heavy wooden platforms shouldered by parishioners of both sexes, first appear in the distance through clouds of copal smoke rising from braziers swung by altar boys in their church attire. Marshals with long, crooked poles raise electric wires crisscrossing the street so that taller floats may pass.

The first float carries the figure of the battered, bleeding Christ, eyes in divine supplication, fallen beneath the weight of the massive cross on which he is soon to be crucified as a common criminal. Lavish arrangements of flowers and fruit from the region decorate this familiar passion scene. Roman soldiers flank the float, jabbing at the statue with their spears, spitting invectives at their pitiful victim. "Why are they doing that to Him?" asks a boy of about three perched on his father's shoulders. "Because they are cruel, and they do not know who He is," answers the parent. Many bless themselves as the float passes, followed by the uniformed *banda,* some twenty musicians playing their ponderously majestic, doleful music recalled over the centuries just for this occasion.

La Dolorosa follows—a life-size statue of grieving Mary—also on a sizable float, borne this time by young women of the parish. Tears streak the Virgin's cheeks, and a sword pierces her heart to signify the pain that she suffers. Again observers bless themselves. Who has not known such sorrow? A mass of worshippers, mostly women dressed in black, many carrying tall, lighted candles, brings up the end of the procession. Spectators disperse and reassemble further along the route to catch still another glimpse of the drama. And then still another. It is as if they do not want the images to disappear, the soulful music to fade. The spectacle inevitably inspires awe. It energizes faith and challenges doubt.

On Good Friday in other Guatemalan locales the horribly bloodied icon of Christ is actually raised on the cross to simulate the crucifixion. Three hours later (after Christ's death), the image is untied from the cross and lovingly lowered, perfumed (with room and underarm spray deodorants), and gently placed in a casket to be borne on the shoulders of local people in a slow, reverential procession throughout the community. In San Andrés Sacabaja, an outlying village in Guatemala's Western Highlands, a living crucifixion (with ropes only, not nails, and not to the death) still takes place. On this holy day young men in the community yearn to play the pain-filled role of Christ.

To many Catholics the passion of Christ is today much more observed, much more meaningful, than is the miraculous ascent into heaven celebrated two days later. They feel closer to God in His down-to-earth suffering than in His heavenly Glory. Here the circumstances of their lives as well as their beliefs are certainly at play. They have discovered in Christ's passion a deeper affinity with humanity as they know it. Thoughts of Calvary pervade their everyday life and ordinary lexicon. In the summer of 2002, for example, when a young girl died of possible medical malfeasance in a Oaxacan hospital, a local newspaper headlined its front page account of the mother's travail: "El Calvario de una madre" (the Calvary of a mother). Readers were meant to understand that phrase as the pain, suffering, injustice, unfairness, and humiliation of the grieving parent. Her plight was to remind them of Christ's agony on the cross.[18] Christian missionaries had planted the seed early in the country's colonial experience.

During the thirteenth and fourteenth centuries in Europe, Dominicans and Franciscans strove to make Christ a living reality, and when they came to the Americas, they did the same among the natives. Missionaries encouraged indigenous peoples whom they sought to convert to empathize with the passion of Christ—to feel, to apprehend, and be moved by the agony of the scourged and belittled prisoner bearing the instrument of his own public execution to Calvary. The missionaries thought that by immersing their acolytes in the sufferings of Christ through plays and pageants, the natives would themselves be moved closer to a mystical union with God, that their natural sympathy for the suffering of a fellow human being would inspire a deeper faith in the divine.

Franciscans especially emphasized the humanity of Christ and concentrated on His excruciating anguish. During a sermon, one Franciscan shed his habit and scourged himself with a heavy iron chain; another walked the fields of his charges barefoot, lugging a huge cross, a cord at his neck and a crown of thorns pressed down upon his head. Painters vied with one another to portray more realistically (or more romantically, appealing to the emotions) the passion and therefore the humanity of Jesus.[19] Their stunning work is still on display, and often venerated, all over Latin America and elsewhere.

It is a long, and perhaps tenuous historical stretch from the early colonial period in Mexico to present-day Tijuana. But cultural traditions, though dynamic and altering over time, can maintain a certain persistence, a tenaciousness which abets their survival. In this case, devotion to Christ with emphasis on the passion has had strong, repetitive reinforcement by Church and family, through images and festivals, poetry and rhetoric. Perhaps such augmentation should be labeled the essence of tradition.

It is this sort of thing—a remembered religious tradition—that one witnessed in midsummer 1999 around Torreón in Mexico's north-central state of Coahuila. A withering drought hounded the region. Livestock died; reservoirs dwindled. More than six thousand people attended a special Mass held in a dried-up river bottom, to ask for relief. Altar boys in the usual Church garb—the long, black gown covered by a white smock—lined a processional route, while in front parishioners in traditional dress shook gourds, waved wands, and danced to an ancestral drumbeat in the supplication of divine help for rain.[20] Likewise, in China since the end of the Cultural Revolution, communities, especially along the south coast, have returned to local religious customs outside of officially sanctioned practices, in long-remembered rites that bring protection and prosperity.[21]

We cannot be sure—we simply do not have sufficient evidence—to assert with any certainty that the spectators who witnessed the execution of Juan Castillo Morales likened it to the painful travails of Jesus Christ. At least some must have sensed the connection—not that in any fashion they thought the soldier divine, but that here was an individual suffering a terrible injustice, if not in relation to the accusations against him, then at least in the prolonged agony and ultimate disgrace in which he died. These days, devotees of Juan Soldado certainly forge just such links. One man says, "The day they shot Juan Soldado, it rained, the sky cried," a reference to the Biblical declaration that the skies darkened as Christ died (Luke 23: 44–45). Another speaks of the execution as "the crucifixion" of the soldier. Others drop additional hints of association: Jesus and Juan, killed by their own people, executed to maintain political order, each fell three times on their way to a ghastly death, both accused common criminals who had actually done nothing wrong; both put to death by the military; scapegoats to satisfy the aims of authority. Unjust, unfair, inhumane, wrongheaded, undeserved; they all add up to grievance and sympathy.

Almost all of the faithful connect the story of Juan Soldado most directly to that of Christ through the concept of martyrdom—not those martyrs of the early Christian church who died for their faith, for their refusal to renounce their belief in Christ as God, but martyrs to justice—those who suffered injustice and died unfairly at the hands of unfettered authority. The mix of circumstance and belief now thickens; the virulent strain of politics along with power, authoritarianism, and arrogance becomes more evident along with those of social imbalance and official corruption. Spirituality, religiosity, piety, and faith are lived within this context.

Mexicans have a popular saying which defines the word *mártir*. When a child has misbehaved, and the mother punishes him or her, and the child protests that the castigation is unfair or unjustified, the mother replies: "No te hagas el mártir"—"Stop pretending you're a martyr," or more directly, "you're no martyr." In other words, "You got what you deserved." When an American tells someone to "Stop being a martyr," it may well refer to a cause that one feels the other has embraced hopelessly, but in Mexico it relates more often to injustice, frequently linked to torture or unwarranted, excessive violence.[22] Today those who venerate Juan Soldado have for the most part declared him innocent of any crime or criminal intentions, and they have created their own versions of what really occurred on the day in 1938 that Olga Camacho was raped and murdered. Unwarranted severity of punishment, especially when a victim is thought to be innocent—even if that assertion of innocence comes after an execution—weighs heavily upon the religious register. "Pity provokes piety. Victims become martyrs, and hence saints, since in the popular mind, these two notions overlap."[23]

Sacred Signs

Now, nearly seventy years after the frightful execution of Juan Castillo Morales, it is difficult to document with much confidence the feelings of spectators and other Tijuanenses who heard and read about the details of the soldier's staged run-for-life. Witnesses remember the event as if it were yesterday—it made that much of an impact—but they were youngsters at the time and can recall few of the sentiments and feelings swarming throughout the community, except that most people thought Castillo Morales guilty. We have seen, however, that doubts existed at the time, and journalists wrote about them. Even today's devotees to Juan Soldado are not explicit about how they or their parents or their grandparents felt about the execution except that it was not justified. Feelings aside, it is known what the curious saw and heard—or say they saw and heard—at the grave site shortly after the execution: blood seeping up through the loosely packed soil that covered the deceased, and the soldier's soul—his ánima—wailing out for justice and vengeance. The faithful are always on the lookout for such signs of God's presence. They are like sentries on a watchtower, anxiously expectant of Christ's promised second coming but also His enduring presence and protection, which is why they respond so enthusiastically to any reports of mysterious spiritual happenings. Moreover, such "signs" are not limited to Christian believers. Popular spiritual practices accompany doctrinal dictates in all faiths, and one great religion may borrow customs from another. When the two slain sons of Saddam Hussein were buried on 3 August 2003 in Iraq, Muslim mourners reported that their remains smelled like perfume, a rose, reminiscent of the "sweet odor of sanctity" said to accompany numerous sainted Christians. Furthermore, although for political reasons the corpses had not been interred for ten days (and were reported by authorities to have badly decomposed), onlookers said the deceased appeared to be asleep; they only had to be awakened, another sign of saintliness for Christians. And akin to the Juan Soldado story, some observers insisted that the sons had died unjustly (they should have been tried in court for alleged crimes) and referred to them as martyrs. For Muslims, "saint" does not carry the same meaning as it does for Christians, and the Qur'an prohibits the worship of saints. Still, a good number of Muslims venerate favorite *walis* (protectors, helpers, benefactors) from whom they ask favors and expect help.[24]

For many, blood carries or conjures up significant religious meaning. For Jews, the blood of the Passover lamb painted on their doors provided for the salvation of the people of God. Christians believe (with varying degrees of intensity) that sins were (are) cleansed by the precious blood of the Lord, hence the redemptive power of blood. Pentecostals sing with unabashed fervor, "There is power, power, wonder-working power in the precious blood of the Lamb." Three or four centuries ago, spectators at public executions swore by the magical curative power of blood shed by repentant criminals. They saw it as a life-giving force which continued to flow after the execution and so scooped it up in a variety of containers for personal use. If a merchant could just catch the blood of a guillotined criminal on his (or her) handkerchief, he was assured a raft of customers in his shop. Crowds at executions also clutched at some of the victim's body parts, especially fingernails and hair, which continue to grow after death. In the maimed body of the executed they did not necessarily see only a by-product of the extravaganza but a possible source of transcendent knowledge or just plain good luck.[25]

When in 1927 Padre Toribio Romo died in defense of the faith during Mexico's Cristero war, which engulfed his remote Jaliscan pueblo of Santa Ana de Guadalupe (pop. 400), parishioners dabbed blood from his mutilated body with cotton swatches preserved to this day in honored remembrance. Their devotion was reinvigorated in May 2000, when the Pope canonized twenty-three martyred priests from the region, among them Father Romo, who is now celebrated along with the others at a flourishing shrine on the outskirts of the revitalized village.[26]

Those who say witnesses saw blood flowing from the grave of Juan Soldado or oozing from the stones which covered it do not speak of any curative properties in the substance, nor do they tie it to sin and salvation. We know not what people said of the matter in 1938, but today those sorts of religious concepts seem to be fading into the past. These more modern spectators interpret stories of the blood only as a sign of God— that God had shed His grace on the fallen soldier. But why this special recognition by the Lord? Because they believe, as taught by the official Church, that in the hierarchy of the heavenly host, martyrs, especially martyrs, but also those who have died unjustly at the hands of other humans, those whose lives have been abruptly and unfairly shortened, sit closest to God. These modern-day martyrs are individuals like Stanley Rother, the liberal-minded Jesuit who was assassinated by the Guatemalan military in 1992 and whose heart, lovingly preserved in a fluid on the altar of the cathedral where he had served, began to bleed profusely soon after his death.[27] Parishioners there understood this as a divine signal, as did those curious, sympathetic, perhaps conscience-stricken but at least concerned individuals and clusters of people who visited the grave site of Juan Castillo Morales that afternoon, or the following day, or surely well within a week of his execution. Doubters said then and do so today that there was no blood or that it was faked, and such skepticism is always an element in these human dramas. As with people who report the appearance of the stigmata, however, it is not a matter of real or fake, an unexplainable mystery or a scientifically proved falsehood, that carries importance, but the meaning and power that these signs possess to move, even transform, people.

Besides, onlookers at the place where Juan died really did see blood, or blood stains, the soldier's blood which had flowed from his riddled body and from his head after he had received the coup de grâce. Likely, a number of visitors thought that blood unjustly shed. At least, spectators at the grave of the fallen soldier were moved, for within hours, or at the most a day or so, they brought flowers to the site and stood blossoms in tin cans filled with water so that the blooms would live for some time after. Someone erected that handmade cross at the head of the grave, and people brought stones, not pebbles but palm-sized stones, which they placed at the site, both to weigh down Juan's restless, troubled soul and to assure him that "We shall not forget." Those stones within weeks grew into an impressive mound. Emotions ran freely and openly, and veneration began. The Juan Soldado devotion was in gestation.

AT THE SAME TIME, Juan's ánima, his soul, remained inconsolable. Visitors said they heard him crying out for justice and vengeance. "I did not do it!" "I am innocent." "Avenge me!" If the soldier yearned for revenge, he also was calling for devotion. Troubled souls need and may request the prayers of the living to help them rest in peace, a common grave site offering that assists the deceased's journey toward eternity.

In the minds of the faithful, ánimas reign just below saints in the heavenly hierarchy, which places them quite close to the Almighty. Yet, as we have seen, ánimas have a mixed reputation among the living. One individual considers them an invaluable assistant in fulfilling one's needs, but another says, "They hang around all the time asking for something. They bother me. I wish they would go away." Some fear that a dissatisfied or unfulfilled ánima can cause misfortune for a person or even terrorize an entire community. But most think ánimas potentially helpful; if you assist them on the road to eternal glory, in gratitude they will ease your earthly pain, or at least pray the Lord to do so.

There are also those ánimas purgando or penando, that is, souls suffering in purgatory or simply wandering aimlessly about, seeking direction toward eternal life. They are frequently depicted in the imagery of the official church as bodies immersed in flames—fire purging their sins. Only their heads can be seen above the fierce blaze, but their faces display no torment, no pain. In fact, these countenances are quite serene, even beautiful and blissful. They are souls with dues to pay but their eventual reward is assured. Hence, they are also ánimas benditas, blessed souls. Prayers by those left behind may induce God's mercy in their behalf.

Animas solas also exist, sad and lonely souls of those who died without family or far from home, and therefore have no one to regale them with prayer. Juan Castillo Morales belonged to this category. While those on earth consider themselves especially obligated to pray for family ánimas, they also display deep reverence for the solas (at times, out of fear), creating special shrines and devotions for them.[28]

One needs to pay attention to souls in pain. Some pray to unknown ánimas who hover in distinct places. A woman in Mexicali regularly offers thanks and solace to an ánima said to inhabit the garbage dump outside of town. She maintains that when she lost a treasured earring, the ánima helped her to find it. In life, the ánima is said to have been a widow who had been abandoned by her sons and forced to work (or rummage) in the city dump, where she foraged for valuables and usable discards which, inadvertently or not, had ended up in the trash. She died scavenging in the garbage pit. Local people must have thought her a good person; perhaps she had uncovered and returned treasured lost items to people.

Whatever her history, she came to be venerated as the Anima of the Garbage Dump, an unfulfilled soul that in return for prayers would help someone to find a lost item, not just in the refuse, but anywhere.[29] Now who could not appreciate an ánima like that?

For many, spirits of the dead hover around places associated with the departed when they lived or where they died. They are sensed by visitors of various faiths at the Anne Frank house and the Dachau prison camp. When innocents die, they cry out for justice: "Undo the wrong"; "Send me [my restless soul] where I belong"; "Justice is the right relationship with God, with one's self and with those around you."[30] Catholic belief in ánimas goes back centuries, and is most prominent along the Mediterranean coast, in Spain, Ireland, England, and in Latin America. In the broadest sense, they are said to be sinful souls suffering in purgatory who need earthly prayers to help pay their penitence and to advance them toward heaven. As all people are in some way sinners, the need for help is extremely widespread. In return for earthly assistance, ánimas intercede before God on behalf of their mortal benefactors. So there is a reciprocal relationship between ánimas and humans, a compelling one that can ameliorate desperation in both directions.

The official Church has not discouraged such exchange, although it insists that rewards from above arrive only through the grace of God and not any revered ánima or saint, whose role is intercessionary, nothing more. A common devotional handbook composed in nineteenth-century Spain, reprinted and used well into the past century, and undoubtedly still consulted in some Spanish towns and villages, lays out the promise of reward for those who pray for the souls in purgatory:

> [The souls] cry out incessantly for their [earthly] benefactors, and the Lord pays attention to them because they are in his grace; and they will cry out even more and will be better heard when they [the deceased] ascend into heaven. And as the favor that is done for them [by humans] by accelerating their progress toward glory is beyond comprehension, so the efficacy with [which] they cry to God for their benefactors is imponderable [cannot be overestimated].

And in the same publication:

> The novena [prayer for an ánima] can be done at any time of the year, and it will be very appropriate to do it *when any special favor is ex-*

pected from the Lord [my emphasis], whether it is for oneself or some-body else; because it is a very efficacious means of putting God in one's debt to make this spiritual alms to His imprisoned and afflicted spouses [ánimas purgando].³¹

With this sort of advice, the Church has no complaint when those in need pray (or seem to pray) *to*, rather than *through*, ánimas or saints such as Juan Soldado. Worshipers at the shrine of Juan in Tijuana say they understand the Church's point of view, but still call Juan himself "muy milagroso," very miraculous, which tends to make the soldier himself the miracle worker. This is only one way in which the faithful constantly rework doctrine to better suit *their* needs for *their* times.

IN TODAY'S COMMON recollection, unsettled ánimas are said to be souls that have left some matter unfinished or promise unfulfilled on earth, hence their uneasiness and clamor for assistance. They need to say good-bye, pay a debt, reveal a secret, or settle a score. Death always leaves tasks undone, so many among the living swear that they have experienced such visitations which are real, explicit, and frequently poignant. Some such retellings have drifted into lore and literature, song and poetry. The most famous among Hispanics concerns La Llorona (the crying woman) whose travail has inspired many versions in diverse locales. Most com-monly, she is said to have been so angered by her husband's infidelity that she drowned their children in a river. In remorseful terror, she tried to find them but could not and died weeping inconsolably on the edge of the stream. Under the circumstances, her deeply saddened ánima cannot rest and relentlessly continues to search for her beloved children. As she wanders, her crying can be heard, not soft sobs but a piercing wail. For some, she has become quite dangerous—or she can be helpful, if per-ceived that way. Parents tell their dawdling children to come inside at night for fear that La Llorona might steal them away as her own. Some see La Llorona as the Angel of Death. She carries the scales of final justice, as does Saint Michael, which makes her a fearsome figure.

Tijuana has its own ánima stories, still repeated, yet unresolved. Best known is that of La Enlutada, the lady in mourning, restlessly searching for her love, or revenge, or simply notoriety. It is said that she was the daughter of a well-known Chinese merchant named Zarco and that around 1930 this beautiful woman wished to marry the man she loved, but her father did not approve of her suitor, and so she lost her desire to live and consigned herself to death. In a state of *artículo mortis* (the moment of death), however, she did marry her beloved and then died. People remember her funeral procession when she rode in an exquisite coach, headed by a young girl dressed as an angel. Women wearing rose- and lily-colored dresses accompanied the cortege. Some carried flowers and others a bow of ribbons, and they buried La Enlutada in Cemetery Number One (the grave site of Juan Soldado). Twenty years passed, but then in 1951 she suddenly reappeared to a taxi driver, also to someone strolling on a street, and two or three times in cabarets. What she said or what she wanted is not stipulated in the tellings, but perhaps we know, for the father who had prevented her marriage and broke her heart died on Christmas Day that year.

But that is not the end of the story. These sorts of legends lodged in supple minds frequently regenerate and mutate. This particular tale took a bizarre turn in 1963 when a local newspaper reported people in town dying mysteriously at night, their faces eaten away to the bone. As reported, it seems that late one night a lady answered a knock on the front door of her residence and encountered the infamous La Enlutada, a phantom woman dressed in black, but whose face was eaten away as if by a hideous disease. The understandably shocked respondent fainted and La Enlutada disap- peared, but news of the incident hurtled through the community, titillat- ing some, frightening others. Other late-night knocks on the door fol- lowed, but the unwelcome visitors soon became two women, and then two women and a man, all with repulsively disfigured faces.

Police discounted the sightings and death reports until one night the pregnant wife of the commandant himself was approached by the ghostly trio and promptly swooned, but apparently did not lose her baby. Now authorities launched an intensive investigation and soon discovered that three inmates—two women and a man—had recently escaped from a leprosarium (actually a forsaken mental hospital) tucked into the rugged La Rumorosa mountains above Mexicali. Authorities quickly appre- hended the suspects, who explained that they were desperately hungry (being ill-fed at the asylum) but ashamed of their appearance, so they knocked on doors at night to beg for food which they ate during the day. How the story concluded is not known, but these matters never end. Reappearances occur. Like that of her counterpart, La Llorona, it is doubtful that the ánima of La Enlutada will ever rest in peace. People may fear, but also need their ghosts.[32]

Also known to Tijuanenses is the ánima of a ballerina who danced at Agua Caliente when the place was in its prime in 1930. She was murdered there by a General Layata and for some time was said to be wandering around bungalows at the plush resort seeking justice. Her ánima has not made its presence known since, but its appearance would not be unexpected.[33]

JUAN SOLDADO'S ANGUISHED ánima was no less insistent around his grave following the execution. Many believe that one's ánima does not depart the site of death for three days, so it makes sense to them that Juan's restless soul could have been heard from at the time. According to one avid devotee of the soldier, Señora Delfina Suárez, who is eighty-eight years old and lives just outside the town of Magdalena, in Mexico's northern state of Sonora, Juan's ánima urged the army captain who she claims had raped and murdered little Olga to turn himself in and to confess his crime:

> Juan appeared to the captain on a back road outside of Tijuana and said, "Señor Captain, I am innocent." But the captain, who was married and also had a lady lover, ignored him.
>
> "Captain, why do you not recognize me?" Juan persisted. "I am Juan Soldado."
>
> In response, the captain walked faster, trying to escape his accuser and soon was headed for a high precipice at the end of the road. As he was about to tumble into the abyss, Juan pulled the captain to safety, and more forcefully declared: "I am Juan Soldado!"
>
> The captain broke down, surrendered to the truth, and returned to town where he confessed the crime to his lover. He then committed suicide.

Delfina said that the captain's lover had told her that story, which parallels many others that implicate one of Juan's superior officers in the death of Olga Camacho.[34] Such tellings are inevitably shaped and shaded by ways in which the devotees have experienced life.

Mexicans, in general, have little confidence or trust in their government or its judicial arm, the result of centuries of official corruption and abuse. In the public mind, explanations of untoward events frequently allege government complicity or conspiracy, so it is not surprising that those who worship Juan Soldado as a saint insist that he was the victim of a military conspiracy, that Juan Castillo Morales had nothing to do with the ghastly rape and murder of Olga Camacho but that an officer in his army unit committed the crime and framed Juan to take the blame. At least, that is what his followers say today in a kaleidoscopic tale of ever-changing detail. In one common version a captain did the deed and then handed Castillo Morales a package containing the little girl's bloody clothing, telling him to get rid of it. Juan did so, but some of the blood got on his uniform, which explains how the spots found on his clothing later implicated him. Some say that no blood appeared on Juan's uniform, but only an apron he was wearing while cutting up some chickens for dinner —it was chicken blood, not human blood on the clothing, but the appearance of any blood on his person or clothing gave Juan's superiors the opportunity to accuse him of the crime. This captain, often identified as Juan's commanding officer, emerges as the bête noir in many versions of the story. One has it that the young soldier happened upon his superior as the officer was raping the girl and that Juan tried to help the victim. Her assailant ran off, and Juan carried the ravaged child to a hospital where she died. In transporting the girl, his uniform became stained with her blood, a detail that the officer quickly used to frame the enlisted man with rape and murder. Another insists that the officer had killed others and that "it was well-known that he had murdered Olga Camacho, but he placed the blame on Juan and took him to a place near the cemetery where the police and soldiers frequently administered the Ley Fuga."[35]

In another telling, it was Juan's fellow soldiers who did him in. His comrades had raped and murdered Olga, and when they came across Juan who had fallen asleep, they placed the girl's bloody clothing next to him. Then they fingered Juan as the assailant and told authorities where they could find him along with the girl's garments.

Still another variant maintains that Juan as part of his military duties customarily carried bags of refuse to a dump outside the headquarters, and that the guilty captain slipped the broken body of the young girl into a bag and ordered Juan to dispose of it. Then the captain informed others that Juan had something more than refuse in one of the bags, and investigators then discovered Olga's corpse in one of the sacks which Juan had been toting, leading to the soldier's arrest and conviction. This story not only explains the crime but develops the character of the fallen soldier: Juan was a good soldier, obedient to superiors, and willing to perform the most menial duties. One version insists that when the captain committed the crime, he ordered Juan Castillo Morales to take the blame, and Juan did so out of military duty.

Some do not connect Juan to the time period of Olga's murder at all. Instead, he is seen as a soldier who came to Tijuana as a Villista (a follower of Pancho Villa) during the Mexican Revolution more than a score of years before the troubles surrounding the Camacho death. When the Villistas rode into town (in reality, none ever did so), rioting and looting followed. Officers took from the rich, even their well-off sympathizers, and kept the booty for themselves. Ordinary soldiers joined the pillage, but superiors forced them to surrender the rewards to those with commissions. One common soldier protested: Juan Soldado. He unabashedly stole from the wealthy but gave the proceeds to the poor, and at the same time, berated his low-rank comrades for turning stolen goods over to their superiors. When the officers learned of Juan's activities, they accused him of being a traitor to their patriotic cause and had him executed. Townspeople, however, recognized Juan as a good soldier and kindly human, unjustly killed, and so began to venerate him as a saint who helped the poor.[36]

The lurid and incomprehensible inevitably creeps into the imaginative reconstruction of sensational stories such as that surrounding Juan Soldado. María Díaz was a teenager in Tijuana when the troubles erupted there in 1938. At the time she heard that Olga Camacho was the daughter of Feliza by a previous marriage, and that General Contreras, who commanded the local military garrison, considered Feliza his novia, his sweetheart. But when he pressed her to marry him, she turned to another suitor. In revenge, the officer ordered Castillo Morales to kidnap Olga on her way to market and to bring the child to him. Juan obeyed his superior, who then gagged and killed the child. Ordered to dispose of the body, the soldier tossed her over a fence. A witness saw the act but could not identify the perpetrator, only that the man involved had blood on his shirt. By radio, the public was urged to look for an individual with a bloody shirt. Juan's common-law wife saw him changing his stained shirt and notified police. Arrest, trial, and execution followed.[37]

The María Díaz account is fantasy, dredged up in fragments and stitched together by hearsay. Yet, to this day Feliza Camacho believes that two people were involved in the rape and murder of her daughter— certainly Juan Castillo Morales, the soldier leaning on the fence whom she questioned near the crime site, but also an accomplice, quite possibly his superior officer. How else can the second set of footprints at the scene be explained? (No other source mentions a second set of footprints.) For her, Juan kidnapped the girl and hurled her over the fence to his accomplice. Then they both took her to the shed where the rape and murder occurred. She does not know the eventual fate of Juan's confederate, but at the time he went free.[38]

All of these stories emanate from a patchwork of tradition, lore, lived experience, and personal predilection. Like all such accounts, they breathe; they change in content and emphasis. But they are not willy-nilly inventions meant to justify a devotion. Better said, they are explanations of why these devotees of Juan Soldado think and act as they do over time, how the travail of the soldier resonates with their own lives and aspirations, and how a despicable criminal can become a revered saint.

7. Criminals and Saints

A s with all explanations concerning religious practices, thoughts, and sensibilities, generalities do not notably clarify how or why criminals (or purported criminals) become saints. Most have been canonized by the people, as opposed to the Church, although the latter has scrubbed clean the personal histories of a good many of its own saints to insure that they meet its standards of virtue. The masses have also done their share to soak their saints in admirable human qualities, and Juan Soldado is no exception. Dissonance occurs because those who are labeled criminals by the state are often considered heroes by the people, or they are seen as criminals unjustly convicted by officialdom, or wrongdoers cruelly mistreated and spitefully punished by government. Popular canonizations which stem from these sorts of circumstances seethe with political recrimination and retaliation. A marvelous example comes to us from the verities of great literature, in this case *The Bridge on the Drina,* by the Nobel Prize winner Ivo Andrić, which claims historical accuracy surrounding the building of the infamous bridge itself. Novelists such as Andrić can chronicle culture in ways that elude most historians. As a Bosnian himself, here he penetrates the soul of his people.

As the Ottoman Turks solidified their control over Bosnia in the second half of the sixteenth century, they sought to improve communications by building a bridge over the Drina River at the town of Visegrad. The Turks, of course, pressed local peasants into the workforce needed to construct the bridge. But Slavs of the region saw that such a structure would serve the Turks more than their own interests and so conspired to sabotage the construction. At night, stone revetments erected during the day suddenly collapsed, and the peasants explained to their masters that a river fairy who did not want the bridge was destroying it.

The Turks were furious and prepared a trap for any human who under the cover of darkness might try to destroy the bridge. Pieces of the scheme fell into place, and they soon had a peasant named Radisav in their grasp. Harsh interrogation followed. Radisav protested his innocence, but finally conceded, "Well, I am in your hands. Do with me what you like."

"You will soon find out what we like," the official replied.

The guards took away the chains [holding the prisoner] and stripped the peasant to the buff. They threw the chains into the heart of the fire and waited. As the chains were covered with soot, their hands were blackened and great patches were left on themselves and the half-naked peasant. When the chains were almost red hot, Merdjan the Gipsy came up and took one end of them in a long pair of tongs, while one of the guards took the other end. . . .

The men brought the chains and wrapped them round the peasant's broad hairy chest. The scorched hair began to sizzle. His mouth contracted, the veins in his neck swelled, his ribs seemed to stand out and his stomach muscles to contract and relax as when a man vomits. He groaned in pain, strained at the ropes which bound him and writhed and twisted in vain to lessen the contact of his body with the red hot iron. His eyes closed and the tears flowed down his cheeks. They took the chain away.

Torture had not loosened the peasant's tongue; further interrogation seemed futile, so the officer in charge ordered that the prisoner "should be impaled alive on the outermost part of the construction work [the bridge] at its highest point, so that the whole town and all the workers should be able to see him from the banks of the river." A town crier announced the execution, and the whole male population of the town, children to old men, assembled to witness it.

The people stood on tiptoe to see the man who had hatched the plot and destroyed the building work. They were all astonished at the poor miserable appearance of the man they had imagined to be quite different [more learned, perhaps, or heroic]. . . . Therefore he seemed to all those there too wretched and too insignificant to have done the deed which now brought him to execution. [In other words, the people had declared him an innocent scapegoat.] Only the long white stake [the impalement stake which he carried on his shoulders] gave a sort of gruesome grandeur to the scene and kept everyone's eyes fixed on it.

The victim was forced to the ground, face down.

[The gipsy] placed the stake on two wooden chocks so that it pointed between the peasant's legs. . . . [He] took the wooden mallet and with measured blows began to strike the lower blunt end of the stake. . . . The body of the peasant writhed convulsively; at each blow of the mallet his spine twisted and bent. . . . At every second blow the gipsy went over to the stretched-out body and leant over it to see whether the stake was going in at the right direction and when he had satisfied himself that it had not touched any of the more important internal organs, he returned and went on with his work . . . He struck a few more times until the [iron-shod] point of the stake reached level with the right ear. The man was impaled on the stake as a lamb on the spit, only that the tip did not come through the mouth but in the back and had not seriously damaged the intestines, the heart, or the lungs. . . .

A murmur and a wave of movement passed through the onlookers on the banks [of the river]. Some lowered their eyes and others went quickly home without turning their heads. But the majority looked dumbly at this human likeness, up there in space, unnaturally stiff and upright.

"Turks, Turks, . . ." moaned the man on the stake, "Turks on the bridge . . . may you die like dogs . . . like dogs."

All those who had been present at the execution of the sentence spread terrible reports through the town and surrounding villages. An indescribable fear gripped the townsmen and the workers. Slowly and gradually a full consciousness of what had happened in their midst in the course of a short November day came home to them. All conversation centered on the man who, high up there on the scaffolding, was still alive on the stake.

The next day, Radisav died.

Now they [the townspeople] looked more boldly up at the scaffolding and the man who had been condemned. . . . They halted for a moment to spit on their palms and say to each other in hushed voices:

"May God pardon him and have mercy on him!"

"Ah, the martyr! It is hard for such as we!"

"Don't you see that he has become a *saint*."[1] (my emphasis)

Such spontaneous popular canonizations sparked by perceived injustice run through the entire history of the Catholic world, from the earliest martyrs through Juan Soldado to the present. Their essence lies in the human condition and the story of Jesus Christ being reworked, albeit with varied details and different motives, over and over again. But matters of justice—or more simply said, fairness—while powerful and strident, have not been the sole forces behind such canonizations. That of Radisav, for example, undoubtedly also carried political implications: his Serb countrymen (for the most part) hated the imperialistic Turks and their pretensions, which made their hideous treatment of one of their own even more odious to spectators. Recall that circumstances as well as belief play into canonizations, whether by the people or the Church.

Criminals as Saints

Criminals thought to be guilty but repentant have also been declared saints by the populace. Remember that the blood and bodies of executed criminals often carried religious significance for spectators at public executions. Such figures were seen as different from ordinary mortals and as kinds of martyrs, closer to God. Therefore, their ánimas carried a special import—these were souls most in need of prayer and in grateful return would more fervently represent human needs to the Almighty.

A special devotion to the ánimas of criminals who had lost their heads to the guillotine emerged several centuries ago in Palermo, Sicily, and a church on what was then the outskirts of town became a pilgrimage site dedicated to their memory. Although executed criminals who had enjoyed higher social status in life were often buried with much pomp in private cemeteries, the repentant convict unclaimed by friends or kin might well have ended up in the graveyard behind the Church of the Beheaded Ones. In life, these venerated individuals may have been brutally violent, but before execution they asked the pardon of their victims and God and renounced untoward violence in all its forms. Spectators remembered and embraced the Biblical dictum: "There will be more joy in heaven over one sinner who repents than over ninety-nine just persons who need no repentance" (Luke 15:7). Hence, the living saw the ánimas of these repentant convicts as close to God and so as protectors against robbers and other dangers. But like all such ánimas and saints, the *decollati* (beheaded ones) did not specialize in only one type of assistance. People who claimed to hear the lamentations of the decollati went to pray for health, material help, relief from misfortune, jobs, luck in the lottery, and love:

> Souls of the beheaded bodies,
> Three hanged, three slain, and three drowned,
> All nine of you join,
> Go into my sweetheart,
> Give him such and such [torments]
> Not to make him die
> But make him come to me.

And as all such popular religion is saturated with other sorts of traditional belief, the petitioners turned to long-held customs for hints of a reply to their prayers:

> Among good auguries are the crow of a cock, the bark of a dog, a whistle, the sound of a guitar or of bells, a song (especially a love song), a knocking on a neighbour's door, the rapid shutting of a window, and the rapid passing of a carriage. On the other hand the mew of a cat is a fatal augury for relatives who are travelling. The bray of an ass, a dispute, the sound of weeping or lamentation, and that of water flung into the road are all evil omens. The chance words overheard from passers-by are also very important, and inferences good or bad are drawn from them.[2]

Although much of Western society has lost or rejected such close connections between mystical signs and the everyday world and belittles such belief as superstition, the majority of mankind still finds wonder and meaning in the echoes of life circling and embracing them. The ambiance at the Church of the Beheaded Ones in Palermo resembles in many ways that now found at the Juan Soldado shrine in Tijuana: the expressive votive drawings, called ex-votos; the faithful at prayer with their rosaries; a petitioner scraping across unforgiving terrain on bloodied knees; the representations of body parts, limbs cured or in need of healing (although in Palermo one sees much larger wax imitations as compared with the mainly small, tin representations in Tijuana); and the myriad ways of giving thanks for miracles received. One major difference, however, concerns the attitude of the Church toward these devotions. In Italy, the Church approves of the cult, not so much to honor the delinquents but their repentance, which is so joyously received in Heaven.

Today not much of the Decollati sanctuary remains, only a side chapel in the main local church, which is overshadowed by modern buildings. A painting of a saint about to be beheaded hangs over a small altar in the chapel, and beneath the altar is a typical depiction of ánimas purgando, souls being purified in a sea of flames. A block away, however, there is a pillar to which a brass plaque is attached. A tortured man, hands bound, hangs by his neck from a gallows depicted in the middle of the plaque. Above the plaque, devotees still place lighted votive candles and the season's flowers.[3] For many Christians (especially fundamentalists) repentance remains the key to salvation.

REPENTANCE MOREOVER CAME (and comes) in many hues. The frenzy of devotion exhibited by Rodrigo Calderón, the fallen Spanish courtier, is but one. As the horses were pulling Damiens apart limb by limb, his confessors approached him for the condemned man's final words. "Kiss me, gentlemen," he said in asking their absolution. Then on 22 March 1760 a French royal guardsman named Jean Corbelet was broken on the wheel for killing a fellow soldier. When strapped to the wheel, he urged the huge crowd witnessing the spectacle to join him in singing the Salve Regina. "At the end of the first verse [sung by the condemned man] the public sang the second, then the condemned man the third, and so on to the end." As the hideous torture continued, Corbelet sang other holy songs with the spectators and asked their forgiveness. Then his voice faded into death.[4]

Not all acts of contrition, however, evidenced such ostentation. Most, in fact, did not, but still could lead to sympathy and popular veneration. In 1969 a thirty-seven-year-old Peruvian, Victor Apaza, murdered his wife, whom he thought unfaithful to him. Two years later, a court sentenced him to death, and shortly thereafter he was executed. Many thought the penalty unduly harsh (normally such cases drew twenty-five years in prison) and politically motivated by internal disputes within the government. Hence, the cry of injustice arose. Also Apaza was said to have been an exemplary prisoner the two years he was held before his execution. While in prison he had worked as an artisan, creatively making children's toys and teaching other inmates to do the same. He also had run a small cafeteria from which he earned a minor income, money that he used to buy materials for making his toys, as well as to support his children and assist the truly destitute in jail with him. After a period of heavy drinking and family abuse, he had converted to Protestant evangelicalism, and while imprisoned studiously read the Bible with other convicts, but evidently at death returned to Catholicism. People called him a "good man," and buried him with much emotion in the public cemetery of his hometown, Arequipa. Flowers and candles soon appeared at the site, then *peticiones* and prayers for relief and favors. Men, women, children, mostly poor, began to speak of the deceased as "muy milagroso" and of favors received from him. Popular canonization followed. To his followers, even those who believed him guilty of murder, Victor Apaza had proved himself to be a "good" person unjustly executed —the harshness of punishment had far outweighed the passion of his crime; therefore, God had vindicated this humble man and responded to his pleas on behalf of those like him on earth.[5] Similarities with the sanctification of Juan Soldado are evident.

WHO KNOWS WHETHER or not Juan Castillo Morales repented at the hour of his death? Only God, for certain. Today few followers mention repentance as the reason for their devotion. Those who do, pray to Juan as an ánima purgando. If he did commit the crime (and a handful of devotees still insist that he did), no one is in more need of prayer than Juan Soldado, and no one would be more grateful for prayers received or more willing to ask the Lord for favors on behalf of his benefactors. When asked how they know that Juan repented, these people simply reply, "How do you know that he did not?" Even if he did not openly, loudly, and clearly, ask forgiveness at the execution, they note that the soldier's ánima (as do all souls) hovered about the grave site for three or four days after his death, and that repentance most likely occurred during that period.

Actually, nothing is known about Juan's religious beliefs, or if he had any at all. At birth, like most children born in Mexico, he probably would have been registered in the Catholic Church in his hometown, Ixtáltepec in the southern state of Oaxaca, but whether or not he practiced Catholic rituals, participated in church functions, or felt close to God, is unknown. Some of the pious say that when about to be shot, he told his military escort, "When I die, ask God to help people to see that I am innocent," which acknowledges a belief in God, His interventionist powers, and insistence upon justice, but it is not repentance, the acknowledgment of guilt and a plea for forgiveness. And his pitiful cries for mercy at the moment of death seem more directed at his executioners than to the divine.

In the case of Juan Soldado, repentance as a stimulus to devotion seems to have faded over time. At the time of the execution, many who came to venerate him said they did so because of his repentance, much as occurred in Sicily with the cult of the beheaded. But as has occurred among many Roman Catholics everywhere, concepts of Purgatory, salvation, and repentance have lost substantial meaning with believers and dimmed into obscurity. On their deathbed, some may solicit God's grace, but the fiery admonition to repent or go to Hell has all but disappeared. Animas purgando has come to mean souls in a sort of limbo, floating about awaiting the call to their reward but not suffering at any way-stop called Purgatory. How rapidly culture adjusts and alters, especially in the vigorous swirl of a fast-growing border city like Tijuana. Rather than stress the need for repentance, those devoted to Juan now explain that "We are all sinners; we all make mistakes; that is to be expected as part of life." For them, God, as always, intervenes in their everyday activities ("si Diós quiere"), but these days is seen as much less fearsome and punishing, more loving, understanding, and comforting, even if still awesome and distant and better approached through His saints.

Saints

Saints provide a connection between heaven and earth. Saints are venerated not because they are different from us, but because they are like us. They are compassionate, humorous, boisterous, forgetful, sometimes uncooperative, capable of revenge, consoling, mysterious, imperfect, and unpredictable. God is glorious, but remote, while saints are family. A saint could be a neighbor, a teacher, a derelict, or a homeless person. At heart, saints are human. That the Almighty is omnipresent and interventionist is at the core of Christian thought, but miracles abetted by saints prove the point in concrete form.

Some still think of saints as extraordinarily virtuous people, which remains the official position of the Church, but in our times human foibles are viewed as understandable, and good works are recognized despite personal shortcomings. There is no one typology which embraces all saints. Instead, saints tend to reflect the politics, social realities, and transcendent religious aspirations in which they developed and became admired. The faithful expect their otherworldly saints to respond to the needs of contemporary times.

IN THE EARLY days of Christianity, when Roman authorities saw such worship as treason against the state, martyrs to the faith became the first saints, canonized by local people who knew them best and in many instances had witnessed their martyrdom. Those left behind wished to remember and venerate their heroic comrades, and to ask their intercession for favors from the Almighty. As these popular canonizations flourished—and not all necessarily resulted from martyrdom—clerics sought to impose discipline on the process, which spawned the tension between official and popular canonizations which exists today. Bishops claimed the right to veto certain canonizations or to postulate as saints individuals not venerated by the general populace. Power was clearly at issue here, but common people persisted in proclaiming sainthood for those who best served their needs—reputed miracle workers with proven results. As the hierarchy of the Roman Catholic Church grew and strengthened, it increasingly demanded control over canonizations. It set standards and bureaucratized sanctification; by the thirteenth century the Pope himself orchestrated the process. The laity listened, willingly venerated the official saints, but never abandoned its prerogative to choose its own saints outside of official sanction, and often surreptitiously. As happens today at the Juan Soldado shrine, the faithful prayed to a scattering of santos, those who responded to their pleadings, some of them of highest standing within the Church, others who were ignored, disapproved, or disdained by that same authority.

But just who deserved canonization? Over time, ideas about saintliness changed. At first considering saints as models of virtue crowned by martyrdom (at the bloody hands of an executioner or through a self-imposed prolonged ascetic life), by the fourteenth century people demanded miracles of their saints with whom they had become more personal and practical. They understood (or claimed to believe) that power and gifts came only from God, but saints had influence with the Almighty, and when miracles resulted, spontaneously or through prayer, saints would be rewarded with devotion by grateful mortals. It was always known that ánimas purgando needed prayers to move beyond purgatory, but saints too seemed to crave adoration.

In its determination to make canonization an institutional monopoly, the Church has instituted a series of guidelines, which it manipulates or ignores to suit current circumstances. Fundamentally, it has always required virtue and miracles of its candidates, but life histories have been cleansed, embellished, and fabricated, and miracle requirements have now been reduced from three to one. Moreover, the famous devil's advocate, whose role it was to strenuously challenge the credentials of proposed saints, has been eliminated from the proceeding. So the Church is now in free fall in its appointment process, balking on cases deemed politically sensitive (like that of the martyred Salvadoran archbishop Oscar Arnulfo Romero), while promoting others—hundreds of others—in places where the religion may be losing its hold (such as Mexico). Even the laity (at least in the United States) complains about the institution's tendency to limit considerations to relatively unknown priests and obscure members of orders, while ignoring those noted for good works which have had significant social meaning in today's world.[6]

The outcry has been quite strident. One set of "daily reflections on saints" argues:

> We need saints who combine charity with a prophetic thirst for justice . . . .

> We need saints immersed in worlds of art, literature, scholarship, political struggle and in everyday life.

> We need prophets who challenge the Church as well as the world to better reflect the justice and mercy of God.[7]

A good many demand that declarations of sainthood return to the vox populi, as in the early days of Christianity. Then the entire Christian community, if it so chose, could proclaim as saints the likes of Mahatma Gandhi or Albert Schweitzer or Father Mychal Judge, who died attending to firefighters at the World Trade Center on 9/11. To date the Church has turned a deaf ear toward such appeals. It seems not to recognize that its saints were never perfect people, that saints have always been part of a tradition of imperfect people. Meanwhile, those who consider themselves

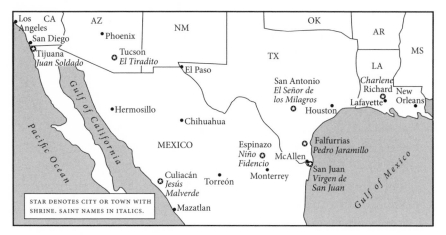

Map 3. Popular Saints Along the U.S. Mexico Border.

to be good Catholics (and not such good Catholics) continue to canonize their own saints.

Popular Saints

No one knows how many saints exist. In 1989 the most authoritative source ran to eighteen volumes and listed more than ten thousand names, perhaps six hundred of them canonized by popes.[8] The present Pope, John Paul II, has well more than three hundred canonizations to his credit, a papal record. But as local communities continue to consecrate their own saints, no one dares estimate how many exist today. We have already met a number of these unofficial saints flourishing today along or reasonably near the U.S.-Mexico border: El Tiradito in Tucson, Sinaloa's Jesús Malverde, and, of course, Juan Soldado in Tijuana. Pedro Jaramillo, a recluse in life, is venerated as a miracle worker in south Texas, as is a teenage girl, Charlene, in Cajun country outside Lafayette, Louisiana, and pilgrimages attract thousands to the Niño Fidencio healing shrine near Monterrey in northeastern Mexico. Each devotion has emerged from its own legend, constantly stirred and thickened by its followers and sampled by the curious and mystified. As with all life stories, aspects have their apparent similarities and detailed differences, all spiced by human idiosyncrasies.

Most saints do not have written biographies. Among those who do, normally prepared under the auspices of the Church, their histories have been found cleansed of negatives and embroidered with exaggerations, inventions, unwarranted assertions, and adulatory fluff, which says much more about the authors and their times (most were written well after the saint's death) than the personality under review. In a good many instances, substantial one-upmanship was involved, as the biographers sought to make *their* subject more admirable than others. Scholars have made a career of picking these writings apart. So we know there are at least a few saints, among many more admirable and even heroic types, who led profligate early lives, thoroughly enjoyed earthly pleasures, never possessed the virtues claimed for them, and may or may not have produced the miracles credited to them.

Some saints probably never lived, but drifted into existence through legends and human creativity. Among the most fascinating of them is a greyhound named Guinefort. The parents of a child in a thirteenth-century French village had left their baby in the care of the family dog while they did some errands. When a serpent threatened the child, the dog killed it, splattering the tot with the snake's blood. The mother and father returned to see their loved one covered with blood and presumed the dog had attacked the baby. So in a rage they threw the dog down a well where it died. However, the animal's innocence was soon established, and it was given a decent burial. Recognizing that the dog had suffered an unjust death, and drawing upon legends of the region, local peasants began to venerate the canine, now regarded as Saint Guinefort. Pilgrimages ensued to the site, from which miracles soon flowed.[9]

No such animal-saints seem to have been worshiped within Christian concepts along the U.S.-Mexico border; however, El Tiradito and probably Jesús Malverde never lived as human beings, but appeared out of tradition and necessity. Located in the old quarter of downtown Tucson, the Tiradito shrine might well have disappeared had not Mexican-Americans interested in preserving their traditions rescued it from the ambitions of redevelopers, and subsequently the city's Chamber of Commerce claimed it as a tourist attraction. Stories of its origin vary in detail, but as we might remember, they revolved around the revenge of an outraged husband over a sexual dalliance between his wife and a younger man, perhaps his son. Mexican lore is replete with such plot lines, especially in those wondrous corridos, peculiarly Mexican popular songs that so often begin with triumphant yelps and end in heartbreaking grief.

In one version of the Tiradito story set in the latter 1800s, the cuck-olded husband catches a philandering railroad worker with his wife and chops the young lover to pieces, scattering his limbs along the rail line, giving another twist to the nickname El Tiradito, or the little castaway. Others prefer the tale of the infuriated husband who killed his wife's paramour with an ax in Tucson and then fled to Mexico. Some make the young suitor a gambler who wandered into town, seduced the wife, and was shot by the husband. Another, which confirms the possible inventiveness of popular religion, occurs at a wedding ceremony, where the rejected suitor of the bride storms into the ceremony, threatens to kill his love, and is accosted by the groom. The melee is broken up by guests, but then townspeople arrive with the blood-stained body of the only priest in town, who was to perform the wedding ceremony, presumably stabbed to death by the crazed suitor. A shrine developed where the priest had fallen.

Even more detailed stories about the origins of the devotion have been spun by the faithful. One brings a somewhat mysterious, handsome young traveler to old Tucson, who stares at an adobe home which formerly belonged to him. Through a window, he sees a couple eating their evening meal. The woman had been his wife; the man appeared to be her new husband. Five years earlier the traveler had been called to Mexico to tend to his gravely ill mother, but now he had returned to reclaim his wife and home. When the woman came to the well in the yard for water, the traveler presented himself. "I thought you dead," she said, and they embraced. Wondering what was keeping his wife, the second husband investigated, found his woman in the arms of another, and plunged a knife into the traveler's chest. Men of the barrio buried the unfortunate victim, and a devotion began at the spot.

Whatever the legend surrounding the shrine—and there are many more marvelous tales being told about its origins—the devotion which began there perhaps a century ago tapped deeply into familiar Hispanic tradition. There was blood at the site; the unsavory, sudden death of an all-too-human person; issues of justice and injustice, of burial in sacred ground; pleas of the sinner for forgiveness. Gradually flowers and candles began to appear at the site deemed to be his grave, and there were reports of miracles: soldiers who returned from the Vietnam conflict unscathed because of prayers to El Tiradito, and a woman who says, "El Tiradito saved the house I was born in from becoming a freeway."

In 1971 the proposed Butterfield Freeway, state planned and federally financed, was to run right through the shrine of El Tiradito. Barrio residents protested, formed preservation committees, and finally had the shrine declared a national monument, which protected it against federally funded intrusions. Now there is an El Tiradito Foundation, which maintains the spot and sponsors events to propagate its remembrance. Still, the tradition may be fading as the barrio around it gentrifies. When I last visited the site in 1999, a few votive candles burned, but there were no written petitions asking favors, no material items expressing thanks for miracles received. No one from among the faithful was present. While evidence exists of the religious belief which generated (or at least developed) the devotion, the local circumstances that prompted and preserved it have yet to be investigated.[10]

By contrast, devotion to Jesús Malverde flourishes, borne by his reputation as the protector saint of drug dealers (*narcotraficantes*), which, of course, spreads his influence everywhere. It is said that he can make cocaine smugglers invisible, protect kingpins of the drug mafia from rivals, and guarantee a good crop of opium poppies and marijuana buds in the mountain-shielded growing fields above his shrine. U.S. drug enforcers frequently find Malverde medallions hanging around the necks of traffickers or on the rearview mirrors of their cars.

Malverde's fame, however, runs far beyond drug matters; his followers assure that he miraculously fulfills a variety of their requests for health, jobs, marriage partners, trucks, safe journey, homes, release from jail, and family reunions. Petitioners write: "Thank you, Malverde, for saving me from drugs," and "Thank you, Malverde, for not having to lose my arm and leg." Another one pleads:

> Dear holy and miraculous Malverde, I am writing this letter so that you'll help me with a problem I have with some friends I had, so that they won't look for me any more. Make them forget the problems we had. Make them please leave my parents and my sister and me in peace. This is what I ask of you, Malverde, that you do this favor. I promise you that when I go to Sinaloa, I'll go visit you, and I'll bring you what I can because I live in Los Angeles, California, Malverde. Your son, Angel Córtez. 15 Sept. 1992.[11]

Of course, drug dealers do not normally identify themselves as such in the shrines of such santos, but in most ways, Malverde is a typical popular santo, discounted by the Church but revered by his petitioners, and like El Tiradito, he probably never walked the earth.

Malverde (a nickname which could mean "camouflaged by banana leaves") seems to have sprung from traditions forged by famous Mexican bandits such as Jesús Arriaga (Chucho el Roto), Heraclio Bernal (the Thunderbolt of Sinaloa), and Santañón in the latter part of the nineteenth century, when the public at large seemed to appreciate the jibes that haughty bandits made at the Porfirian dictatorship then in power. All lived, were granted some Robin Hood–type qualities by their admirers, but were most appreciated for their hair-raising escapes from authorities before their eventual capture, thanks to betrayal by a gang member. Newspapers gleefully reported their escapades, but no such documentation exists for Malverde, whose real name might have been Jesús Juárez Mazo according to some novelists and historical investigators. In his heyday, Malverde is said to have been a brigand who robbed the rich to serve the poor. Police seriously wounded him in a shootout near the state capital at Culiacán, and he retreated for recovery to the surrounding mountains, but gangrene set in and death approached. As a final noble gesture, however, Malverde had a comrade turn him in to police so that the companion could collect the reward on the bandit's head and distribute it to the needy. The governor was pleased to get his tormentor and promptly had him hanged from a tree on the outskirts of town. As already noted, the legend is that the governor also refused to allow the body to be buried—but even folklore does not reveal whether or not Malverde's accomplice ever received his reward. It is not known precisely what triggered the devotion; those circumstances remain unstudied. It could have been the cruelty of punishment or denial of burial in sacred ground. Or did his reputation as a generous bandit precede him to the grave?

In the late 1970s Sinaloa's government designed a new state house to be built on the site occupied by Malverde's grave. As the bulldozers went to work, hundreds, perhaps thousands, of the santo's followers protested. They could not prevent the project from going forward as devotees of El Tiradito did in Tucson, but they exacted an agreement from the governor to dedicate a nearby vacant lot to the shrine and another space in the vicinity to the grave itself, including the mound of stones covering it. The struggle over the shrine attracted widespread media attention, which generated new interest in (and devotion to) the saint, depicted in his images as a handsome, neatly groomed young man, at times wearing a black fedora. At the same time, in mountains throughout the region the military engaged in the ferocious Operation Condor, rooting out marijuana and opium plant growers, frequently humble farmers, and uncovering narcotics dealers, petty and otherwise. It is said that at this juncture Malverde became revered as the patron saint of drug traffickers.[12] Here is an example of how changed circumstances revise needs and can alter the character and reputation of a local saint. Juan Soldado underwent a similar transformation.

UNLIKE JESÚS MALVERDE and El Tiradito, whose worldly existence is doubtful, El Niño Fidencio thrived as a faith healer, renowned throughout a vast region of the United States and Mexico during the first third of the twentieth century. While recorded details of his early life are sketchy, extraordinary photographs, many of them reproduced as picture postcards, confirm his role as a healer. One such photo shows him cutting five feet off the floor-length hair of a young girl, who gave up her beautiful hair in thanks for a cure received.

His name was José Fidencio Síntora Constantio, born in November 1898 into a large family but orphaned by age ten. As a youth he drifted into various locales and worked as a miner, a field hand, and a ship's cook until settling down at the age of twenty-three on an hacienda called Espinazo, which his uncle managed, outside the industrial city of Monterrey. Family and neighbors were the first to experience his healing powers, which he insisted had come from God. He claimed to have been given his mission by the Holy Spirit under a tree on the hacienda and later spoke of other visions of holy personages. The German spiritist who owned the hacienda thought of El Niño as a spiritualist medium and circulated photographs of the healer, whose fame rapidly spread. In 1928 the sickly (or hypochondriacal) president of Mexico, Plutarco Elías Calles, paid El Niño a visit while on a political tour of the region. Nothing precise is known of what transpired between the president and the healer, but they met together for three hours, and reports are that El Niño used bees' honey and wraparound bandages to cure Calles of a malady. Reports of the event created a sensation and attracted thousands of pilgrims to Espinazo. (No photos of the president at Espinazo were allowed, however.) By 1930 the hacienda had become a community center with three barbershops, branch banks, post and telegraph offices, butcher shops, and grocery stores supporting some fifteen thousand people. On special occasions, such as the healer's birthday, crowds might reach fifty thousand.

Not only is El Niño Fidencio credited with curing various illnesses—cancer, tuberculosis, insanity, blindness, leprosy, dropsy, birth defects, and intestinal diseases are among the most frequently mentioned—but he also delivered babies, amputated broken limbs with pruning shears, extracted molars with pincers, and removed growths with shards of glass. One photo postcard shows a young man with a grotesquely swollen knee, hands clutching his lower thigh as a tourniquet, while Niño Fidencio slices open the afflicted knee with a piece of glass. El Niño once said that some wealthy people gave him a modern operating table and surgical instruments, but he never used them. He and his thirty helpers relied on traditional medicines and practices shaped by his own imaginative innovations—rolling people in the dirt and swinging the mentally ill in giant circles on a swing—along with God's grace. He massaged the sick with his own saliva, and concocted a healing paste of tar, soap, soot, honey, and herbs. He had more than two hundred different herbs on hand, which he mixed into a vat containing fruits and plants to make a healing substance.

Nor were the miracles he ascribed to the divine limited to health. He resolved family, legal, and land disputes, helped the lovelorn, and provided financial and material relief. He accepted no money for his services, but for his own well-being accepted some clothing or food—candy, fresh eggs, fruit, a chicken or goat—from grateful devotees. He was said to have been a humble man, with blue eyes and yellowish skin, often childlike in voice and mannerisms, a virgin who never married, given to yoga and meditation as well as astral projections.

Many nights he planned special entertainment for his visitors, a chorus line of girls singing and dancing in the main salon at the complex. He frequently joined in, singing in a strong, female voice which resembled that of the incomparable Lola Beltrán, the queen of Mexican ranchero music who died in 1996. Believing that humor aided healing, he would don female clothing, or a cowboy outfit, or hats of various styles, and might parade with an umbrella or two. El Niño had two mascots, a huge turkey that strutted around with spread tail feathers and a toothless mountain lion named Concha.

He died in 1938; some insist that he had lapsed into a trance but that doctors killed him when they did a premature autopsy. Regardless, his work is carried on by *curanderos,* said to be infused with the spirit of El Niño. Over the years, the number of followers at Espinazo has oscillated. Today the crowds are dwindling. Many of the curanderos (most are women called *materias;* men are referred to as *cajones*) who claimed to have special spiritual connections to El Niño have now died, and there are increasingly fewer novices to replace them, as young people pursue other interests. But faith in Niño Fidencio continues. More than twenty thousand people, half of them Mexican-Americans, attended the healer's birthday anniversary in 1999, some wearing purple T-shirts saying, "In the name of God, we walk with Niño Fidencio into the new millennium." More than five hundred shrines honoring him stretch across Mexico. Although the Catholic Church still declines to recognize him as a saint, the Mexican government has registered the movement as the country's newest religion. A cabinet next to his tomb displays bottles preserving tumors, kidney stones, and teeth said to have been extracted by El Niño and his assistants. The faithful still come mainly for health. They explain that medical costs have risen everywhere else, but at Espinazo care and cures remain free.[13]

EQUALLY FERVENT TODAY is devotion to Pedro Jaramillo, a reputed miracle maker who lived in a small, humble dwelling on a bank of the Olmo River outside of the whistle-stop hamlet of Falfurrias, south Texas, in the early twentieth century. Born in Guadalajara, Jaramillo for unknown reasons journeyed northward into the Rio Grande Valley, where he worked in a liquor store. One day he complained of an affliction in his nose and for relief lay face down in the mud of the Olmo. He repeated the ritual for three days, and the malady disappeared. Soon after, while he was asleep at home, a voice came to him to announce his healing powers, and for the next twenty-five years he exercised his curing abilities as "The Healer of Los Olmos." Some of his prescriptions still exist: for a cure-all, "Bathe seven nights, at whatever hour you choose, entirely nude, soaping yourself in cold water"; for athlete's foot he recommended that sufferers pour tomato juice in their boots. Lore has it that when he advised a rancher to eat a chicken egg daily for his illness, the patient substituted a turkey egg and therefore was not cured. Don Pedrito never claimed that he himself possessed special healing capabilities; he attributed all such cures to the will of God, who had chosen him as an intermediary. He died in 1908 with his reputation radiating over a large region.[14]

I visited the Pedro Jaramillo shrine in Falfurrias on Saturday, 17 April 1999. It is much larger than the Juan Soldado shrine in Tijuana, much more orderly and better maintained. A statue of the santo stands prominently to one side. Votive candles give light to the dim interior. Labels on the candles show to whom devotion is addressed or indicate a favor being sought—sometimes both. Some carry images of well-known saints, others that of the hunchback of luck (some believe that God specially graces the physically deformed), King Solomon, John the Conqueror, or Pancho Villa. One carries the image of an ajo macho, a special type of garlic clove used as medicine to be hung over a doorway for protection—shades of vampire stories. Another features a horseshoe for luck, and others a spider web or a puppet on strings, asking help to escape the control of some person or institution. There are labels that solicit steady work, astral strength, death to an enemy, a saintly death for oneself, peace of mind, help in controlling personal feelings, or the blessings of a *tapa boca* (shut up), meant to quiet people who talk too much. Here you have so-called popular religion—or better said, simple religiosity—at work, the faithful making individual choices about what they think or feel may bring them earthly results from an otherworldly source, whether it be by way of official Church doctrine, traditional lore, black magic, custom, or personally adjusted Church teachings.

Within this wondrous tapestry of votive candles, people are asking Don Pedrito's assistance for all sorts of maladies and aspirations in their lives. This is confirmed by the petitions for help and notes of thanks for favors received which cover the walls of the shrine—among them a legal petition to terminate a parent-child relationship, a plea to help a youngster play minor league baseball (there are many requests from athletes looking for improved skills and a place on a team roster), a newspaper article reporting a car wreck and asking recovery for teenagers badly injured in the accident, and many requests for assistance in arranging legal papers for citizenship, a car license, legal immigration status, and divorce. There are also political campaign posters among the petitions, placed by local candidates for city aldermen. Are they asking for divine help or more mundanely, the votes of those at the shrine? Undoubtedly both. Same for the plethora of business calling cards on the walls representing a notary public; a construction worker; janitorial services; cellular phone and pager providers; lawnmower repair; a musical group; automobile, tax, television, plumbing, and electrical services; manicures and hairdos; and the training and showing of horses. In some respects, the inside walls resemble a community bulletin board covered with a sheen of spirituality.

In a corner of the shrine a curandero is at work, a middle-aged man from Colombia who came to the area at the behest of his brothers to work in the petroleum business and then became interested in and studied curandismo. He wears a priestlike cloak to keep evil spirits away. Now he is putting a blessing on the head of a middle-aged woman asking his help. He is invoking the power of Pedro Jaramillo, and grace is said to radiate from his hands to the woman, whom he does not touch. Power emanates from the Lord, who sheds his grace on Don Pedrito, who passes it on to the curandero and then the woman to be healed. In another instance, the curandero waves incense burning in an aluminum pan over a woman and her child. He rubs ointment on the back of still another person. He picks up her right arm and manipulates it, so as to loosen the shoulder joint. He tells her to breathe deeply. Then the curandero pulls a curtain stretched on a cord around the healing scene so that the patient is shielded from view. Said to involve bathing different parts of the body with a variety of fluids, the healing activities take place for more than an hour behind the curtain. There is no hurry in these procedures. Others seated in the shrine patiently await their turns.

For all those who solicit his help, the curandero carefully addresses their individual problems, in a strong, clear voice explaining what they must do to get well. One man comes with a letter from his doctor recommending a treatment which the sick man does not understand. The curandero studies the letter and then explains its contents to the patient. The curandero does not criticize medical doctors nor the drugs they recommend. In fact, he blesses prescription drugs brought to him for scrutiny. When he blesses them, the infirm seem to be relieved and convinced of their possible effectiveness. In some manner, probably unexplainable, prescription drugs, magic, spirituality, and traditional cures work in tandem at the shrine to produce wellness, physical, psychic, material, and spiritual. Healing in its various expressions is by far the greatest favor asked of popular saints.

CHARLENE, WHO IS revered as a saint in southwest Louisiana, lived for only twelve years, and it is her manner of dying that has led to veneration. Born in 1947, she grew up in Cajun Country, a region noted for its generally congenial but sometimes sharply contentious people, a taste for hog's headcheese, scrumptious crawfish gumbo, étouffeé, Saturday night dances, fiddle and accordion competitions, deep Roman Catholic religiosity, and economic dependence on petroleum and rice production. Her father was a public employee, and she grew up in modest circumstances with five brothers and sisters, seemingly a cheerful and confident little girl, competitive in sports and spiritually inclined. In July 1959 she fell sick, was checked into a local hospital, was diagnosed with acute lymphatic leukemia, and thirteen days later she died. The family buried Charlene in her home farming community of Richard (near Lafayette), a region noted for its recognition of signs from heaven: an image of the face of the crucified Christ etched into a frosty window, blood dripping from the crown of thorns on his head; or a figure of the Virgin Mary shaped from the leaves and branches of a large oak tree. (More than thirty thousand people came to view that image when it first appeared in the mid-1990s.) Today Charlene's grave has become a pilgrimage site for those in need as well as the curious. Most come from a radius of twenty-five miles, but tour buses also arrive with visitors from much more distant places.

Those who seek Charlene's official canonization by the Church are convinced of her saintliness and miracle-working powers. Their sentiments arise from testimonials by people who tended to the girl as she lay dying in considerable pain: when visited by a priest, she said: "O.K., Father, whom am I to suffer for today?"[15] Those for whom she suffered (a remembrance of Christ's selfless suffering) are said to have become well, and the devotion now is centered at her grave site, where visitors leave their written petitions, mostly concerning health but also other necessities, along with their thanks for miracles granted, coins, flowers, candles, and Rosaries. Said about Charlene's interventions:

I was told by doctors that I had cancer. I was operated on then. I am still as well as can be, all because of Charlene's prayers.

I visited Charlene's tomb and prayed to her, especially for good weather to save our rice crop. It had been raining for some time almost every day. Since Tuesday we have had no rain and are able to cut our rice, thanks to Charlene.

I put her picture . . . in my front room. I pray to her for whatever I need. . . . She answers my prayers so fast I can't believe it. I went to her grave once.[16]

Parents visiting the grave topped with its large, plain, rectangular block of marble set on a marble slab (graves are above ground here because the water table is so shallow) hold up Charlene, her virtue and charity, as good examples for their children. There is an aura of sanctity about the place.

A survey conducted at Charlene's grave site in 1992 showed her admirers to be predominantly Cajun, female, married, middle-aged (although their ages covered the spectrum from twenty to eighty), and Catholics who regularly attend Mass. They were better educated, more likely to be employed, and earned incomes higher than Louisianans as a whole. In other words, they were solidly middle class. Most had learned of Charlene through their families and community acquaintances. One-third came to ask for health assistance, and another third for help with personal problems connected with their work, finances, and family. Many visited just to pray, to find peace—and 20 percent out of plain inquisitiveness.[17] By and large, the pilgrims seemed to be experiencing the same sorts of life's difficulties faced from time to time by the rest of us. Most assuredly, these people were *not* marginal, oppressed, politically motivated, at war with the Church or society, or suffering deprivation; they were not delusional religious fanatics, nor did they fret much about the preeminence of New Orleans to the east, or their reputation as "coon-ass Cajuns." In fact, they kind of liked the nickname "coon-ass." Instead of only searching for a modern, social science explanation for devotion to Charlene, one might better admit the presence of mystery, consider the power of faith, and wander down those corridors of spirituality long trod by believers and seekers.

During those periodic oil crises or hurricanes that smite the region, devotion to Charlene becomes especially ardent, and while her followers credit numerous miracles to her intervention, the local bishop has yet to confirm any of them or to forward the girl's credentials for sainthood. Quite recently a mother whose newborn baby was near death prayed to Charlene for assistance, and the stricken tot survived. A miracle to most who witnessed the recovery, it was discounted by the bishop, because doctors were present at the recovery. Even though the attending physician swore in writing that modern medicine could not explain the sudden recuperation of the dying child, the bishop found the evidence tainted and insufficient for consideration by the Vatican.

Official hesitancies, however, do not dim devotion to santos canonized by the people. An assistant district attorney explained: "I am convinced that God is letting her become of service to us in southwest Louisiana."[18] In a mood that harks back centuries, each community desires its own patron (protector) saint, and French-Canadian Cajuns, Catholics in the main, but also Methodists, Presbyterians, and Baptists, living amongst the bayous of Evangeline country west of New Orleans have their own in Charlene.

Juan Soldado

As did Charlene, Pedro Jaramillo, El Niño Fidenicio, and most other popular saints, Juan Soldado also lived—as Juan Castillo Morales. His followers, however, know nothing of his life history, nor do they believe it necessary to do so. Despite general sentiments within official Catholicism that its saints have lived virtuous lives, ordinary Catholics do not necessarily hold their canonizations to such standards. It is the miracle-producing aspect of a saint's persona that counts. Furthermore, by leaving the biographical details of a saint's life blank, devotees are free to fill in the vacancies as they see fit. So far, this has only occurred in random snippets limited to the period following the soldier's arrival in Tijuana until the rape and murder of Olga Camacho. No one knows when military duty brought Castillo Morales to the border town, how long he had been there before the crime, or anything much of his official duties, social life, or recreational preferences. Because newspapers reporting the arrest and execution of Juan (that is, those papers discovered for this study) did not examine his background, at least in print, the faithful have no foundation on which to build a life history. In any case, they feel no inclination in that direction.

Some claim to have known the soldier casually before the crime. Alejandro Borja, who owned and operated an automobile service station near the comandancia, said that he and the soldier often chatted at the station. Just before the murder, he said, Juan was despondent because he was quarreling with his wife. "It was said that he mistreated his wife. Anyhow, they were not getting along very well."[19] If this could be verified, it would be important, because it would give that mysterious woman a motive for turning over her common-law husband's bloody clothes to the police and then hostilely confronting him at the interrogation.

Mariano Mendivil, owner of the grocery store across the street from the military headquarters, said Juan on occasion bought merchandise in his shop, that he was a polite young soldier, cheerful and chatty, and that he could not believe that such a person had committed the horrible crime.[20] Others confirmed the soldier's kindness and good nature. One of the faithful says that she saw the soldier playing with local children on several occasions. He tossed a ball with them and bought them ice cream. Many say simply that Castillo Morales was a good soldier and an amiable lad. Juana Valdez, a child living in Tijuana when the troubles occurred, ties Juan's good works to the origins of devotion. She explains that "Juan Soldado's mother was a poor widow living in Tijuana who depended upon her son to provide food and maintain the household. Every morning after her son's death, the mother would wake up and see a meal and sometimes money left at her front door. Juan [his ánima] came back from the dead every morning to bring his mother more food. Because of this miracle, everyone in town began to see Juan as somewhat of a santo who *had* to be innocent of such a crime" (emphasis added).[21]

This image-building procedure is seen most clearly in the clay statuary of the soldier sold at the two commercial booths vending Juan Soldado materials—scapularies, photographs, prayer cards, key chains, and other trinkets—outside the main gates to the cemetery that contains Juan's shrine. These two merchants have had a monopoly on Juan Soldado paraphernalia for decades. One of them, Juan Iglesias, asserts that a relative, working at home, first molded and then painted the original ceramic statutes of the soldier—a nice-looking young man with decidedly Anglo facial features, handsomely dressed in his green military uniform, cap on his head, black necktie, belt, and boots, standing at attention, hands cupped at his sides.[22] As these figures, which are sold for $5 to $7, are hand-painted, slight variations appear. For example, Juan is sometimes given a trimmed, black moustache on his upper lip, thick black eyebrows, brown or black eyes, long sideburns, darker skin, or a more angelic, somewhat impish countenance, resembling the wide-eyed cherubs so common to decorations in Mexican churches built in the colonial period. But by and large the impression remains the same: a young, smartly uniformed soldier, ready to obey orders. In fact, as statuary, Juan's age seems to be dropping. Where he once appeared to be about twenty years old, he now seems to be approaching fifteen or sixteen with a serene look that radiates virginity and innocence. No doubt, the image is being cleansed of any semblance of wanton youthfulness.

The statues, of course, in no way resemble Juan Castillo Morales, whose black-and-white newspaper photographs prove him to have been mestizo, with not deeply Indian facial characteristics but decidedly those of a mixed-blooded Mexican who looked to be every one of his twenty-four years. The merchant explains that the sculpture was modeled after the photo of Castillo Morales that accompanied his original army enlistment papers—when the soldier was only eighteen. As was the custom, the military had sent a copy of that photograph to the enlistee's parents, and that after the execution the picture had been circulated. None of this explanation is creditable; rather it can be seen as a creative imagination hard at work.

There are always surprises at the shrine; details change, new icons and offerings appear, stories about the soldier change. The faithful impulsively rearrange the images, prop up new floral arrangements, here and there stuff in recent peticiones and thank-yous. At the 2002 celebration of Juan's birthday, paper fliers carried a newspaper photo of Juan Castillo Morales behind bars at the time of his imprisonment. The text indicated that the case had been reinvestigated through contemporary newspapers and the soldier's innocence confirmed. The fliers had been left by a devotee fulfilling a *manda*, or vow: in exchange for a favor received, the recipient had agreed to research the crime in order to prove the injustice of Juan's execution. Of course, Juan in the picture looked nothing like Juan as venerated. The faithful thought the picture a fake and tossed it away. Several years earlier a local historian investigating the Juan Soldado story showed the pious a similar picture at the shrine and asked if they recognized the image. They scoffed and said it looked like the devil.

I noted an alteration on the plaster bust of Juan Soldado on the main altar. There was Juan with his customary soldier's cap, but a first lieutenant's silver bar had been pinned above the brim over the frontal military insignia. Juan had been promoted in rank. Here was Juan Soldado, heralded as everyone's common soldier, a soldado raso, the lowest of the low, representative of the masses, the poor and humble, those who were frequently drafted into military service by force, suddenly and inexplicably promoted to officer status, perhaps not sharing in the means and prestige of the bourgeoisie, but distinguished, if not elitist. Who had "promoted" Juan? For what reason? Was this a working man who had worked his way up? Was it meant to shout that "Our Juan is among the best?" No one questioned at the shrine that day in 2001 or on succeeding visits seemed to notice the promotion; no one said that it would alter their devotion in any way. It amounted to a small detail with meaning to one of the followers but none of the others. One suspects that the shrine is filled with just such personal touches, the kind that parents perform to make their children seem distinguished and extra-special.

Give and Take

While many religious people may choose to address the Divine directly, most Catholics prefer the services of a go-between—someone close to God but less awesome, less exalted and so more apt to respond to a human being's trivial needs, and therefore more approachable. Under the circumstances, it makes sense to have an intercessor, an advocate, who is acquainted with the heavenly terrain. So the needy turn to saints (and ánimas, who are considered close to sainthood) whom they find more like family, and they expect these saints to carry their concerns to the Almighty. In exchange, they promise to extol the saint with prayer and devotion. The premise is that saints need humans as much as people need saints.[23]

Saints, you see, inhabit a hierarchy in which there is mobility in both directions. Recognition of their holiness helps to maintain and perhaps enhance their standing in the community of saints. Many saints have emerged from obscurity to veneration. Saint Jude is an example. Jude was only a minor saint with a small following in Central and South America when in the 1920s Claretin missionaries began to work in Chicago's Hispanic barrio. The Claretins built a church, but when the Depression struck, could not make the mortgage payments. The head of the mission had a personal devotion to Jude and brought an image of the saint to his parish. In search of a patron of their own, the Hispanics adopted Saint Jude; the church survived. Veneration and miracles followed, and Jude stands famous today as the patron of hopeless causes (mortgage payments included). However, there is always the threat, always the pos-

The Juan Soldado shrine with its red-brick entranceway in Municipal Cemetery Number One, Tijuana. (Author's photo)

A young woman prays before the standard image of Juan inside the shrine. Other devotees have left flower arrangements and lighted candles to venerate the saint and ask for favors. (Author's photo)

A bust of Juan inside the shrine, surrounded by petitions for assistance. (Author's photo)

Above: The outer walls of the shrine are covered with plaques thanking Juan for favors received. (Author's photo)

Left: The faithful venerate Juan with a variety of poignant, custom-made remembrances. (Author's photo)

An amateur painting honors Juan in the shrine. It links God to Juan through the Rosary: the Lord has granted a miracle to the painter through Juan Soldado. (Author's photo)

Fulfilling a manda—a promise made to Juan Soldado in exchange for a favor received—a young man approaches the shrine across rough pavement on his knees, accompanied by a loud, brassy banda, famous in the Mazatlán region of Mexico. (Author's photo)

A woman, assisted by members of her family, fulfills her manda to Juan with a painful crawl on bloodied knees through the cemetery. (Author's photo)

Above: Outside the cemetery a variety of Juan Soldado paraphernalia is sold, along with items honoring others in the expansive conglomerate of saints. (Author's photo)

Right: Tijuana's wax museum features a figure of Juan Soldado in an exhibit that is also a site of veneration. The wax representation of Juan portrays him as a mature adult rather than the lad seen at the shrine. (Author's photo)

Shrines to Juan appear elsewhere as the devotion spreads, this one at Magdalena in Mexico's northern State of Sonora. (Author's photo)

The shrine outside Abreojos, midway down the Pacific side of the Baja California peninsula, is isolated and simple. (Author's photo)

The interior of the Abreojos shrine is cluttered with petitions for assistance, a number of them from Mexican soldiers stationed in the district. Some pictures of soldiers and military identification cards line the frame of the painting behind the image of Juan. Images of St. Martin de Tours, the Roman soldier who gave his cape to a destitute traveler and then converted to Christianity, are also prevalent here. (Author's photo)

The Shrine of the Miracles in downtown San Antonio, Texas, is privately owned and has rigid visiting hours. Religious articles sold inside the shrine finance its upkeep and support the owners. Its altar displays various santos, popular and official. Worshipers may place their favorite icon with the group. The popular santo Pedro Jaramillo sits with his full beard near the center of the photograph. (Author's photo)

The Pedro Jaramillo shrine in Falfurrias, in south Texas, is well-known through the region and beyond. The santo sits inside, a donation box close by. (Author's photo)

For protection against harm, the faithful frequently wear scapularies featuring their favorite saint. This one to Jesús Malverde, the so-called patron saint of drug dealers, is popular throughout Mexico and beyond. (Photo: Rebecca Giménez)

An elaborate home altar in Ixtáltepec, Juan Castillo Morales's birthplace. No one there knows that one of their sons is now venerated as a saint in Tijuana, and none of the town's altars carry his bust. (Author's photo)

sibility, of being downgraded, of falling back into obscurity, as has happened to other saints, how many will never be known. So it is thought that Saint Jude welcomes and rewards devotion to his cause.[24]

If Jude worries about his status, imagine the concern of Juan Soldado. Considering the size of Tijuana, his base of adoration is quite thin. Some in town think that he was guilty of rape and murder and that reverence toward him is fostered by the devil. The great majority of inhabitants, brushed by the wings of secularization, accord him no reverence at all. One might conclude that Juan's role as a santo is precarious and requires unceasing devotion for support. Followers consider him "muy milagroso," very miraculous, and their thanks are effusive. So far, so good, but . . .

Such adoration is part of the ethical agreement that exists between these sacred beings and mortals. Saints are naturally appreciated in their role as intercessors; as figures of power, they are treated with respect and courtesy, but there is no guarantee that a particular saint will respond to a human cry for help. In this case, flattery may well get you somewhere. Under the circumstances, the relationship between humans and saints becomes, and always has been, recognized as reciprocal, which does not mean evenly balanced or fair. You can barter with saints, but if you want to get, you have to give. Or if you do get, you had better be ready to repay. Failure to reciprocate can lead to anger and revenge.

An aura of patronage permeates this close association between humans and saints. Towns and people, of course, have long worshiped their patron saints, not only for their protective powers but also as conduits for assistance from the Divine. God, as always, is the supreme patron, but there are many other lesser patrons, saints and ánimas among them, with substantial power to ease one's passage through the hazards of life. But the relationship between patrons and their clients is never (meant to be) one-way; patrons do not normally grant favors as handouts. They demand a return, whether it be loyalty, publicity, money, a gift, or prayer. Those who have confidence in the advocacy of Juan Soldado leave peticiones in the shrine which honors him—most often scraps of paper requesting a favor or writings scribbled on the wall—and in return make a *promesa* or manda, often written but reinforced orally, which asserts that if their request is granted, they will repay Juan with special devotion, which can be material representations, spiritual incantations, or both.

Pleas by believers to other santos and ánimas generally adhere to the same pattern. Promesas are serious vows, which if not fulfilled before one dies, can have catastrophic repercussions. Commonly at family get-togethers a legend called "La Promesa" is retold:

> There was a young couple just married who after a year had a baby boy. One day the baby got sick, and doctors said his life could not be saved. The couple prayed in church for their child's recovery and promised that if this occurred, they would give the boy to a Catholic orphanage. Through a miracle the child got well, but the parents did not deliver him to the orphanage and in due time forgot their promesa. The boy grew to handsome manhood, and after many years the family returned to church. As they knelt in front of the altar, the young man turned to stone. The couple cried for forgiveness, but the stern punishment from heaven endured. The parents had not kept their promise.[25]

A woman remembers that as a teenager, "When my brother was sick, I made a promesa that if he got better, I would make a pilgrimage to San Juan de los Lagos [a famous Mexican pilgrimage site]. I kept putting it off until my grandmother told me what would happen if I died before I fulfilled it"—that her soul, her ánima, would never be at rest. Another woman confirms with a classic story of unfinished business: "All through my childhood I heard mother make promises (vows) and ask for miracles. She once told me the story of a lady who had asked for a miracle and had promised to go to the San Juan [shrine] in return. However, this lady died before she could go. So she [her ánima] was seen several times by her friends and relatives whom she asked to pay for her offering [at the shrine]." This same woman tells the story of a friend who was ill and prayed to be cured. She was healed but did not keep her vow to repay the Virgin Mary for her help, and soon after became ill again and died.[26] Mexican immigrants in the United States frequently recall the need to return to their homeland to fulfill a promesa for fear that sudden death will leave their ánima adrift.

HOW DO BELIEVERS choose a particular saint to venerate? After all, there are thousands to choose from in the burgeoning community of saints. In former times, towns picked their patron saint by the holy person's reputation or by divine signal, perhaps an appearance to a resident; through a local devotion of unknown origins, or simply by lottery.

Now saints tend to be chosen in accordance with their avowed specialty. Certain saints have long been known for their particular aptitudes; Saint Blaise for throat disease, Saint Barbara for protection against sudden death and fire, Saint Margaret guarded people at childbirth, and Saint Erasmus eased intestinal problems. Nowadays, the list is long and frequently whimsical, recorded in practical writings such as *Aunt Carmen's Book of Popular Saints* and *Heaven Can Help Us: The Worrier's Guide to the Patron Saints*.

Aunt Carmen recommends specific prayers for San Martín de Porres, who specializes in social justice; Santa Gertrudis la Magna, patron saint of students; Santa Bárbara, who aids architects and builders; the Holy Child of Atocha, helper of miners and prisoners; San Isadore, patron saint of farmers, often asked for rain; San Pascual Bailón, patron saint of shepherds and cooks; and Santa Rita, who like Saint Jude specializes in impossible causes.[27] Worriers are advised to consult with Saint Agnes or Saint Catherine if their problem concerns love, Saint Theresa for anxiety, Saint Anthony of Padua for missing objects, and Saint Thomas Aquinas if faced with a difficult school exam. Saint Hubert helps hunters, Saint Brendan, sailors; and Saint Benedict, cave hunters as well as victims of poisoning. There are specific saints to be consulted for various diseases, difficult births, sterility, wounds and fractures, deaf mutes and the blind.[28] Juan Soldado is said to be the migrants' saint, assuring safe passage and employment for those who cross the U.S.-Mexico border, legally and otherwise. Jesús Malverde is revered for his protection of drug dealings. Whatever one's predicament, it seems that there is a saint who has the specialized knowledge and skills to address it.

And apparently one need not even approach a santo for relief; any another person considered to be blessed with the grace of God will do. Bruce Wilkinson, an American minister dedicated to Bible study and teaching, recently uncovered an obscure Biblical character named Jabez, who asked God to "enlarge my territory, that Your hand would be with me, and that you would keep me from evil, that I may not cause pain! (First Chronicles 4: 9–10)." Wilkinson interpreted the phrase "enlarge my territory" as "Surely, I was born for more than this." He then broadened his vision: "If Jabez had worked on Wall Street, he might have prayed, 'Lord, increase the value of my investment portfolios.' When I talk to presidents of companies, I often talk to them about this particular mindset. When Christian executives ask me, 'Is it right to ask God for more business?' my response is, 'Absolutely.'" That did it. Wilkinson's discovery, published in a slim volume by a religious press, has sold ten million copies and remains perched at the top of several best-seller lists. Jabez became the holy patron of corporate and petty capitalists, and apparently a good many other more ordinary working people who sought to enlarge their "territory," whether or not for Godly purposes.[29] Recently, the publisher donated thousands of copies to America's prison population, presumably to nourish forlorn futures with dreams of material success.

A SAINT'S SPECIALTY is often an outgrowth of tasks performed while on earth. Hence, Saint Joseph is the patron saint of carpenters. Other specialties originate from miracles attributed to that particular saint, the story passed through generations by word of mouth, and, in some cases, later confirmed in writing. Statues or paintings of saints often carry an emblem which indicates a detail of their life story. An example is Saint Appollonia, a martyred saint, who had her teeth smashed out with a club as part of her torture. When believers later fleshed out her life history, her symbol became a pair of pincers holding a giant molar. No wonder she became the patron saint of those suffering a toothache.[30] But in no way does a saint's specialty limit the holy person's miracle-producing powers. Juan Soldado, for example, may be dubbed the patron saint of immigrants by the media, but less than one-tenth of the peticiones addressed to him for assistance concern the needs of migrants in crossing the border from Tijuana and finding security in the United States. Even fewer thanks for miracles received seem to be from migrants, although many expressions of gratitude do not specify the favor received.

For their part, those seeking help do not necessarily limit their request to a specialty-saint, or even to any one saint. As evidenced by the collection of saintly icons present in most shrines, petitioners not only address the saint to whom the shrine is dedicated, but also others that they believe may benefit their cause. Once inside the Tijuana chapel, most address their prayers only to Juan Soldado, but more than a fourth also pray to other divinities, such as the Virgin of Guadalupe, Saint Jude Tadeo, El Niño de Atocha, and to the Lord Himself.[31] Elsewhere, at their home altars, in church, or when they are moved to do so regardless of the moment or location, they direct their devotion to a wide variety of santos. In other words, Juan Soldado is not the only saint who they venerate, and they do not hesitate to call on others from the whole panoply of holy personages as suits their requisites, and whims.

It would be unusual to visit a Mexican shrine dedicated to a particular saint that did not also prominently display an image of the Virgin of Guadalupe. Icons of Martin de Tours, the Roman soldier who shared his officer's cape with a shivering beggar and then converted to Christianity, are commonly seen on altars honoring a fellow soldier, Juan Soldado. In downtown San Antonio, Texas, huddled in the shadow of a busy, elevated freeway, is a chapel, a rather large one containing several rows of benches for the faithful, dedicated to El Señor de los Milagros, the crucified Christ. The shrine lies on private property, and its owners impose rigid visiting hours, but the faithful come and go in a steady stream. The image itself, Jesus suffering on the cross, is said to have been brought to this spot, then a tiny colonial outpost, by Spanish missionaries at the start of the nineteenth century. The devotion, neither encouraged nor disdained by the official Church, is therefore nearly two centuries old. The altar over which the cross is displayed is cluttered with pictures, icons, and remembrances of fifty or sixty representatives of the legion of saints. Each visitor is free to bring an image of a favorite saint, and the outpouring of peticiones, flowers, votive candles, expressions of gratitude, and iconography is so great that it requires continual cleanup by the guardian-owners of the shrine.[32] The reason for this proliferation of santos is not only because believers have their favorites, but because petitioners do not hesitate to shop around for the saint most favorably disposed to their needs. For their part, not only do saints appear to be somewhat vain and insecure, but they also may be fickle. That is, while mortals do not hesitate to select as patrons those saints who cooperate with their requests, saints aid some who ask for assistance and offer devotion, but not others. Why this is so is one of the mysteries that helps to sustain the vitality of the faith.

BELIEVERS REACT TO a saint's hesitancies or rejection in myriad ways. A presumption is that a saint's repudiation stems from the sinfulness of the petitioner, or a lack of faith. But those asking favors rarely ascribe such failings to themselves. Who has not sinned? Doubt is natural, if not indispensable, in one's search for faith. A middle-aged woman at the Juan Soldado shrine who has known disappointments with saints says, "It is all up to God. God's will. You can pray to Juan Soldado all you want for the recovery of a friend who is dying of disease, but if God wants that person to die, there is nothing that Juan Soldado can do about it." When asked why she did not pray for help to Saint Francis Xavier, widely venerated for his miracles in her Sonoran hometown of Magdalena, Delfina Suárez said that she tried to do so, "pero no me hace caso" (but he is not paying attention). "He did not offer me anything. For some reason, God did not want it to be so."[33] Therefore, she turned, with better results, to Juan Soldado.

A ritual commonly performed at the Juan Soldado shrine in Tijuana involves bringing small stones and placing them in front of Juan's bust inside the shrine. The stones, larger than pebbles but not rocks, are said to have come from the spot in the cemetery where Juan Castillo Morales fell dead, and therefore carry a kind of sacredness. But in fact the stones can come from anywhere. When one asks for a favor, the petitioner takes one of these stones from the altar, and if the favor is granted, is obligated to return it to the shrine for another's use. So the stones are in constant rotation. Origins of the ritual are unknown. One of the faithful explained that, "It must come from our Aztec past," which meant that some practices at the shrine which cannot be fathomed are credited to native tradition, a matter of pride for many Mexicans. One lady showed me a stone from the shrine that she had been carrying in her purse for ten years. She said her prayers had not yet been answered, "but they will be, and then I will return the stone. Juan Soldado is a busy man, but my turn will come. I am sure of that."[34]

Not all petitioners are that patient with the tardiness or failures of their santos. They may provoke, or even defy, the images to force what they want out of them. If the images do not respond, they may hit, threaten, insult, or punish the saint. They may hang the figure upside down or lock the santo in a drawer until a request is granted. When farmers do not receive the rain they implore from their patron, San Isidro, they are prone to bury him headfirst in one of their fields. Saints who do not perform from home altars are often turned around or covered up or made to stand, face to the wall, in a corner, like a punished child. If a saint repeatedly fails to deliver, the image may be banished for good. Those who tidy up a saint's shrine normally expect a favor in return. If they do not receive it, they might say: "I fulfilled my obligation to you. I cleaned up your place, and you are not carrying out your obligation to me." If such a scolding does not work, they might declare in anger: "I refuse to honor you," toss the statue out of the shrine, and secure a different one to take its place.

A good many people do not wait to learn whether or not a santo is paying attention to them; they aim to get the saint's attention from the start and let him or her know that they mean business. Some will print up prayer cards with the saint's special oration and a list of his or her miracles on the back, instead of the front side. It is like saying to that saint: "We know your special prayer and your reputation for miracles. And if you wish recognition on the front of the card, then you must perform for us." It is taken for granted that the santo understands rejection and will grant the petition in order to resume accustomed status. For any number of believers, Saint Anthony is the saint who finds lost objects. So when believers lose or misplace their keys or eyeglasses, a letter or a book, some do not simply ask Saint Anthony for help but impulsively hang him outside a window, face down, threatening to leave him there until he indicates where the lost item can be found. If and when it is, the santo will be returned to his niche.[35]

Many residents of Chicago—Catholics, Protestants, and Jews—believe that Saint Joseph can help you sell your house. To invoke his assistance, one may buy a Sell-My-House kit at any number of outlets (Sears and Catholic Church gift shops included) and follow the enclosed instructions: bury Saint Joseph in the back yard, head down, facing the house to be sold. When (and if) it is sold, recover and clean the icon, give thanks, and place it in an honored site. Father Richard Fragomeni, an associate professor of sacramental theology at Chicago's Catholic Theological Union, explains why people believe in the efficacy of Saint Joseph to sell homes:

> Most saints have a specialty which relates to an aspect of their lives. Saint Joseph, of course, was a carpenter, and was also the head of the Holy Family. He provided Jesus with a home. As a family grows and needs a new home, they ask the assistance of Saint Joseph to provide them a good home, just as he did for his family. So it is easy to understand why they pray to him. Saint Blaise is another example of a helpful saint. He once tended a child who was choking to death on a fish bone. Now it is customary for people with throat ailments to pray to Saint Blaise. On the day commemorating the saint's death—February 3—believers commonly go to church to have their throats blessed.

In this way, prayers to particular saints become a pious practice. Father Fragomeni remembers that his mother used to hang an image of the Virgin Mary on her clothesline to insure that the wet clothes received a warming sun. He admits that such devotions carry an aspect of magic and superstition, "but many people are in great need of help, and what works for them, works. People are trying to secure some power over what seems out of their control." The official Church neither rejects nor abhors such piety. "There is concern, however, that if the plea to a saint does not produce desired results, the person might lose all faith [in God]." As for Saint Joseph and home sales, "It is alright to pray to him, but one should also get a good real estate agent."[36]

Even the Virgin Mary may be scorned and tested. In an example from late medieval France:

> A widow had only one child whom she tenderly loved. On hearing that this son had been taken [in war] by the enemy, chained and put in prison, she burst into tears, and addressing herself to the Virgin, to whom she was especially devoted, she asked her *with obstinacy* [emphasis added] for the release of her son; but when she saw at last that her prayers remained unanswered, she went to the church where there was a sculptured image of Mary, and there, before the image, she said:—"Holy Virgin, I have begged you to deliver my son, and you have not been willing to help an unhappy mother! I've implored your patronage for my son, and you have refused it! Very good! Just as my son has been taken away from me, so I am going to take away yours, and keep him as a hostage!" Saying this, she approached, took the statute of the child on the Virgin's breast, carried it home, wrapped it in spotless linen, and locked it up in a box, happy to have such a hostage for her son's return. Now, the following night, the Virgin appeared to the young man, opened his prison doors, and said:—"Tell your mother, my child, to return me my son now that I have returned hers!" The young man came back home to his mother and told her of his miraculous deliverance; and she, overjoyed, hastened to go with the little Jesus to the Virgin saying to her:—"I thank you, heavenly lady, for restoring me my child, and in return I restore yours!"[37]

Statues of divinities carrying a child are especially attractive to those in need. On some, the child is attached to the icon by a screw. Disappoint the petitioner, and the santo may lose the child—at least temporarily.

Such approaches replicate the means by which family disputes are often resolved: disappointment and spontaneous rage precipitate revenge, compromise and love bring resolution. All this is part of the give-and-take between santos and human petitioners. There is no way of knowing how many petitioners have abandoned Juan Soldado out of frustration, but regardless of disappointments, any number maintain patient faith in him convinced that their turn will come.

IN THIS TELLING, the foundation of the devotion to Juan Soldado has emerged as a rich composite of circumstances and belief which portrays Tijuana and its populace around 1938. The gruesome manner of the public execution accorded a young soldier convicted of murder and rape, set against a background of social agitation caused by national politics, fallout from the Depression, the stress of growth and change all pressed people to ponder their perceptions of the calamitous events surging about them. It challenged (and in some cases confirmed) their sense of justice as administered by the state, raised the specter of their own complicity (by silence or otherwise) in the horrid affair, and heightened their spiritual sensibilities pertaining to divine intervention in worldly affairs. Adoration followed, miracles occurred, a saint was born. As with most relationships between santos and their followers, this association had both practical and material elements mingled with abiding religiosity. Worshipers begged the grace of God for material betterment on earth but at the same time honored the supremacy of the Lord in their lives and recognized the domination of divine will over earthly power.

As it developed, the entire devotion displayed precedents cemented into centuries of Christianity as practiced by ordinary believers, more specifically in Latin Catholicism: canonizations by the people, construction of life histories, emphasis on miracles, reciprocity between saint and petitioner, the pragmatic nature of the exchange, and the time-proven practices at the shrine, along with the wary stance of the official Church. As religiosity billows in constant interplay between the daily lives of mortals and their spiritual beliefs at the time, it is subject to both slow, wrenching change in long-cherished traditions and also relatively abrupt, spontaneous adjustments to accommodate more immediate challenges in daily living. Even the comparatively new devotion in Tijuana has seen substantial change since its inception.

Few of those who witnessed the horrendous events which inaugurated the devotion are alive today, nor have any written memoirs of those days come to light. But a good deal of vivid personal testimony about the calamity has been passed down orally through family networks, so that we are now well within our third generation of devotees to Juan Soldado. We should meet some of these people, learn what we can of their thinking about the fallen soldier, reflect upon their spirituality, develop a profile of those visiting the shrine along with a sense of where the devotion seems to be headed. The largest crowds pay their respects to the santo on San Juan Day, 24 June, and on the Day of the Dead, 2 November. I was there on San Juan Day, 2000.

8. Closer to God

C emetery Number One, Tijuana, 24 June 2000: The day celebrates
John the Baptist on the Catholic calendar, but the steady stream
of people coming here is honoring Juan Soldado. They have proclaimed it the birthday of Juan Castillo Morales, although we really
do not know the exact day of the soldier's birth. He died in February 1938
at age twenty-four, so he was born in 1913 or 1914. Giving him a birthday
fills in a blank in his life history, but the date itself is not important to his
followers. It is the celebration that counts. Visitors, accompanied by a
smartly dressed mariachi group in their typical bolero jackets and tight-
legged pants with silver buttons strung along the seams, will sing to him
with gusto "Las Mañanitas," the Mexican birthday song. Other types of
musical units will also be present: three-piece *conjuntos* (guitar, base,
and accordion) common to Norteño music, and big brass bands called
bandas, defined by their large drum, blaring out tunes associated with
Mazatlan and surroundings. Additionally, there will be strolling guitarists
in street clothes, and a teenager or two with boom boxes blasting out
modern rock. It will be a loud, colorful scene, with families seated on
tombstones near the Juan Soldado shrine eating their pollo, carne asada,
tamales, pizza, or hamburgers swimming in hot chile sauce and drinking
Cokes and Tecate beer in the shadows of small trees to avoid the full force
of the summer heat that by noon will approach ninety degrees. These
sorts of chatty, sometimes raucous celebrations have long gone hand-in-
glove with Mexican religiosity.

The cemetery usually opens at 9 A.M., but the heavy, rusting iron gates
swing back a half hour early to accommodate expected crowds. The

gatekeeper, a middle-aged woman, gripes about having to open early and receiving no extra hourly wage. This is a municipal cemetery, and the city pays her to be there from 9 A.M. to 4 P.M., with no overtime pay possible. Furthermore, she is not convinced that Juan Soldado is really a saint. Still, she is willing to tell his followers what she knows of the soldier and direct them to his shrine. She may not be sure about Juan's saintliness, but acts as if she is hedging her bets.

Outside the gate, two entrepreneurs who sell Juan Soldado mementos set up their mobile stalls. They have been selling there for years and seem to have a monopoly on the business. They sell pictures of Juan in scapularies and in cheap metallic frames, nothing that resembles Juan Castillo Morales, but representations of the healthy, innocent, white-skinned, young teenager who has become Juan Soldado. Plaster busts of the re-crafted soldier are also on sale, along with votive candles labeled with a prayer to the santo and a variety of seasonal flowers, some of them shaped into a garland or some other simple decoration.

At 10:20 A.M. a mariachi band dressed in *charro* outfits approaches. They have been paid $200 an hour by a middle-aged man who lives outside of Los Angeles to serenade himself in the company of Juan Soldado. The man is fulfilling a manda, repaying Juanito for a favor received. He promised Juan mariachi music on his birthday in exchange for a miracle (which he declined to discuss) and, along with his family, has kept his promesa for the past four years. (Most promesas are fulfilled in a single visit.) One of the hallmarks of this pilgrimage site is the way in which the faithful come as families with many children in tow. Fathers often carry children on their shoulders; mothers cradle them in their arms. The youngest baby here today is only two weeks old, but his mother wanted him to meet Juan as early in life as possible. Parents explain the story of Juan Soldado to their children; they take the youngsters inside the shrine itself, where they help them to light candles and to touch the bust of the santo. They point out the hundreds and hundreds of peticiones that cover the inside walls of the shrine and the plaques giving thanks for miracles received. Then they gather as family outside the shrine to praise Juan and eat their picnic lunch.

The shrine itself is unpretentious. It started off as an uncovered grave site piled with stones, a cross, votive candles, flowers, and other offerings, peticiones in their various forms, and gratitude expressed by crutches, bunches of human hair, clothing, eye patches, car parts, and other appropriate material goods. By the 1950s the bare metal chassis of four cars formed the supports of a shelter over the grave. Devotees piled parts of wrecked automobiles—doors, fenders, side panels, headlights—against the framework. The shrine resembled an auto junk yard. Why the auto parts? At that time, migrants found crossing the tortuous La Rumorosa mountain pass above Mexicali by bus, car, or truck more hazardous than illegally crossing the international border at Tijuana's Colonia Libertad, then separated from the United States only by a strand of barbed wire. Skeletons of ruined vehicles lying in the crevices of La Rumorosa proved the point. Migrants who successfully traversed the hazard brought auto parts to the shrine to thank Juan Soldado. Or they delivered parts to ask for a safe return. Testimonials to successful passage piled up at the shrine.

The faithful constructed a wooden building in the 1960s to shelter followers and protect the site. A decade or so later a fire, thought to have been ignited by a votive candle, burned it down. Devotees soon rebuilt the shrine, this time of cinder blocks, now plastered over and painted a vibrant medium green. Marble and metal plaques giving thanks cover the outside walls. As there is no space for additional plaques on the walls, they are simply stacked up next to the shrine or propped up on nearby tombstones. Although much smaller and with only one room, the structure resembles many of the humble homes clinging to the steep hillsides surrounding the core of the city: functional, with only a front door and a window or two, and in some cases a jerry-rigged addition tacked on. As they consider Juan family and treat him as such, it is only natural that they would want him to feel at home—*their* home.

The shrine is only ten feet square with a roof ten feet high, that slopes to nine at one end allowing rain to run off. Leading to the front door is a twenty-two-foot-long walkway, its roof supported by an open colonnade of arches and pillars of bright red brick. The inside of the shrine can accommodate only four to six visitors at any one time, so it is not unusual, particularly on special days, to see a long line of devotees patiently waiting their turn to enter the chapel. Votive candles keep the inside hot, stuffy, and filled with the smell of burning wax, but no one seems to mind. A few of the candles have been lit to honor divine figures other than Juan Soldado. Several candles carry representations of the Virgin of Guadalupe, others San Martín Caballero or El Niño de Atocha, a favorite of mineworkers. There is little space left on a central table for votive candles in their glass holders, so some just stand their candle offering in hot, melted wax dribbled on the floor. The altar up front is covered with statues of various santos; a plaster cast of the Virgin of Guadalupe; live, paper, and plastic flowers set in vases; colorful flower wreaths in various shapes and sizes; balloons, petitions, photos, paintings, and other offerings of the faithful, all flanking a bust of Juan Soldado in a glass case. Usually the door to the case is locked shut, but today it is open, so that the faithful can touch the bust of Juan and leave a petition right next to him.

Some stranger might consider the setting unkempt and cluttered; indeed, no attempt is made to keep it orderly. For this is not a Church chapel, its contents maintained, dusted, and normally securely protected from devotional touch except by the approved. This is a people's shrine, everyone's chapel, and the faithful cram into it to find a niche for *their* special petition, to touch Juanito physically, to rub their own faces, arms, and shoulders with some of the moisture, even soot and grime, that covers the glass encasement containing the beloved soldier's figure, and to say a prayer, to shed a tear, to express their concern and care for the one they venerate.

These pious people (and Latinos in general) seek and need contact with material things. Religious statues in Our Lady of Sorrows Church in Edinburg, Texas, no longer have fingers. They have been broken off by parishioners touching and tugging on them over and over again. These people feel closer to those they can touch. Dealing with the dead is not an abstract matter, which is why they clean up and decorate the graves of departed ones each 2 November, designated as the Day of the Dead, and why they reject any notion of cremation. Nothing is held back in these moments. Their love and care of those faithful to Juanito is palpable and moves all who witness it. The experience, for even the most doubt-burdened or cynical, neutral or agnostic observer, is enchanting.

There are few furnishings inside the shrine. Prayer stands flank the altar, and a long metal table for candles extends down the center of the modest building. A padlocked metal box for monetary offerings stands at the entranceway; today it overflows with dollars and pesos, so much so that one of the faithful has asked a caretaker at the cemetery to stuff the bills inside the box so that none of the money can be pocketed by an interloper. Indeed, thefts of money and artifacts at the shrine (and other grave sites in the cemetery) is a continuing problem. Dentures and eye glasses are stuffed here and there; crutches, arm splints, and leg braces are piled in corners; and wedding gowns, baby clothes, and bunches of hair from the head ("I have cut my treasured long hair so that you may have it in thanks") hang on the walls, along with an assortment of milagros, small tin representations of legs, arms, and hearts, images of body parts representing favors both requested and received. A girl who requested and received a "guaranteed" date for her school prom has left her corsage in thanks. Hand-crocheted baby shoes thank Juan for a safe child delivery. There is a picture of four blind children asking for sight. Among the most expressive offerings in the chapel are the *retablos,* tender amateur paintings on canvas and metal, or wooden carvings, which glorify Juan, often in the company of a notable divine personage, such as the Virgin of Guadalupe or another favored saint. One pencil sketch portrays Juan as an older, much more mature young man than do the plaster figures of the soldier. Another hangs a Rosary around his neck. None of the representations in this chapel is the work of a trained artist. They stem from a full heart rather than a trained hand, and are highly reflective of the needs and devotion of their donors.

A NEW MARIACHI band arrives at 11 A.M.—two trumpets, five regular guitars, and a guitarrón (a much larger stringed instrument, played like a bass guitar but carried by the musician), hired by a swarthy young man, perhaps twenty years old, dressed in blue jeans, T-shirt, and a baseball cap turned backwards. He is accompanied by two other youthful males. Friends? Acquaintances? Bodyguards? Who knows? The young man struts and swaggers around, resembling a bullfighting matador who has just completed a graceful pass with a cape or achieved a single-thrust kill of the beast. This fellow obviously is full of himself and has money. Twice he returns to the chapel with large bundles of candles to be lighted in honor of Juan Soldado. He seems to be buying candles by the dozen. His comrades do not enter the shrine. When asked for a few words about his presence, he declines with *más tarde,* later on. Most people at the shrine *want* to talk about Juan Soldado and their personal manda to him, but this young man refuses, suspicious of questions asked by a gringo who could be a police investigator posing as a curious spectator. Those involved in illegalities seek Juan's protection as much as anyone else and are understandably hesitant to chat with obvious outsiders about their devotion.

At noon three other people approach the shrine to pay a manda. They have crawled on their knees some fifty yards over a rough cobblestone pathway flanked by pine, eucalyptus, pepper, and cypress trees from the entrance of the cemetery to the shrine. Family members are with them. As the penitents progress toward their goal, one family member spreads a long carpet in front of them to somewhat protect their knees, but it remains a rugged, painful crawl. Some others have done the same but without the carpet. Their knees become bruised and bloody. They need to stop frequently to ease the pain, but they never leave their knees. Onlookers pay them little attention. It is as if the pilgrims are doing what is expected of them, or that their style of devotion is no one's business but their own. Family members may chat about miracles received by those in their own group, but they do not delve into the devotional needs and finds of others. Their privacy is respected. None of the public witnessing, the so-called open sharing common among evangelical groups, occurs at the shrine, where the atmosphere is friendly and chatty, but not preachy.

There is a second Juan Soldado *capilla*, or little chapel, on a ridge at the back or southern end of the cemetery, near where the soldier is said to have fallen and met his death. The devoted say that blotches of his blood lie beneath it. A woman praying at the site claims that this was the original shrine, that a wealthy, well-known person received a great miracle there and in gratitude built the lower shrine and had the soldier's relics, his bones, reburied there.[1] This upper chapel is constructed in chalet-style, slightly larger than the principal shrine below but much more open with its peaked ceiling and wide-open entrance. A niche built into its main altar contains the well-known image of Juan Soldado loosely woven into cloth. The insignia on the soldier's military shirt have been plucked from the image, much as early Christians in search of relics picked at the clothing or even the bones of their saints. The material around Juan's left hand, stretched down his side, has been loosened and a live rose placed in its clutch, as the pious bring him ever more closely into their lives. Near and around the image, votive candles give off their flickering light, and with its many petitions, assorted artwork, and kneeling benches, this shrine resembles its counterpart lower in the cemetery. But on the cement floor at the foot of this upper altar lies an offering of three fresh (at least, uncooked) eggs set in a bed of now-hardened red wax.

Over the centuries, the Church has often complained that veneration of saints publicly proclaimed outside its jurisdiction carried semblances of magic, superstition, and witchcraft. Indeed, caretakers of the Tijuana cemetery say that at night, when it is closed, and the gates are locked, unknown people have engaged in strange rituals at various grave sites. Remnants have been found the following day: animal bones, feathers, blood, scratches in the soil, as if some ancient rites had taken place and their celebrants faded into the darkness. As regularly occurs at the Pedro Jaramillo shrine in south Texas, it is not unusual for the faithful to combine traditional healing practices with their petitions for saintly assistance, and it is generally assumed that aspects of these ceremonies are founded in the occult. The manner of dress and instruments employed by a curandero are said to have magical qualities. Even those who believe in the power of saints admit that the devil may not be far off. In this instance, however, the eggs carried no evil omen. They had been placed there by a person who had been cured by a curandero praying through Juan Soldado and ultimately to God. Eggs rubbed on afflicted parts of the body are a common remedy in the astonishing stock of curing agents used by curanderos; the eggs draw the poison from sicknesses. The ailing individual had made Juan a promesa: Heal me and I will offer you the eggs in return, and the person fulfilled the manda. Here one witnesses the blending of Catholicism as practiced at the shrine with customs long embedded in everyday knowledge. Faith is the essential ingredient common to each.

In another instance of this meld, a woman warns that one should not light one votive candle with the flame of another. Why not? Because if you do, the troubles of the person who lit the original candle will be passed on to you. A sort of contagion will occur. Better to light a candle with a match.[2] Those in search of betterment select from a smorgasbord of religiosity and practicality. Naturally, they rely on proven help, but when one choice does not work, they try another, or several others, and many times their selections overlap. In some ways, they are not so different from the rest of us with troubles.

The Faithful

As with any such gathering, there is considerable diversity among the nearly five hundred people visiting the shrine this sunny day. A profile of the group drawn by questionnaire from more than a hundred of the faithful shows them to be about two-thirds female, of all ages with most between twenty-five and forty, almost two-thirds of them married. Almost all had some formal education, but half had not completed primary school. Yet half of the other half, or 25 percent of the total, had finished high school and a handful studied beyond. Some 20 percent lived and worked in the United States, and another 10 percent were employed across the line but lived in Tijuana. Jobs covered the spectrum, with most in unskilled labor involving public works, housing, waiters and waitresses, repair helpers, flower sellers, shop employees, janitors, vegetable packers, and factory workers. A quarter considered themselves professionals—teachers, nurses, bureaucrats, secretaries, merchants, accountants, musicians—or skilled laborers, such as carpenters, printers, auto mechanics, painters, electricians, and tailors. One-fifth of the women said they were housewives. Overall, only 10 percent claimed to be unemployed, but a significant number, approaching 20 percent, declined to give their work status, which might indicate a good deal of clandestine, illegal, unmentionable, or embarrassing activity among these individuals. This is not surprising given the hustling, innovative, unpredictable, often dangerous ways Tijuanenses engage to make ends meet.

Only one-tenth of the group polled had been born in Tijuana. The others came from all over the republic, but 40 percent of them claimed western central Mexico as their birthplace, and another 10 percent northwestern states. But these migrants were not newcomers to the city; they had lived in Tijuana an average of fifteen to twenty years. Thus far, the picture drawn of these devotees to Juan Soldado greatly resembles that of Tijuanenses as a whole, although social statistics for the city are notoriously unreliable. Still, it seems that those visiting the shrine on San Juan Day are neither destitute nor forsaken, and may well be more stable and better off than a good many of their fellow, local citizens.

All call themselves Catholics, meaning they were baptized Catholics and hope to die Catholics. Almost half say they go to Mass every week, and another tenth every two weeks, so they see no discrepancy between their devotion to Juan Soldado and formal church attendance, even if local bishops have emphatically denied Juan any saintliness. In fact, those who venerate Juan Soldado go to church more often than the city's other Catholics. A third first heard of Juan Soldado through family, most often "mama," and another third by way of friends, fellow workers, neighbors, and acquaintances, most of whom claimed that Juan had helped them. Some others first visited the shrine because they lived near the cemetery or learned of the miracle worker in casual conversation with fellow shoppers, or via television programs, newspaper articles, or simply stories circulating around town. One said Juanito came to him in a vision, another that his father had known the soldier.

Only a sprinkling made their first visit out of curiosity. A few others had first come as children, brought there by their parents, but most came to ask for help: to cross the border without a hassle, get off drugs, find a residence in public housing, to secure a passport, request a cure, to get decent employment, have a husband stop drinking, to discover a lost mother, become pregnant, or more generally, "Just to know him [Juan Soldado]," "to ask favors," and "to solve problems." It cannot be determined how many visited Juan once, or several times, and then decided not to return, discarding him as their patron for lack of satisfactory return. A third of those surveyed visit the shrine only once a year, usually on this day, his birthday. Another third come several times a year, perhaps monthly. Almost 15 percent pay a weekly call, but a good many say, "when I can," or "when I am in town," "not often," "when I feel like it," or "when I need a miracle." As a group, they have been coming to the chapel for an average twenty years. There were a few "first timers," but many had been visiting for several years, and over 40 percent for more than ten years. Virtually all consider Juan "muy milagroso," or very miraculous.[3]

ENOUGH OF STIFF statistics. It is unconscionable to reduce these warmly chatty, festive, proudly devoted people to stark statistics. Flesh and bones need to be added to the numbers. Listening to them with all their doubts, frankness, and sincerity is a pleasure.

A sixty-two-year-old divorced woman with only one year of formal education, who was born in Bachíniva in the state of Chihuahua but now lives in Mexicali, has been coming to the shrine for sixteen years. Still, she harbors uncertainties: "I know very well he is not a saint, because he is not recognized by the Pope, but he makes miracles. He has done them for me. I have a lot of faith in him."

A taxi driver, forty years of age, with a primary education, born in Guadalajara and transplanted to Tijuana in 1970, explains that some years back he got into trouble with the law over marijuana possession and looked to Juan Soldado for help, which he received. (He declined to elaborate on the type of assistance obtained.) He has been coming to the shrine once a month for ten years, and for protection from all sorts of problems encountered by taxi drivers, he carries water from the cemetery in his cab. The man says he is Catholic, but he does not go to Mass, and every decade he visits the famous image of the Virgen de Talpa, outside of Guadalajara, "de rodillas," on his bare knees, scraping across the pavement to pay his respects.

Born in Michoacan, this seventy-year-old man has lived in Tijuana for forty-eight years. He picked cherries and peaches as a seasonal worker in the United States, and with his wife has been visiting the shrine for twenty years. He recognizes that nothing is known of the background of Juan Castillo Morales or the crime of which he was convicted but he hopes for the best: "They say that Juan was a good boy, but who knows?"

A woman, fifty-four years old, is from Nayarit and lives in San Diego, where she works in a hospital. She first came to Juan Soldado for help with her unspecified troubles: "I don't know much of his [the soldier's] background or the crime, but I would like to know the truth." While his background remains unsettled in her mind, she adores him as a miracle worker.

The same sorts of doubts concern a fifty-three-year-old bachelor from Veracruz, who has lived in Tijuana for thirty years: "There are lots of things they may say about him [Juan Soldado], but who knows if it's true or a lie." Yet his devotion to Juan remains strong.

Another woman from Nayarit, fifty-nine years of age, who has lived in Tijuana for forty years, could not have children. She asked Juan Soldado for help, and within four months she had adopted a two-year-old daughter. "Juan Soldado makes miracles. Because he died unjustly, God gave him the *don* [the power] to make miracles."

Stories and legends about Juan Soldado led a seventy-three-year-old woman, born in San Lorenzo, Sinaloa, and a resident of Tijuana for forty-eight years, to devotion. Now she comes to fulfill a manda. Her son was in an accident, and doctors wanted to amputate his arm. She asked the help of Juan Soldado, and the arm was saved: "Those who die in a brutal manner have miracle-working powers."

A seventy-four-year-old woman, a native of Zapotiltic, Jalisco, who lives in Los Angeles, is at the shrine to ask for the release of a nephew from the Los Angeles County Jail. The court sentenced the nephew to eight years in jail on a narcotics charge, then reduced it to six years. A hearing for reduction of sentence was held in April, and she asked Juan to have her nephew freed. He was, and now she is fulfilling her promesa.

National television brought Juan Soldado to the attention of a woman, age fifty-six, born in Veracruz but now living in Mexico City. She came to the chapel to ask Juan's help for an elderly friend who was about to lose his home. There is no tradition of taking and returning stones at similar shrines honoring others in Veracruz, but she took a stone from the Juan Soldado chapel hoping for a miracle. Her friend did not lose his home, and today she is in Tijuana to return the stone.

Visiting from Mexicali, a sixty-three-year-old woman entered the chapel with four other people, and Juan Soldado spoke to one of them, telling her of his innocence and how his superior officer had framed him. He then told her how to reinvigorate the fertility of her brother's farm-land: light five red candles, sprinkle water and sugar on the property that does not seed. She did so, and the following year's crop was bountiful.

Before attempting to cross the border illegally, young men normally go to their mothers to ask their love and blessing for safekeeping. The son of this sixty-seven-year-old woman from Guadalajara, who now lives on the outskirts of Tijuana, had no time for this familial act. His *coyote* (smuggler) was impatiently awaiting him. So he went to Juan Soldado and asked for protection, which he received. Now the mother is grateful and is fulfilling her son's manda.

Juan Castillo Morales appeared in a dream to a forty-three-year-old man who makes cardboard cartons in Tucson but lives to the south in Naco, Sonora, which adjoins the border. Juan identified himself and told him of his unfortunate past and urged a visit to his shrine. Friends helped the man to make the connection with Juan Soldado in Tijuana. There the man discusses his needs with Juan, and a bond has grown between them.

The graduate of a U.S. university, this forty-seven-year-old woman who works in an American hospital and lives in Chula Vista (south of San Diego) says that her father knew Juan Castillo Morales and believed in his innocence. Juan, she said, had lived in Tijuana as a young lad, loved children, and organized games for children so that they would not get into trouble and become vagrants. She is the one respondent who concluded that such a good person had to be innocent of any crime.[4]

These testimonials are hardly unique, nor were they specially skimmed from the survey or from the hundreds reviewed during my visits to the shrines. They are typical of the warm, friendly, human, and diverse ways in which individuals have come to know Juan Soldado. They represent the fascinating (but not unblemished) face of religiosity with all its doubts, frowns, magic, longing, innocence, gratitude, hopes, and needs. Among the irregular patterns, we encounter the invention and embellishment of the soldier's life story, the uneasy flight of his ánima seeking new recruits to venerate him, the use of custom and magic to restore fertility in the land, the belief that those who die suddenly and unjustly are blessed. Many shelter doubts about Juan's background and his role in the crime, but evince a willingness to suspend disbelief in the name of miracles granted, a thoroughly pragmatic approach to problem solving: what works, works. Certainly, these devotees are not inflexible religious fanatics, nor do they wallow in superstition and ignorance. They are as modern as the next person on the street, and more creative than many in dealing with their problems. Juan Soldado does not necessarily represent any court of last resort for them, but an alternative approach to the Almighty whose grace is evident in miracles received.

AT 4 P.M. A STREAM of pilgrims still approaches the shrine, some crawling long distances on their now-battered knees to pay their respects to the santo. A group of women recite the Rosary out loud and sing traditional Catholic hymns at the entrance to the chapel. It is the sort of thing one hears and witnesses over and over again at Roman Catholic prayer meetings or services and is a persuasive reminder of how deeply the devotion to Juan Soldado is rooted in traditional Catholicism. They have brought the Church to Juan and vice versa. Meanwhile, cemetery personnel are already starting to clean up the site, placing perishable flowers and fruit in piles to be burned. They are anxious to go home. An hour later, they announce the closing of the cemetery, and the pilgrims slowly begin their departure, some making a final sign of the cross at the shrine. They pass right by, but pay no attention to, the Camacho family burial vault, a handsome marble structure that stands out among more common graves with their simple slabs and headstones. Olga is not there, but in Cemetery Number Two, just up the street. Her part in the drama appears to be forgotten.

Now the gates to Cemetery Number One are closed and padlocked. A car pulls up with out-of-town license plates, and four people get out, one of them a young man in his early twenties, who explains that the family group is on vacation from Guadalajara, and that he read about Juan Soldado in a book about Mexican santos and wished to photograph the shrine. As a Charismatic Catholic, he says that he does not believe that

Juan Soldado is a saint or that the miracles attributed to Juan are bona fide. Still, the devotion is a curiosity and an example of how Catholics stretch their faith.

The caretaker in charge, wearied by the day's pressures, declines to reopen the gate—"No se puede"—it just is not possible. He suggests that the visitors return the next day. They say they cannot, but perhaps they will.

The Church and Juan Soldado

The Roman Catholic Church has its rules and policies concerning the selection of saints, but they are flexible, subject to political expediency, at times contradictory in application, and ignored by much of the laity. Priests and bishops are hardly of one mind about the canonization process and the amount of parishioner participation to be tolerated. Bishops tend to be the guardians of the faith; they are the ones to decide whether or not a process toward sainthood should be forwarded to Rome for more formal investigation. And bishops are not easy to move. Local priests may or may not sympathize with their congregation's pressures for a canonization, but it is the bishop who can nip the process in the bud, normally by tabling the request of the faithful, that is, delaying and impeding any investigation until advocates get worn out trying or die off. In the early days of Christianity, when believers fervently, but randomly, proclaimed their saints, bishops endorsed some of them simply to gain some control over the process. For centuries, however, ultimate authority has rested with the popes, who have used it to fulfill the requirements of the Church, as they and their councils determine and interpret them. A lack of firm guidelines and the elasticity of choice at the highest echelons of the institution have encouraged consternation and protest among believers, who tend to shape and cast their own religiosity regardless of official dogma.

Devotions to the borderland santos to whom we have been introduced are all in flux, some of them suspended in a web of bureaucratic hopelessness, others off on their own and flourishing. Charlene seems to be stymied in southwest Louisiana. The major promoters there are patiently working with the bishop who has convinced them that their case is not yet strong enough—no certifiable miracle has yet occurred—and that "these things take time." Meanwhile, the faithful continue to give thanks at the girl's grave site for miracles granted. There seems to be less of a press for El Tiradito's canonization in Tucson, where parish priests in the area of the "Sinner's Shrine" are split over the merits of the devotion. Some say that any devotion which reinforces the faith and brings people closer to God is virtuous and worthy of clerical support. Others note the propensity of the devil to pose as a positive good while doing evil. Niño Fidencio, who faced vituperative denunciations from the Church and media during his earthly ministry, still draws the devoted to Espinazo. Continuing resistance by the Church blocks any possibility of official recognition, but has in no way diminished belief in El Niño's healing powers or his ability to produce miracles. Jesús Malverde faces a similar standoff with the Church in Sinaloa, but belief in his protective energy continues to spread and deepen. There is much sympathy among clergy in south Texas for devotion to Pedro Jaramillo, although some decry it as superstition and ignorance. Under the circumstances, there can be no official movement toward sainthood, although many swear to have benefited from his saintliness.

Within the Church's hierarchy of possibilities, Juan Soldado seems on the same plane as Pedro Jaramillo. Bishops decry, ignore, or try to remain neutral by nominally appreciating devotion to him, while assuring the faithful that Juan does not meet the criteria for sainthood. Once a year, in a formal ceremony, bishops in Tijuana's cathedral bless the sacred images of their parishioners, but when one bishop came across prayers and pictures of Juan Soldado in the stack to be blessed, he tore them up and tossed them aside. Nevertheless, pictures of Juan and printed copies of the special prayer dedicated to him continue to appear in the cathedral, on private home altars, and in the wallets and pocketbooks of his followers. As with El Salvador's Bishop Romero, the Church believes that Juan Castillo Morales may have been unjustly executed, but that he is not a martyr to the faith because he died for political reasons. In 1982, the then-Bishop of Tijuana, Jesús Posadas y O'Campo (who was killed in a shootout between drug lords outside the Guadalajara airport in 1993), issued a formal statement concerning Juan Soldado. It is the only such pronouncement that we have from a prelate:

> If Juan Soldado is a Saint, he has to meet three conditions [criteria]. A man is able to have his defects; is able to have many qualities, but also deficiencies, including psychological ones. And this is above all, be-

cause all men are able to become saints. In the second place, he must have displayed heroic Christian virtues: faith, hope, and above all, a love of God and of himself, and finally a saint must be officially canonized and recognized as such by the Church.

As for Juan Soldado, the first condition is clear. He was a man of our race, of our times, of our history, and of our conditions. As far as heroic virtues, history must judge that, but it seems that he was really and precisely a model of virtue, according to the eyewitnesses that there are. Because he died through the injustice of a false accusation that they [the authorities] brought against him for something that he had not done, in their hearts people believe him to be a victim. In this way, they consider this man a saint because he unjustly suffered.

The Church has not recognized him [as a saint], because in order to recognize a person as a saint one needs a long process, and it is very difficult to prove the virtues that he [Castillo Morales allegedly] practiced.

As a result, from the position of the Church we cannot confirm that Juan Soldado might be a saint.

The bishop hesitates at this point, and then sighs:

People, many people of good will and a sense of piety, go to the tomb [of Juan] to ask God's intercession, and God may listen to them, and if it is what He wishes, and given their faith along with the righteousness of their intention, . . .

His excellency again pauses, then:

Well, they come to this intercessor [Juan Soldado], who according to tradition and history, died unjustly because of a false accusation. God knows [the truth]. But we can hope that in the infinite mercy of The Lord, he will be welcomed among His saints.[5]

Priests working in the vicinity of Juan Soldado shrines essentially follow the bishop's lead. Only a handful attempt to steer their parishioners away from the devotion, utilizing charges of superstition and ignorance to make their point. A priest at Tijuana's Catholic seminary, Mario Valderrama, says, "The people who believe in Juan Soldado are largely ignorant and of lower social status. The superstitiousness of these people also plays a large role in their belief in Juan."[6] Father Francisco Javier

Salcido, whose parish includes Magdalena, Sonora, explains: "People call themselves Catholics because they were baptized in the Church. . . . They believe in Juan Soldado through ignorance. They have many santos, one for each thing: lost keys, their health, or to find a sweetheart for their son. They believe in Juan Soldado through ignorance, but is it better to eliminate devotion to him than to leave the people with no faith at all?"[7] Most priests answer that question "No." Padre Antonio Ollos blessed and said Mass at the inauguration of the Magdalena shrine, and a Spanish missionary did the same at the soldier's shrine outside the fishing village of Abreojos on Baja California Sur's Pacific coast. Father Eduardo Samaniego of San Diego's Christ the King barrio church says with conviction: "Do not take peoples' devotion from them," and adds, "We are made in the image or likeness of God. There is God in us. When people come to me and say, 'I have seen a vision,' I then ask, 'What has this done for your life? How has this changed your life for the better?' When they explain, I encourage belief in the vision. Imagination is fine if it brings us closer to God."[8]

Father Salvador Cisneros of Tijuana stresses that a person's santo is his or her protector. "The saint is not only a moral symbol. It is someone who actually protects. People want protection, and for those who venerate Juan Soldado, he is the santo closest to their lived experience. The Virgin Mary wants people to do better; Juan Soldado grants miracles despite bad behavior."[9] Once again the emphasis: devotees consider Juan to be one of *their own* and sympathetic to *their* necessities.

The faithful in Tijuana do not overly criticize the Church for its reluctance to consider Juan Soldado for sainthood, and they have not advocated his candidacy in any formal way. They note that it can be centuries before the Church gets around to certifying the sanctity of an individual whose saintliness has long been popularly recognized, and they offer the Peruvian San Martín, along with their own country's Juan Diego, as examples. The people proclaimed them saints during the colonial period of Latin American history; the Church canonized San Martín in 1962 and Juan Diego in 2002. In short, they find the Church lagging, but are confident that Juan Soldado's moment shall arrive. A devotee puts it this way: "Why should I care whether or not the Church has anything to do with Juan Soldado? I speak to him and God listens in."[10] A typically practical Jesuit, Gil Gentile, sums it up, "Traditionalists think of Juan Soldado as magic and superstition. Others see him as important as Jesus.

Then they bypass Jesus and pray to Juan Soldado. The devotion does not fit into official Church teachings. It does not speak for the hierarchal Church. *It just happens.*"[11]

Dynamic Devotions

Devotions, such as that to Juan Soldado, are never static; they are always percolating, being reshaped and remodeled. How can it be otherwise, when the interplay between those circumstances and beliefs which led to the adoration in the first place are so different from those generating the devotion today? A thin residue of an earlier mix may remain, but the requisites and aspirations of the pious fluctuate and are transformed by the realities and fantasies of their own age. When veneration began, Tijuana was a physically cohesive town of less than fifteen thousand inhabitants, principally lodged on a small mesa. Now its population is estimated to be nearly two million; the city sprawls for miles in a crazy-quilt pattern over the abrupt hills and canyons of the surrounding countryside and down to the sea.

Tijuana is a stew of people. What was in 1938 a relatively insignificant, loosely patrolled, and easily negotiated border post is now the most crossed international line in the world, tightly guarded from the U.S. side, and smothered in bureaucratic rigamarole. Today's formidable waves of migration dwarf the ripples of the 1930s, and while tourism remains important, the city is far less dependent on it than it was in the earlier years. None of the virulent crime that currently pervades Tijuana was evident in the late 1930s, which is why the ghastly rape and murder of Olga Camacho so spontaneously jolted the community into deadly turmoil. Protestantism possessed only a tiny toehold in the town sixty years ago, but now an evangelical presence is notable in the city. Consumerism, materialism, secularization—those hallmarks of bustling modern cities— have created opportunities, raised expectations, torn at family ties, as well as community traditions and comradeships; they have strained public services, frustrated bureaucrats, worried spiritual leaders, forced individualism on many who fear it, encouraged artistic creation, and made Tijuana both a beacon of possibility and siren of disaster. While the cost of living is higher than in most other parts of Mexico, so is per capita income, which is second only to the luxury resort town of Cancún. Increasingly, migrants who once saw Tijuana only as a jumping-off platform for the United States now come to stay, to make it their workplace and their home. Much of this effervescence is reflected at the shrine of Juan Soldado. It can be seen in the petitions that the pious address to the santo, in their creative reconstructions of the story that gave rise to the devotion, and in their wonderment over (or indifference toward) official Church doctrine concerning the role of saints, the destination of one's soul, and a person's relationship to the divine.

JUAN SOLDADO, HOWEVER, does not only belong to his reverent followers. He has become associated as well with the secular city at large; he is a vital part of Tijuana's history and recognized as such. As a steadfast common soldier, he also represents the nation. Furthermore, he is increasingly the object of attention for the media as well as the arts, and the subject of academic inquiry. Almost everyone in Tijuana and in southern California's Latino community has heard of Juan Soldado, and while relatively few people venerate him as a saint or have ever been to his chapel, they know the outlines of his story, even as they hesitate to pronounce judgment on its veracity.

The earliest (discovered) newspaper account of the devotion appeared in the *San Isidro Border Press* nearly nine months after the execution of Juan Castillo Morales. It verified that worship was flourishing at the grave site during annual Day of Dead rites on 2 November 1938. Two weeks later the *San Diego Evening Tribune* investigated reports that the soldier's pleading voice was luring scores of young ladies to the scene, where they were said to pray for his soul and petition for assistance in solving a personal problem. Some found their wishes for marriage quickly granted.

These women had gone to the cemetery on 1 November to place flowers on the graves of loved ones, and on passing the spot where Juan fell dead, they claim to have heard an unearthly voice: "I am innocent. I sacrificed myself for the sake of another." It was thought to be that of the soldier's restless ánima crying out for justice and peace. "Burning candles, they kneel and offer prayers. They snatch up and throw rocks, cans, and other missiles 'to drive away the evil spirits.'" The reporter concluded that the place "is attaining the aspects of a shrine."

A photo that accompanied the article shows a well-established shrine, covered with flowers and large rocks. Tin cans hold water to preserve freshly cut flowers, and at one end stands an elegant tall standard featuring a religious image, its top protected by an arched roof and floral coronas (crowns) hanging from its wooden arms. Such standards stake out one's claim to a place. The writer did not understand the significance of the rocks, cans, and offerings left at the grave and lamented the "ever-increasing pile of debris around the grave," which "offers mute testimony to the strange rites on the hillside."[12] Strange to the reporter, perhaps, but obviously well understood by the faithful.

Tijuana's most-read Spanish-language newspaper, *El Hispano Americano* (circulation 4,500), ridiculed the *Tribune*'s piece and in large headlines labeled it "calumniosa," slanderous. It insisted that young ladies of Tijuana should not be accused of practicing rites which resemble those of the "black-lipped pico de pato of central Africa" (a reference to natives distinguished by their large, round lip pieces). The article, it assumed, must have been the work of an elderly *Tribune* correspondent who had lived in Tijuana for twenty years, did not speak Spanish, and undoubtedly received his misinformation from his drinking buddies, making fun of him in a local cantina which they all frequented.[13] Border people often respond to perceived cultural slights with sharp invective.

For the next three decades Juan Soldado's paper trail is thin. Printed stories focused more on the crime and its aftermath than on the devotion itself. In 1946, *Detective Internacional*, published in Tijuana, saw a crime wave caused by the unfettered growth of population and tourism during World War II sweeping town and called for harsh and immediate punishment for those responsible. The magazine noted that the failure to bring Juan Castillo Morales to justice promptly (that he was not shot on arrest or turned over to the mob for its brand of justice) had ignited riots that led to the destruction of public buildings, which were the main symbols of order and authority. "Venal or partial justice in which the delinquent is not punished delivers to the community a life of revenge and justice at its own hands."[14] So much for the devotion based largely on a supposed injustice dealt the accused, but then most townspeople who recalled the events thought the soldier guilty.

El Imparcial, another Tijuana newspaper, published a special section in 1952, which recapitulated the riotous happenings fourteen years earlier. While its focus was on the repression of union involvement in the turmoil, it presented a detailed and balanced account of the crime, discussed the evidence against Castillo Morales, found it compelling but noted that many mistakenly thought the soldier innocent and prayed for his salvation. "The popular mind is highly fickle and easily led to believe that which many times is not the truth."[15] One of the photographs accompanying the text shows Juan's grave site covered with stones, flowers, and a large cross which carried a plaque dated 1950 on which Salvador M. González thanked Juan Soldado for saving him from a "prison so great" coupled to hopes that God had taken the soldier to His holy kingdom. Three other crosses at the site also attested to miracles received.

The media's relentless search for human interest stories revived interest in Juan Soldado in the 1980s, and by then the press and television had a "hook." As debate over the impact of Mexican immigration on American labor, social services, and schools became more strident, lives of the migrants came under closer scrutiny, and those most sympathetic to the plight of migrants soon discovered Juan Soldado. Mainly in the Southwest and southern California, in telling their life stories, migrants increasingly referred to the protective powers of the santo who had helped them to evade the net woven by American authorities to snare illegal entrants. One miracle escape blended into another, and the media soon crowned Juan as the patron saint of migrants, much as drug enforcement in the state of Sinaloa had made Jesús Malverde the patron saint of narcotics dealers.

Santos may have their specialties, but they are also approached in more general ways, and petitions left at shrines are sure indicators of community concerns. When in the early 1990s the Texas state legislature passed a law making automobile insurance mandatory, an inordinate number of photocopies of car registrations and licenses appeared on the walls of the Pedro Jaramillo chapel in Falfurrias. The shrine lies in the largely Hispanic Rio Grande Valley, one of the poorest regions in America. Many there could not afford automobile insurance, so they took their chances with noncompliance and relied on Pedro Jaramillo for protection. Judging by the proliferation of "thanks for the miracle received" messages scratched across the faces of those photocopies, the santo had responded to the necessity.[16]

About the same time, the Virgin of San Juan shrine, situated in the farming community of San Juan deep in the Rio Grande Valley, experienced a swarm of petitions accompanied by photos of young Latino men and women in military uniform. The devotion itself has a spectacular history. In the 1940s, Father José Azpiazú, the Spanish missionary priest whose parish included San Juan, became disturbed by reports that some members of his congregation had begun to worship several vague lines on a rock that they imagined to be an outline of the Virgin Mary. Father Azpiazú noted that many of his parishioners had migrated there from the major Mexican pilgrimage site at San Juan de los Lagos. To counter what he considered a spurious cult, he traveled to the Mexican shrine and commissioned a statue of the Virgin of San Juan for his own church. En route, Father Azpiazu and his companions nearly suffered a fatal accident and considered their escape a confirmation of divine sanction for their commission.

When they learned of the experience of their priest and the arrival of the new image of the Virgin, parishioners and other Catholics from throughout the region flocked to the devotion, supported by their donations and those of others from throughout the United States and Mexico. Contributions reached half a million dollars, which financed a large, attractive church at the locale. In the fall of 1970 the power of its blessed image was confirmed when an angry preacher, distraught at the success of this rival church, crashed a light plane into the structure, killing himself, burning the building nearly to the ground, but injuring no one and leaving the statue of the Virgin intact. Repair dollars flooded in, and within a decade a veritable cathedral marked the site, graced by the miraculous Virgin on its main altar and with a beautifully appointed chapel for supplicants to one side. In 1991, attached to the walls of this chapel were the extraordinary number of photographs of young people in military service with the petitions: "Bring my son home safe and sound"; "Protect my daughter against harm"; "Let my son serve his country well"; "Help my daughter to do her duty bravely." The Gulf War was in progress; the valley had contributed a disproportionately large number of volunteers to the war effort, and the shrine unmistakably exhibited the moment's community concerns along with its pride.[17]

CERTAINLY, WITH TIJUANA well-known as a springboard for illegal (and legal) entry into the United States, petitions for assistance in making it across the line and finding safe haven on the *otro lado* are to be expected. As a group they comprise some 10 percent of all petitions left at the Juan Soldado shrine. My favorite concerns a young man who four times had crossed the border illegally, was discovered, and turned back by authorities. Determined to make another try, he asked Juan to "turn off the computers of the migra," so that even if again caught, his past failures would not be recalled.

With Operation Gatekeeper (stricter measures against illegal migrants inaugurated by the U.S. government along the border on 1 October 1994) and the heightened overall security imposed after 11 September 2001 now making it more difficult to cross, the assistance of Juan Soldado is more eagerly sought. I recently met a young man at the shrine in desperate need of the santo's help. I was inside taking notes when he approached me (an obvious gringo), speaking pretty fair English, mixed with Spanish:

"What goes on in here?" he asked.

I explained that this was the Juan Soldado shrine.

"I know nothing of these sorts of things," he said. "I am not very religious. Who is Juan Soldado?"

I briefly related the story as told to me by devotees.

"Well, I have just been kicked out of the United States, four days ago, and I need to go back there to see my wife and two kids. I have no money, and was wandering down a street in downtown Tijuana when a woman told me that I should talk to Juan Soldado about my problem. She told me how to get here."

"A wife and two children?" I inquired.

"Yes, I crossed over four years ago and found work around Los Angeles. I met this American woman from Louisiana, and we've been living together. Now we have two tiny children, one two, the other a baby."

The fellow, in his late twenties, said he was from the city of Parral, on the southern edge of the state of Chihuahua. "I don't know what to do. I want to get back to my wife and kids, but maybe I will have to return to my family in Parral."

He said that he held a well-paying job, earning $12.50 an hour at a toy store in Long Beach, California, when migration authorities swept in, rounded up, and deported (dumped into Tijuana) all illegal suspects.

"When I first went into the United States, I paid a coyote $1,000 to take me across. Now the coyotes are asking $1,800, and I have no money at all."

"So now you are here to speak to Juan Soldado?"

"Well, I guess so. The woman on the street told me that he was muy milagroso and specialized in helping migrants. But I have no idea what to do in here."

"Maybe you can light a candle and ask for assistance. People *do* say that he grants miracles."

"OK, I'll give it a try. Oh, by the way, can you spare me a little money for something to eat? I have not eaten for a couple of days, and I am really hungry."

I handed him a $5 bill.

"Muchas gracias. That's my first miracle from Juan Soldado."[18]

PUBLIC AND SCHOLARLY interest in Juan Soldado has thrived in the last decade or so. It began in 1987 with an exposition including photographs and testimonials at the Centro de la Raza in San Diego's famous Balboa Park. Newspapers touted the exhibit and sent reporters to the shrine to develop their own accounts of the devotion. Television soon weighed in with its versions, carrying the story nationwide through its Hispanic network. Also in 1987, the newspaper *ABC* reinvestigated the crime and its context and brought the history of the devotion up to date in a series of detailed stories that ran for six weeks. In 1999 the *Los Angeles Times* syndicated an article which within two weeks showed up in the *Philadelphia Inquirer*. Other outlets that cater to Hispanic culture have further spread the story. A modernistic painting of Juan, surrounded by symbols like the Virgin of Guadalupe and with the skyline of Los Angeles in the background, has been printed as a picture postcard. Televisa, one of Mexico City's most watched TV stations, featured the Juan Soldado story in its popular "Santos y Santones" (Church-canonized saints and people's saints) program in 2002.

Tijuana itself has kept pace. Television accounts periodically replay for local interest. Members of the city's historical society have diligently pursued leads to the story, while scholars on both sides of the line have published on the topic. In 1990 a folklorist concluded in her *Leyendas de Tijuana* that even if Juan were unjustly executed, he is no saint, and she suggested that the shrine survives only because it is a moneymaker for unnamed parties who regularly empty the shrine's coin box of its donations.[19] Even if they did so, they would not get rich. For many years the contributions, collected by a nearby neighbor, were used for public improvements in the colonia—for a day-care center, a children's outdoor park, the local school, and to pave the main pathway to the Juan Soldado chapel with stones and cement. Robbers have periodically pried open the box for its contents. As the cemetery is municipal, however, the city government recently reinforced the coin box, took over collections, and added them to the municipal budget, totaling about $100 a month.[20]

Although revenue produced at the Juan Soldado chapel is meager, shrines can be enormous moneymakers. Saint Jude's in Chicago and the chapel celebrating the Virgin in Lourdes, France, are examples of modern, highly capitalized operations. San Juan thrives on donations in south Texas, as does Charlene in Louisiana, where a drive is now underway to repair recent hurricane damage to the church. Donations at the Malverde shrine have financed the purchase of thousands of wheelchairs and crutches for the infirm along with coffins for families who could not afford a decent burial for a loved one.[21]

Compared to these moneymakers, Juan Soldado is a pauper, and many devotees believe that shrines ought not be used to produce revenue, especially if the recipients are in some way suspect. The sale of candles and a few other relatively inexpensive devotional articles inside the shrine itself finances the El Señor de los Milagros chapel in San Antonio and provides a living for its owners. Remember, however, this shrine is privately owned on private property. Some who worship there recall the story of Christ and the moneylenders in the temple. They find such commerciality irreverent, but so far their protests have been ignored.

Similar charges of crass commercialization now circle the new Toribio Romo shrine in tiny Santa Ana de Guadalupe, where Beethoven's Fifth Symphony echoes from speakers attached to electric light poles, and the local church runs the Pilgrim's Restaurant, where it sells T-shirts that carry the image of the martyred santo. Tourism is financing a prosperity that the pueblo and parish have never known. Says the priest in charge, thirty-nine-year-old Gabriel González Pérez, "We are not trying to make money on people's faith. We simply want to give the people who visit us the best service we can."[22]

SAINTS HAVE THEIR special prayers, most of them cut from the same mold by manufacturers of prayer cards and votive candles, who wrap paper printed with the prayers around the candles they sell. As Juan Soldado is a small devotion, it has not attracted large commercial operations, so vendors outside Cemetery Number One write and photocopy his prayer to paste on votive candles. For those who wish to address Juanito, here is his prayer:

Praise the Holy Almighty, in the name of the Father, the Son, and the Holy Ghost, Who with His infinite mercy has shed His grace, indulgences, and miracles on my dear brother and protector Juan Castillo Morales.

In the name of God Almighty and in the spirit and soul of Juan Soldado, with heartfelt righteousness and overwhelming faith in your infallible help, I confide in you all the worries that morally and materially torment me, never doubting for a minute that my good wishes will be fulfilled, providing that the Lord and you in particular agree.

At this point you make your petition for assistance, and then continue:

As you know Juanito, my petition is just, and all I need is your support to rid myself of the immoral and material things that are consuming me.

Brother Juan, the soldier, I beg of you, do not deny me your protection in this difficult task.

I consign myself to God's mercy and your infallible help, and I promise from this moment on to be among those devoted to you. Amen.

This prayer is steeped in traditional Catholicism, confessional at its core. "Help me, Juan, with the moral and material problems which are consuming me." What the Church meant (or used to mean) by such problems originated in the Ten Commandments—no stealing, jealousy, killing, adultery, false gods, and the rest—but none of the petitions left at the shrine address these sorts of issues. Instead, today there are pleas to solve family dilemmas, fulfill common material needs, restore health, obtain legal documents, assure safe passage across the border, find love, attain good school grades. The oration reeks of humbleness and guilt; the petitions address daily needs and aspirations. Here we see the religiosity of mainly ordinary people at work, leaning on the structure of their cultural heritage for support, while refashioning its inner substance to deal with their contemporary concerns.

Moreover, the formal prayer to Juan Soldado carries a certain formulaic stiffness not often present in the passionate, personal sentiments of those who venerate him. For example, here is a poem that one of the pious posted at his shrine:

Poem to the Miraculous Soldier

You are yourself a soldier
To me, a kind soldier

Like the guerrilla [warrior] you were in the past,
And now in the present you are a miracle worker.

Soldier, warrior against evil
As such you have always conquered and won
Over devils who know not the truth
Because as such [a warrior-soldier], you are able to help lamentable
    and suffering people.

There are some who say you are an assassin
Others thank you for your deeds
In my opinion, you are but
A saintly soldier, guardian of the just.

For my part, I give to you thanks,
For the favor or assistance that you rendered me.
With you, I now continue on my voyage
With this petition that you inspired and fulfilled.

This poem cannot be expressed with its deserved poignancy in English, but the imagery is at the same time simple and majestic. Juan Soldado, a heroic soldier defends the republic against invaders (likely thought of as the French imperialists in the 1860s), and is now a miracle worker. He is a national warrior, but also a warrior of God, such as Saint Michael the Archangel, relentlessly struggling against Satan and his minions who personify deceit and evil. Yes, there is controversy over his past, but no matter (an example of Mexican forgiveness—who has not sinned?). For he presently basks in God's eternal grace and watches over us, the good and righteous (imperfect beings but ones who have harmed no others). The writer concludes: Thank you, Juanito, for past favors, as well as this request (unknown) which you inspired me to make and which you fulfilled. I happily and confidently walk with you on my path through life.

Heaven truly touches earth through Juan Soldado. Yes, he is appreciated as a miracle worker, a patron, by those who have such faith in him, but more widely among the citizenry at large, he is a symbol of *our* country's glorious past and a celebrated icon in *our* city's history. You may worship the soldier if you wish, but even if not, you can hallow his presence in our midst.

9. John the Soldier

A universal Juan Soldado has long reigned among Mexican heroes. A working man or campesino, he is the soldado raso, the common soldier, who since its inception has defended the nation with unstinting valor and honor against all enemies and does not hesitate to lay down his life for the Tricolor. He is officially celebrated on the Día de los Soldados, organized by the defense ministry around banquets and parades, but the public better knows him from literature, movies, and lusty corridos, where he cavorts with his fellow *juanes* (johnnies) in a picaresque life against a backdrop of his country's lore and legends. Other countries have had their counterparts—during the U.S. Civil War, Johnny Reb zealously defended the Southern cause, while Johnny Turk turned back the British and Australians at Gallipoli. But none of these seem to be remembered in quite the same way as Mexico's juanes, who make pacts with the devil as well as with God.

An undated tale from the U.S.-Mexico border has this Juan receiving his military discharge with meager pay that he used to buy three pieces of bread for his journey home. En route, he met an elderly man seated by the side of the road who said he was hungry. When he gave the old man a piece of his bread, Juan did not know that this was Saint Paul. A short time later he met a beggar who also asked for bread. Juan did not recognize the beggar as Saint Peter, but after complaining about a country of beggars, gave the humble man his second piece of bread and continued on his way. Juan turned angry when he met a third party who asked for bread, but he surrendered his final piece to this stranger, who turned out to be God. In response to his generosity, the Almighty offered the ex-soldier His blessing along with whatever else he desired. Juan replied that he wished that his knapsack had magic powers. The Lord told Juan that when he wished for something, just say "Todo a mi mochila," everything in my knapsack, and the command will be obeyed.

Juan continued on his trip. When he got hungry, he went to a bakery, said "Todo a mi mochila," and his knapsack soon bulged with pan dulce and other baked delicacies. At night he needed a place to sleep, but there were no vacancies at rooming houses, so he bedded down in an abandoned house, even though a stranger warned him the dwelling contained ghosts. During the night Juan heard chanting and awoke to find a legion of devils hovering around him. "Todos a mi mochila," he ordered, and the devils jumped into his knapsack.

Juan is now rich. He uses the devils in his financial dealings, insuring that he stays wealthy. But every night before he goes to bed, Juan puts his money for safekeeping in a bank, and in this manner he has amassed a fortune.[1] Mexico's juanes may come to military service as down-and-outs, but they are astute, streetwise, pragmatic, and know with whom to make a deal. Whether or not devotees in Tijuana's Cemetery Number One ascribe such attributes to *their* Juan Soldado, they surely want him to make a deal.

SOON AFTER THE riots and execution of Juan Castillo Morales a movie titled *Juan Soldado, o Venganza* (Juan Soldado, or vengeance) was filmed in Tijuana. The timing is intriguing. The plot has nothing to do with the roiling events that preceded it; the project must have been planned for a national audience well before then. But with its romantic glorification of the military, one wonders whether or not it was rushed along to salve wounds opened by the army's harsh repression of the riots which had swept the town. As it turned out, the military seemed to suffer few repercussions from either its role in quelling the turbulence or its use of public execution and the Ley Fuga to punish the accused. The attitude then was that the army did what it had to do, or at least what it was expected to do, in such circumstances, and had the authority to punish one of its own as it saw fit. It raised a few eyebrows, but little else, beyond unwittingly generating the devotion to Juan Soldado.

Mexican and Hollywood moviemakers frequently filmed in Tijuana, where labor was cheap and attractive buildings, such as those in the Agua Caliente complex, formed an engaging, ready-made set. Louis Gasnier, a

French moviemaker noted around the world for his avant-garde work, directed *Juan Soldado*. He hired thousands of Tijuanenses as extras, including soldiers from the local garrison. Filming began on 12 October 1938, as part of the town's Columbus Day (now Día de la Raza) celebration.[2]

The movie was a *ranchero* (romantic cowboy) melodrama, said to be infused with the *pocho* (culturally mixed) spirit of the border. The *New York Times* reviewer called it the "best horse opera seen in [Spanish] Harlem's Teatro Hispano in many a day" and offered this synopsis of the plot:

> Emilio Tuero, possessor of good looks and a pleasing singing voice, is excellent as the young rancher who joins the army after his little place has been ravaged and his small son killed by desperados under the orders of a bandit leader who poses as a wealthy real estate man and takes advantage of the citizens' terror to buy up their land at ridiculous prices.
>
> Before the hero, with the aid of the Fourteenth Infantry [Juan Castillo Morales's former outfit], has avenged himself and cleaned up the gang, the audience sees plenty of fighting, several fiestas and some touching scenes involving María Luisa Zea (more fetching than ever), as his faithful wife, and Lucha Altamirano in the role of a ranch owner who loves him vainly, but too well. For persons familiar with Mexico, the story is far from incredible.[3]

The film's message is clear. A handsome young rancher, terrorized by lawless marauders, cannot undo his afflictions by himself, or even with the assistance of family or friends. Therefore, he joins the army and uses the military's force and reputation to root out the evildoers and return stability to a romantically colorful, peaceful and law-abiding society. It is the administration's newly professionalized army that insures justice and domestic tranquillity in Mexico. Other Mexican films entitled *Juan Soldado* were made in 1914 and 1919, but attempts to track them down have proved fruitless. As they were made during and just after the fighting phase of the Mexican Revolution, their content—even as potboilers— would be interesting, especially for their depictions of the military.

TIJUANA NOW HAS a wax museum, open since 5 February 1993, featuring a potpourri of international, national, and local figures of historical, political, and entertainment fame. Only two directly relate to Tijuana itself: Juan Soldado, and the mythical Tia Juana (Aunt Jane), which speaks to the paucity of local historical heroes. Instead of figures who have distinguished the city's past, one sees representations of national figures: the Aztec king Moctezuma; the revered nineteenth-century president Benito Juárez; and naturally Pancho Villa and Emiliano Zapata, along with the current president of Mexico, Vicente Fox, and the presidential aspirant Luis Donaldo Colosio, who was assassinated on 23 March 1994, in Tijuana. Galleries also feature international notables such as Mahatma Gandhi, Ayatollah Khomeini, Fidel Castro, Bill Clinton, and Mikhail Gorbachev. The present Pope appears with Noah, Abraham, and Daniel, with Moses in the background, and just down the corridor another alcove displays an array of movie, singing, and other entertainment stars.

The wax representation of Juan Soldado presents him as a neatly dressed soldier of the Fifth Infantry Battalion, but somewhat older in the face, darker of skin, and deliberately more realistic in countenance than plaster figures of the soldier sold outside the cemetery. The identification placard posted on the platform on which Juan stands simply mentions him as a soldier unjustly accused of a murder he did not commit, but does not specify that crime as the rape and murder of an eight-year-old girl. The immediate area has become another shrine to Juan Soldado. Rosary beads hang around the soldier's neck, votive candles burn at his side, and petitions and offerings pile up around him, so many that they are cleaned up and discarded monthly by the museum's staff. In tone and content, the peticiones are much the same as those left at chapels in the cemetery. Many are written on the backs of tickets bought to enter the museum. A pharmacist wants his business to prosper; a child asks not to be reproached by his schoolteachers. One person left 50 pesos ($5) for a fulfilled favor, another a cigarette to help himself to stop smoking. Make my parents stop fighting; help me to cross the border to bring money to my pueblo; allow me to become pregnant. "I do not want to be rich. I just want to get ahead because I am miserable." Fix my car; help my son to get organized; bring me luck in the lottery. Help us to get married; bring my father back so that we can reunite the family; demand justice for our family before [a college administrator, name mentioned] at UCLA; get my brother over the line along with all the boys from my village. The litany of hardship and frustration goes on and on and on.

In reality, however, relatively few museum visitors say a prayer or leave a message at the site. Instead they see Juan as they might any curious historical figure, someone they may have heard about in school, from family or friends, or on TV but of no personal import to their lives. Parents explain to their children that he was a soldier unfairly treated and for whom the townspeople generally hold much sympathy, but no details of the soldier's life or his ignominious end seem to be known. An observer might comment that some think him a saint, but nothing more than that is said—except that he is part of Tijuana's history. Maybe that is enough, a strong lesson in itself.

Schoolteachers take their pupils to the shrine in the cemetery. Boy Scout leaders bring their troops. Students take polls and write term papers about Juan Soldado, not necessarily because they believe in his sanctity, but because he is an important personage in local history and because soldiers like him defend the patria. Speaking casually to citizens around town, one gathers that relatively few venerate him, just a few thousand in a city of millions. "I learned from my mother that only the Church can name saints," says César Laniado, a merchant, and someone else that, "My patron is the Virgin of Guadalupe, and I have received favors from her." Others aver that, "I do not believe in such things," or "I am a Protestant and need no saints to talk to God for me." Some call the devotion "all superstition," or admit, "I am Catholic, but no longer a practicing Catholic." They leave the story of Juan Soldado at, "Se dice . . . ," it is said that, and their explanation quickly dribbles off into "¿Quién sabe?" who knows. Yet most know him as a historical figure like all such juanes poised to protect the nation, and essential as part of local tradition. In border towns, nationalism can be strident, even virulent. Tijuanenses need to get along with their neighbors to the north, but they still enjoy twisting the tiger's tail.[4]

Today's Petitions

Not all of the faithful by any means visit Juan Soldado shrines only to ask for favors. Or they do not do so every time. When asked why they came this particular day, they might say, "Just to be near Juan," or "To see how he is doing," "To make sure that he is safe," or "Just to say hello." They love this young soldier like a son, or brother, or someone close to their heart. From time to time, devotees visit just to bask in the serenity of the place. "I feel at peace here." "It is a holy place, and I feel myself in touch with God." These are people taking comfort in the shadow of the Almighty. Just being there transcends the mundane of routine daily life; it relieves the burden, and encourages one to think about more fortunate times to come. They might find something there to remind them of paradise. Some say that it makes them happy just to see someone else blessed.

Most, however, visit Juan to ask for specific favors meant to resolve pressing concerns and to bring immediate relief in the here and now. Only one petition read among several thousand in the past decade concerned broad political or social issues. That one asked for peace in the world, for the end of wars and global conflict, and the elimination of atomic bombs and such weaponry. By its wording, it seemed to have been written by a school pupil who had been impressed by a frightening civics class. But no other petitions asked for social justice, aid for the poor, or political reform.

Every now and then a petition approaches the dark side. In keeping with a long-held tradition that spirits can both heal and harm, one might ask Juan Soldado to punish an enemy, to bring bad luck upon an individual, to hurt the feelings of someone who has injured those of the petitioner. These sorts of requests may shade into black magic, and there are those who think that Juan Soldado is in league with the devil. Latinos believe that Satan also inhabits their world, and for some, Juan Soldado has his subterranean side. The Church itself warns that the devil appears in many guises, and while most priests approve of devotions that they believe bring the faithful closer to God, there is always concern that a false prophet can do the opposite. Allan Figueroa Deck, a liberal priest who has written sympathetically about Latino religious sensibilities, says the Church must carefully weigh the devotion to Juan Soldado for fear that it might be leading its followers away from the true faith rather than toward it. Satan may be at work in Cemetery Number One.[5]

Despite an occasional anomaly, petitions to Juan Soldado concern pragmatic needs. Some shudder that such materialism is at odds with the spiritual, but religion has always been practical and the spiritual meshed with the material. Father Gil Gentile explains that the petitions concern material needs "because they [the supplicants] need them. But at the same time they are looking for meaning, some kind of truth that is bigger than they are. Their faith allows them to *aguantar*—to bear up—*seguir adelante*—to keep on trucking. It gives them fuel. There are moments of grace, and grace comes in unlikely ways. Grace may be seen as divine energy. It is ammunition that you receive from God."[6]

Father Gentile in his own earthy words has expressed the nature of popular religiosity itself. It is not an either/or approach to the mundane or the spiritual. Most often, the faithful are visiting both at the same time, whether they or others realize it. This is how spirituality infuses the lives of all believers. It is their fuel for betterment.

PETITIONERS AT THE Juan Soldado shrines seek divine energy to solve problems familiar to us all. Individual needs surpass superficial similarities on the petitions. Their words are intensely personal and frequently moving. They make compassionate observers want to help, but the matter is in other hands:

> Please allow our family a good personal relationship so that our parents do not suffer. In return, I PROMISE not to fight with my brothers and sisters.

> Help my mother through her operation. I promise to bring her here personally to see you.

> Good soldier: I ask you with all my heart and all my faith that Benny has his child with him forever. Good soldier: help me as I am a mother, and like your mother, I suffer for my children. I promise to come with Benny and his son, and each will light three candles to you.

> [A business card] Larry McClements, Oakwood Multi-Media Services, Woodland Hills, California. [When contacted, he says he does not venerate Juan Soldado, but that four years ago he left a card at the shrine, "just in case." And how has business gone since then? "I have had very good luck."][7]

> Care for my mother, as I am going to the other side [the United States] to work for awhile.

> Thank you for helping my son to graduate from Redlands High School [in southern California]. [As she promised to do, she has left a photocopy of her son's diploma leaning against a bust of Juan Soldado.]

My love, a helicopter pilot, was killed in a crash of his helicopter. Bring me more information about the accident. Bring him back to me.

[Another business card] William H. Sutherling, M.D., Epilepsy and Brain Mapping Program, Los Angeles. [Dr. Sutherling denies leaving his card at the shrine. He claims to know nothing of Juan Soldado or the soldier's miracles. He is a scientist. Perhaps one of his patients left the card there—hedging bets between Dr. Sutherling and Juanito.][8]

Help me to find work, as Christmas is approaching.

Help me to have a better relationship with my mother, and to find a good man as soon as possible.

[An official U.S. notice of alien verification of illegal status appears on the wall. The notice states that the person named had presented a false U.S. birth certificate as proof of citizenship, that she misrepresented her true identity, and that therefore her visa application was denied. Now the woman wants help from Juan Soldado.]

Your mother also suffered, so help me, a mother, to keep my son with me forever.

Thank you for fulfilling my mother's request that I score a [soccer] goal [in a championship game]. [An attached newspaper clipping confirms the goal.]

Help that my sweetheart [male] never deceives me.

Unite me with this woman. If so, I promise . . . I really do not know what to promise, but I will promise something.

[On the picture of a 1980s station wagon] Gracias.

Make me a good soldier like you. The best. Strong and valiant.

Thank you for the miracle of caring for my brother. I did not believe in your miracles. I ask you to pardon me for not believing in your miracles. Today I believe in you.

I am from Tijuana. One day let me pass to the U.S.A. through the great door [customs and immigration] without hiding from anyone.

Juan Soldado, I ask you to care for my family, and I give you thanks, although I am not a Catholic.

[A banner carries the inscription: U.S. Army. Fort Roberts, California, and a poem to a sweetheart] And my constant prayer will be: That God may keep you safe for me.

Thanks for the miracles. You know powerful people work with the devil [to torment me].

[A police wanted poster from the Fresno, California, Sheriff's Office is on the wall.] Here is the man who killed my daughter [who was married to the suspect]. I ask that you help me by bringing him to justice. Thank you. [A Fresno detective confirmed the man's capture, trial, conviction, and sentence to life imprisonment. The suspect had fled to Tijuana, where a friend convinced him to turn himself over to authorities, who subsequently delivered him to Fresno detectives. The detective in charge said that it would have been difficult to apprehend the defendant had it not been for the lucky break in Tijuana. He said he knew nothing of Juan Soldado's miracles, but . . .][9]

Juan Soldado, I thank you for all that you have granted me. Give me strength so that I can solve my problems. I am a very lonely woman. I have my husband and daughter, but you know that I love another man, because we have come here together [to see you]. Please make sure that he never abandons me.

Fulfill my greatest dream. Let me win the lottery.

SOME SIXTY OUT of one hundred devotees who go to the shrines ask favors for themselves, family, or others. Many also come to give thanks for miracles received. As is commensurate with their times, more and more petitions concern immigration issues and family breakups. One can read these pleas and feel the effects of Operation Gatekeeper clamping down on visa and green card applications, raising barriers to illegal crossings, and monitoring the border with greatly augmented armed forces supported by the highest technology. Equally obvious is the stress that daily life in Tijuana is placing on families. Such may be symptomatic of all big-city life today. But relative to its space and resources Tijuana is seriously overpopulated and in many ways ungovernable. Corruption is rampant, security compromised, poverty widespread, and without a doubt Tijuana's heady, no-holds-barred ambiance has ruptured communal bonds. Just a decade ago there were only occasional references to family breakdown among petitions at the Juan Soldado chapel, but today they are too common to go unnoticed: bring my brothers home, make daddy stop mistreating mama, get my brother off drugs, help papa with his drinking problem, don't let my husband leave me, tell my wife to be faithful, make my sister stay in school, find me decent-paying work so that I do not have to leave my family for the other side, get my brother out of jail, make us one family again. There is a photograph on the wall in the main shrine of an American couple with children posed in serapes and sombreros in a cart being pulled by one of those famous zebra-striped donkeys. Scribbled on the picture is the request: Juan Soldado, please hold this happy family together.

Altered Beliefs

Just as flux is evident in the types of favors asked of Juan Soldado over the years, so is it in the spiritual beliefs that the faithful have brought to the devotion since its inception. Whereas the soldier's alleged repentance had ignited the initial veneration, now repentance is rarely, if ever, mentioned as the stimulus for worship of him. Injustice is now considered to be the root cause. For the first generation of worshipers veneration became a cleansing, while for the second and third generations, whose parents have emphasized the unfair treatment accorded the soldier, the issue has become justice. Besides, the concept of repentance as the means to eternal bliss has virtually disappeared from all Catholicism, along with notions of salvation and Purgatory. God today is seen as much less demanding and more loving, so there is less need to repent, especially for minor transgressions, as defined by the faithful, not the Church. Hellfire and damnation are all on their way out, along with crippling guilt. With the slow fading of these beliefs (some find the erosion has been occurring over centuries), a person's life history has become less important in judging that individual's merits. By and large, the background of Juan Castillo Morales is unimportant to his followers. If it meant anything to them, they would create an early life for him. As it is, they simply devise a few favorable references apropos the soldier's residence in Tijuana and let it go at that. Moreover, there is benefit in denying Juan Soldado an early life, for it allows the faithful to imagine it as they wish, if at all, and therefore proclaim him to be "everyone's saint."

When queried about the soldier's background or even the origins of devotion to him, meaning the crime and execution, increasing numbers of devotees know or care less and less. Only a decade ago, relatively few knew the soldier as Juan Castillo Morales, but almost all had their versions of what had occurred in 1938. Now 10 to 15 percent profess to know nothing of the circumstances surrounding the devotion—only that Juan Soldado is said to be muy milagroso. He grants miracles, and that is all they need to know. In past centuries, devotees are known to have chosen miracle-working saints over those of professed moral virtue, but today's sole emphasis on favors received is new and eye-opening. Certainly, the kind of world in which we live has helped to realign our priorities. Secularization, science, commercialization, consumerism, acquisitiveness, and materialism have altered values, morals, and ultimately culture. The reforms of Vatican II created gaps through which Catholics increasingly explore alternatives. The day most important to Catholics in this border region—at least the day when church is most attended—is no longer Easter or Christmas but Ash Wednesday, when the faithful receive ashes they can see and touch as a protective for next year's fortunes or even life itself.[10] Tijuana is being swept along by the tidal wave of today's sensibilities and has no traditional bulwarks to stem the onrush. Of those who worship Juan Soldado, only a handful make the annual trip home to celebrate the day of the patron saint of their natal towns and villages. Some others still go, but "not often," "when I happen to be there," "at times," or every two, four, or ten years. But by and large, that once essential festivity has been eliminated from their calendar, and there is nothing in Tijuana to replace it.

Judging by attendance on major feast days—Saint John's Day, 24 June, and the Day of the Dead, 2 November—cemetery custodians say that the devotion to Juan Soldado is losing its luster, not in fervency, but in numbers. Indeed, there does seem to have been a diminution in the last several decades. A priest remembers, "People do not venerate him as much as they did in the 1950s. Since the 1970s, his following has died down. There used to be processions for Juan on certain holy days, and people used to crawl on their knees to the shrine. Today there are never processions, and it is rare for believers to crawl on their knees to the shrine. People's reverence for Juan is not what it used to be."[11]

The most recent falloff might be attributed to economic difficulties. People at the 2002 birthday celebration for Juan said they came less often because they could not spare the money to get there or to buy flowers, candles, and other offerings once they did so. But measuring spirituality by attendance, whether it be church or shrine, is a notoriously inadequate means of judging faith, and no one can know the true or even approximate number of devotees to Juan Soldado. Inmates at the Tijuana jail create likenesses of Juan and hang them on strings around their necks; innumerable residents carry representations of Juan on their person. On the other hand, tattoo parlors on both sides of the border report little call for representations of Juan on the bodies of their customers. In considering the strength of devotion, it would be crucial to have some sense of how many have requested favors, received no response, and decided to pursue other venues. Nevertheless, of those celebrating Juan's birthday in the year 2000, about 10 percent said it was their first visit, so a small, but steady stream continues to nourish the devotion.

Even if visitation at Tijuana's main shrine has diminished, chapels elsewhere evidence the spread of veneration for Juan (see map 4). Examples are located in the northern Sonoran town of Magdalena and another outside the fishing village of Abreojos, halfway down the Pacific side of the Baja California peninsula. The Magdalena chapel grew from a mother's desperation to free her teenage son from the Tucson city jail where in 1950 he was being held on drug-trafficking charges. The mother learned of Juan Soldado through a friend and went to Tijuana to petition for her son's release, promising to venerate Juan in return. Three months later, authorities released the young man—no prosecution, no trial, no criminal record. In gratitude and with the help of friends and neighbors, the mother and her husband built a chapel honoring Juan Soldado on their property. For years devotees came from throughout the region to celebrate San Juan Day with a fiesta—carne asada, corn, beer, and mariachis— at the site. Meanwhile, the grateful mother made annual pilgrimages to Cemetery Number One in Tijuana, where she claims to have received other miracles from Juan Soldado. "Juanito protects me from mal de ojo [jealousies]) and susto [frights]," so her religiosity is fused (as is so much religiosity) to traditional beliefs far from orthodoxy.[12] In the Magdalena

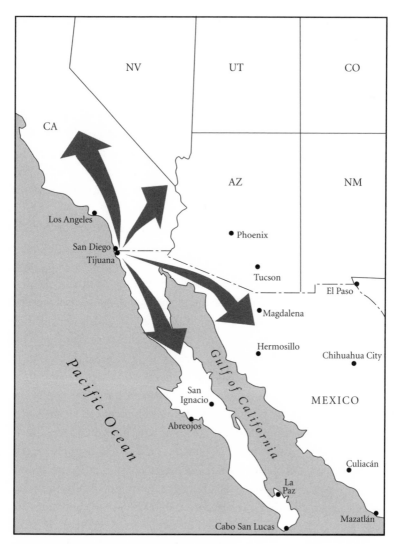

Map 4. The Expanding Juan Soldado Devotion.

chapel itself, a statue of Juan stands next to an image of the Sacred Heart of Jesus. The expected variety of votive candles includes many to Saint Francis Xavier, patron saint of the town. On one wall is a large picture of Saint Lazarus, the leper, with dogs licking him clean of his infirmities. Little tin milagros abound. These days the chapel remains locked against thieves who steal the milagros and other icons, but a caretaker nearby keeps a key for the faithful and curious.

Much less is known about the origins of the shrine outside Abreojos. The chapel is set in high desert terrain with the great ocean bay famed as a spawning ground for whales off in the distance. Residents of the area say that some decades ago a woman fulfilling a manda to the soldier fashioned a niche out of a wooden box, put a plaster bust of Juanito inside, and placed the small reliquary in the crotch of a tree growing from the bottom of an arroyo near the present shrine. A subsequent flash flood spilled down the arroyo and washed away the oratory. Townspeople from Abreojos combined skills and revenue to build a larger, more secure chapel on nearby higher ground. Their Spanish missionary priest blessed the structure and said an inaugural Mass there.

The inside resembles its somewhat smaller counterpart in Tijuana. The altar is covered with floral designs and images of many saints along with retablos and other offerings of the faithful. A crude divining stick, evidently used to locate underground water in the habitually parched area, hangs from the ceiling. Soldiers who patrol the transpeninsular highway some fifteen miles east periodically visit the shrine, leaving their pictures, petiticiones, and even small pieces of military equipment on the main altar. Most of their requests concern the fear of being sent off to war, of being killed or stranded far from home. They seem to empathize with a fellow soldier who died far from abode and family.[13]

At present, general devotion to Juan Soldado might best be characterized as wide but thin. Prayer cards to him have turned up far south in Oaxaca, in the eastern port of Veracruz, and in the nation's capital. Similar evidence can be found in many American cities, and veneration is growing in southern California. There is, however, no determined, systematic effort to establish new shrines and followings in population centers, such as those being promoted by the followers of Niño Fidencio. Devotions such as all these come and go. They may flicker briefly, and then burn out. Embryonic movements recently embraced the slain rock star Selena, the assassinated Mexican presidential candidate Luis Donaldo Colosio, and the center of the spectacular international custody battle, Elián González; but they seem not to have prospered—at least, not yet. Devotions may thrive for a year or two, or even a century, and then wither and die. Longtime survival seems to require official endorsement by the Church, and we already know how long, political, and idiosyncratic the approval procedures can be. Rome certainly will not consider the case of Juan Soldado until a verifiable confession turns up absolving

Juan Castillo Morales of any complicity in the rape and murder of Olga Camacho—and perhaps not even then.

And Now Olga

The Camacho family crypt lies in Tijuana's Cemetery Number One, not a dozen paces from the shrine of Juan Soldado. The mutilated body of eight-year-old Olga was buried there on 15 February 1938, the day before her accused rapist and murderer was publicly executed for the crime in the same cemetery. Camacho family members convinced of the guilt of Juan Castillo Morales watched with scorn the growth of the Juan Soldado devotion. They openly taunted the believers, shouted angry words at them, called them uncivilized pagans, and worse. Even if they felt sympathy for the slain young girl and her family, the devotees continued to venerate Juan, their miracle worker. Finally, the Camachos could stand the contradiction no more. Why should little Olga rest so close to her assassin and be subject to the cynicism of his followers? So they moved the child to the new Cemetery Number Two, which opened in 1940 just three blocks down the street. Today the child's grave remains there, unmarked, surrounded by a plain iron fence. Caretakers can identify the spot, but say that few seem to care. On the Day of the Dead 2002, Juan's shrine was piled high with flowers, candles, and many other offerings. The money box inside was overflowing with donations. All day long the scene was immersed in festivity. By contrast, Olga's grave was marked by only two bunches of flowers, one artificial, the other real, placed in tin cans sunken slightly into the hard dirt that covers her grave. Although there was considerable activity in the cemetery, no one visited her resting place.

It would seem that given the strong Catholic tradition of devotion to young virgin girls who suffered tragic deaths, the faithful would make Olga rather than her presumed assassin the object of veneration in Tijuana. This has happened with Charlene in Louisiana's Cajun country, and Ingmar Bergman's dramatization of Scandinavian legend in *The Virgin Spring* (1960) burned the sacred image into the filmgoer's imagination. Moreover, following her rape and murder in Anzio, Italy, on 5 July 1902, veneration centered on twelve-year-old Maria Goretti rather than her assassin, a local boy who thirty years later attended her canonization by Pius XII. So one wonders why none of this adoration has been accorded Olga. No one seems to have pondered matters of God's grace in the dilapidated wooden garage where her ravished body was discovered and where her blood stained the soil, nor did they (as far as is known) visit her grave site in any numbers in search of signs of an Almighty presence. Today a handful of devotees to Juan Soldado claim that Olga's ánima still cries out for justice, as did that of Castillo Morales, but no one seems to pay it any heed. Instead, Juan's followers said they bonded more closely with the soldier because Olga died an innocent and needed no prayers to repose close to God, and because the blatant injustice of Juan's execution flooded their consciousness and stirred their emotions so that his experience melded with their own. Finally, the signs and miracles at the soldier's grave confirmed for them the Lord's presence, while no such portents have been reported from the child's burial site.

More detached analysts say today that the rape itself deprived Olga of veneration, that as a generality, and even more so some seventy years ago, Mexicans (and others, especially men) thought that a raped girl was a spoiled girl who was not worthy of marriage or even acceptance in her family home. Frequently people reasoned that the victim had somehow invited the act, or at least did not resist it. Indeed, several who witnessed (or participated in) the troubles in 1938 remember Olga as coquettish, an impish, spirited youngster who encouraged attention. At least, they say, such was a rumor at the time.

At the 2002 birthday celebration for Juan in the cemetery, an experimentally minded local poet named Heriberto Yépez decided to test for any semblance of devotion to Olga Camacho. He digitally computed a photograph of Olga, added a prayer to her, and printed out cards for distribution at the Juan Soldado shrine. He called his project "interventionist art" and wanted to learn how devotees to Juan would react when confronted with an image of Olga. Most offered little response; many did not recognize her as the victim of the accused rapist-murderer. A few indicated that a small devotion to the young girl was already quietly active, but none reported a miracle received by way of Olga. One man stated that he hoped that the child would become muy milagroso, because she then could form a partnership with Juan and as a couple they would be even more powerful intercessors.[14] Yépez also placed some of his cards on Olga's grave, but they aroused no special attention. All in all, the experiment seems not to have stimulated any devotion to Olga or aroused much interest in that possibility, but perhaps it is too early to tell.

The Camachos do not welcome attempts to sanctify Olga. They do not want her to become a santa and testily rejected the Yépez project as unwarranted meddling. Over the years, the family has refrained from discussing even among themselves the girl's death and the veneration of her supposed killer. The subject remains too painful for them. Several members of the family would like to move Olga's remains back to the Camacho crypt in Cemetery Number One, but they dread the sensationalism that such change would engender. Better to leave the little girl where she rests, hopefully in some state of peace.[15]

As It Is

So was Juan Castillo Morales guilty or innocent? Followers of Juan Soldado have already decided, not so much on material evidence, but on their convictions about earthly justice and heavenly grace. God sent signs to these people, who have a lively attachment to the unseen and spiritual, and then worked through the soldier to produce miracles, and is continuing to do so. That sealed the verdict for them, and the stories they weave around it are only so much embellishment. Faith is their touchstone, and when they tell you that their veneration of Juan Soldado is a matter of faith, it probably means "You really do not understand"—or it could be a polite slap in the face: "I believe and you do not." "I have faith" can also be a defensive mechanism against the attack of others: "This belief is mine, not yours." Faith, normally larded with doubt, exists in various forms and intensities which can be neither measured nor weighed. Under the circumstances, the devotion to Juan Soldado is best seen as simply something that the faithful *need* to do.

For the great majority of outsiders, veneration of Juan Soldado is mere curiosity. Some think it a foolish superstition, others pay it no special attention but respect those who do. A good number of us dangle between secular and spiritual sensibilities, gyrating between logic and belief, between rationality and mysticism, unable or unwilling to catch hold of either pole. To be sure, the soldier's ordinary-looking shrine in Tijuana's Cemetery Number One exudes the unfathomable, radiates the incomprehensible. Best for all, I think, to leave it at that.

NOTES

1. NOTIONS OF JUSTICE

1 Interviews with Feliza Camacho on 12, 20, 27 Aug. and 5 Sept. 2000 at the Tijuana home of her daughter Conchita.

2 *San Diego Sun*, 12 March 1937.

3 *Los Angeles Examiner*, 16 Feb. 1938; *San Diego Sun*, 29 June 1937. For examples of continuing front-page coverage of these events in a Tijuana newspaper, see *El Hispano Americano*, 7 Sept. 1934, 4 Jan. and 7 March 1935. In mid-1934 the sensational kidnapping and ransoming of June Roberts, age six, in Tucson, Arizona, also commanded press attention. See *El Hispano Americano*, 5 and 12 May and 15 June 1934.

4 *San Diego Sun*, 6 March 1937 and 16 April 1937; *San Diego Union*, 12 and 15 March 1937.

5 The description of these events was culled from twenty-one newspapers that covered the story in some depth. Interviews and scattered snippets published in books, journals, and magazines added details. To footnote every tidbit of information would hopelessly clutter the text and unduly burden the reader. Nevertheless, substantial direct quotations do carry a citation as do large blocks of material taken from a single source. Newspapers from Feb. 1938 consulted for this portion of the book include *Calexico* (California) *Chronicle*, *Daily News* (Los Angeles), *Chicago Daily Tribune*, *El Excelsior* (Mexico City), *El Hispano Americano* (Mexicali and Tijuana), *Los Angeles Examiner*, *Los Angeles Times*, *El Nacional* (Mexico City), *Oaxaca Nueva* (Oaxaca, Mexico), *La Opinión* (Los Angeles), *San Diego Evening Tribune*, *San Diego Sun*, *San Diego Union*, *San Francisco Chronicle*, *San Francisco Examiner*, *San Ysidro* (California) *Border Press*, *St. Louis Post Dispatch*, *El Universal* (Mexico City), and *El Universal Gráfico* (Mexico City). Two Tijuana newspapers later published detailed reports: *El Imparcial*, special section, Aug. 1952, and *ABC*, articles by Arturo Alvarez López, from 12 Aug. to 11 Sept. 1982. Information on the interrogation of Mariano Mendivil is from his widow,

Delfina Roberta (Babi) Madrid Viuda de Mendivil, interviewed on 5 Sept. 2000 in her Tijuana residence. An example of a printed snippet is *Historia viva de Tijuana*, 163–64.

6　Interviews with José Carmareña Iñíquez on 17 and 22 August 2000 at his Tijuana home.

7　*Los Angeles Examiner*, 17 Feb. 1938. The conflict between the coroner's report, which stated that the murder had preceded the rape, and the soldier's version was never resolved in newspaper or other written accounts.

8　*San Diego Evening Tribune*, 16 Feb. 1938.

9　Telephone interview with Joseph Orantes, former chief of the crime laboratory of the San Diego Police Department, 25 Sept. 2000 at his residence. On evaluating today's confessions see *New York Times*, 1 Nov. 2002.

10　Local, national, and international circumstances leading up to and surrounding the crime, trial, and its aftermath are detailed in part II of this book.

11　*San Diego Union*, 11 Feb. 1937 and 15 Feb.1938.

12　*St. Louis Post-Dispatch*, 16 Feb. 1938.

13　*San Diego Union*, 5 July 1937.

14　*San Diego Union*, 27 March 1998. The Huejutla tragedy is also detailed in Quiñones, *True Tales from Another Mexico*, 31–51.

15　Among the witnesses was José Camareña. Another witness to the rioting was Manuel Cecena, interviewed on 27 Oct. 2000 at his Chula Vista home. For the hesitancy of authorities in smaller towns to unleash repressive forces on a citizenry that includes their friends and neighbors, see Spierenburg, *The Spectacle of Suffering*, 102–3.

16　The destruction is carefully catalogued in Universidad Autónoma de Baja California (UABC), Instituto de Investigaciones Históricas (IIH), Archivo, IIH, Dir. Gral. de Gobierno, 10.105. Documents pertaining to Baja California in the Archivo General de la Nación (AGN) in Mexico City have been photocopied and reclassified with an IIH number at the Instituto de Investigaciones Históricas at UABC in Tijuana. Hereafter, such documents will be cited only by their IIH number, although the copies also carry an AGN classification. The frantic flurry of communications between government offices during the crisis in Tijuana are in IIH, Leg. Lázaro Cárdenas, Exp. 11.49, and AGN, Ramo Presidenciales, Lázaro Cárdenas, "Encuentros sangrientos," 541.1/104.

17　*San Diego Evening Tribune*, 15 Feb. 1938.

18　*San Diego Sun*, 15 Feb. 1938.

19　Among several newspapers that carried Associated Press accounts of this conversation, see *El Excelsior*, 16 Feb. 1938.

20　*San Diego Sun*, 15 Feb. 1938.

21　*San Francisco Examiner*, 16 Feb. 1938; *El Excelsior*, 16 Feb. 1938.

22　When a Mexican institution carries the word "autónoma" in its title, it indicates that in terms of governance, it is free of direct government control. In this case, however, the Press and Publicity Department lay within a cabinet-level secretaría responsible for domestic peace, an agency which certainly would have managed its own publicity. "Autónoma" here was meant to convey the idea of impartiality and objectivity, hardly the truth as verified by its brief and only release concerning the deadly mayhem in Tijuana.

23 *San Diego Evening Tribune*, 16 Feb. 1938.

24 *San Diego Sun*, 16 Feb. 1938.

25 Interview with Carlos Escandón, 4 Aug. 2000 in his Tijuana home. Today he laughs at one repercussion of these happenings: some four decades after the burnings in Tijuana, a noted local businessman visited Señor Escandón in his office saying that he had a photo of him kicking hard at the gates of the comandancia during the rioting, in other words breaking the law and challenging authority. Unless Escandón gave him a considerable amount of money, the extortionist threatened to release the photo to the press. Escandón brusquely ordered the intruder from the office. In the mid-1970s the incriminating photo appeared in a Mexico City newspaper, but authorities never followed the lead. Escandón, now approaching ninety, speaks of the entire incident with pride.

26 *San Diego Union*, 17 Feb. 1938.

27 Interviews with José Camareña, 17 and 22 Aug. 2000 at his Tijuana residence. Researchers who desire to use the archive of Mexico's Secretaría de la Defensa Nacional (the national military defense archive) must apply for permission and state precisely what documentation is being requested. If entry is granted, staff bring appropriate documents to the researcher. I requested the trial record of the Juan Castillo Morales courts martial, materials concerning the military's role in suppressing the riots, and the service records of Castillo Morales, Governor Sánchez Taboada, and Manuel Contreras. In his response, the director of the archive, Brig. Gen. D. E. M. Juan Manuel de la O González, graciously granted me permission to see the service records of Sánchez Taboada and Contreras. He said that no records for Castillo Morales or his trial could be located, nor were there any documents in the archive pertaining to the troubles in Tijuana. I wrote the director on 23 Oct. 2002; his office responded on 19 Nov. 2002. I thank the general and his staff for searching for these materials.

28 *San Diego Evening Tribune*, 16 Feb. 1938.

29 *La Opinión*, 18 Feb. 1938; *San Diego Sun*, 17 Feb. 1938. *La Epoca* repeated the same details in slightly different order on 18 Feb. 1938. For Dubin, see *El Hispano Americano*, 8 August 1935.

30 The article is reproduced in F. M. Rodríguez, *Trinchera obrera*, 53.

31 Quiroz Cuarón, *La Pena de muerte en México*, 56–62, 74–75.

32 Zugasti, *El Bandolerismo*, 15–16.

33 From the 117-minute documentary *Berkeley in the '60s*, Mark Kitchell, director and writer, 1990.

34 The *Los Angeles Examiner* published a vivid account of the execution on 18 Feb. 1938:

> TIJUANA, Mexico, Feb. 17.—Swift-moving justice of the "Law of Flight" today sped Juan Castillo Morales, 24-year-old soldier, to a murderer's grave in the military [*sic*] cemetery on the outskirts of this riot-torn border city.

Three volleys fired by his comrades cut short the "escape" of the private, whose confession of the sex-murder of 8-year-old Olga Consuelo Camacho incited the riots which took three other lives Monday.

It was to appease the wrath of the mob of more than 1,000 men and women that Gen. Manuel Contreras invoked "el ley del fugo" to effect the dramatic graveyard execution.

At Sunrise

As the first rays of the sun poked above the rugged hills which form the eastern border of the Tijuana Valley, two heavily armed guards awakened the condemned man in his cell.

"I am not afraid to die," [Castillo] Morales boasted with forced bravado.

Between several ranks of soldiers, standing at attention with fixed bayonets, he was hurried into an armored military van.

Vengeful citizens hurled threats and invectives at the man as [he] was sped through the city streets.

Firing Squads

Awaiting him at the small, hilltop cemetery were two firing squads, a small crowd of his would-be lynchers—and a newly turned grave.

The fateful moment, which he feared most and which enraged citizens had demanded, had arrived.

Defiance, courage, vanity, melted from the doomed slayer.

He didn't want to "escape," he insisted.

Begs Cigaret

After begging a cigaret from one of his guards, he was shoved from the van.

Led to the brow of the knoll, the youth was released with a quick jab of a bayonet.

Inhaling deeply from his last cigarette, he turned and ran.

With the speed of a frightened animal he twisted and turned.

He hurdled a short barbed-wire fence. Then another.

Meanwhile, barked commands were heard. He'd had his "chance" [to escape].

Guns blazed. [Castillo] Morales faltered, regained his feet, staggered on.

Second Volley

Then a second volley rang out. The fleeing man pitched flat on his face. He tried desperately to get up.

His writhing was the mute command for the third and final volley.

He rolled over—very still.

Marching briskly to his side, an officer leaned quickly over the prostrate form, pressed the muzzle of his automatic to the forehead—fired the "shot of mercy."

Scattered cheers were voiced by the spectators as a doctor pronounced [Castillo] Morales dead.

With scant ceremony the soldiers buried him as the crowd dispersed to spread the news of the execution through the city.

Other reporters and eyewitnesses filled in further details. Much of the event was confirmed in an interview with Dolores Becerra Antón, 9 Oct. 2000, in her Chula Vista home. Her nephew Manuel attended the execution.

2. AFTERMATH

1   *San Diego Evening Tribune*, 18 Feb. 1938.
2   *San Ysidro* (California) *Border Press*, 25 Feb. 1938.
3   *San Diego Herald*, 17 Feb. 1938. For the *Herald*'s diatribes against Tijuana see its editions of 2 and 9 Dec. 1937.
4   *San Diego Union*, 17 Feb. 1938.
5   Rodríguez, *Trinchera obrera*, 52–54.
6   *El Excelsior*, 21 Feb. 1938.
7   U.S. National Archives, Record Group 165, U.S. Military Intelligence Reports, 1919–1941, W 100.2, Mexico: G-2, Reel 6, Nos. 1,000–1,001: "Regulations for Garrison Commanders. . . . Promulgated July 1, 1933, and signed by President Abelardo Rodríguez."
8   U.S. National Archives, Record Group 59, Records of the Department of State Relating to the Internal Affairs of Mexico, 1930–1944, Consular Reports, Lower California, #281, Smale telegram to Secretary of State, 16 Feb. 1938. Further references to this source are labeled "Consular Reports," along with number of report, author, recipient, and date.
9   Consular Reports, #284, Smale to Secretary of State, 18 Feb. 1938.
10 Ibid.
11 *San Diego Sun*, 15 Feb. 1938.
12 Tijuana Gobierno Municipal [municipal archive], Registro Civil, Año 1938, No. 40, el 18 Feb. 1938; *San Diego Union*, 19 Feb. 1938.
13 *El Imparcial* (Tijuana), Aug. 1952 (special edition).
14 One example among many articles about Jesús Malverde: *Christian Science Monitor*, 15 June 1998, 1, 7. Starr, *Catalogue of a Collection of Objects Illustrating the Folklore of Mexico*, 130. Jesús Malverde is discussed with appropriate citations in part III of this book.
15 Interview with Ramón Camacho, 28 July 2000, at his Tijuana home. A photograph of the Afghan memorial appears in *National Geographic*, June 2002, 92–93.
16 Beliefs of those who venerate Juan Soldado are elaborated in part III of this book.
17 Interviews with those who venerate Rother in 1998 and 2002 in Santiago Atitlán. The missionary's pastorate in the Maya town, including letters written to his family when he was threatened by the military, is poignantly recalled in *The Shepherd Cannot Run*.
18 E-mail discussions with Sylvia Carlock, 19 Feb. 2002 and 28 April 2003; interview with Ms. Carlock, 10 March 2003, Anaheim, Calif. Ms. Carlock, who lives in Garden Grove, Calif., writes for the Orange County *Excelsior* and is also a freelance writer specializing in Mexican culture. My sincere gratitude to her for her personal insights and valuable contributions to this project. The classic Mexican

novel concerning the ánima is Rulfo, *Pedro Páramo*. For succinct comments on the ánima in Latino thought see Parker, *Popular Religion and Modernization in Latin America*, 195–99, 202, 213.

19 For some such accounts see *El Imparcial*, Aug. 1952, 4, 5, 15. Also, the Tijuana newspaper *ABC* published a recapitulation of these events between 12 Aug. and 11 Sept. 1982; see esp. 28 Aug. 1982.

20 *San Ysidro Border Press*, 11 Nov. 1938.

21 Interviews with Feliza Camacho, 12, 20, 27, 29 July and 5 Sept. 2000, at the Tijuana home of her daughter Conchita.

22 Interview with Conchita Camacho, 29 July 2000, at her Tijuana home.

3. TIJUANA

1 An excellent recent book on Lourdes is Harris, *Lourdes: Body and Spirit in the Secular Age*. Equally good for Marpingen is Blackbourne, *Marpingen: Apparitions of the Virgin Mary in Nineteenth-Century Germany*.

2 El Tiradito, Charlene, and El Niño Fidencio, along with other such santos, are discussed more fully in part III of this book.

3 For the paintings see Crosby, Lindsay, and Crosby, *The Cave Paintings of Baja California*. The literature on Baja California is large and rapidly growing. The books, in general, are of uneven scholarly quality but still a delightful read.

4 Bustamente, *Historia de la Colonia Libertad*; interview with Carlos de la Parra, a civil engineer with a Ph.D. in urban development, who conducts his research activities at El Colegio de la Frontera (Tijuana), 27 Nov. 2001, in his office. Ing. Parra greatly enhanced my understanding of the locale's geography, topography, and water resources. My sincere thanks to him for his expertise, clarity, and patience.

5 Antonio Padilla Corona, "Imagen urbana de Tijuana," in Piñera Ramírez and Ortiz Figueroa, eds., *Historia de Tijuana, 1889–1989*, 1:103–20. See also Padilla's finely researched book *Inicios urbanos del norte de Baja California*. A valuable overview of early Tijuana appears in Ricardo Morales Lira and Alfonso García Cortez, "La Revolución también es una calle," 19–23. Although lacking analysis, the work of Aguirre Bernal, *Tijuana, su historia, sus hombres*, contains valuable statistical, biographical, documentary, and ephemeral data for the study of Tijuana from its origins through much of the last century.

6 Hart, *Empire and Revolution*, 37, 512.

7 Quoted in Pourade, *The Glory Years*, 79.

8 Summers, *Buenos Días, Tijuana*, 12–14; de Baca, "Moral Renovation of the Californias," 30–31; Padilla, "Imagen urbana," 73–76; M. Taylor, "Land of Much in Little," 479; and Ridgely, "The Man Who Built Tijuana: 'Sunny Jim' Coffroth and the Freewheeling Days of the High Roller," 58. For a new overview concerning the founding and development on Tijuana's so-called vice industry, see L. D. Taylor, "The Wild Frontier Moves South," 204–29.

9 Padilla, "Imagen urbana," 74; de Baca, "Moral Renovation," 4; Summers, *Buenos Días, Tijuana*, 39; and Shantz, "The 'Mexicali Rose' and the 'Tijuana Brass,'" 58.

10   Quoted in Ridgely, "Man Who Built Tijuana: 'Sunny Jim' Coffroth," 58.

11   Kirk, "Hour's Visit to Mexico," 501–2.

12   Summers, *Buenos Días, Tijuana*, 17–19, 23–24.

13   Nevins, *Operation Gatekeeper*, 50–55.

14   Secretaría de Relaciones Exteriores (México), Archivo, Legajo 28166, Baja California, reported in *San Diego Union*, 20 Dec. 1912. For the invasion of Tijuana by radical leftists see the fine article by L. D. Taylor, "The Magonista Revolt in Baja California."

15   De Baca, "Moral Renovation," 43.

16   Schantz, " 'Mexicali Rose,' " 323, 332–33, 366–67; Piñera Ramírez and Ortiz Figueroa, *Historia de Tijuana*, 1: 96–98; de Baca, "Moral Renovation," 10, 47–49; Price, *Tijuana*, 50; and Summers, *Buenos Días, Tijuana*, 30–31. Long's obituary appears in *San Diego Tribune*, 19 Feb. 1962 and *San Diego Union*, 25 Feb. 1962.

17   Ridgely, "Man Who Built Tijuana: 'Sunny Jim' Coffroth," 98; Piñera Ramírez and Ortiz Figueroa, *Historia de Tijuana*, 1: 96–98.

18   *San Diego Union*, 19 April 1915.

19   Cantú still lacks a good biography, but for aspects of his life and work (and antics) see Hall, *Oil, Banks, and Politics*, 9–16, 54–58, 166–67; de Baca, "Moral Renovation," 9–11, 42; Schantz, " 'Mexicali Rose,' " 65–67, 171–74, 180–224, 238, 331, 346, 551, 557; Sandos, "Northern Separatism During the Mexican Revolution," 191–214; *Historia viva de Tijuana*, 50, 119; Buffington, "Prohibition in the Borderlands," 19–38; Werne, "Esteban Cantú y la soberanía mexicana en Baja California," 1–30; Rodríguez González, "La Figura y época de Esteben Cantú (1914–1924) en el Archivo Nacional de los Estados Unidos," 163–70; Rathbun, "Facts About Lower California," 9. In 1919 the federal government sent a member of its treasury department to the district to report on the region's economic condition. For his report see Rolland, *Informe sobre el Distrito Norte de la Baja California*.

20   De Baca, "Moral Renovation," 55–56.

21   Ibid., 75; Ridgely, "Tijuana, 1920."

22   Woods, "A Penchant for Probity," 107.

23   *New York Times*, 6 June 1920.

24   De Baca, "Moral Renovation," 77–78, 131–32, and 154; Schantz, " 'Mexicali Rose,' " 315–16; Summers, *Buenos Días, Tijuana*, 33; Tello Villalobos, *Tijuana*, 71–72, 90–93; Elia Flores Sotelo, "La Ultima de nos vamos: una apuesta de reflexión sobre el campo de diversión," in Castillo Udiarte, et al., *La Revolución*, 38; Sandez de Gutiérrez, "Nuestra concina, un *collage*," 2: 407–10. The first Rodríguez administration officially outlines its budgets and achievements in Abelardo Rodríguez, *Memoria administrativa del gobierno del Distrito Norte de la Baja California, 1924–1927*.

25   *Historia viva*, 16, 33, 69, 131; Summers, *Buenos Días, Tijuana*, 40.

26   Sandez de Gutiérrez, "Nuestra cocina," 407–10; Price, *Tijuana*, 56; *Historia viva*, 41, 31–32. The original Caesar salad recipe called for 1 cup French bread croutons, ⅓ cup olive oil, 2 garlic cloves, 1–2 tsp. anchovy paste, 1 bunch romaine lettuce, salt and pepper to taste, juice of one lemon, 1 tsp. Worcestershire sauce, and 1 coddled egg.

27 Thomas, *The Wanderer*, 9, 24.

28 Ibid.; Price, *Tijuana*, 54–55; Ridgely, "Inside Tijuana," 98.

29 *Historia viva*, 15, 30, 66, 156; Tello Villalobos, *Tijuana*, 119–20. In his interview on 4 Aug. 2000, Carlos Escandón, of school age himself when Obregón opened, expressed the attitudes of teenagers at the time.

30 Aikman, "Hell Along the Border," 17–23.

31 Buffington, "Prohibition in the Borderlands," 30.

32 For the Peteet case see ibid., 30–31; de Baca, "Moral Renovation," 13–18; and the fascinating recent revision, Cabeza de Baca and Cabeza de Baca, "The 'Shame Suicides' and Tijuana," 603–35.

33 James M. Smallwood, ed., *Will Rogers' Weekly Articles: The Coolidge Years, 1925–1927* (Stillwater, Okla., 1980), 2:163–66.

4. MEXICO FOR MEXICANS

1 De Baca, "Moral Renovation," 76, 79–80; *Historia viva de Tijuana*, 103; Tello Villalobos, *Tijuana*, 88–95; Ruiz González, *Por fin habla Buchito sobre la zona libre*, 259–60, 286.

2 An excellent article on the early formation of Tijuana's labor unions is Samaniego López, "Formación y consolidación de las organizaciones obreras in Baja California, 1920–1930." See also de Baca, "Moral Renovation," 122; Vásquez Hoyos, "La Revolución," 59–60; IIH, Leg. Emilio Portes Gil, Exp. 1.76, and Leg. Lázaro Cárdenas, Exp. 17.4; Piñera Ramírez and Ortiz Figueroa, *Historia de Tijuana*, 1: 98–99, 146; *Historia viva*, 47–48, and Ridgely, "Tijuana, 1920," 111.

3 IIH, Leg. Pascual Ortiz Rubio, Exp. 1.20, 9 Sept. 1930.

4 Bustamente, *Historia de la Colonia Libertad*, 13.

5 Interview with Carlos de la Parra, 27 Nov. 2001, at El Colegio de la Frontera; *Historia viva*, 174; *El Hispano americano*, 20 July 1930 and 26 July 1938.

6 Mercado Díaz de León, *Los Pioneros de la medicina en Tijuana*, passim. My thanks to Dr. Gonzalo R. Ballon-Landa, specialist in infectious diseases, San Diego, for his expert assistance in interpreting data from *Pioneros*. Tello Villalobos, *Tijuana*, 103; Cornelius, "Nation Building, Participation, and Distribution," 476, n. 37.

7 Kiyoko Nishikawa Aceves, "De la internacionalización de Tijuana," in Castillo Udiarte et al., *La Revolución*, 86–87; *Historia viva*, 22, 39, 51–52, 75, 80, 170, 177.

8 Kluckhohn, *The Mexican Challenge*, 159.

9 *Historia viva*, 43; *Labor* (Tijuana), 6 March 1937.

10 *Historia viva*, 66–67, 75, 119.

11 Ibid., 15–16, 38–39, 47, 63, 175–76; José Armando Estrada Lázaro, "Veinte años de deporte tijuanense," 195–98, 211–13; interview with A. E. Sada, who played baseball in Tijuana in the 1930s, 24 Sept. 1996, in San Diego; Tello Villalobos, *Tijuana*, 118–19; *Labor*, 16 Jan., 6 Feb., and 13 March 1937; *El Hispano americano*, 18 Nov. 1938; Mario Ortiz Villacorta, "Clubes sociales," in Piñera Ramírez and Ortiz Figueroa, *Historia de Tijuana*, 2: 223–49.

12 Mercado Díaz de León, *Pioneros*, passim.

13 Interviews with Feliza Camacho, 12, 20, 27 Aug. and 2 Sept. 2000 in Tijuana.

14 Proffitt, *Tijuana*, 84; IIH, Leg. Abelardo Rodríguez, Leg. 514-39/1-114, Lic. M. J. Casellas Díaz, Prof. M. Quirós, et al., to Presidente Rodríguez, 11 Oct. 1932.

15 *San Diego Union*, 7 March 1891.

16 Carlos Franco Pedroza, "La Iglesia católica en Tijuana: Origen y desarrollo," in Piñera Ramírez and Ortiz Figueroa, *Historia de Tijuana*, 2: 253–71.

17 Diocese of San Diego, Historical Archive, *Diocesan Heritage*, 112–14. *The Southern Cross* (diocesan newspaper, San Diego), 21 Oct. 1931 and 26 Aug. and 16 Dec. 1932. See also file records listed by churches in diocesan archive: "San Ysidro, Our Lady of Mount Carmel, 1926–1936," Alloero to Dolan, 28 July 1930, and 5 March 1932; "National City, Saint Anthony, 1929–1973," Nuñez to Cantrell, 14 Aug. 1931.

18 Gamio, *The Life Story of the Mexican Immigrant*, 63. I am aware that Manuel Gamio's conclusions about the attitudes of Mexican migrants to the United States in the late 1920s are under scholarly review, and properly so. The only material from his work used in this book are direct quotations from the surveys he collected. Interpretations of those interviews are my own.

19 Ibid., 4, 21, 25, 58, 244, 116, 161–62.

20 *The Southern Cross*, 21 Oct. 1931, 12 and 26 Aug. 1932, and 6 Jan. 1933; *Diocesan Heritage*, 112–14. Diocese of San Diego, Historical Archive: File, "San Ysidro, Our Lady of Mount Carmel," Alloero to Cantwell, 12 July 1926 and 28 July 1930; File, "National City, Saint Anthony," Núñez to Cantwell, 14 Aug.1931; File, "Calexico, Our Lady of Guadalupe, Buddy to Labrador, [1937]; File, "Yuma, Saint Thomas Mission," Pudlowski to McGueken, 21 March 1936.

21 Secretaría de la Economía Nacional, Dirección General de Estadística, *Sexto Censo* 16, 31.

22 Gregory, *American Exodus*, 7–9.

23 *Los Angeles Times*, 10 June 2001.

5. RIDING THE ROLLER COASTER

1 The rich tapestry of Agua Caliente must be stitched together from bits and pieces of material strewn across widespread sources. For a sampling, see de Baca, "Moral Renovation," 127–31, 140–41; Profitt, *Tijuana*, 135, 170–71, 194–7; Piñera Ramírez and Ortiz Figueroa, *Historia de Tijuana*, 1: 104–5, 115–18, 123–28, and 2: 168–69; Tello Villalobos, *Tijuana*, 74–75; Price, "Tijuana Ethnology," 55; *Historia viva*, 61, 109–10; *San Diego Union*, 1 Jan. 1931; Schantz, "'Mexicali Rose,'" 340, 355–56, 376–78; IIH, Leg. Ortiz Rubio, Exp. 1.52; Leg. "Zona Libre," Exp. 16.11. Bowman's obituary appears in *San Diego Union*, 21 April 1949. Laura Hillenbrand treats the raucous ambiance of Tijuana during the 1930s in her best-selling book *Seabiscuit*, esp. at 14–16 and 99–101.

2 The hotel's "Service" booklet contained the rules. My gratitude to Andre Williams for furnishing a copy of the booklet. Williams, an enthusiastic aficionado of local history with homes in both Carlsbad, Calif., and Tijuana, collects ephemera on Tijuana's past, which he graciously shared with me. His rich collection pro-

vided many valuable parcels of social and cultural history as well as photographic images for this book. Thank you, Andre.

3 IIH, Leg. Lázaro Cárdenas, Exp. 8612. This document details salaries of workers at Agua Caliente in accordance with the contract dated 14 June 1937 between the owners of the resort and the worker's union there. Also, Proffitt, *Tijuana*, 198; De Baca, "Moral Renovation," 145, and *Historia viva*, 132.

4 De Baca, "Moral Renovation," 140–41.

5 Proffitt, *Tijuana*, 170–71.

6 De Baca, "Moral Renovation," 143–44 and 152–54.

7 Piñera Ramírez and Ortiz Figueroa, *Historia de Tijuana*, 1: 129–34; de Baca, "Moral Renovation," 137. Consul Reports (U.S. National Archives, Record Group 59) detail the impact: Frank Bohr, Mexicali, #93, "Political Review for November, 1931," 30 Nov. 1931; Smale, Ensenada, #97, "Political Review for December, 1931," 31 Dec. 1931; Bohr, #99, "Political Review for January 1932," 2 Feb. 1932; Smale, #181, "Political Review for October 1934," 31 Oct. 1934; Smale, #194, "Political Review for March 1935," 31 March 1935; Howard A. Bowman, Mexicali, #230, "Political Situation in Mexicali Consular District," 16 April 1936; and Smale, #245, "Political Report for September 1936," 30 Sept.1936. For more general comments see Nevins, *Operation Gatekeeper*, 33; de Baca, "Moral Renovation," 152–54, 159; Gregory, *American Exodus*, 78–79. Standard books on the deportations include Hoffman, *Unwanted Mexican-Americans in the Great Depression*, and Balderama, *Decade of Betrayal*. In his article concerning repatriations during the Cárdenas regime, Fernando Saúl Alanís Enciso argues that while the federal administration made elaborate plans to resettle numbers of repatriates in Baja California, it did little to implement the program. See his "La Colonización de Baja California con mexicanos provenientes de Estados Unidos (1935–1939)."

8 The best account of San Diego during the depression is San Diego Writers' Project, *San Diego: A California City*. See also Eddy, "The Visions of Paradise." For a solid study of the U.S. Navy impact on San Diego see Shragge, "Boosters and Bluejackets"; chap. 7 covers "vice" and the Navy's concerns about Tijuana. Some of his findings appear in "'I Like the Cut of Your Jib.'" Shragge now directs the UCSD Civic Co-Operative, which catalogues sources of local history. His assistance in calculating the contributions of the Navy to the regional economy for this book is gratefully acknowledged.

9 The request is detailed in IIH, Leg. "Zona Libre," Exp. 16.11. See also Irigoyen, *El Problema económico de las fronteras mexicanas*, 2: 433–34, 452. Also Nevins, *Operation Gatekeeper*, 43; *Historia viva*, 45–46; Piñera Ramírez and Ortiz Figueroa, *Historia de Tijuana*, 1: 130–33; Tello Villalobos, *Tijuana*, 125–26; Proffitt, *Tijuana*, 194, 224; Ruiz González, *Por fin habla Buchito*, 17, 241–42. Consular Reports, Bowman, Mexicali, #182, "Politcal Review for October 1934," 31 Oct. 1934; #198, "Political Review for May 1935," 31 May 1935.

10 De Baca, "Moral Renovation," 146–47; *Historia viva*, 106–7; IIH, Leg. "Zona Libre," Exp. 16.11, 16.

11 For the Chamber's tourist guide: IIH, Leg. Abelardo Rodríguez, Exp. 7.50.

12 De Baca, "Moral Renovation," 159.

13 These changes are well documented in IIH, Leg. "Zona Libre," Exp. 16.11.

14 Inspectors from Mexico's Treasury Department reported results of the Free-Trade Zone on 27 March 1935. See their report in IIH, Leg. "Zona Libre," Exp. 16.11. For diversity in Tijuana's economy between Jan. and June 1937, see El Hablador (Tijuana), 16 Sept. 1937.

15 San Diego Herald, 25 July 1935.

16 Interview with César Laniado, 11 Sept. 2000, in his workplace in Tijuana.

17 IIH, Leg. Abelardo Rodríguez, Exp. 1.27, Navarro to Presidente, 29 Nov. 1933; and interview with Delfina Roberta (Babi) Madrid de Mendival, 5 Sept. 2000, in Tijuana. Mariano was her husband.

18 Kluckhohn, Mexican Challenge, 159–63. Alan Knight has assessed the Cárdenas epoch in several articles and chapters in books; see "Cardenismo: Juggernaut or Jalopy?"; "Revolutionary Project, Recalcitrant People: Mexico, 1910–1940"; and "The Rise and Fall of Cardenismo, c1930-c1940 Also good on Cardenismo is Hamilton, The Limits of State Autonomy. A fine overview is Hernández Chávez, La mecánica cardenista.

19 For seizure of the Colorado Land Company's property see Dwyer, "Between Peasants and the Leviathan"; and Kerig, El Valle de Mexicali y la Colorado River Land Company, 1902–1946.

20 Samaniego López, "Formación y consolidación," 329–62.

21 Diocese of San Diego, Historical Archive, File: "San Ysidro, Our Lady of Mount Carmel, 1926–36," J. R. Núñez, inventory, 13 Dec. 1935. Calexico (Calif.) Chronicle, 3 Nov. 1934; IIH, Leg. Lázaro Cárdenas, File 14.11, J. Rosendo Nuñez to Presidente, 27 March 1935. Consular Reports, Bowman, Mexicali, #185, "Political Review for November 1934," 30 Nov. 1934; #233, "Political Review for April 1936," 30 April 1936.

22 Diocese of San Diego, Historical Archive, File: "Calexico, Our Lady of Guadalupe, 1923–1936," Joseph Higgins, Calexico, to Bishop John J. Cantwell, Los Angeles, 15 Feb. 1923.

23 Ibid., American Catholic Congregation to Cantwell, 3 June 1930.

24 Documentation for this acrimonious exchange may be found in the archive of the San Diego Diocese. See file: "Our Lady of Guadalupe [San Diego], 1936–1967." The Thomson letter to Buddy is dated 21 Oct. 1940. Albert L. Pulido writes about the case in "Mexican-American Catholicism in the Southwest."

25 De Baca, "Moral Renovation," 158.

26 Consular Reports, Smale (Ensenada), #202, "Political Report for July 1935," 31 July 1935. Many have commented on effects of the closing: Smale, #206, "Political Report for Aug. 1935," 31 Aug. 1935; Bustamante, Historia de Colonia Libertad, 18; Historia viva, 147; de Baca, "Moral Renovation," 161–63; Piñera Ramírez and Ortiz Figueroa, Historia de Tijuana, 1: 143–44.

27 IIH, Leg. Lázaro Cárdenas, Exp. 16.15, Olachea to Cárdenas, 26 Dec. 1934.

28 Archivo General de la Nación (AGN), Ramo Presidenciales, Lázaro Cárdenas, Exp. 564.1/65, Magaña to Cárdenas, 20 Oct. 1935.

29   Consular Reports, Bowman, Mexicali, #213, "Voluntary Report, Prevailing Politi-
     cal and Economic Situation in Mexicali Consular District," 21 Oct. 1935.
30   *San Diego Union*, 21 Feb., 22 March, 4 Aug. 1936; Consular Reports, Smale,
     Ensenada, #224, "Political Review for January 1936," 29 Feb. 1936. AGN, Ramo,
     Cárdenas, Exp. 437/67, "varios [letters]," Treviño to Cárdenas, 20 April 1936.
31   Consular Reports, Smale, Ensenada, #254, "Suspension of Navarro," 25 Feb. 1937.
32   Consular Reports, Smale, Ensenada, #252, "Political Review of January, 1937," 30
     Jan. 1937; *San Diego Union*, 24 Feb. 1937.
33   Piñera Ramírez and Ortiz Figueroa, *Historia de Tijuana*, 1: 134–36; *San Diego
     Union*, 23 Feb. 1937; Dwyer, "Between Peasants," 678. Professor Joseph Stout of
     Oklahoma State University, who is researching post-revolutionary military affairs
     in Mexico's National Defense Archive, kindly provided me with a copy of the
     service record of Sánchez Taboada, which is lodged in the "Cancelados" section of
     the archive. (Sánchez Taboada was born in 1895 to a middle-class farming family
     in the State of Puebla. Following his seven-year-stint as governor of Baja Califor-
     nia Norte, he became the country's Secretary of the Navy; he died in 1955.) The
     service records of Contreras could not be found by the archivists. My apprecia-
     tion to this good colleague for his endeavor on my behalf.
34   *San Diego Herald*, 30 June 1938.
35   *Historia viva*, 61–62, 78, 86–87, and 120. Consular Reports, Smale, Ensenada,
     #260, "Political Report for April 1937," 30 April 1937; #263, "Political Report for
     May, 1937," 31 May 1937; #264, "Political Report for June, 1937," 30 June 1937. Tello
     Villalobos, *Tijuana*, 111; *San Diego Sun*, 23 Feb., 7, 11–13 March, 13 May, 9–11, 28
     June, 14 Sept., 5 Nov., 11, 29–31 Dec. 1937; *El Hispano americano*, 2 April 1937; *San
     Diego Union*, 23–24 Feb. 1937.
36   *San Diego Sun*, 3 Jan. 1938.
37   *San Diego Sun*, 4 Jan. 1938.
38   *San Diego Sun*, 5–6, 14 and 25 Jan. 1938.
39   *San Diego Union*, 28 Jan. 1938.
40   *San Diego Sun*, 13 Feb. 1938; also *San Diego Union*, 28 Jan. 1938. And see Piñera
     Ramírez and Ortiz Figueroa, *Historia de Tijuana*, 1: 159–60; *San Diego Sun*, 27
     Jan. 1938.
41   Piñera Ramírez and Ortiz Figueroa, *Historia de Tijuana*, 1: 159–60; *San Diego
     Sun*, 15 Feb. 1938.

6. WITNESS TO EXECUTION

 1   There are many journalistic accounts about Jesús Malverde. Among the most
     recent and informative are Daniel Sada, "Cada piedra es un deseo," *Letras libres* 15
     (March 2000): 32–37; *La Jornada* (Mexico City), 10 and 11 Aug. 2000; Quiñones,
     True Tales, 225–32.
 2   A full file of newspaper clippings and other materials on the Tiradito story and
     shrine exists in the archives of the Arizona Historical Society, Tucson, Ariz. See
     especially, ephemera files, "Tucson," "Neighborhoods," "Barrio Libre," and Place

Folders, "Tucson," "Wishing Shrine." See also Gamio, *Mexican Immigration to the United States*, 124–27. Juan Soldado is considered along with El Tiradito in Griffith, "El Tiradito and Juan Soldado."

3 See the sections "The Trial" and "Punishment" and their notes in chap. 1.

4 Quoted in Foucault, *Discipline and Punish*, 3–5.

5 Puppi, *Torment in Art*, 24.

6 Ibid., 20.

7 Johnson, *Death Work*, 54.

8 Web pages of Morning Edition, National Public Radio (www.npr.org), visited 1 May 2001; printouts of 30 April program on executions on file with author.

9 Bessler, *Death After Dark*, 31–33; *St. Louis Post Dispatch*, 21 May 1937.

10 Merback, *The Thief, the Cross, and the Wheel*, 156.

11 Spierenburg, *Spectacle of Suffering*, 193.

12 Camus, *Reflections of the Guillotine*, 5–6.

13 Interview with Socorrito Flores (Octavio's widow), 4 Aug. 2000, Tijuana.

14 Interview with Alejandro Borja, eye witness to the execution, 17 Aug. 2000, Tijuana.

15 See note 8 to this chapter.

16 L. J. Taylor, "The Worst Death Becomes a Good Death," 243–44.

17 Ibid., 244–61.

18 *El Imparcial* (Oaxaca City), 11 July 2002. I have attended numerous Holy Week celebrations in Antigua, most recently in 2002 and 2003.

19 Brading, *Mexican Phoenix*, 143–45.

20 *New York Times*, 1 June 1999.

21 Ibid., 7 April 2000.

22 E-mail from Javier Villa, University of Illinois, Chicago, 31 May 2000.

23 Vauchez, *Sainthood in the Later Middle Ages*, 151.

24 *Los Angeles Times*, 4 Aug. 2003. A good article on *walis* is Denny, " 'God's Friends,' " 69–97.

25 Merback, *The Thief, the Cross, and the Wheel*, 18, 32, 97, 129, 271; Barber, *Vampires, Burial, and Death*, 64.

26 *New York Times*, 14 Aug. 2002. Also, conversation with Javier Villa, 4 Jan. 2003, Chicago.

27 See *The Shepherd Cannot Run*. Residents of Santiago Atitlán, interviewed in 1997 and 2002, confirmed the incident of the flowing blood.

28 Garciagodoy, *Digging the Days of the Dead*, 11.

29 Interview with José R. Ruiz, University of California, San Diego, 14 Sept. 2000, San Diego. His mother, who lives in Mexicali, related the story to him.

30 Interview with Father Eduardo Samaniego, pastor, Christ the King Roman Catholic Church, San Diego, 3 Feb. 1998, at the church.

31 Christian, *Person and God in a Spanish Village*, 94–95.

32 *Historia viva*, 31, 52, 140, 181.

33 Ibid., 31–32.

34 Interviews with Delfina Suárez, 2–4 Oct. 1997, at her Magdalena home.

35 Vega, "¿Quién es Juan Soldado?"
36 Ibid.
37 Gunn, "Juan Soldado: Murderer to Saint."
38 Interviews with Feliza Camacho, 13, 20, 27 Aug., 2 Sept. 2000, Tijuana.

7. CRIMINALS AND SAINTS

1 Andrić, *The Bridge on the Drina*, 34–54.
2 Hartland, "The Cult of Executed Criminals at Palermo," 173–74.
3 The fascinating cult of the Decollati (beheaded ones) is discussed, ibid., 168–79; M. P. Carroll, *Veiled Threats*, 142–45; and Franzonello, "Il Culto delle Anime Decollate in Sicilia." My thanks to colleagues Joanne Ferraro (San Diego State University), John Marino (University of California, San Diego), and Daniela Traffano (Centro de Investigaciones y Estudios Superiores, Oaxaca) for help in procuring, reading, and analyzing this thesis.
4 Puppi, *Torment in Art*, 51, 54.
5 Van Ronzelen de González, "Victor Apaza."
6 The literature on the subject is vast and often polemical. For a reasonably balanced introduction (but with a strong point of view) see Woodward, *Making Saints*. The appropriate book on every scholar's list is P. Brown, *The Cult of Saints*. Those interested in the relationship between official and popular religion (a troublesome dichotomy, to be sure) should consult the Vatican's *Directory on Popular Religion and the Liturgy: Principles and Guidelines* (Vatican City, 2001). In interesting ways it closes the gap between the two poles. (As of this writing, the document can be found on the Vatican's Web site: www.vatican.va/roman_curia /congregations)
7 Ellsberg, *All Saints*, 4.
8 Woodward, *Making Saints*, 51.
9 Schmitt, *The Holy Greyhound*.
10 See note 2 to chap. 6.
11 Quiñones, *True Tales from Another Mexico*, 225–26.
12 Reference to medallions is from *Christian Science Monitor*, 15 June 1998. For other Malverde sources, see note 1 to chap. 6.
13 In recent decades, El Niño Fidencio has attracted considerable professional research. For examples see Garza Quirós, *El Niño Fidencio y el fidencismo*; Riley, "Fidencio, El Niño Fidencio"; Macklin and Crumrine, " 'Santa' Teresa, El Niño 'Santo' Fidencio, and 'San' Damian." Full newspaper accounts include *The Monitor* (McAllen, Texas), 25 Oct. 1992; *San Diego Union-Tribune*, 12 Nov. 1999; *La Opinión* (Los Angeles), 14 Sept. 2002. A popular devotional manual is *La Verdadera novena del ánima de Malverde* (Santa Ana, Calif., 1996). A beautiful photographic account of the devotion with significant text is Gardner, *Niño Fidencio*.
14 *Corpus Christi* (Texas) *Caller Times*, 20 Feb. 1999. The best scholarly work on Pedro Jaramillo is Romero, "Don Pedrito Jaramillo, the Emergence of a Mexican-American Folk Saint." See also Hudson, ed., *The Healer of Los Olmos, and Other*

Mexican Lore, and Malagamba, "Don Pedrito Jaramillo, una leyenda mexicana en el sur de Texas."

15   Gutierrez, *Charlene*, 28.

16   Ibid., 85–106, section titled "Others Who Believe."

17   Sociology professor Thomas C. Langham of Our Lady of the Lake University, San Antonio, Tex., conducted the survey in July 1992. He reported his findings the following year at the Southwestern Social Science Association meeting in New Orleans. He continues to work on the Charlene case. My sincere gratitude to him for permission to use portions of his research data. Thanks are also due to Stephen Vincent of Lafayette, who for many years has conducted research on the Charlene canonization process. His frankness and insights were invaluable to me.

18   Gutierrez, *Charlene*, 99.

19   Interview with Alejandro Borja, 17 August 2000, Tijuana.

20   Interview with Delfina Roberta (Babi) Madrid de Mendivil, 5 Sept. 2000, Tijuana.

21   Vega, "¿Quién es Juan Soldado?"

22   Interview with Juan Iglesias, 19 Jan. 2003, at cemetery.

23   Scholars and others who investigate saints as intercessors widely recognize this reciprocal relationship. For examples see Ingham, *Mary, Michael, and Lucifer*, 98–100; Fenn, *The Persistence of Purgatory*, 5, 8–9; Christian, *Person and God*, xv, 55–56, 64–65, 119–32, 172–80; Kenny, "Patterns of Patronage in Spain"; Duffy, *The Stripping of the Altars*, 183–86; Gregory, *Salvation at the Stake*, 307–8; Vauchez, *Sainthood in the Later Middle Ages*, 444–46, 462–65; Orsi, *Thank You, St. Jude*, 112–15; and Pia DiBella, "Name, Blood, and Miracles," 59.

24   Orsi, *Thank You, St. Jude*, 3–9. The Pope removed Saint Philomena from the list of saints in 1969 for lack of evidence that she ever existed. At the same time he downgraded celebrations for Saints George and Christopher.

25   Glazer, ed., *Flour from Another Sack*, 164–65.

26   Ibid., 20.

27   Mora, *Aunt Carmen's Book of Practical Saints*, 111–18.

28   La Plante and LaPlante, *Heaven Can Help Us*, passim.

29   Wilkinson, *The Prayer of Jabez*, 13–14, 41–42; *New York Times Book Review*, 20 Nov. 2001, 47.

30   Duffy, *Stripping of the Altars*, 179–80.

31   Statistical percentages which appear in this and following sections of part III are the result of a survey taken at the Juan Soldado shrine on 24 June 2000. A total of 103 individuals (out of approximately three hundred adults and two hundred children) responded to eighteen questions prepared on a survey sheet. Two previous trial runs helped to modify the questionnaire and the approach. Initially, individuals were simply presented with the form and asked to respond, but their answers were too direct and short (clipped off) to be of much use. I then tried to administer the survey verbally, but my gringo-Spanish accent again truncated answers. On 24 June 2000 (San Juan Day) I assembled a team of eight native-speakers (long-time friends and professional colleagues, mostly from Tijuana) who administered the questionnaire from the time that the cemetery opened

(8:30 A.M.) until it closed (5 P.M.). They surveyed one member of nearly all the families who visited the shrine that day. The results were extraordinary, because respondents not only provided answers capable of later computer analysis, but frequently chatted beyond the specific question asked, detailing aspects of their religiosity and rendering personal insights (often poignant and colorful) that greatly enriched the entire study of this devotion.

My extreme gratitude to the team members is in order. Two Mexican graduate students, Flor Salazar, and her husband, Sergio Canedo Gamboa, helped to design and test the questionnaire, which they then administered along with others. Flor is finishing her Ph.D. dissertation at Bristol University in England and Sergio his at the University of California, San Diego. With us that day were my former student and now colleague Raúl Rodríguez González, who is the director of the library and teaches history at the Centro de Enseñanzas Técnicas y Scientíficas (CETYS) in Tijuana; José Armando Estrada, a historian now employed at the local branch of the Consejo de Cultura y Arte in Tijuana, who also teaches history at CETYS; Ariel Mojica, a senior student of Armando's who specializes in religious history; and Daniel Vega, then a graduate student in Latin American Studies at San Diego State University. All of these spirited, intelligent people not only lent me heaps of their youthful energy in administering questionnaires but provided cultural insights that greatly informed my study in progress. Finally, Matt O'Hara, who recently completed his dissertation in Mexican history at the University of California, San Diego, and is now an assistant professor of history at New Mexico State University, enthusiastically assisted in the computerization of the project and careful compilation and analysis of the results. Sincere thanks to all.

Further endnotes in chap. 8 relative to this *inquesta* will be cited as "Survey." (Respondents were not asked to give their names.)

32 Shrine visited on 14–15 April 1998, and 18–19 March 2002. Brief descriptions of the shrine appear in Arnold, "The Folk-Lore, Manners, and Customs of the Mexicans in San Antonio, Texas," and Gamio, *Mexican Immigration to the United States*, 122–24.

33 Interview with Delfina Suárez, 2 Oct. 1997, at her Magdalena home.

34 Interview with María Teresa García, 17 June 2000, Tijuana.

35 Interview with David Ungerleider Kepler, Jesuit priest, assistant to the rector at Universidad Iberoamericana (Tijuana), 2 Nov. 2002, Tijuana.

36 Telephone interview with Father Richard Fragomeni, Catholic Theological Union (Chicago), 7 February 2003.

37 Adams, *Mont Saint Michel and Chartres*, 245–46.

8. CLOSER TO GOD

1 Interview with María del Carmen Hernández of San Diego, 2 Nov. 2002 at the shrine.

2 Related by the Mexican anthropologist Jorge Durand, now specializing in migration studies, by e-mail, 25 May 2000. Durand mentions Juan Soldado in his excellent book coauthored with Patricia Arias, *La Experiencia migrante*, 181–90.

3 Survey (see note 31 to chap. 7). Comparisons with the general population of the city are drawn from *Tabulados básicos*. The calculations are general, because my background questions did not exactly match those for the *Tabulados básicos* census. The distinction between a santo who is "milagroso" and one who is "muy milagroso" is not clear. Some say the difference lies with the success (or lack of it) that an individual petitioner has experienced with a saint. If the requested favor is received, then the saint becomes "muy milagroso." If not, the saint remains only "milagroso."

4 Survey.

5 *ABC*, 11 Sept. 1982.

6 Kamburoff, "The Cult of Juan Soldado," Appendix 4.

7 Interview with Father Francisco Javier Salcido, 3 Oct. 1997, Magdalena.

8 Interview with Father Eduardo Samaniego, Christ the King Roman Catholic Church, San Diego, 3 Feb. 1998, at the church.

9 Interview with Father Salvador Cisneros, 17 Feb. 1998, Tijuana.

10 Interview with María Teresa García, 17 June 2000, Tijuana.

11 Interview with Father Gil J. Gentile, 25 May 2000, at Saint Vincent de Paul Society, San Diego.

12 *San Diego Evening Tribune*, 16 Nov. 1938.

13 *El Hispano Americano* (Tijuana), 18 Nov. 1938.

14 "Un día, Tijuana cego de ira," *Detective Internacional* (Tijuana) 2, no. 50 (1 June 1946): 1.

15 *El Imparcial* (Tijuana), [n.d.] Aug. 1952.

16 I visited the shrine in the spring of 1996.

17 For the San Juan shrine, see Robert E. Wright, "The Faith of the Migrants: Texas and New Mexico in Historical Perspective," paper delivered at the Conference of U.S. and Mexican Historians, Fort Worth, Texas, 20 Nov. 1999; *The Monitor* (McAllen, Tex.), 9 Nov. 1993 and 8 June 1997. I visited the shrine several times in the late 1990s and interviewed Father Juan Nicolau there on 11 April 1998.

18 The exchange took place in the cemetery on 14 April 2000. For obvious reasons the name of the migrant is omitted.

19 *The Reader* (San Diego), 29 Oct. 1987; *San Diego Tribune*, 31 Oct. 1987; *San Diego Union*, 2 Nov. 1987; *Los Angeles Times*, 18 July 1997; *Philadelphia Enquirer*, 1 Aug. 1997. Díaz Castro, *Leyendas de Tijuana*, 221–28. The *ABC* series ran from 12 Aug. to 11 Sept. 1982.

20 Interview with Eduardo Guzmán, caretaker at Cemetery Number One, 21 Oct. 2001.

21 *Christian Science Monitor*, 15 June 1998.

22 *New York Times*, 14 Aug. 2002.

9. JOHN THE SOLDIER

1   Aiken, *Mexican Folktales from the Borderlands*, 94–95.

2   "'Juan Soldado' fue filmado por una compañía Tijuanense," *El Mexicano en la cultura*, no. 54 (5 Feb. 1972).

3   Ibid.; *New York Times*, 24 July 1939; García Riera, ed., *Historia documental del cine mexicano*, 1: 213–14.

4   Interview with César Laniado, 11 September 2000, Tijuana. The other comments quoted here were spontaneously offered by his customers.

5   Telephone interview with Father Allan Figueroa Deck, who teaches at Loyola Marymount University in Los Angeles, 22 July 1997.

6   Interview with Father Gil J. Gentile, 25 May 2000, at Saint Vincent de Paul Society, San Diego.

7   Telephone conversation with Larry McClements, 14 Nov. 2002.

8   Telephone conversation with Dr. William H. Sutherling, 20 Nov. 2002.

9   Telephone conversations with the Fresno County Sheriff's Department, Detective Division, Oct. 2002.

10 Interview with Father Eduardo Samaniego, pastor, Christ the King Roman Catholic Church, San Diego, 3 Feb. 1998, at the church.

11 Kamburoff, "Cult of Juan Soldado," Appendix 4.

12 Interviews with Delfina Suárez, 2–4 Oct. 1997, at her Magdalena home.

13 I visited the Abreojos shrine on 8–10 Aug. 1997 and conducted interviews with priests, devotees, and others in the district. Two of my fine History of Mexico students, Eric Fern and Keith Berkley, who were working in Abreojos at the time, brought this shrine to my attention and arranged interviews with the local townspeople. They left a petition at the shrine asking that they receive a good grade in the course, and they did. I thank them for their spirited support on the project.

14 Interview with Heriberto Yépez, 24 June 2002, Tijuana.

15 Interview with Ramón Camacho, 28 July 2000, Tijuana. Olga was his cousin.

SOURCES

ARCHIVES

Archivo de la Parroquia de La Asunción Ixtáltepec (Oaxaca).
Archivo General de la Nación (Mexico City), Ramo Presidenciales; cited as AGN.
Archivo General del Estado de Oaxaca.
Arizona Historical Society (Tucson).
Church of Jesus Christ of Latter-Day Saints (San Diego), Regional Genealogical Library and Computer Center, Genealogical Records.
Diocese of San Diego, Historical Archive, Parishes.
Tijuana, Gobierno Municipal, Registro Civil, Difuntos.
Tijuana, Instituto Municipal de Arte y Cultura, Archivo Histórico.
Universidad Autónoma de Baja California (Tijuana), Instituto de Investigaciones Históricas, Archivo Histórico; cited as IIH.
United States National Archives, Record Group 59, Records of the Department of State Relating to the Internal Affairs of Mexico, 1930–1944, Consular Reports, Lower California; and Record Group 165, U.S. Military Intelligence Reports, 1919–1941.

NEWSPAPERS

ABC (Tijuana)
Calexico (Calif.) Chronicle
Chicago Daily Tribune
Christian Science Monitor
Corpus Christi (Texas) Caller Times
Daily News (Los Angeles)
La Epoca (Tijuana)
El Excelsior (Mexico City)
El Hablador (Tijuana)

El Hispano Americano (Tijuana and Mexicali)
El Imparcial (Tijuana)
Labor (Tijuana)
Los Angeles Examiner
Los Angeles Times
El Nacional (Mexico City)
New York Times
Oaxaca Nuevo (Oaxaca City)
La Opinión (Los Angeles)
The Reader (San Diego)
San Diego Evening Tribune
San Diego Sun
San Diego Union
San Francisco Chronicle
San Francisco Examiner
San Ysidro (Calif.) *Border Press*
St. Louis Post Dispatch
El Universal (Mexico City)
El Universal Gráfico (Mexico City)

BOOKS, ARTICLES, AND PAPERS

Acosta Montoya, David. *Precusores del agrarismo y el asalto a las tierras en el estado de Baja California.* Mexicali, 1985.

Adams, Henry. *Mont Saint Michel and Chartres.* New York, 1986.

Aguirre Bernal, Celso. *Tijuana, su historia, sus hombres.* Mexicali, 1975.

Aiken, Riley. *Mexican Folktales from the Borderlands.* Dallas, 1980.

Aikman, Duncan. "Hell Along the Border." *American Mercury* 5 (May 1925): 17–23.

Alanís Enciso, Fernando Saúl. "La Colonización de Baja California con mexicanos prevenientes de Estados Unidos (1935–1939)." *Frontera Norte* 13 (July–Dec. 2001):141–63.

——. "Los Projectos de Manuel Gamio para el estudio de la migración mexicana a Estados Unidos (1925–1930). *Boletín*, Fideicomiso Archivos, Plutarco Elías Calles y Fernando Torreblanca, No. 42 (Jan.–April 2003).

Almada Díaz, Manuel. *Historia contemporanea de Tijuana: Siglo XX.* Ciudad Juárez, 1994.

Almáraz, José. "Law and Justice." *Annals of the American Academy of Political Science* 208 (March 1940): 39–47.

Andrić, Ivan. *The Bridge on the Drina.* Chicago, 1959.

Ariès, Philippe. *The Hour of Our Death.* New York, 2000.

Arnold, Charles A. "Folklore, Manners, and Customs of the Mexicans in San Antonio, Texas." Ph.D. diss., University of Texas, Austin, 1928.

Arreola, Daniel D. "Across the Street Is Mexico: Invention and Persistence of the Border Town Curio Landscape." *Yearbook of the Association of Pacific Coast Geographers* 61 (1999): 9–41.

Arreola, Daniel D., and James R. Curtis. *Border Cities: Landscape, Autonomy and Place Personality.* Tucson, 1993.

Baca, Vincent Z. C. de. "Moral Renovation of the Californias: Tijuana's Political and Economic Role in American-Mexican Relations, 1920–1935." Ph.D. diss., University of California, San Diego, 1991.

Balderama, Francisco E. *Decade of Betrayal: Mexican Repatriation in the 1930s.* Albuquerque, 1995.

Bantjes, Adrian A. "Iconoclasm and Idolatry in Revolutionary Mexico: The Dechristianization Campaigns, 1929–1940." *Mexican Studies/Estudios Mexicanos* 13, no. 1 (winter 1997): 87–120.

Barber, Paul. *Vampires, Burial, and Death: Folklore and Reality.* New Haven, 1988.

Baring-Gould, Sabine. *Virgin Saints and Martyrs.* New York, 1901.

Bax, Mart. *Medjugorje: Religion, Politics, and Violence in Rural Bosnia.* Amsterdam, 1995.

Becker, Marjorie. *Setting the Virgin on Fire: Lázaro Cárdenas, Michoacán Peasants, and the Redemption of the Mexican Revolution.* Berkeley, 1995.

Bell, Catherine. *Ritual: Perspectives and Dimensions.* Oxford, 1997.

Bella, Robert N., and Philip E. Hammond, eds. *Varieties of Civil Religion.* New York, 1980.

Belting, Hans. *Likeness and Presence: A History of the Image before the Era of Art.* Chicago, 1994.

Benítez Zenteno, Raul, and Gustavo Cabrera Acevedo. *Tablas abreviadas de mortalidad de la población de México, 1930–1960.* Mexico City, 1967.

Berger, Peter. "Secularism in Retreat." *National Interest* (1996): 3–12.

Bergman, Susan. *Martyrs.* Maryknoll, N.Y., 1996.

Bessler, John D. *Death in the Dark: Midnight Executions in America.* Boston, 1997.

Biles, Robert E. "The Position of the Judiciary in the Political Systems of Argentina and Mexico." *Lawyer of the Americas* 8 (1976): 287–318.

Blackbourn, David. *Marpingen: Apparitions of the Virgin Mary in Nineteenth-Century Germany.* New York, 1994.

Bokovy, Matthew F. "Peers of Their White Conquerors: San Diego, Public Memory, and the Politics of Cultural Heritage in Southern California, 1880–1940." Book manuscript.

Brading, David A. *Mexican Phoenix: Our Lady of Guadalupe: Image and Tradition across Five Centuries.* New York, 2001.

Brand, Norton F. *The Mexican Southland.* Fowler, Ind., 1922.

Branton, Pamela Hart. "The Works Progress Administration in San Diego County, 1935–1943." Master's thesis, San Diego State University, 1991.

Brasseur, Charles. *Viaje por el istmo de Tehuántepec.* Mexico City, 1981.

Brenner, Anita. *Idols Behind Altars.* New York, 1929.

Brown, Jim. *Riding the Line: The United States Customs Service in San Diego, 1885–1930. A Documentary History.* Washington, 1991.

Brown, Peter. *The Cult of the Saints: Its Rise and Function in Latin Christianity*. Chicago, 1981.

——. "The Saint as Exemplar in Late Antiquity." *Representations* 1, no. 2 (spring 1983): 1–25.

Brown, Raymond E. *The Death of the Messiah: From Gethsemane to the Grave. A Commentary on the Passion Narratives of the Four Gospels*. New York, 1993.

Buffington, Robert. "Prohibition in the Borderlands: National Government–Border Community Relations." *Pacific Historical Review* (1993): 19–38.

Burkhart, Louise M. *Holy Wednesday: A Nahua Drama from Early Colonial Mexico*. Philadelphia, 1996.

Bustamente, Jorge A. *Historia de Colonia Libertad*. Tijuana, 1990.

——. "Mexican Immigration and the Social Relations of Capitalism." Ph.D. diss., University of Notre Dame, 1975.

Butler, Matthew. "Keeping Faith in Revolutionary Mexico: Clerical and Lay Resistance to Religious Persecution, East Michoacan, 1926–1929." *The Americas* (July 2002).

Cabeza de Baca, Vincent, and Juan Cabeza de Baca, "The 'Shame Suicides' and Tijuana." *Journal of the Southwest* 43, no. 4 (winter 2001): 630–35.

Caciola, Nancy. "Through a Glass Darkly: Recent Work on Sanctity and Society." *Comparative Studies in Society and History* 38 (1996): 301–9.

Cahill, Thomas. *Desire of the Everlasting Hills: The World Before and After Jesus*. New York, 1999.

Calles, Plutarco Elías. *Correspondencia personal, 1919–1945*. 2 vols. Mexico City, 1991.

Camp, Roderic Ai. *Mexican Political Biographies*. Tucson, 1976.

——. *Mexican Political Biographies, 1933–1993*. Austin, 1981.

Campos, Anthony John. *Mexican Folk Tales*. Tucson, 1977.

Camus, Albert. *Reflections of the Guillotine*. Michigan City, Ind., 1959.

Cantú Jiménez, Esteban. *Apuntes históricos de Baja California Norte*. Mexico City, 1957.

Carmichael, Elizabeth, and Chloë Sayer. *The Skeleton at the Feast: The Day of the Dead in Mexico*. Austin, 1992.

Carroll, John T., Joel B. Green, et al. *The Death of Jesus in Early Christianity*. Montville, N.J., 1996.

Carroll, Michael P. *Madonnas That Maim: Popular Catholicism in Italy since the Fifteenth Century*. Baltimore, 1992.

——. *Veiled Threats: The Logic of Popular Catholicism in Italy*. Baltimore, 1996.

Castanien, Pliny. *To Protect and Serve: The History of the San Diego Police Department and Its Critics, 1889–1989*. San Diego, 1993.

Castillo Udiarte, Roberto, Alfonso García Cortez, and Richardo Morales Lira, compilers. *La Revolución también es una calle . . . Vida cotidiana y prácticas culturas en Tijuana*. Tijuana, 1996.

Chamberlain, Eugene Keith. "Mexican Colonization Versus American Interests in Lower California." *Pacific Historical Review* 20, no. 1 (Feb. 1951): 43–55.

Christian, William A., Jr. *Local Religion in Sixteenth-Century Spain*. Princeton, 1981.

——. *Moving Crucifixes in Modern Spain*. Princeton, 1992.

———. *Person and God in a Spanish Valley*. Princeton, 1989.

Cooper, David D. *The Lesson of the Scaffold*. London, 1974.

Cornelius, Wayne A. "Nation Building, Participation, and Distribution: The Politics of Social Reform under Cárdenas." In *Crisis, Choice, and Change: Historical Studies of Political Development*, edited by Gabriel A. Almond, Scott C. Flanagan, and Robert J. Mundt. Boston, 1973.

Cronon, David E. "American Catholics and Mexican Anticlericalism, 1933–1936." *Mississippi Valley Historical Review* 45 (Sept. 1958): 201–30.

Crosby, Harry W., Lowell Lindsay (editor), and Joanne H. Crosby (illustrator). *The Cave Paintings of Baja California: Discovering the Great Murals of an Unknown People*. El Cajon, Calif., 1998.

Cruz, Victor de la. *El General Charis y la pacificación del México postrevolucionario*. Mexico City, 1993.

Cruz Martínez, Pbro. Nicolás. *Cincuenta años de historia del seminario diocesano de Tijuana: 1940–1990*. Tijuana, 1991.

Cunningham, Lawrence S. *The Meaning of Saints*. New York, 1980.

Curiel Martínez, Juan Luis. *Foradores de Tijuana*. Tijuana, 1993.

Dedina, Serge Louis. "The Political Ecology of Transboundary Development: Land Use, Flood Control, and Politics in the Tijuana River Valley." Master's thesis, University of Wisconsin, Madison, 1991.

Delgado, Juan José. *Los Migrantes en Tijuana*. Mexico City, 1996.

Denny, Frederick M. " 'God's Friends': The Sanctity of Persons in Islam." In *Sainthood: Its Manifestations in World Religions*, edited by Richard Kieckhefer and George D. Bonds. Berkeley, 1988.

Deursen, A. T. Van. *Plain Lives in a Golden Age: Popular Culture, Religion, and Society in Seventeenth-Century Holland*. Trans. Maarten Ultec. New York, 1994.

Devlin, Judith. *The Superstitious Mind: French Peasants and the Supernatural in the Nineteenth Century*. New Haven, 1987.

Díaz Castro, Olga Vicenta. *Narraciones y leyendas de Tijuana*. Mexico City, 1981.

Diócesis de Tijuana. *Plan pastoral, 1989–1994: Hacia una iglesia nueva*. Tijuana, 1989.

Dolan, J. P. *The American Catholic Church Experience*. Garden City, N.Y., 1985.

Domingo, Pilar. "Rule of Law, Citizenship, and Access to Justice in Mexico." *Mexican Studies/Estudios mexicanos* 15, no. 1 (winter 1999): 151–91.

Drimmer, Frederick. *Until You Are Dead: The Book of Executions in America*. New York, 1990.

Dueñas Montes, Francisco. *Datos y documentos para la historia de Baja California*. Mexicali, 1984.

———. *Territorio norte de la Baja California: Temas históricas, 1931–1953*. Mexicali, 1991.

Duffy, Eamon. *The Stripping of the Altars: Traditional Religion in England, 1400–1580*. New Haven, 1992.

Durand, Jorge. *Mas allá de la línea: Patrones migratorios entre México y Estados Unidos*. Mexico City, 1994.

Durand, Jorge, and Patricia Arias. *La Experiencia migrante: Iconografía de la migración México-Estados Unidos*. Guadalajara, 2000.

Dwyer, John J. "Between Peasants and the Leviathan: The Expropriation and Spontaneous Seizure of American-Owned Agricultural Property in Mexico, 1934–1941." Ph.D. diss., University of Illinois, Urbana-Champaign, 1998.

Eddy, Lucinda. "The Visions of Paradise." *Journal of San Diego History* 41, no. 3 (summer 1995): 154–238.

Eire, Carlos M. N. *From Madrid to Purgatory: The Art and Craft of Dying in Sixteenth-Century Spain.* New York, 1995.

Ellsberg, Robert. *All Saints: Daily Reflections on Saints, Prophets, and Witnesses in Our Times.* New York, 1997.

Espín, Orlando O. "Popular Catholicism among Latinos." In *Hispanic Culture in the U.S.: Issues and Concerns*, edited by Jay P. Dolan and Allan Figueroa Deck. Notre Dame, 1994.

Espinosa, Victor M. "El Día del emigrante y el retorno del purgatorio: Iglesia, migración a los Estados Unidos y cambio sociocultral en un pueblo de los Altos de Jalisco." *Estudios sociológicos* 17, no. 50 (1999): 375–418.

———. "Doy grácias: Hacer el norte: Las Esperanzas de los migrantes." *La Brecha* no. 89 (4 July, 1999): 3–7.

Estrada Lázaro, José Armando. "Veinte años de deporte tijuanense." In *Historia de Tijuana, 1889–1989: Edición conmemorativa del centenario de su fundación*, vol. 2, edited by David Piñera Ramírez and Jesús Ortiz Figueroa. Tijuana, 1989.

Evans, Richard J. *Rituals of Retribution: Capital Punishment in Germany, 1600–1987.* New York, 1996.

Ezell, Edward Clinton. *Small Arms of the World.* Hamburg, 1983.

Farmer, David Hugh. *Oxford Dictionary of Saints.* Oxford, 1987.

Fenn, Richard K. *The Persistence of Purgatory.* New York, 1995.

Figueroa Deck, Allan. "The Challenge of Evangelical/Pentecostal Christianity to Hispanic Catholicism." In *Hispanic Culture in the U.S.: Issues and Concerns*, edited by J. P. Dolan and Allan Figueroa Deck. Notre Dame, 1994.

Forty, Ralph. *San Diego's South Bay Interurban.* Glendale, 1987.

Foucault, Michel. *Discipline and Punish: The Birth of the Prison.* Trans. Alan Sheridan. New York, 1979.

Franzonello, Lucia. "Il Culto delle anime decollate in Sicilia." Tesi di Laurea. Università de Palermo, 1946.

Gamio, Manuel. *The Life Story of the Mexican Immigrant.* New York, 1971.

———. *Mexican Immigration to the United States: A Study of Human Migration and Adjustment.* Chicago, 1930.

García Canclini, Nestor. *Tijuana: Casa de toda la gente.* Mexico City, 1989.

Garcíagodoy, Juanita. *Digging the Days of the Dead: A Reading of Mexico's Día de los Muertos.* Niwot, Colo., 1998.

García Riera, Emilio. *Historia documental del cine mexicano*, vol. 1. Mexico City, 1969.

Gardner, Dore. *Niño Fidencio: A Heart Thrown Open.* Albuquerque, 1992.

Garza Quirós, Fernando. *El Niño Fidencio y el fidencismo.* Monterrey, 1991.

Gaxiola, Francisco Javier. *Memorias.* Mexico City, 1975.

Gilbert, James Carl. "A Field Study in Mexico of the Mexican Repatriation Movement." Master's thesis, University of Southern California, 1934.

Gil Durán, Ileana. "La Influencia del tourismo en el nacimiento y desarrollo inicial de Tijuana, 1888–1910." *Journal of the Pacific Coast Council on Latin American Studies* 2, nos. 1-2 (issue ed. Reynaldo Ayala; 1989): 31–37.

Glazer, Mark, ed. *Flour from Another Sack and Other Proverbs, Folk Beliefs, Tales, Riddles, and Recipes.* Edinburg, Texas, 1994.

González, Adolfo. "Historical Case Study: San Diego and Tijuana Border Region Relationship with the San Diego Police Department, 1957–1964." Ph.D. diss., University of San Diego, 1995.

González Viaña, Eduardo. *Sarita colonia viene volando.* Lima, 1990.

Gordon, Bruce, and Peter Marshall, eds. *The Place of the Dead in Medieval and Early Modern Europe.* New York, 2000.

Goulart, Ron. *The Tijuana Bible.* New York, 1989.

Gregory, Brad S. *Salvation at the Stake: Christian Martyrdom in Early Modern Europe.* New York, 1999.

Gregory, James N. *American Exodus: The Dust Bowl Migration and Okie Culture in California.* New York, 1989.

Griffin, Ernst C., and Larry R. Ford. "Tijuana: Landscape of a Cultural Hybrid." *Geographical Review* 66 (1976): 435–47.

Griffith, James S. *Beliefs and Holy Places: A Spiritual Geography of the Pimería Alta.* Tucson, 1992.

——. *A Shared Place: Folklife in the Arizona-Sonora Borderlands.* Logan, 1995.

——. "El Tiradito and Juan Soldado." *International Folklore Review* (1987): 75–81.

Gudeman, Stephen. "Saints, Symbols, and Ceremonies." *American Ethnologist* 3, no. 4 (Nov. 1976): 707–29.

Guevara Santillán, Manuel. *Estadísticas y gráficas de Tijuana.* Tijuana, 1979.

Gunn, Jeffrey. "Juan Soldado: Murderer to Saint." Research paper, Writing of History, San Diego State University, 30 April 1991.

Gutierrez, Barbara Lenox. *Charlene.* Lafayette, La., 1988.

Hall, Linda. *Oil, Banks, and Politics. The United States and Post-Revolutionary Mexico, 1917-1924.* Austin, 1995.

Hamilton, Nora. *The Limits of State Autonomy: Post-Revolutionary Mexico.* Princeton, 1982.

Harley, R. Bruce, and Catherine Louise LaCoste, eds. *Readings in Diocesan Heritage.* Vol. 11: *Most Reverend Charles Francis Buddy, First Bishop of San Diego, 1936–1966.* San Diego, 1991.

Harris, Ruth. *Lourdes: Body and Spirit in the Secular Age.* New York, 1999.

Hart, John M. *Empire and Revolution: The Americans in Mexico since the Civil War.* Berkeley, 2002.

Hartland, E. Sidney. "The Cult of Executed Criminals at Palermo." *Folk-Lore* 21 (June 1910): 168–79.

Hawley, John Stratton, *Saints and Virtues.* Berkeley, 1987.

Hefley, James, and Marti Hefley. *By Their Blood: Christian Martyrs of the Twentieth Century*. Grand Rapids, Mich., 1996.

Heilbron, Carl H., ed. *History of San Diego County*. San Diego, 1936.

Hernández, Alberto H. "Transformaciones sociales y pluralismo religioso en cinco ciudades fronterizos." In *Política y poder en la frontera*. Mexico City, 1992.

Hernández Chávez, Alicia. *La Mecánica cardenista*. Vol 16 of *Historia de la revolución mexicana, 1934–1940*. Mexico City, 1979.

Herzog, Lawrence A. *Where North Meets South: Cities, Space, and Politics on the U.S.-Mexico Border*. Austin, 1990

Hillenbrand, Laura. *Seabiscuit: An American Legend*. New York, 2001.

Historia de Tijuana: Semblanza general. Tijuana, 1985.

Historia viva de Tijuana. Tijuana, 1996.

Hoffman, Abraham. *Unwanted Mexican-Americans in the Great Depression: Repatriation Pressures, 1929–1939*. Tucson, 1974.

Hudson, William Mathis, ed. *The Healer of Los Olmos, and Other Mexican Lore*. Dallas, 1966.

Ingham, John M. *Mary, Michael, and Lucifer: Folk Catholicism in Central Mexico*. Austin, 1986.

Irigoyen, Ulises. *El Problema económico de las fronteras mexicanas. Tres monografías: Zona libre, puertos libres y perímetros libres*. 2 vols. Mexico City, 1935.

James, William. *The Varieties of Religious Experience*. New York, 1982.

Johnson, Robert. *Death Work: A Study of the Modern Execution Process*. Belmont, Calif., 1998.

Kamburoff, Brian. "The Cult of Juan Soldado." Research paper, Writing of History, San Diego State University, 30 April 1991.

Kelly, Michael, ed. "Introduction [and] First Annual Report of the Board of Health of the City of San Diego for the Year Ending December 31st, 1888." *Journal of San Diego History* 48, no. 4 (fall 2002): 280–84.

Kemp, Eric Waldram. *Canonization and Authority in the Western Church*. London, 1948.

Kenny, Michael. "Patterns of Patronage in Spain." *Anthropological Quarterly* 33, no. 1 (Jan. 1960): 14–33.

Kerig, Dorothy Pierson. *El Valle de Mexicali y la Colorado River Land Company, 1922–1946*. Mexicali, 2001.

Kieckhefer, Richard. "The Cult of Saints in Popular Religion." *Explor* 7 (1984): 41–47.

Kieckhefer, Richard, and George D. Bond, eds. *Sainthood: Its Manifestations in World Religions*. Berkeley, 1988.

Kirk, Henry S. "Hour's Visit to Mexico." *Illustrated Overland* 40 (Dec. 1902): 499–502.

Kluckhohn, Frank L. *The Mexican Challenge*. New York, 1939.

Knight, Alan. "Cardenismo: Juggernaut or Jalopy?" *Journal of Latin American Studies* 26, part 1 (Feb. 1994): 73–107.

———. "Corruption in Twentieth-Century Mexico." In *Political Corruption in Europe and Latin America*, edited by W. Little and E. Posada-Carbo. London, 1996.

———. "The Political Economy of Revolutionary Mexico, 1900–1940." In *Latin America, Economic Imperialism and the State: The Political Economy of the External*

Connection from Independence to the Present, edited by Christopher Abel and Colin M. Lewis. London, 1985.

——. "Popular Culture and the Revolutionary State in Mexico, 1910–1940." *Hispanic American Historical Review* 74, no. 3 (1994): 393–444.

——. "Revolutionary Project, Recalcitrant People: Mexico, 1910–1940." In *The Revolutionary Process in Mexico: Essays on Political and Social Change, 1880–1940*, edited by Jaime Rodríguez O. Los Angeles, 1990.

——. "The Rise and Fall of Cardenismo, c1930-c1940." In *Mexico since Independence*, edited by Leslie Bethell. New York, 1990.

Langmuir, Erika. *Saints*. London, 2001.

Langston, Edward Lonnie. "The Impact of Prohibition on the Mexican–United States Border: The El Paso–Ciudad Juárez Case." Ph.D. diss., Texas Tech University, 1974.

La Plante, Alice, and Clara La Plante. *Heaven Help Us: The Worrier's Guide to the Patron Saints*. New York, 1999.

Laurence, John. *A History of Capital Punishment*. New York, 1960.

LeGoff, Jacques. *The Birth of Purgatory*. Chicago, 1986.

León Zavala, Ramiro. *Panorama histórico de la educación técnica en Tijuana, B.C., 1939–1986*. Tijuana, 1986.

Lieuwen, Edwin. *Mexican Militarism: The Political Rise and Fall of the Revolutionary Army, 1910–1940*. Albuquerque, 1968.

MacFarland, Charles S. *Chaos in Mexico: The Conflict of Church and State*. New York, 1935.

McGaffey, Ernest. "Bull-Fighting in Tijuana." *Outing* 77 (Nov. 1920): 75–76.

Macklin, B. June, and N. Ross Crumrine, " 'Santa' Teresa, El Niño 'Santo' Fidencio, and 'San' Damian: The Structural Development of Three Folk Saints' Movements, Northern Mexico." *Comparative Studies in Society and History* 15 (1973): 89–105.

Malagamba, Amelia. "Don Pedrito Jaramillo, una leyenda mexicana en el sur de Texas." In *Entre la mágica y la historia: Tradiciones, mitos y leyendas de la frontera*, compiled by José Manuel Valenzuela Arce. Tijuana, 1992.

Maldonado, Luis. *Génesis de catolicismo popular: Inconsciente colectivo de un proceso histórico*. Madrid, 1979.

Markides, Kyriakos S., and Thomas Cole. "Change and Continuity in Mexican-American Religious Behavior: A Three-Generation Study." In *The Mexican American Experience: An Interdisciplinary Anthology*, edited by Rodolfo O. de la Garza et al. Austin, 1985.

Marrow, James. H. *Passion Iconography in Northern European Art of the Middle Ages and Early Renaissance*. Kortdrijsk, Belgium, 1979.

Martin. R. L. "Mexican Prospects." *Yale Review* 25 (March 1936): 511–36.

Martis, Kenneth C. "United States International Land Border Crossing: San Ysidro, California." Master's thesis, San Diego State College, 1970.

Merback, Mitchell B. *The Thief, the Cross, and the Wheel: Pain and Spectacle of Punishment in Medieval and Renaissance Europe*. Chicago, 1999.

Mercado Díaz de León, Dr. Rafael. *Los Pioneros de la medicina en Tijuana*. Mexico City, 1985.

Mercado Díaz de León, Dr. Rafael, and Irma Cháirez Hernández, "Médicos pioneros, primeros hospitales y asociaciones médicas." In *Historia de Tijuana, 1889–1989: Edición conmemorativa de centenario de su fundación*, vol. 1, edited by David Piñera Ramírez and Jesús Ortiz Figueroa. Tijuana, 1989.

Meyer, Jean. *Período 1924–1928. Estado y sociedad con Calles*. Vol. 11 of *Historia de la revolución mexicana*. Mexico City, 1977.

Michaels, Albert L. "The Crisis of Cardenismo." *Journal of Latin American Studies* 2, no. 1 (1971): 51–79.

Molinar, Paul. *Saints: Their Place in the Church*. New York, 1965.

Mora, Pat. *Aunt Carmen's Book of Practical Saints*. Boston, 1997.

Morales Lira, Ricardo, and Alfonso García Cortez. " 'La Revolución también es una calle . . .' (de frentes, fronteras y cruces culturales." In *La Revolución también es una calle . . .*, compiled by Roberto Castillo Udiarte, Alfonso García Córtez, and Ricardo Morales Lira. Tijuana, 1996.

Morgan, David. *Visual Piety: A History and Theory of Popular Religious Images*. Berkeley, 1998.

Mulder-Bakker, Anneke B., ed. *The Invention of Saintliness*. London, 2002.

Mullin, Robert Bruce. *Miracles and the Religious Imagination*. New Haven, 1996.

Nevins, Joseph. *Operation Gatekeeper: The Rise of the "Illegal Alien" and the Making of the U.S.-Mexico Boundary*. New York, 2002.

Neza: Organo mensual de la sociedad nueva de estudiantes juchitecos. Oaxaca, 1986.

Novales Castillejos, Mario. "Informe general sobre la exploración sanitaria del municipio de Asunción Ixtáltepec, estado de Oaxaca." Trabajo que presenta para su examen profesional de médico, cirujano y partero. Universidad Nacional Autónoma de México, 1946.

Oktavec, Eileen. *Answered Prayers: Miracles and Milagros along the Border*. Tucson, 1995.

Oles, James. *South of the Border: Mexico in the American Imagination, 1914–1917*. Washington, 1993.

One Hundred Saints: Their Lives and Likenesses Drawn from Butler's "Lives of the Saints" and Great Works of Western Art. New York, 1993.

Orsi, Robert A. *Thank You, St. Jude: Women's Devotion to the Patron Saint of Hopeless Causes*. New Haven, 1996.

Padilla Corona, Antonio. *Inicios urbanos del norte de Baja California: Influencias e ideas, 1821–1906*. Mexicali, 1998.

Parker, Cristián. *Popular Religion and Modernization in Latin America: A Different Logic*. Maryknoll, N.Y., 1993.

Peel, J. D. Y. "Syncretism and Religious Change." *Comparative Studies in Society and History* 10, no. 2 (Jan. 1968): 121–41.

Pia DiBella, Maria. "Name, Blood and Miracles: The Claims to Renown in Traditional Sicily." In *Honor and Grace in Anthropology*, edited by J. G. Peristiany and Julian Pitt-Rivers. New York, 1992.

Piñera Ramírez, David, Jorge Martínez Zepeda, Catalina Velázquez Morales, and Antonio Padilla Corona. "Apuntes para la historia de la música en Baja California." *Meyibó* 2, no. 6 (1985): 7–26.

—— and Jesús Ortiz Figueroa. *Historia de Tijuana, 1889–1989: Edición conmemorativa del centenario de su fundación.* 2 vols. Tijuana, 1989.

Ports, Uldis. "Geraniums vs. Smokestacks: San Diego's Mayoralty Campaign of 1917." *Journal of San Diego History* 21, no. 3 (summer 1975): 50–56.

Pourade, Richard. *The Glory Years.* San Diego, 1964.

Prewett, Virginia. "The Mexican Army." *Foreign Affairs* 19 (1941): 609–20.

Price, John A. "Tijuana Ethnology: The Cultural Nature of an International Border." Photocopy of typescript. University of Texas at Austin, Benson Latin American Collection, 1969.

——. *Tijuana: Urbanization of a Border Culture.* Notre Dame, Ind., 1973.

Proffitt, T. D., III, *Tijuana: The History of a Mexican Metropolis.* San Diego, 1994.

Puente México: La Vencindad de Tijuana con California. Tijuana, 1991.

Pulido, Alberto López. " 'Cuando iba con Juan Soldado, de volada pasaba': Crossing Borders Through the Stories of Chicano/Latino Religions." Hispanic Lecture in Theology and Religion, the Hispanic Institute of Theology, Drew University, 23 April 1998.

——. "Mexican American Catholicism in the Southwest: The Transformation of a Popular Religion." *Perspectives in Mexican American Studies* 4 (1993): 93–108.

Puppi, Lionello. *Torment in Art: Pain, Violence, and Martyrdom.* New York, 1991.

Quiñones, Sam. *True Tales from Another Mexico: The Lynch Mob, the Popsicle Kings, Chalino, and the Bronx.* Albuquerque, 2001.

Quiróz Cuarón, Alfonso. *La Pena de muerte en México.* Mexico City, 1962.

Radelet, Michael L. *Facing the Death Penalty: Essays on Cruel and Unusual Punishment.* Philadelphia, 1989.

Rathbun, Morris M. "Facts About Lower California." *The Mexican Review* 1 (1917): 9, 13.

Ridgely, Roberta. "Inside Tijuana." *San Diego and Point Magazine* 20, no. 8 (June 1968).

——. "The Man Who Built Tijuana: 'Sunny Jim' Coffroth and the Freewheeling Days of the High Roller." *San Diego and Point Magazine* 18, no. 3 (Jan. 1966) (part 1 of a 10-part series entitled "The Man Who Built Tijuana" by Ridgely).

——. "Tijuana, 1920. Prohibition Pops the Cork," *San Diego and Point Magazine* 19, no. 7 (May 1967) (part 4 of a 10-part series entitled "The Man Who Built Tijuana" by Ridgely).

Riley, Luisa. "Fidencio, El Niño Fidencio." *Luna Córnea* no. 9 (1996): 4–15.

Roca, Hernán de la. *Tijuana In.* Mexico City, 1932.

Rodríguez L., Abelardo. *Autobiografía.* Mexico City, 1962.

——. *Memoria administrativa del Gobierno del Distrito Norte de la Baja California, 1924–1927.* Mexicali, 1993.

Rodríguez, Francisco M. *Baco y birjan: Una historia sangrante y dolorosa, de lo que fué, y lo que es Tijuana.* Tijuana, 1968.

———. *Trinchera obrera: Una historia sangrante y dolorosa de lo que fué, y lo que es Tijuana*. Tijuana, 1977.

Rodríguez González, Raúl. "La Figura y época de Esteben Cantú (1914–1924) en el Archivo Nacional de los Estados Unidos: Un informe preliminar." *Meyibó* 3, nos. 7–8 (1988): 163–70.

Rolland, Modesto C. *Informe sobre el Distrito Norte de la Baja California*. Mexicali, 1993.

Romandía de Cantú, Graciela. *Exvotos y milagros mexicanos*. Mexico City, 1978.

Romero, Octavio. "Don Pedrito Jaramillo: The Emergence of a Mexican-American Folk Saint." Ph.D. diss., University of California, Berkeley, 1964.

Ronzelen de González, Teresa van. "Victor Apaza: La emergencia de un santo. Descripción y analysis del proceso de formación de un nuevo culto popular." *America indígena* 45, no. 4 (Oct.–Dec. 1985): 647–68.

Rubel, Arthur J., Carl W. O'Nell, and Rolando Collado-Ardón. *Susto: A Folk Illness*. Berkeley, 1984.

Rubin, Jeffrey W. *Decentering the Regime: Ethnicity, Radicalism, and Democracy in Juchitán, Mexico*. Durham, N.C. 1997.

Ruffin, C. Bernard. *The Days of the Martyrs: A History of the Persecution of Christians from Apostolic Times to the Time of Constantine*. Huntington, Ind., 1985.

Ruíz González, Wulfrano. *Por fín habla Buchito sobre la zona libre*. Tijuana, 1988.

Rulfo, Juan. *Pedro Páramo*. New York, 1994.

Russell, Louise. "Legendary Narratives Inherited by Children of Mexican-American Ancestry: Cultural Pluralism and the Persistence of Tradition." Ph.D. diss., Indiana University, 1977.

Ryan, Frank. *The Labor Movement in San Diego: Problems and Development from 1887–1957*. San Diego, 1959.

Samaniego López, Marco Antonio. "Formación y consolidación de las organizaciones obreras en Baja California, 1920–1930." *Mexican Studies/Estudios Mexicanos* 14, no. 2 (summer 1998): 329–62.

———. "Surgimiento, luchas e institucionalización del movimiento obrero en Tijuana." In *Historia de Tijuana, 1889–1989: Edición conmemorativa de centenario de su fundación*, vol. 2, edited by David Piñera Ramírez and Jesús Ortiz Figueroa. Tijuana, 1989.

Sánchez Guzmán, Salvador. "Estudio previo del problema palúdico en Ixtáltepec, Oaxaca." Tésis para obtener el título de médico cirujano y partero, Universidad Nacional de México, 1947.

Sánchez Lara, Rosa María. *Los Retablos populares: Exvotos pintados*. Mexico City, 1990.

Sanders, Thomas Griffin. *Tijuana: Mexico's Pacific Coast Metropolis*. Indianapolis, 1987.

Sández de Gutiérrez, Graciela. "Nuestra cocina, un *collage*." In *Historia de Tijuana: Edición conmemorativa del centenario de su fundación, 1889–1989*, vol. 2, edited by David Piñera Ramírez and Jesús Ortiz Figueroa. Tijuana, 1989.

Sandos, James A. "Northern Separatism During the Mexican Revolution: An Inquiry into the Role of Drug Trafficking, 1919–1920." *The Americas* 41, no. 2 (Oct. 1984): 191–214.

——. "Prohibition and Drugs: The United States Army on the Mexican-American Border, 1916–1917." *Pacific Historical Review* 49, no. 4 (Nov. 1990): 621–45.

San Diego Writers' Project, Works Progress Administration, State of California. *San Diego: A California City.* San Diego, 1937.

Schantz, Eric Michael. "All Night at the Owl: The Social and Political Relations of Mexicali's Red Light District, 1913–1925." *Journal of the Southwest* 43, no. 4 (winter 2001): 549–602.

——. "The 'Mexicali Rose' and the 'Tijuana Brass': Vice Tours of the United States–Mexico Border, 1910–1965." Ph.D. diss., University of California, Los Angeles, 2001.

Schmitt, Jean Claude. *The Holy Greyhound Guinefort: Healer of Children since the Thirteenth Century.* New York, 1983.

Schneider, Luis Mario. *Cristos, santos y vírgenes: Milagros y devociones que abren las puertas del cielo desde los santuarios mexicanos.* Mexico City, 1995.

Schroeder, Susan. "Tijuana's Elite Healers: The Blending of Western Medicine with Ritualistic Cures." *Journal of Latin American Lore* 16, no. 2 (winter 1990): 233–58.

Schuler, Friedrich E. *Mexico between Hitler and Roosevelt: Mexican Foreign Relations in the Age of Lázaro Cárdenas, 1934–1940.* Albuquerque, 1998.

Secretaría de la Economía Nacional, Dirección General de Estadística. *Quinto censo de población, May 1930.* Mexico City, 1940.

——. *Sexto Censo de población, 1940.* Mexico City, 1940.

The Shepherd Cannot Run: Letters of Stanley Rother, Missionary and Martyr. Oklahoma City, 1984.

Shragge, Abraham J. "Boosters and Bluejackets: The Civic Culture of Militarism in San Diego, California, 1900–1945." Ph.D. diss., University of California, San Diego, 1998.

——. " 'I Like the Cut of your Jib': Cultures of Accommodation Between the U.S. Navy and Citizens of San Diego, California, 1900–1951." *Journal of San Diego History* 48, no. 3 (summer 2002): 230–55.

Smith, Lacey Baldwin. *Fools, Martyrs, Traitors: The Story of Martyrdom in the Western World.* New York, 1997.

Smyth, Damian Barry. *The Trauma of the Cross: How the Followers of Jesus Came to Understand the Crucifixion.* New York, 1999.

Sodi, Carlos. *El Procedimiento penal mexicano.* Mexico City, 1937.

Spencer, Daniela, and Bradley A. Levinson, "Linking State and Society in Discourse and Action: Political and Cultural Studies of the Cárdenas Era in Mexico." *Latin American Research Review* 34, no. 2 (1999): 227–45.

Spierenburg, Pieter. *The Spectacle of Suffering: Executions and the Evolution of Repression: From a Preindustrial Metropolis to the European Experience.* New York, 1984.

Starr, Fredrick. *Catalogue of a Collection of Objects Illustrating the Folklore of Mexico.* London, 1899.

——. *In Indian Mexico: A Narrative of Travel and Labor.* Chicago, 1908.

Starr, Kevin. *Americans and the California Dream.* New York, 1973.

Stegemann, Ekkehard W., and Wolfgang Stegemann. *The Jesus Movement: A Social History of Its First Century.* Minneapolis, 1999.

Stephen, Lynn, and James Dow, eds. *Class, Politics, and Popular Religion in Mexico and Central America.* Washington, 1990.

Summers, June Nay. *Buenos Días, Tijuana.* Ramona, Calif., 1974.

Tabulados básicos: Baja California. XII censo general de población y vivienda: 2000. Aguascalientes, Mexico, 2001.

Taylor, Larissa Juliet. "The Worst Death Becomes a Good Death: The Passions of Don Rodrigo Calderón." In *The Place of the Dead: Death Remembrance in Late Medieval and Early Modern Europe,* edited by Bruce Gordon and Peter Marshall. New York, 2000.

Taylor, Lawrence D. "The Magonista Revolt in Baja California: Capitalist Conspiracy or Rebellion de los Pobres." *Journal of San Diego History* 45, no. 1 (winter 1999): 2–31.

———. "The Mining Boom in Baja California from 1850 to 1890 and the Emergence of Tijuana as a Border Community." *Journal of the Southwest* 43, no. 4 (winter 2001): 463–92.

———. "The Wild Frontier Moves South: U.S. Entrepreneurs and the Growth of Tijuana's Vice Industry, 1908–1935." *Journal of San Diego History* 48, no. 3 (summer 2002): 204–29.

Taylor, Marian. "Land of Much in Little." *Overland* 63 (May 1914): 479.

Taylor, Michael C. "Why No Rule of Law in Mexico? Explaining the Weakness of Mexico's Judicial Branch." *New Mexico Law Review* 27 (1999): 142–66.

Tello Villalobos, Arturo. *Tijuana: El Principio, su nombre y semblanzas monografía en 1930 y gráfica de 1887–1945.* Tijuana, 1999.

Theilmann, John M. "A Study of the Canonization of Political Figures in England by Popular Opinion, 1066–1509." Ph.D. diss. University of Georgia, 1977.

Thomas, Edward C. *The Wanderer in Tijuana, Baja California, Mexico.* Los Angeles, 1922.

Toor, Frances. *A Treasury of Mexican Folkways: The Customs, Myths, Beliefs, Fiestas, Dances, and Songs of the Mexican People.* New York, 1947.

Troxell, Harold C., et al. *Floods of March 1938 in Southern California.* Washington, 1942.

Tweed, Thomas A. *Our Lady of the Exile: Diasporic Religion at a Cuban Catholic Shrine in Miami.* New York, 1997.

Valenzuela Arce, José Manuel. *El Movimiento urbano popular en Tijuana: Reconstrucción testimonial.* Tijuana, 1987.

———. "Por los milagros recibidos: religiosidad popular a través del culto a Juan Soldado." In *Entre la mágia y la historia: Tradiciones, mitos y leyendas de la frontera,* compiled by José Manuel Valenzuela Arce. Tijuana, 1992.

Vásquez Hoyos, Liliana. "La Revolución: Las Mil y una barras: Espacio social, cotidanidad, y cultura urbana." In *La Revolución también es una calle. . . . ,* compiled by Roberto Castillo Udiarte, Alfonso García Córtez, and Ricardo Morales Lira. Tijuana, 1996.

Vauchez, André. *Sainthood in the Later Middle Ages*. New York, 1997.

Vaughan, Mary Kay. *Cultural Politics in Revolution: Teachers, Peasants, and Schools in Mexico, 1930–1940*. Tucson, 1997.

Vega, Daniel. "¿Quién es Juan Soldado?" Research paper, History of Mexico, San Diego State University, 30 April 2000.

La Verdadera novena del ánima de Jesús Malverde (nació en 1870 y murió el 3 de mayo de 1909). Santa Ana, Calif., 1996.

Weber, Msgr. Francis J. *Century of Fulfillment: The Roman Catholic Church in Southern California, 1840–1947*. Mission Hills, Calif., 1990.

Werne, Joseph. "Esteban Cantú y la soberanía mexicana en Baja California." *Historia mexicana* 30, no. 1 (July–Sept. 1980): 1–30.

White, Owen P. "Art of Drink on the Mexican Border." *American Mercury* 17 (July 1929): 271–77.

Wilkinson, Bruce. *The Prayer of Jabez: Breaking through to the Blessed Life*. Sisters, Ore., 2000.

Wilson, Charles M. "Crime Detection Laboratories in the United States." In *Forensic Science: Scientific Investigation in Criminal Justice*, edited by Joseph L. Peterson. New York, 1975.

Wilson, Stephen. *Saints and Their Cults: Studies in Religion, Sociology, Folklore, and History*. New York, 1983.

Woods, Gerald. "A Penchant for Probity: California Progressives and Disreputable Pleasures." In *California Progressivism Revisited*, edited by William Deverell and Tom Sitton. Berkeley, 1994.

Woodward, Kenneth L. *Making Saints: How the Catholic Church Determines Who Becomes a Saint, Who Doesn't, and Why*. New York, 1990.

Wright, Pearl Couser. "Religious *Fiestas* in San Antonio." Master's thesis, St. Mary's University of San Antonio, 1946.

Yamagata, Larry M. "Tia Juana River Valley: A Conflict in Change." Master's thesis, San Diego State University, 1973.

Zamora, Julian. *Los Mojados: The Wetback Story*. Notre Dame, Ind., 1971.

Zenteno Quintero, René Martín. "Del Rancho Tijuana a Tijuana: Una Breve historia de desarrollo y población en la frontera norte de México." *Estudios demográficos y urbanos* 10, no. 1 (1995):105–32.

Zerón Medina, Fausto. "Informe general médico-social sobre el municipio de Ixtáltepec del estado de Oaxaca." Trabajo que para su examen profesional de médico cirujano partero. Universidad Nacional Autónoma de México, 1943.

Zugasti, Julián. *El Bandolerismo: Estudio social y memorias históricas*. Madrid, 1982.

INDEX

Tijuana (*cont.*)

92; relationship of, with San Diego, 8, 15, 26–27, 79, 81, 84, 91, 103, 134, 145, 148; religious life in, 127–33, 155–58, 265; sentiment toward the U.S. in, 56, 59, 105, 142, 267, 279; wages and income in, 56, 141, 150–51, 160, 265. *See also* Movie industry, in Tijuana

Tijuana history and development: early history, 79, 83–86; in World War I, 91, 101; in 1920s, 96–100; in 1930's, 78–79; in 1940s, 267; immigration from other parts of Mexico, 81, 91, 99, 125, 265–66; wax museum of history, 277–79. *See also* Baja California Norte; Riots of February 1938; Tijuana local government

Tijuana local government, 11, 24–25, 125; police and fire departments, 5, 22–24, 29, 98, 148; public works, 60, 91, 98–99, 142, 158, 160; Parque Teniente Guerrero, 98, 113–14; territorial governors, 160–63. *See also* Cantú, Lt. Col. Esteban; Contreras, Gen. Manuel; Rodríguez, Abelardo; Sánchez Tabaoda, Lt. Col. Rudolfo

Tijuana social and cultural life: around 1900, 86; in 1920s, 96–99; in 1930s, 78, 107–14, 142–43, 153, 265; today, 265–66, 283–85; education and schools, 99–100, 112–13, 134, 153–54; radio station, 134; social organizations, 125; sports, 113, 124–25. *See also* Tijuana tourism

Tijuana tourism, 56, 58–59, 76, 91, 97, 148, 151, 158; early, 82–85; in 1920s, 93–95; in 1930s, 137, 147; celebrity visitors, 89, 92, 96–97, 107, 140, 144, 165; as contact with wider world, 133–34; curio and souvenir businesses, 82, 86, 148; dependence on alcohol sales of, 92, 146; effect of casino closure on, 160–65; effect of Depression on, 143–44, 148, 152–53; hotels, 82–83, 85, 96–97, 104; prices, 139, 147; sporting events, 82–83, 86, 88, 104, 124; tax revenues generated by, 90–91, 98, 142, 161; U.S. Navy sailors and, 91, 101, 145; zebra-striped donkeys, 111, 284. *See also* Bars; Casinos; Horseracing; Prostitution, in Tijuana

Tijuana River dam, 98, 106–7, 110, 125

Tiradito, El, 76, 175–76, 211–14, 262

Torres, Padre Juan, 155–57

U.S. anti-Mexican sentiment, 102, 151–52, 156, 164

U.S. consul reports, 55–59, 161–63

U.S. Navy, 91, 101, 145

Virgin of San Juan (Tex.), 75–76, 268–69, 272

Withington, Carl, 87, 104, 137

Yasuhara, Soo, 96, 124

Paul Vanderwood is Professor Emeritus of Mexican History at San Diego State University. His authored works include *The Power of God Against the Guns of Government: Religious Upheaval in Mexico at the Turn of the Nineteenth Century* (1998); *Disorder and Progress: Bandits, Police, and Mexican Development* (rev. and enlarged ed., 1992); and *Disorder and Progress: Bandits, Police, and Mexican Development* (1981). He coauthored (with Frank N. Samponaro) *War Scare on the Rio Grande: Robert Runyon's Photographs of the Border Conflict, 1913–1916* (1992) and *Border Fury: A Picture Postcard Record of Mexico's Revolution and U.S. War Preparedness, 1910–1917* (1988).

Vanderwood, Paul J.

Juan Soldado: rapist, murderer, martyr, saint /

Paul J. Vanderwood.

p. cm.—(American encounters/global interactions)

Includes bibliographical references and index.

ISBN 0-8223-3404-6 (cloth: alk. paper)

ISBN 0-8223-3415-1 (pbk.: alk. paper)

1. Castillo Morales, Juan, d. 1938—Cult.

2. Mexico—Religious life and customs. I. Title. II. Series.

BL2530.M4V36 2004   972'.23—dc22   2004009138